21世纪高等院校国际经济与贸易专业精品教材

国家级双语示范课程教材

省级社会科学著作类优秀成果奖

Documents for International Business Bilingual Coursebook

3rd edition

国际商务单证 双语教程 （第三版）

杨静 主编

东北财经大学出版社
Dongbei University of Finance & Economics Press
大连

图书在版编目（CIP）数据

国际商务单证双语教程 / 杨静主编 .—3 版 .—大连：东北财经大学出版社，2019.3（2020.11重印）

（21世纪高等院校国际经济与贸易专业精品教材）

ISBN 978-7-5654-3416-7

Ⅰ.国… Ⅱ.杨… Ⅲ.国际贸易–票据–双语教学–高等学校–教材 Ⅳ.F740.44

中国版本图书馆 CIP 数据核字（2019）第 002688 号

东北财经大学出版社出版

（大连市黑石礁尖山街 217 号 邮政编码 116025）

网　　址：http://www.dufep.cn

读者信箱：dufep@dufe.edu.cn

大连雪莲彩印有限公司印刷　东北财经大学出版社发行

幅面尺寸：185mm×260mm　　字数：471 千字　　印张：17

2019 年 3 月第 3 版　　　　　2020 年 11 月第 7 次印刷

责任编辑：蔡　丽　　　　　　责任校对：蓝　海

封面设计：冀贵收　　　　　　版式设计：钟福建

定价：38.00 元

教学支持　售后服务　　联系电话：（0411）84710309

版权所有　侵权必究　　举报电话：（0411）84710523

如有印装质量问题，请联系营销部：（0411）84710711

Preface of Third Edition
第三版前言

　　本书是为培养涉外经济部门所需的既能熟练掌握外贸专业知识,又能熟练运用专业英语从事进出口业务的复合型人才而专门编写的教材,旨在帮助学习者在熟练掌握专业知识的基础上用英语进行商务活动,并熟练掌握国际贸易相关条款和单证制作。本书可作为高等院校国际贸易、国际商务、国际物流、商务英语等专业学生的教材,也适合作为外销员、单证员和跟单员的工具书,还可供制单员在资格考试前复习、练习使用。

　　本书中英文对照,操作性强。本书兼顾外贸专业和非外贸专业人员的需要,采用英汉对照的方式介绍进出口贸易过程中经常遇到的单证缮制及相关问题,为学习者提供一个在学习专业知识的同时提高英语应用能力的平台。本书所选用的外贸单证案例内容全面、新颖,具有典型性和普遍性,非常适合双语案例教学。本书与《国际商务单证实训教程》配套使用,方便学习者进行实践操练,真正实现了学做结合。

　　本次修订打破了以知识体系为线索的传统编写模式,以一票贸易单证操作的工作流程为主线,以培养职业核心能力为目标,以工作任务为导向进行内容设计和编排,充分体现学练结合、任务驱动、工作过程导向的编写模式,注重对贸易单证操作能力的训练,紧紧围绕工作任务的需要来选取内容,并通过综合训练和案例分析等形式,体现对读者鲜明的可持续职业能力培养的特色。

　　本次修订体现了以下三个特点:

　　一是前瞻性。本书的修订是在对外贸企业进行充分调研的基础上进行的,充分吸收了外贸企业在单证操作过程中的最新做法和最新案例。

　　二是实用性。本书的修订做到了教材内容与企业操作内容相衔接,操练题均来自外贸企业的操作实例。

　　三是可操作性。本书的修订打破了以知识体系为线索的传统编写模式,以一票外贸单证操作的工作流程为主线,先提出任务,让读者带着任务去学习,学完后再练习,所有内容学完了,一票单证业务也就掌握了,学习的过程就如在做外贸单证,具有很强的可操作性。

　　在本书编写过程中,刘艳萍、陆秋娥、朱海平、钟良健、朱良华、张堂云、凌华、戴君益、魏格坤等帮助校对书稿,在此表示感谢。同时,本书参考了同类教材,并得到了外贸企业专家和银行国际结算专家的精心指导和帮助,在此一并表示真诚的感谢。书中存在的不足之处,敬请各位专家、读者批评指正。

本书配套学习网站是 http://www.nclass.org/vc/99464161 或 http://www.nclass.org/cb/99464161。同时,东北财经大学出版社网站(http://www.dufep.cn)提供免费的 PPT 等教学资源。

编　者

2018年12月

Contents
目　录

Sample Index
样单索引

Chapter 1

Overview of International Trade Documents
外贸单证概论

Learning Objectives

◆ 重点掌握外贸单证的分类;掌握外贸单证的作用和外贸单证工作的基本要求;了解外贸单证工作的重要性。

Guide Case

A Case of Loss of More than $6,000

On April 12, 2018, a bank in Hong Kong, China opened an L/C for $540,000, in which the shipment time was on August 15, the validity was on August 30, and the trade contract number listed thereon was "CN1830325". On August 9, the beneficiary presented the negotiation documents, in which the trade contract numbers listed were "CNI830325". According to the beneficiary export company's claim, their first contract numbers always are "CNI" and the issuing bank's L/C must be mistaken. Therefore the beneficiary insisted on the company's official number and all the contract numbers of documents were written as "CNI830325". The negotiating bank did not take seriously, and considered that the importer was easy to find out, so it accepted negotiation to send the documents and made reimbursement to the reimbursing bank. The reimbursing bank New York branch as the issuing bank's reimbursing bank also drew $540,000 into the negotiation bank's account on August 9.

But the telex by the issuing bank on August 13 refused to pay; the reason was that "documents can't be in conformity with the L/C". Because the contract numbers of the documents were not in conformity with the L/C indeed, the negotiating bank couldn't argue, completely in a passive position. After the local middlemen's in Hong Kong, China and the applicant's consultation for many times, this batch of documents with "discrepancies" was accepted by accommodating on September 14, but the issuing bank lodged compensation for $6,108.75.

---

6 000 多美元损失的案例

中国香港某银行于 2018 年 4 月 12 日开来一张信用证,金额为 540 000 美元,装运期为 8 月 15 日,有效期至 8 月 30 日,该证所列贸易合同编号为"CN1830325"。8 月 9 日受益人交来议付单据,所有单据中的贸易合同编号均为"CNI830325"。据受益人出口公司称,他们的合同编号历来以"CNI"为字首,开证行的来证肯定搞错了。因此,受益人坚持以该公司正式编号为准,把单据中的合同编号均写为"CNI830325"。议付行对此未认真对待,以为进口方易于查清,遂接受议付寄单,并向偿付行索汇。开证行的偿付行即该行的纽约分行于 8 月 9 日亦将货款 540 000 美元划入议付行在该行的账户。

但是,开证行于 8 月 13 日来电表示拒付,理由是"单证不符"。由于单证的合同编号的确与信用证不符,议付行无法提出抗辩,完全处于被动地位。后经中国香港当地中间商与开证人多次协商,这批有"不符点"的单据于 9 月 14 日虽被通融接受,但以开证行要求补偿利息 6 108.75 美元而告终。

1.1 Meaning, Role, and Significance of International Trade Documents 外贸单证的含义、作用与重要性

1.1.1 *Meaning of International Trade Documents* 外贸单证的含义

A document is an official paper that serves as proof or evidence of something. Documents lie at the heart of all international trade transactions. Most international trades are done on the basis of delivery against documents and payment against documents. Uniform Customs and Practice for Documentary Credits (ICC No. 600)(UCP600) provides that: "Banks deal with documents and not with goods, services or performance to which the documents may relate."

单证是可作为证明或证据的正式文书。单证是国际贸易交易的核心。单证是国际贸易交货和付款的主要依据。《跟单信用证统一惯例》(国际商会第 600 号出版物,简称 UCP600)规定:"银行处理的是单证,而不是单证可能涉及的货物、服务或履约行为。"

1.1.2 *Role of International Trade Documents* 外贸单证的作用

For different departments (customs, banks, exporter, importer, insurance company, government, etc.), international trade documents have different roles. However, there is one same point, international trade documents provide proof of ownership of goods at any time and place throughout the transaction and are very important to all the departments.

To the exporter, documents provide an accounting record of a transaction, a receipt for goods shipped, the means for export clearance of the goods, as well as information and instructions to the many individuals, companies and governmental agencies that transport, handle, or inspect the shipment.

To the importer, documents provide an accounting record of a transaction, assurances that the goods ordered are the goods shipped, and the means for clearing goods through customs at the country of destination.

To the shipping company and freight forwarder, documents provide an accounting record of a transaction, instructions on where and how to ship the goods, and a statement giving instructions for handling the shipment.

To the banks, documents provide instructions and accounting tools for collecting and disbursing payments.

To the country of export and its regulatory agencies, documents provide a means of evaluating risks, valuing a shipment and tracing the point of loss in a coverage claim.

To the country of import and its regulatory agencies, documents provide proof of the right to import, statistical and census information regarding the goods imported, evidence that the goods imported will not harm the health and safety of its citizens, and an accounting tool for assessing duties and fees.

国际贸易单证在不同的部门(如海关、银行、出口商、进口商、保险公司、政府等)有不同的作用。然而,相同点是国际贸易单证是贯穿整个交易的物权凭证,并且对所有的部门来说都是非常重要的。

对于出口商来说,单证提供了交易的会计记录、装运货物的收据、货物出口清关工具,并为负责运输、处理或检查货物的个人、公司和政府机构提供信息和说明。

对于进口商来说,单证为交易提供会计记录,确保订购的货物是装运货物,并提供目的国海关清关工具。

对于船运公司和货运公司来说,单证为交易提供会计记录,为货物提供装运地点和装运方式说明,并为装运管理提供说明。

对于银行来说,单证可作为说明和收付款的结算工具。

对于出口方及其监管机构来说,单证为评估风险、货运定价和跟踪索赔范围内的损失点提供一种凭证。

对于进口方及其监管机构来说,单证为货物进口权、与进口货物有关的统计和普查信息提供证明文件,证明进口货物不会损害公民的健康和安全,是评估税费的会计工具。

1.1.3   Significance of International Trade Documents
外贸单证的重要性

Document is an indivisible part of international trade. It refers to the preparation and examination of documents involved in a transaction. The major purpose of documents is to provide a specific and complete description of the goods so that they can be correctly processed for transport, insurance, payment, customs clearance, etc. For most transactions in international trade today, without documents there will be no possibility of transactions. Considering its importance this chapter is solely devoted to the introduction to the basic requirements and information source of export documents, and the explanation of the major documents used in export trade.

The importance of documents, in a sense, can be amplified by saying that in some international transactions the exchange of documents takes priority over the exchange of goods. This is well illustrated in those contracts signed under the trade terms such as FOB/FCA, CFR/CPT and CIF/CIP, where the delivery of goods from the seller to the buyer is symbolized by the handover of title documents, rather than the actual delivery of physical goods. As these types of transactions take a large portion of the total volume of trade, the importance of documents hence can not be underestimated.

Without proper documents, neither sellers can send goods out of their countries and collect payments, nor can buyers release goods without problems. A smooth transaction heavily relies on the correct preparation and presentation of relevant documents at different stages. It is crucial for both the seller and the buyer to acquire sufficient documents skills to be qualified practitioners. In the meantime, compared with importers, exporters are more susceptible to the impact of documents. It is an essential condition for exportation in the first place. In order to get through the mandatory supervision and control of the customs, presentation of required documents is the prerequisite. Lack of necessary documents or presentation of wrongly-made documents is among the most common reasons for delayed release of cargos from the customs.

This also applies to importers when they are handling the import customs formalities. In addition, documents serve as the proof of fulfillment of contract for the sellers. Most of the obligations listed on the sales contract could be reflected on the availability of certain documents or the certain content of a document. A bill of lading, for example, indicates the details of the seller's performance of transportation. Sometimes the buyer requires some documents to ensure that the goods delivered are what he expects. A certificate of quality may be required to guarantee the quality of the product. As a result, by evidence of documents, exporters prove that they have delivered the right goods at the right time to the right place in the right manner. Furthermore, in most cases exporters have to use documents in their collection of payment. If we recall the payment issues, one thing is obvious that most of the popular payment terms ask for documents, especially a bill of lading as title documents. Unable to provide the required documents, the exporter will have trouble in setting payment for its goods delivered.

单证是国际贸易不可分割的一部分。它是指涉及单证的单证准备和单证审查。单证的主要目的是具体和完整地描述货物,以便货物在运输、投保、支付和清关等时能得到正确的处理。在当今的国际贸易中,大多数的交易不可能在无单的情况下完成。考虑到单证的重要性,本章专门对出口单证的基本要求和信息来源进行介绍,并对出口贸易中的主要单证进行详细的解释。

在某种意义上,单证的重要性可以放大到如此程度:在一些国际贸易中,单证的交换优先于货物的交换。我们可以从以 FOB/FCA、CFR/CPT 和 CIF/CIP 术语成交的合同中看出端倪。在这些合同中,卖方对买方货物的交付以交易单证的交付为凭据,而不是以实际货物的交付为凭据。这种类型的交易在总贸易量中占了很大一部分,因此单证的重要性是不能被低估的。

没有正确的单证,卖方不能将货物送出国门和收到货款,买方也无法正常地提取货物。

一笔交易能够顺利进行,极度依赖于每个阶段相关单证的正确制作和提交。对买卖双方来说,具备应有的制单能力是成为合格的外贸从业人员的重要因素。同时,相对于进口商来说,出口商更容易受到单证的影响。首先,单证是实现出口的必要条件。要通过海关的强制性监管和控制,提交规定的单证是前提条件。必要的单证不齐全或提交的单证有误是通关延误的普遍原因。

对进口商来说,单证也是办理进口清关手续的一个重要内容。另外,单证也是出口商履行合同义务的证据。销售合同上列出的大部分义务可以通过取得某些特定单证或某张单证上的特定内容反映出来。例如,提单可以说明出口商履行装运货物的细节。有时,进口商要求提供一些单证,从而确保所装运的货物如其所期盼;可能还需要提供品质证书以保证产品质量。通过单证,出口商可以证明其已经在正确的时间、以正确的方式将正确的货物装运至正确的地点。另外,在大多数情况下,出口商需要使用单证来结汇。再回到付款这个主题,我们可以很明显地看到,大多数颇受欢迎的付款方式都以附带单证为条件,尤其是作为交易凭证的提单。如果不能提供规定的单证,出口商就不能为已装运的货物顺利结汇。

1.2　Main Kinds of International Trade Documents 外贸单证的主要类型

There are several kinds of documents used in international trade. In many cases, documents issued by one entity (e.g. the bill of lading issued by a shipping or logistics company) may be required by more than one entity (e.g. the importer, the customs authority of the country of import). The following is a brief summary of the kinds of international trade documents. Each will be treated in detail in the chapters that followed.

1.Transaction Documents

They are the documents the buyer and the seller generate to form the basis of their agreement to sell and purchase specific goods under specific terms and conditions. Transaction documents include the letter of inquiry, request for proposal, proposal, letter of intent, purchase order, contract of sale, proforma invoice, and commercial invoice. Not all transactions require each of these documents.

2.Transport Documents

They are the documents issued by the logistics company as a receipt and contract for carriage of the goods to the stated destination. These organizations also issue insurance and inspection certificate. All international transactions involving the transport of goods require some form of bill of lading.

3.Import Documents

These documents are required by the customs authority of the country of import and vary greatly from one country to another. The minimum documents' requirement is an entry form and a commercial invoice. However, many other forms may be required, especially if the imported merchandise is sensitive (e.g. animals, weapons, drugs, food), if the importer is requesting special tariff treatment under an import program (e.g. GSP, NAFTA) or if the import comes from certain countries.

Import documents generally include import licenses and permits, commercial invoice, bill of lading, certificate of origin, import declaration, and inspection certificate. In certain countries, consular invoice, insurance certificate, international exchange documents and bank draft may be required.

4.Banking Documents

These documents are required by the banks especially through a documentary letter of credit or documentary collection procedure. Banking documents include the application for letter of credit or documentary collection, collection order, draft or acceptance, order to open an L/C, documentary L/C, L/C advice, order amendment, amendment notification, and order of assignment. Related documents include those which make part of a document package for the importer for the import clearance of the goods in the country of destination.

5.Special Documents

Special documents are documents required by the importing or exporting country for special commodities. They include export license for natural resources, import license for important goods (weapons, ammunition, etc.), documents relevant with quota. Documents related to specialized goods and trade sensitive countries provide the greatest challenge to traders.

国际贸易主要使用几类单证。多数情况下,一个实体开出的单证(比如由船运公司或者物流公司开具的提单)可能被不止一个实体(比如进口商、进口国海关等)所需要。以下是外贸单证的简单分类。每类单证将在后面章节中做详细介绍。

1.交易单证

交易单证是买卖双方缮制的,构成了在特定条款和条件下卖或买特定商品所达成的协议的基础。交易单证包括询盘函、报盘函、递盘/报盘、意向书、购货订单、销售合同、形式发票和商业发票。不是所有的交易都需要全部这些交易单证的。

2.运输单证

作为货物装运到指定目的地的收据和合同,运输单证由物流公司开具。这些物流公司也开具保险和检验证书。所有涉及货物运输的国际贸易都要求某种格式的提单。

3.进口单证

各进口国海关当局对进口单证都做了要求,并且不同国家的要求也截然不同。对进口单证的最低要求是提供报关单和商业发票。但是在很多情况下,提供其他形式的单证也很必要,特别是当涉及敏感度较高的进口商品(如动物、武器、药品和食物)时;当进口商要求在某项进口协定下(如普惠制或《北美自由贸易协定》)享受特别关税待遇时;或当进口商来自于某些特定的国家时。

进口单证通常包括进口许可证和批文、商业发票、提单、原产地证书、进口报关单和检验证书。在某些国家,领事发票、保险凭证、外汇单证和银行汇票可能被要求提供。

4.银行单证

银行要求银行单证,特别是在通过跟单信用证或跟单托收程序进行贸易的情况下。银行单证包括信用证申请书或跟单托收申请书、托收委托书、汇票或承兑汇票、开立信用证通

知书、跟单信用证、信用证通知、变更通知、修改通知书和变更安排书。相关单证包括了进口
商在目的国进口货物通关所需要的单证。

5.特殊单证

特殊单证是进口国或出口国针对特殊商品而要求提供的单证。其包括自然资源出口许
可证、重要商品(如武器、弹药等)进口许可证,以及与配额相关的单证。与特殊商品和贸易
敏感国家相关的单证对交易者来说挑战最大。

1.3　Parties to International Trade Documents　外贸单证当事人

The core of every business transaction is a buyer and a seller, and specialized parties.

1.Exporter/Seller

In most transactions the exporters/sellers are responsible for the documents required by the export authorities, the importers/buyers, or the banks in documentary collection or letter of credit. However, not all the documents listed below are required in all transactions. The exporters/sellers may issue/provide the documents as follows,and soon:

(1)Transaction documents:including proposal, bid or quotation, contract for sale of goods, proforma invoice, and commercial invoice, and so on.

(2)Export documents:including export license, export declaration, and inspection certificate, and so on.

(3)Transport and insurance documents:including packing list, and bill of lading/air waybill, and so on.

(4)Banking documents:including documentary collection order and bank draft / bill of exchange, if documentary collection is used;including bank draft/bill of exchange, if documentary letter of credit is used.

(5)Special documents:including certificate of origin, consular invoice, and so on.

2.Importer/Buyer

Importer/buyer has primary responsibility for preparing a number of documents required by the customs authorities of the country of import. Since these documents are easily secured by the exporter in the country of export, the importer is responsible for notifying the exporter of the documents required. The importer/buyer may issue/provide the documents as follows:

(1)Transaction documents:including request for proposal or request for quotation, bid or quotation, contract for sale of goods, proforma invoice, and commercial invoice.

(2)Transport and insurance documents:including packing list and bill of lading / air waybill.

(3)Banking documents:including letter of credit application, if documentary letter of credit is used.

(4)Import documents:including import permit/license, special customs invoice, customs declaration and other specialized documents.

3.Export Authority

Export authority has three major responsibilities: law enforcement, revenue collection and census. The following is a list of the basic export documents required by most countries:

(1)Export license/permit.

(2)Export declaration, including destination control or ultimate consignee statement.

(3)Bill of lading.

(4)Commercial invoice.

(5)Certificate of origin.

(6)Inspection certificate.

4.Import Authority

Import authority has three major responsibilities: law enforcement, revenue collection and census. Importers often use customs brokers to assist in import formalities. The following is a list of the basic import documents required by most countries:

(1)Import permit/license.

(2)Import declaration.

(3)Bill of lading.

(4)Commercial invoice.

(5)Certificate of origin.

(6)Inspection certificate.

5.Freight Forwarder/Logistics Company

International freight forwarders are in the business of moving goods from one country to another. Logistics companies are in the business of planning and controlling the flow of raw materials, work in progress, or finished products from point of origin to point of destination. Documents issued by the logistics company are as follows:

(1)Bill of lading.

(2)Insurance certificate.

(3)Inspection certificate.

6.Customs Broker

Customs brokers assist in all aspects of clearing imported goods through customs. They handle the sequence of customs formalities and other details critical to the legal and speedy import and export of goods. Documents issued by the customs broker are as follows:

(1)Application for import license and import permit.

(2)Import declaration.

(3)Special customs invoice.

(4)Documents and applications related to refunds and drawback.

7.Freight Carrier (Shipping Line, Airline, Railroad, Barge Line, Courier)

Freight carriers are in the business of moving goods from one country to another. Carriers range from huge ocean shipping lines that move ships that load quantities of crude oil or grain, to courier companies that handle small package shipments of less than one-half kilogram.

It is very important to realize that some carriers are specialists in only one mode of transport. Since international shipments often require more than one mode of transport (sea , air , and land),it may be necessary to use a shipper (or a logistics company) that can act as a "multimodal transport operator" which takes responsibility for the entire shipping process from point of origin to point of final destination.

Documents issued by freight carriers are as follows :

(1)Bill of lading.

(2)Insurance certificate.

(3)Air waybill.

8.Government Regulatory Agency

Government regulatory agencies are in the business of enforcing specific laws and regulations designed to protect the economic well-being in addition to the health and safety of their citizens. The government regulatory agencies in US include : Food and Drug Administration , Animal and Plant Health Inspection Service , and Consumer Product Safety Commission.

Documents issued by government regulatory agencies are as follows :

(1)Certificate of inspection.

(2)Phytosanitary certificate.

(3)Veterinary health certificate.

(4)Safety testing certificate.

(5)Fumigation/sterilization certificate.

(6)Dangerous goods certificate.

9.International Bank

International banks handle all aspects of international payments from importers to exporters , including the documentary collection and the letter of credit. Documents issued by the international banks are as follows :

(1)Documentary collection order.

(2)Documentary letter of credit.

(3)Documentary letter of credit amendment.

(4)Documentary letter of credit advice.

(5)Bank draft/bill of exchange.

10.Insurance Company

Insurance companies provide coverage by contract to indemnity or guarantee another party against risk of losses by stated perils , such as the risk of loss or damage to shipments of cargoes in international trade. Some of the large logistics companies have their own insurance companies as subsidiaries. Documents issued by insurance companies are insurance policies or insurance certificates.

11.Attorney

Attorneys and law firms are in the business of providing legal advice to clients. The role of attorneys varies greatly from country to country. The contract for sale of goods is issued by the attorney.

12.Inspection Company

Inspection companies are in the business of providing testing services for exporters, importers, export authorities and import authorities. Inspection companies are often licensed by government agencies or have professional affiliations with recognized industry groups. Some countries require that samples of products be sent in advance of the full shipment to laboratories within the country of import for testing, while others are satisfied with certificates generated in the country of export prior to shipment.

Documents issued by inspection companies are as follows:

(1)Certificate of inspection.

(2)Phytosanitary certificate.

(3)Veterinary health certificate.

(4)Safety testing certificate.

(5)Fumigation/sterilization certificate.

(6)Dangerous goods certificate.

(7)Quality certificate.

13.Notary Public

Most countries have appointed or commissioned individuals who are given authority to identify and certify the identity of persons who sign documents with proof of their signatures. In some countries, such as England, France and Germany, these individuals often have special legal training, while in other countries they can be qualified after a short course, test and background check. Some countries have no provision for such commissioned persons, in which event consular, judicial or legal professionals will often be used to fulfill authentication requirements.

The key documents "certified" or "notarized" by notaries are:

(1)Limited power of attorney.

(2)Contract and inspection certificates.

(3)Consular invoice.

14.Chamber of Commerce

Chambers of commerce provide export education, country market information, assistance with export documents and trade leads.

Documents issued by chambers of commerce are as follows:

(1)Certificate of origin.

(2)Certificate of free sale.

15.Consular Office

Consular official or office of country of import, located in the country of export, is often empowered to "certify" certain documents or forms required for the eventual import of goods.

Documents issued by the consular office are as follows:

(1)Commercial invoice.

（2）Customs invoice.

（3）Consular invoice.

所有商业交易的核心都离不开买方、卖方以及专业化当事人。

1.出口商/卖方

在大多数交易中,出口商/卖方负责向出口国当局、进口商/买方,以及跟单托收或者信用证交易下的银行出具其所要求的单证。然而,并不是所有交易都需要下面列出的全部单证。出口商/卖方可能出具或提供的单证如下:

（1）交易单证,包括询价、投标或报价、货物销售合同、形式发票、商业发票等。

（2）出口单证,包括出口许可证、出口报关单、检验证书等。

（3）运输和保险单证,包括装箱单、提单/航空货运单等。

（4）银行单证。如果采用跟单托收,银行单证包括跟单托收单和银行汇票;如果采用跟单信用证,银行单证包括银行汇票。

（5）特殊单证,包括原产地证书、领事发票等。

2.进口商/买方

进口商/买方的主要责任是准备进口国海关当局所要求的单证。由于出口国的出口商很容易获取这些单证,进口商负责通知出口商所需的单证。进口商/买方可能出具或提供的单证如下:

（1）交易单证,包括报价函、投标或报价、商品销售合同、形式发票和商业发票。

（2）运输和保险单证,包括装箱单、提单/航空货运单。

（3）银行单证。如果使用跟单信用证,需提供信用证申请书。

（4）进口单证,包括进口许可证、特殊的海关发票、海关报关单和其他专门的单证。

3.出口方当局

出口方当局有三个主要职责:执法、征税和普查。下面列举了大多数国家要求的基本的出口单证:

（1）出口许可证。

（2）出口报关单,包括目的地管制声明或者最终收货人声明。

（3）提单。

（4）商业发票。

（5）原产地证书。

（6）检验证书。

4.进口方当局

进口方当局有三个主要职责:执法、征税和普查。进口商经常雇用报关员协助办理进口事宜。下面列举了大多数国家要求的基本的进口单证:

（1）进口许可证。

（2）进口报关单。

（3）提单。

（4）商业发票。

（5）原产地证书。

（6）检验证书。

5.货运代理/物流公司

国际货运代理公司的业务是将商品从一个国家运输到另一个国家。物流公司的业务是计划和控制原材料、在产品或成品的流动,从供应地运输到目的地。物流公司出具的单证如下:

(1)提单。

(2)保险凭证。

(3)检验证书。

6.报关员

报关员协助办理所有货物进口清关手续。货物能否合法、快速进出口,他们处理清关手续的顺序和其他的细节至关重要。报关员出具的单证如下:

(1)进口许可证申请书和进口许可证。

(2)进口报关单。

(3)特殊海关发票。

(4)与退货和退款有关的单证和申请书。

7.货运承运人(班轮、航空、铁路、驳船、快递)

货运承运人的业务是将商品从一个国家运输到另一个国家。承运人的范围广泛,可以是用海洋班轮运载批量原油或粮食的大公司,也可以是运送不到500克小包装货物的快递公司。

有些承运人只在一种运输方式上是行家,明确这一点非常重要。由于国际货运往往需要不止一种的运输方式(海运、空运、陆运),因此,可能有必要用到托运人(或物流公司),他们能扮演多式联运经营者的角色,负责将货物从供应地运输到最终目的地的整个货运过程。

货运承运人出具的单证如下:

(1)提单。

(2)保险凭证。

(3)航空运单。

8.政府监管机构

政府监管机构的职责是强制执行为保证经济健康运行以及保护公民的健康和安全而制定的特定的法律、法规。在美国,这些政府监管机构包括:食品和药物管理局、动物和植物检验检疫局,以及消费者产品安全委员会。政府监管机构出具的单证如下:

(1)检验证书。

(2)植物检验检疫证书。

(3)兽医卫生证书。

(4)安全检测证书。

(5)熏蒸/消毒证书。

(6)危险品证书。

9.国际银行

国际银行负责处理进口商对出口商的国际支付,包括跟单托收和信用证。国际银行出具的单证如下:

（1）跟单托收单。

（2）跟单信用证。

（3）跟单信用证修改书。

（4）跟单信用证通知书。

（5）银行汇票。

10. 保险公司

国际贸易中，保险公司通过合同提供保险，担保合同另一方在遭受约定危险导致的损失（比如货物运输损失或损坏风险）时能够得到赔偿。一些大型的物流公司有其自己的作为其子公司的保险公司。保险公司出具的单证是保险单或保险凭证。

11. 律师

律师和律师事务所给客户提供法律建议。不同国家的律师，角色大不相同。律师制作货物销售合同。

12. 检验公司

检验公司负责为进出口商、进出口方当局提供商品检验服务。检验公司常常由政府机构或专业公认行业组织颁发牌照。一些国家要求商品样本在全部装运前预先寄进口国实验室进行检验，而另外一些国家则要求在发货之前出口方出具证书即可。

检验公司出具的单证如下：

（1）检验证书。

（2）植物检验检疫证书。

（3）兽医卫生证书。

（4）安全检测证书。

（5）熏蒸/消毒证书。

（6）危险品证书。

（7）品质证书。

13. 公证人

大多数国家任命或委任个人鉴定单证的签字。在一些国家，如英国、法国和德国，公证人通常拥有专门的法律培训，而在另外一些国家，公证人可以在短期培训、测试和背景调查后取得资格。一些国家没有委任这些人，在此情况下，领事、司法或法律专业人士经常履行鉴定责任。

公证人要"鉴定"或"公证"的主要单证是：

（1）有限授权委托书。

（2）合同、检验证书。

（3）领事发票。

14. 商会

商会提供出口培训、国家市场信息，协助出具出口单证，并提供贸易导向。

商会出具的单证如下：

（1）原产地证书。

（2）自由销售证书。

15.领事办公室

进口国在出口国设的领事官或领事办公室,经常被授权为最终进口货物所需的某些单证或表格提供证明。

领事办公室出具的单证如下:

(1)商业发票。

(2)海关发票。

(3)领事发票。

1.4 Basic Requirements for International Trade Documents 外贸单证的基本要求

So far, there has been no well-established standard for documents in international trade. In addition, documents' requirements may differ from transaction to transaction and from country to country, largely. The differences mainly lie in areas such as the types needed, content and languages used, etc. Whatever differences there might be, generally speaking, documents for every transaction should meet such basic requirements as correctness, completeness, conciseness, cleanness and promptness.

迄今为止,还没有任何确定的标准来规范国际贸易单证。此外,每个国家、每笔交易对单证的要求都不同。这些差异主要存在于几个领域,如单证的种类、内容、语言等。不管这些差异是什么,一般来说,每笔交易的单证都应该满足正确、完整、简洁、清洁和迅速等要求。

1.5 Checklist for Documents Errors 单证纠错内容

(1)Check typing errors in the name of commodity, figures such as quantity, package number, unit price and total amount, insurance amount, insurance premium, etc.

(2)Check spelling errors in the names and addresses of the parties concerned.

(3)Avoid redundant, unnecessary or ambiguous words or expressions in such terms as the name, quality, quantity, time or place of shipment, etc.

(4)Avoid correction on the face of the documents.

(5)Mark the date of each document clearly.

(6)Check the title of each document to make them the same as the stipulation of the L/C. For instance, an insurance certificate is not acceptable when the L/C requires an insurance policy.

(7)Make sure some documents' reference numbers required to be mentioned in other documents are correctly presented.

(8)Prepare exactly the same numbers of originals and duplicates as required.

(9)All documents must be properly issued, signed and sealed by the right party.

(10)Arrange the documents according to the order of the issuing date on the documents.

　　(1)审查商品的名称和数量、包装号码、单价、总额、保险金额、保险费等数字是否有打印错误。

　　(2)审查有关各方的名称和地址是否有拼写错误。

　　(3)避免在名称、质量、数量、装船的时间或地点等条款上出现冗余的、不必要的或模糊的词语或表达。

　　(4)避免在单证表面进行修改。

　　(5)每份单证的日期都清楚标示。

　　(6)确定每份单证的标题与信用证规定的一致。例如,若信用证要求的是保险单,那么银行不接受保险凭证。

　　(7)若要求标示相关单证的参考号码,那么应确保该单证的参考号码在其他单证上被正确标示。

　　(8)正本和副本的数量应符合规定。

　　(9)所有的单证都应由正确的当事人出具、签署和盖章。

　　(10)应根据单证上的签发日期顺序排列单证。

1.6　Relevant International Regulations and Practices 相关国际规则与惯例

1.International Regulations and Practices Relevant with Contract

The United Nations Convention on Contracts for the International Sale of Goods (CISG) strives to create a uniform international sales law, and to regulate the rights and obligations of buyers and sellers in international transactions for the sale of goods. Until now, a number of countries that account for two-thirds of all world trades have joined the CISG, and the number is on the rise.

2.International Regulations and Practices Relevant with International Payment

　　(1)International Regulations and Practices for Collection: The Uniform Rules for Collections No. 522 (URC522).

URC522 underlines the need for the principal and/or the remitting bank to attach a separate document, the collection instruction, to every collection subject to the Rules, that makes it very clear that banks will not examine documents, particularly not to look for instructions and addresses problems in respect of documents against acceptance (D/A) and documents against payment (D/P), and clearly indicates that banks have no obligation to store and insure goods when instructed.

　　(2)Uniform Customs and Practice for Documentary Credits No.600 (UCP600).

Uniform Customs and Practice for Documentary Credits (UCP) is a set of rules on the issuance and use of letters of credit. The latest version, called the UCP600, formally commenced on July 1st, 2007.

UCP600 applies to any documentary L/C when the text of the L/C expressly indicates that it is subject to UCP600. UCP600 is binding on all parties to the L/C unless expressly modified or excluded by the L/C.

3.International Regulations and Practices Relevant with Trade Terms

（1）Warsaw-Oxford Rules 1932.

（2）Revised American Foreign Trade Definitions 1990.

（3）International Rules for the Interpretation of Trade Terms 2010 (INCOTERMS 2010).

4. International Regulations and Practices Relevant with Transportation for International Trade

（1）International Regulations and Practices Relevant with Ocean Transportation：

①International Convention for the Unification of Certain Rules of Law Relating to Bills of Lading,1924 (Hague Rules).

②Protocol to Amend the International Convention for the Unification of Certain Rules of Law Relating to Bills of Lading (The 1968 Brussels Protocol/Visby Rules).

③The United Nations Convention on the Carriage of Goods by Sea,1978 (Hamburg Rules).

④CMI Uniform Rules for Sea Waybills,1990.

（2）International Regulations and Practices Relevant with Carriage of Goods by Road：Convention on the Contract for the International Carriage of Goods by Road (CMR).

（3）International Regulations and Practices Relevant with Carriage of Goods by Rail：Convention Concerning International Carriage of Goods by Rail (CIM), Agreement on International Railroad through Transport of Goods (CMIC).

5. International Regulations and Practices Relevant with International Cargo Transportation Insurance

（1）China Insurance Clause (CIC).

（2）W/W Clause.

（3）Institute Cargo Clause (ICC).

6.International Regulations and Practices Relevant with International Trade Arbitration

（1）Convention on the Recognition and Enforcement of Foreign Arbitral Awards,1958.

（2）UNCITRAL Arbitration Rules,1976.

（3）UNCITRAL Model Law on International Commercial Arbitration,1985.

1.与合同相关的国际规则与惯例

《联合国国际货物销售合同公约》力求建立一个能够规定国际货物销售交易中买卖双方的权利和义务的统一的国际销售法。到目前为止,世界上2/3的国家已经加入了该公约,这个数字还在上升。

2.与国际支付相关的国际规则与惯例

（1）托收业务中的国际规则和惯例:《托收统一规则》(国际商会第522号出版物,简称URC522)。

URC522强调客户和/或托收行有必要在每一笔遵守该规则的托收业务中特别附上一个单独的文件——托收指示,在其中清楚指出银行对于委托人提交的托收单证不予审查,尤其是对与承兑交单(D/A)和付款交单(D/P)有关的指示和地址问题,银行不予核对,并明确指出,银行在办理托收业务时没有义务对商品进行储存和投保。

(2)《跟单信用证统一惯例》(国际商会第600号出版物)。

《跟单信用证统一惯例》(UCP)是一套适用于信用证开立和使用的规则。最新版本为国际商会2007年7月1日颁布的第600号出版物,简称UCP600。

UCP600适用于所有在正文中标明按照该惯例办理的跟单信用证。除非信用证明确修改或排除了该惯例,否则,该惯例对一切相关当事人均具有约束力。

3.与贸易术语相关的国际规则与惯例

(1)《1932年华沙–牛津规则》。

(2)《1990年美国对外贸易定义修订本》。

(3)《2010年国际贸易术语解释通则》(INCOTERMS 2010)。

4.与国际贸易运输相关的国际规则与惯例

(1)与海洋运输相关的国际规则与惯例:

①《统一提单的若干法律规定的国际公约》(1924年)(《海牙规则》)。

②《修改统一提单的若干法律规定的国际公约议定书》(《1968年布鲁塞尔议定书》《维斯比规则》)。

③《联合国海上货物运输公约》(1978年)(《汉堡规则》)。

④《1990年国际海事委员会海运单统一规则》。

(2)与公路货运相关的国际规则与惯例:《国际公路货物运输合同公约》(CMR)。

(3)与铁路货运相关的国际规则与惯例:《国际铁路货物运输公约》(CIM)和《国际铁路货物联合运输协定》(CMIC)。

5.与国际货物运输保险相关的国际规则与惯例

(1)中国保险条款 (CIC)。

(2)仓至仓条款。

(3)协会货物条款 (ICC)。

6.与国际贸易仲裁相关的国际规则与惯例

(1)《承认及执行外国仲裁裁决公约》(1958年)。

(2)《联合国国际贸易法委员会仲裁规则》(1976年)。

(3)《联合国国际贸易法委员会国际商事仲裁示范法》(1985年)。

1.7   Skills of Making Documents
制单技巧

1.Payer's Identification

Payer, drawee, payor.

2.Consignee's Identification

Consignee, cargo receiver, receiver.

3.Identification of Loading Port and Port of Delivery

Loading port, port of loading, port of shipment, port of unloading, port of delivery, discharging port, port of discharge, port of debarkation.

4.Time Sequence of Making Documents

The dates of issuing documents should be consistent with logic and international practice. The bill of lading date usually is the key to confirm the dates of other documents. Draft date should be later than the date of bill of lading, invoice date and other documents' dates, but not later than the validity of the L/C. The relationship of all documents' dates is as follows:

(1)The invoice date should be on the first date of all the documents.

(2)The bill of lading date should not be earlier than the shipping date stipulated in the L/C.

(3)The policy date issued should be earlier than or equal to the date of the bill of lading (generally, 2 days early than the date of the bill of lading), but not earlier than the invoice date.

(4)Packing list date should be equal to or later than invoice date, but must be before the date of the bill of lading.

(5)The date of certificate of origin should not be earlier than the invoice date, but not later than the date of bill of lading.

(6)The date of commodity inspection certificate should not be later than the date of bill of lading, but not too much earlier than the date of bill of lading, especially fresh, easy to be bad goods.

(7)The date of beneficiary's certificate shall be equal to or later than the date of bill of lading.

(8)The shipping date should be equal to or late than the date of the bill of lading within 3 days.

(9)The date of certificate of shipping company should be equal to or early than the date of the bill of lading.

1.付款人的表示方法

如 payer、drawee、payor。

2.收货人的表示方法

如 consignee、cargo receiver、receiver。

3.装货港和卸货港的表示方法

如 loading port、port of loading、port of shipment、port of unloading、port of delivery、discharging port、port of discharge、port of debarkation。

4.制作单证的时间顺序

各种单证的签发日期应符合逻辑和国际惯例。通常提单日期是确定其他单据日期的关键。汇票日期应晚于提单、发票和其他单证的日期,但不能晚于信用证的有效期。各单证日期的关系如下:

(1)发票日期应在各单证的日期之首。

(2)提单日不能早于信用证规定的装运期。

(3)保单的签发日应早于或等于提单日期(一般早于提单2天),但不能早于发票日期。

(4)装箱单日期应等于或迟于发票日期,但必须在提单日之前。

(5)原产地证书日期应不早于发票日期,但不迟于提单日期。

(6)商品检验证书的日期应不晚于提单日期,但也不能过分早于提单日,尤其是鲜活、容易变质的商品。

（7）受益人证明日期应等于或晚于提单日。

（8）装船日期应等于或晚于提单日3天以内。

（9）船运公司证明日期应等于或早于提单日。

1.8   Main Links of Procedure of Export Documents 出口单证流程要点

The procedure of export documents can be shown by Figure 1-1.

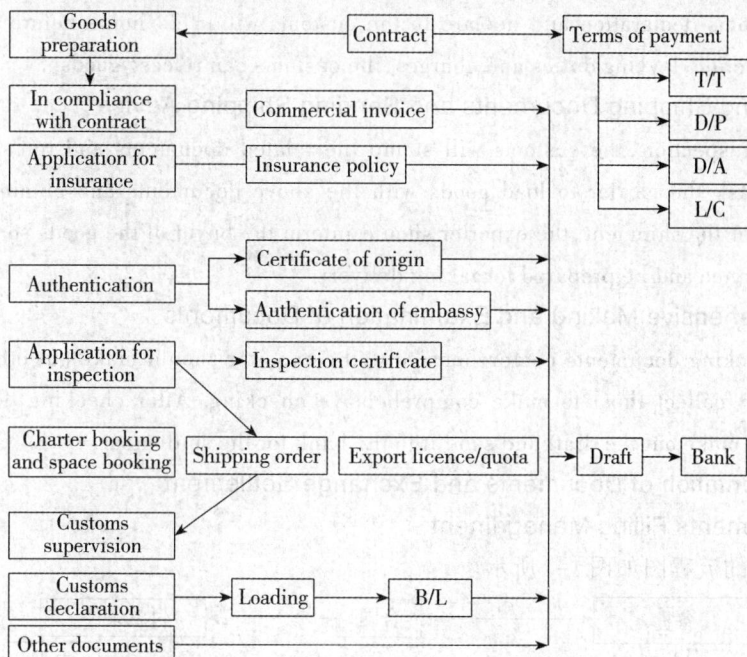

Figure 1-1   Procedure of Export Documents

1.Order Handling and Goods Preparation

According to requirements of the contract or the L/C, the related person should urge the factory or the warehouse to arrange goods and should check the description, quality, quantity, specification, packing and shipping mark of goods to make sure goods are of good quality and are well packed. Besides, make sure that the quantity of goods meets the need and the shipping mark is clear.

2.Urging, Examining and Amending an L/C

Try to urge the importer to open the L/C if he fails to open it in due course. After receiving the L/C, the exporter should register and check it and should ask for amendment to it if he finds some problems.

3.Application for Commodity Inspection

When goods are listed in the catalogue of inspection or are required to be inspected by the contract or the L/C, Lgoods must undergo the inspection and quarantine carried out by the inspection authority before getting the customs clearance bill or the inspection certificate.

4.Application of Commodity Insurance

Covering insurance for the contract on CIF basis, the exporter should cover the goods transportation insurance with the insurance company and get insurance documents before shipping goods.

5.Authentication of Diplomatic Missions

The diplomatic missions or other authorized organizations authenticate the identification of the signer of one file to certify the validity of the file.

6.Handling Export Consignment

Filling in export shipping note. Obtaining the shipping order.

7.Handling Export Declaration

After handling the consignment and obtaining the shipping order, the consigner should fill in the export customs declaration and declare to the customs within 24 hours before loading. After checking, inspection, levying duties and charges, the customs can release goods.

8.Obtaining Shipping Documents and Sending Shipping Advice

After the inspection, the customs will stamp the related documents and release goods. The consigner can ask the carrier to load goods with the above documents and obtain the shipping documents. After the shipment, the exporter should inform the buyer of the goods so that the buyer can cover insurance and be prepared for taking delivery.

9.Comprehensive Making and Examination of Documents

When checking documents comprehensively, the exporter should make out other documents accordingly and collect them to make comprehensive checking. After checking documents, the exporter should make out the draft and send it to the bank for the settlement.

10. Presentation of Documents and Exchange Settlement

11. Documents Filling Management

出口单证的流程图如图1-1所示。

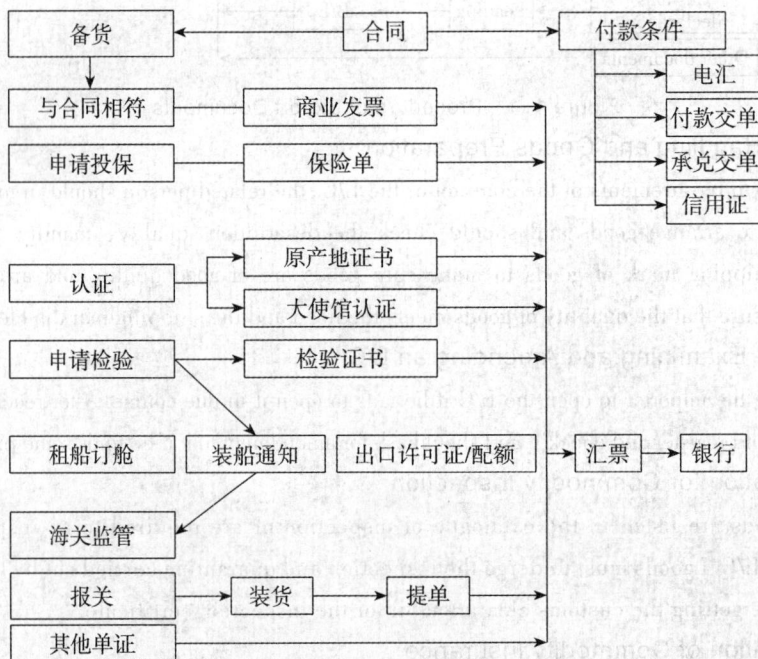

图1-1 出口单证流程图

1.收发订单与备货

根据合同或者信用证的要求,相关人员应该敦促厂方或者仓库备货;同时,为了确保货品的质量和包装完好,应该派人员对货品的描述、质量、数量、说明书、包装以及唛头进行检查;此外,要确保货品的数量无误以及唛头的字迹清晰。

2.催证、审证与改证

如果进口商到期还未能开证,出口商应该敦促进口商办理开证手续。在收到信用证之后,出口商应该进行登记、核实,发现问题后应该及时修改信用证。

3.货物检验申请

合同或信用证中所列货物必须接受检查时,必须经检验机构检验和检疫之后才能获得清关单或检验证书。

4.货物投保申请

以到岸价合同为基础投保,出口商应该与保险公司办理货物运输保险并在货物装运之前取得保险单证。

5.外交使团认证

外交使团或其他授权机构对文件签署者进行身份认证,证明文件的有效性。

6.办理出口托运手续

填写出口装货通知单,获取装货单。

7.办理出口报关手续

在办理托运手续和获取装货单后,委托人应该填写出口报关单并在装货前的24小时内报关。在审查、检验和缴纳关税和费用后,海关才予以放行。

8.取得装运单证和发放已装船通知

货物进行检验之后,海关将在相关的单证上盖章并允许货物通行。委托人可以根据上述单证要求承运人装载货物并获取装运单证。在装运后,出口商应该通知买方使得买方及时投保,并做好交接的准备。

9.综合制单与审单

出口商对单证进行综合的审核时,应该填写相应的其他单证,并逐一进行综合的审核。在审核完单证之后,出口商应该填写汇票,并送至银行进行结算。

10. 交单结汇

11. 单证归档管理

1.9　General Procedure of Import Documents
进口单证的一般程序

(1)Application of the quota certificate or the import license.

(2)Application of opening the L/C.

(3)Amendment to the L/C.

(4)Charter, shipping space booking and insurance.

(5)Examination of documents and payment of international exchange.

(6)Application of goods inspection and the customs clearance.

（1）申请配额证明或进口许可证。

（2）申请开立信用证。

（3）修改信用证。

（4）租船、订舱与投保。

（5）审查单证与支付外汇。

（6）货物报检申请和清关。

1.10 Methods of Examining Documents
审单的方法

The basic ways of documents review are longitudinal auditing method and lateral auditing method.

1.Longitudinal Auditing Method

On the basis of the L / C and UCP600, the documents specified should be checked, the contents of the documents should comply with the provisions of the L/C and UCP600 and achieve "consistent documents".

2.Lateral Auditing Method

Other provisions of the documents should be reviewed centered with the commercial invoices to make relevant content consistent with each other.

单证审核的基本方法有纵向审核法和横向审核法。

1.纵向审核法

以信用证和UCP600为基础,对规定的各项单证进行审核,各单证的内容要符合信用证和UCP600的规定,做到单证相符。

2.横向审核法

单证的其他规定应该以商业发票为中心进行审核,使有关内容互相一致,做到单单相符。

1.11 Key Projects of Examining Documents
审单的重点项目

Drafts, invoices, transport documents and insurance policies are the key projects of examining documents.

汇票、发票、运输单证和保险单是审单的重点项目。

1.12 Key Points Reviewed and Common Discrepancies of Main Documents
主要单证的审核要点及常见不符点

Under the L/C, documents presented must be audited one by one. The followings are the key points reviewed and common discrepancies of main documents (Table 1-1).

Table 1-1   Key Points Reviewed and Common
                              Discrepancies of Main Documents

Types of Documents	Key Points Reviewed	Common Discrepancies
Commercial Invoice	(1) The invoice should be issued by the beneficiary i.e. the opener should be consistent with the beneficiary's name and address of the L/C (2) The description of goods such as name of commodity, quantity, unit price, packing, price terms and contract number, must be in strict accordance with the L/C (3) The payee / bearer of invoice shall be the applicant and the payee should be consistent with the applicant's name and address of the L/C (4) The invoice date can be earlier than the issuing date and shall not be later than the presentation period and the expiry date of the L/C (5) The invoice amount should be the same as the draft amount. Unit price and trade terms of invoice should be consistent with the L/C. The bank is not responsible for checking the detail calculation process or the arithmetic results (6) The signature of the invoice generally is not needed, unless otherwise stated in the L/C (7) The port of shipment, the port of discharge, shipping mark, quantity and weight of invoice should be consistent with other documents listed	(1) The opener of invoice is not the beneficiary of the L/C (2) The name of invoice does not conform to the stipulations of the L/C (3) The payee / bearer of invoice is not in conformity with the requirements of the L/C (4) The name of importer is different with the applicant of the L/C (5) The quantity, invoice amount and unit price do not agree with the L/C or are not within the allowed margin of increase or decrease in the L/C (6) The description of the goods of invoice is inconsistent with the description of the goods in the L/C (7) The loading port or the port of destination on the invoice does not agree with the bill of lading
Packing List/Weight List	(1) The name and copies of documents must be consistent with the requirements of the L/C (2) The number and date of packing list must be exactly the same as the invoices' (3) Generally, packing list / weight list do not show unit price and total amount (4) The size of packages, packing materials, the means of packing, gross weight/net weight/tare weight must be consistent with the invoices'	(1) Packing list/weight list does not conform to the stipulations of the L/C (2) Number and date of packing list do not agree with the invoices' (3) The consignee and signature of packing list are wrong (4) The contract number and destination of packing list do not agree with the invoices' (5) The specifications and packing of packing list are wrong (6) The name of goods, shipping mark, gross weight, etc. are wrong

Continued

Types of Documents	Key Points Reviewed	Common Discrepancies
Bill of Lading	(1) The number of copies of full set of bill of lading must be presented as the requirement stipulated in the L/C (2) The payee/bearer of bill of lading should be filled in the requirement of the L/C (3) The notify party of bill of lading should be consistent with the provisions of the L/C (4) The consignor of bill of lading shall be consistent with the beneficiary of the L/C (5) The bill of lading should indicate the name of the carrier and be signed by the carrier or its agent, the master or his agent (6) Unless there are special provisions, the bill of lading shall be clean on board bill of lading (7) When the price term is CFR or CIF, freight column marked should be "Freight Prepaid" or "Freight Paid". When the price term is FOB, freight column marked should be "Freight Collect" (8) The date of the bill of lading should be not later than the latest shipping date stipulated in the L/C (9) The bill of lading date should be not later than 21 days after the date of shipment (If the L/C has other regulations, it should be according to its provisions) (10) Number, shipping mark, quantity, name of vessel and voyage contained in the bill of lading should be consistent with the invoice. Description of goods is available, but must not conflict with the invoices'	(1) The types of the bill of lading submitted are not consistent with the stipulations of the L/C (2) Fail to submit the full set of effective bill of lading (3) The name of the shipper is inconsistent with the L/C (4) The name of the consignee is inconsistent with the L/C (5) The name of the notify party does not agree with the L/C (6) Not properly endorsed (if required) as stipulated in the L/C (7) The bill of lading submitted is not clean (8) The information listed in the shipping documents such as name, packing and quantity of goods are not in conformity with the L/C (9) Freight prepaid or freight collect is not proved as stipulations in the L/C (10) Not indicate the name of the carrier
Certificate of Origin	(1) Documents should be signed by the agency the letter of credit designated. If there is no regulation, documents issued by the beneficiary are also acceptable (2) Name of commodity, marks, quality, quantity and price of the relevant goods records should be consistent with the L/C, invoice and other documents (3) Ensure that the country of origin recorded in the certificate of origin conforms to the requirements of the L/C (4) The issuing date should not be later than the date of shipment	(1) The specy of certificate of origin submitted does not agree with the L/C (2) The agency of certificate of origin does not conform to the requirements of the L/C (3) The goods information specified in the certificate of origin does not agree with the L/C, invoice and other documents (4) The country of origin recorded in the certificate of origin does not match the requirements of the L/C (5) The issuing date of the certificate of origin is after the date of shipment

Continued

Types of Documents	Key Points Reviewed	Common Discrepancies
Insurance Policy	(1) Only insurance companies or underwriters or their agents have the right to issue the insurance documents (2) Under the CIF and CIP, the insured or the beneficiary is the seller. The insurance policy in negotiable form shall be endorsed by the insured (3) Banks accept the insurance documents, certificates of insurance and insurance declarations. Insurance policy can replace certificate, but the certificate of insurance can not take the place of the policy (4) The same currency must be used to issue the insurance document as to open the L/C. The minimum amount of insurance amount shall be the CIF or CIP value plus 10%, or the bigger one of 110% of total amount of the L/C for payment, acceptance or negotiation and 110% of the invoice value (5) Original copies of insurance policy shall conform to the requirements of the L/C (6) The date of the insurance policy should not be later than the issuing date of the B/L (7) Coverage should comply with the stipulations of the L/C (8) Compensation place should comply with the stipulations of the L/C, usually in the importing country (9) Name of vessel, route, port, date of shipment listed on the insurance policy should be consistent with the bill of lading (10) Description of goods should list the name of commodity, marks, quantity and so on, and should be consistent with the invoice, bill of lading and other shipping documents	(1) The type of the insurance policy does not conform to the stipulations of the L/C (2) The insurance policy is not issued by the insurance company or underwriter (3) The currency or amount of insurance does not agree with the L/C (4) The description of the goods on the insurance policy does not agree with the L/C (5) The insurance amount in lowercase or uppercase is inconsistent with each other. The amount in words is not correct (6) Port of shipment or port of discharge does not agree with the stipulations of the L/C (7) Coverage doesn't agree with the stipulations of the L/C. For example, make a mistake in taking failure to delivery risk as TPND (8) Not provide a full range of insurance documents (9) Insurance policy without endorsement or endorsement is not correct (10) The date of insurance policy is later than the date of bill of lading

Continued

Types of Documents	Key Points Reviewed	Common Discrepancies
Inspection Certificate	(1) It should be issued by the issuing agency stipulated by the L/C (2) Inspection items and contents should accord with the requirements of the L/C. If inspection results are not in conformity with the requirements of the L/C, the buyer can refuse to pay (3) The date of inspection should not be later than the date of shipment, but not too early, otherwise it will lead to the failure test	(1) The types of the inspection certificate submitted do not agree with the L/C (2) The issuing institutions of the inspection certificate do not conform to the requirements of the L/C (3) Inspection items and contents do not conform to the requirements of the L/C. Inspection results are not in conformity with the requirements of L/C (4) The inspection date is later than the date of bill of lading, or fresh, perishable commodities are inspected too early
Bill of Exchange / draft	(1) Under L/C, the draft should list drawn clause including the issuing bank, L/C number and the issuing date which should be consistent with the L/C (2) The currency and the amount should be in conformity with the stipulations of the L/C. The amount in lowercase or uppercase is inconsistent with each other. Draft amount in general should be 100% of the invoice value, and no more than the L/C amount (3) The payer of draft shall be the issuing bank or the paying bank specified. If the paying bank is not provided by the L/C, it should be the issuing bank and the applicant should not pay (4) The issuer of draft shall be the beneficiary, usually exporter, and should be consistent with the beneficiary's name and place of the L/C (5) The payment deadline of draft shall be consistent with the L/C (6) The issuing date of draft must be within the validity of the L/C. It should not be earlier than the invoice date (7) The payee of draft is usually the negotiating bank (8) The issuer of draft must sign and seal. Draft without the signature and seal of the issuer is invalid	(1) The issuing date of the draft is later than the validity of the L/C (2) The sum of the draft is greater than the amount of the L/C (3) Uppercase and lowercase of the amount of the draft is in not conformity with each other. The amount of draft in words is not accurate, or fails to fill "ONLY" (4) The currency does not agree with the invoice or the L/C (5) The payment deadline does not conform to the stipulations of the L/C, or the date of payment is not clear (6) The contents of the draft have been changed (7) The number of copies of the draft submitted is not correct (8) Drawn clause is not listed according to the stipulations of the L/C (9) Fail to or be wrong to list the L/C number (10) The issuer fails to sign and seal

在信用证项下,所提交的单据必须进行逐一审核。表1-1为主要单证的审核要点及常见不符点的说明。

表1-1　　　　　　　　　　　　　主要单证的审核要点及常见不符点

单据种类	审核要点	常见不符点
商业发票	(1)发票应由信用证受益人开立,即开立人应与受益人的名称、地址一致 (2)商品的名称、数量、单价、包装、价格条件、合同号码等描述,必须与信用证严格一致 (3)发票的抬头应为开证申请人,即抬头应与信用证开证申请人的名称、地址一致 (4)发票日期可以早于开证日期,不得迟于最迟交单日期和信用证到期日 (5)发票金额应与汇票金额相同,发票单价、贸易术语应与信用证相符。银行不负责核对详细核算过程或算术计算结果 (6)发票一般不需要签字,除非信用证另有规定 (7)发票上的装运港、卸货港、唛头、数量、重量应与其他单证所列一致	(1)发票的开立人不是信用证受益人 (2)发票名称不符合信用证规定 (3)发票的抬头与信用证要求不符 (4)进口商名称与信用证上的开证申请人不同 (5)货物数量、发票金额及单价与信用证不一致或不在信用证允许的增减幅度之内 (6)发票对货物的描述与信用证中对货物的描述不相符 (7)发票上的装运港或目的港与提单上的不一致
装箱单/重量单	(1)单据的名称和份数必须和信用证要求相符 (2)装箱单的号码、日期与发票上的完全相同 (3)装箱单/重量单一般不显示单价和总金额 (4)货物包装大小/件数、包装材料、包装方式、毛重/净重/皮重等需与发票上的一致	(1)装箱单/重量单不符合信用证规定 (2)装箱单上的号码、日期与发票上的不一致 (3)装箱单上的收货人、签发人是错误的 (4)装箱单上的合同号、目的地与发票上的不一致 (5)装箱单上的规格、包装有误 (6)货名、唛头、毛重等有错漏之处
提单	(1)提单必须按信用证规定的份数全套提交 (2)提单的抬头应按信用证要求进行填写 (3)提单上的通知人应与信用证的规定相符 (4)提单上的发货人应与信用证的受益人一致 (5)提单应标明承运人名称,并经承运人或其代理人签字或船长或其代理人签字 (6)除非信用证有特别规定,提单应为清洁已装船提单 (7)价格术语为CFR或CIF时,运费栏应注明"Freight Prepaid"或"Freight Paid";如价格术语为FOB,运费栏应注明的是"Freight Collect" (8)提单日期不得迟于信用证所规定的最迟装运日期 (9)提单的交单日期不得迟于装船日期后21天(信用证有其他规定者按其规定) (10)提单所载件数、唛头、数量、船名、航次等应和发票相一致。货物描述可用总称,但不得与发票上的相矛盾	(1)提交的提单种类与信用证规定不相符 (2)未提交全套有效的提单 (3)托运人的名称与信用证不相符 (4)收货人的名称与信用证不相符 (5)通知人的名称与信用证规定不一致 (6)未按信用证规定正确背书(如果需要的话) (7)提交了不清洁的提单 (8)装运单证中所列货物的名称、包装、数量等信息与信用证规定不相符 (9)未按信用证规定证明运费已付或运费到付 (10)未注明承运人的名称

单据种类	审核要点	常见不符点
原产地证书	(1)单证应由信用证指定机构签署；如果没有规定，则受益人出具的单据也可以被接受 (2)货物名称、唛头、品质、数量及价格等有关商品的记载应与信用证、发票以及其他单证一致 (3)确保原产地证书记载的原产国符合信用证要求 (4)签发日期不迟于装船日期	(1)提交的原产地证书种类与信用证规定不一致 (2)原产地证书的出证机构不符合信用证要求 (3)原产地证书上记载的货物信息与信用证、发票及其他单证不一致 (4)原产地证书记载的原产国与信用证要求不一致 (5)原产地证书的签发日期在装船日期后
保险单	(1)只有保险公司或保险商或其代理方才有权签发保险单证 (2)在 CIF、CIP 贸易条件下，被保险人或受益人是卖方。可流通的保险单应由被保险人背书 (3)银行接受保险单证、保险凭证和保险申报单。保险单可以代替保险凭证，但保险凭证不能代替保险单 (4)保险单证必须使用与信用证相同的货币开立。最低保险金额应为 CIF 或 CIP 价格的金额加10%，或者信用证要求付款、承兑或议付金额的110%与发票金额的110%两者中取金额较大者 (5)保险单正本份数应符合信用证要求 (6)保险单日期不应晚于提单签发日期 (7)承保险别应符合信用证规定 (8)赔偿地点应符合信用证规定，一般是在进口国 (9)保险单上所列的船名、航线、港口、装运日期应与提单一致 (10)商品描述应列明货物名称、唛头、数量等，并应与发票、提单及其他运输单据一致	(1)保险单的种类不符合信用证规定 (2)保险单不是由规定的保险公司或保险商出具 (3)保险货币或金额与信用证规定不一致 (4)保险单上对货物的描述与信用证规定不一致 (5)保险金额大小写不一致或大写金额不正确 (6)装货港或卸货港与信用证规定不一致 (7)投保险别与信用证规定不一致，如误把交货不到险当成偷窃、提货不着险 (8)未提供全套保险单证 (9)保险单未经背书或背书不正确 (10)保险单日期迟于提单日期
检验证书	(1)应由信用证规定机构签发 (2)检验项目及内容应符合信用证的要求。检验结果如与信用证要求不符，买家可拒付 (3)检验日期不得迟于装运日期，但也不得过早，否则会导致检验失效	(1)提交的检验证书种类与信用证规定不一致 (2)检验证书的出证机构不符合信用证要求 (3)检验项目及内容不符合信用证要求。检验结果与信用证要求不符 (4)检验日期晚于提单日期，或鲜活、易腐烂商品检验过早

续表

单据种类	审核要点	常见不符点
汇票	（1）信用证名下汇票应列出出票条款，其中开证行、信用证号码及开证日期应与信用证相符 （2）货币名称和金额应与信用证规定相符，且大小写金额一致。汇票金额一般应为100%的发票金额，且不超过信用证金额 （3）汇票付款人应为开证行或指定的付款行。若信用证未规定付款行，应为开证行，不应以申请人为付款人 （4）汇票出票人应为受益人，通常是出口商，且应与信用证受益人名称、地点相符合 （5）汇票付款期限应与信用证规定相符 （6）汇票出票日期必须在信用证有效期内，不应早于发票日期 （7）汇票收款人通常为议付行 （8）汇票的出票人必须签字盖章，无出票人签字盖章的汇票被视为无效汇票	（1）汇票的出票日期迟于信用证有效期 （2）汇票金额大于信用证金额 （3）汇票金额大小写不一致或汇票大写金额不准确，大写金额最后漏填"ONLY" （4）货币名称与发票或信用证不一致 （5）汇票付款期限与信用证规定不符，或未明确付款日期 （6）汇票的内容被更改 （7）汇票提交的份数不正确 （8）未按规定列明出票条款 （9）漏列或错列了信用证号码 （10）出票人未签字盖章

1.13　Processing Methods of Problem Documents
有问题单证的处理方法

Importers (applicants) focus on auditing whether documents conform to an L/C and whether the goods are consistent with documents. After audit if any problems were found, they should be recorded in the audit form and reported to business department and finance department. If importers (applicants) decided to refuse to pay after audit, they should state discrepancies stipulated in documents and L/C clauses on the documents arrival notice under the import L/C, and build a special seal for finance within the time returned to the bank.

In accordance with the relevant provisions of the UCP600 and ISBP, the issuing bank must review these documents within a reasonable time, the next day up to five working days after receipt of the relevant the documents, and make the decision of the payment or refuse to pay. If the issuing bank audits the documents and finds that there are substantial discrepancies in the surface of the negotiating documents and decides to refuse to pay, it shall promptly notify the sender in telecommunications not later than fifth banking day since the second day of the receipt of documents. If the issuing bank audits the documents and finds that there are no substantial discrepancies and agrees to pay, it shall immediately give the applicant (importer) to audit the relevant documents copies under the L/C, the documents arrival notice and confirmation, and limit him to reply in 3 days so that the issuing bank can notice in 5 working days.

进口商(开证申请人)审单的重点是审查单证是否相符以及单货是否相符。审查后如发现单证有问题,要记录在审单记录表上,及时上报业务部门和财务部门。当进口商(开证申请人)审查后决定拒付时,应在进口信用证项下单证到达通知书上列明单证与信用证条款规定的不符点,并加盖财务专用章在银行规定的时间内返还银行。

按照UCP600和ISBP有关规定,开证银行必须在收到有关单证次日起5个工作日的合理时间内审核这些单证,并做出付款或者拒付的决定。如果开证银行审核并发现议付单证表面与信用证条款有实质性不符点而决定拒付,应立即以电讯方式通知寄单人,不得迟于收到议付单据的第2天起第5个银行工作日。若开证银行审核议付单据表面与信用证条款后认为无实质性不符点或拟同意付款,应立即将信用证项下有关单证复印件、单证到达通知书和确认书一并交给开证申请人(进口商)审单,限其在3天内答复,以使开证行能在5个工作日内对外通知。

Training Case 1-1

A Case of Discrepant Documents

In April 2018, our party a certain oils and foodstuff import and export company clinched a deal with British George trading company for a cottonseed oil business, the total number was 840 metric tons and partial shipments were allowed. The terms of shipment in the L/C were regulated as follows: "840 M/Tons of cottonseed oil. Loading port: Guangzhou. Partial shipments are allowed in two lots, 460 M/Tons to London not later than September 15, 2018. 380 M/Tons to Liverpool not later than October 15, 2018."

Our company made shipment for 305 metric tons of goods to London on August 3 in Huangpu port, and planed to continue shipment of 155 metric tons in late August. Two batches shipped to London totally were 460 metric tons. 305 metric tons were shipped to Liverpool in late September. The rest of 75 metric tons would continue to be shipped. After negotiation, the exporter sent documents and applied to the issuing bank for claiming accordingly.

Two discrepancies were put forward after documents were presented to the issuing bank: One was that partial shipments referred in the L/C was 460 metric tons to London, 380 metric tons to Liverpool, rather than two lots each place. The second was the discrepant loading port. The L/C required the loading port in Guangzhou port, but to goods' loading port was Huangpu port.

Our exporter promptly replied message in the retort: (1) "Partial shipments are allowed in two lots" in the L/C should be interpreted as partial shipments were allowed in two batches of shipment. (2) It was well known that Huangpu port was one of the ports in Guangzhou. Therefore, our bank thought that documents were in compliance with the terms of L/C and the issuing bank should immediately pay advances. But the end result was that the issuing bank asked us to compensate for the losses, the part of goods shipped not yet could be delivered after L/C amendment.

单证不符点的争议案

　　我方某粮油进出口公司于2018年4月与英国乔治贸易公司成交一笔棉籽油生意，总数量为840公吨，允许分批装运。来证中对装运条款规定如下："840 M/Tons of cottonseed oil. Loading port：Guangzhou. Partial shipments are allowed in two lots，460 M/Tons to London not later than September 15，2018，380 M/Tons to Liverpool not later than October 15, 2018."（840公吨棉籽油。装货港：广州。允许分两批装运：460公吨棉籽油不迟于2018年9月15日运到伦敦，380公吨棉籽油不迟于2018年10月15日运到利物浦。）

　　我方公司于8月3日在黄埔港装运305公吨货物至伦敦，计划在8月末再继续装运155公吨。两批共为460公吨，均装运至伦敦。9月末装运305公吨至利物浦，其余75公吨将继续装运。出口商办理议付后即向开证行寄单索汇。

　　单据到开证行后被提出两处不符点：一是信用证所指分批装运是指装运至伦敦者为460公吨，装运至利物浦者为380公吨，而非两地各分两批；二是装运港不符，信用证要求在广州港起运，而来货起运港为黄埔港。

　　我出口商当即复电反驳：（1）来证中"Partial shipments are allowed in two lots"应解释为在两批装运中允许再分批装运。（2）众所周知，黄埔港是广州市的一个港口。因此，我方银行认为单证相符，开证行应立即予以偿付垫款。但最终结果是，开证行要求我方赔偿损失，未发运部分待修改信用证后再行发运。

　　资料来源　封文丽. 国际结算实务与案例分析[M]. 北京：冶金工业出版社，2013：127.

Key Terms

examining documents 审单

Exercise

◎ *Case Analysis*

One of our export companies received an irrevocable letter of credit from abroad, noticed and confirmed by a certain foreign bank within the territory of China. When the export company was to deliver the relevant documents to negotiation bank after the date of shipment, it was informed by the foreign bank, due to the issuing bank is declared bankrupt, that the bank was not liable for negotiation or payment of the L/C, but could accept the business which entrusted to the buyer by our export company directly. What do you think we should do to deal with this? Please describe the reasons briefly.

　　我出口公司收到国外开来的不可撤销信用证一份，由设在我国境内的某外资银行通知并加保兑。我出口公司在货物装运后，在拟将有关单据交银行议付时，忽接该外资银行通知，由于开证银行已宣布破产，该行不承担对该信用证的议付或付款责任，但可接受我出口公司委托向买方直接收取货款的业务。对此，你认为我方应如何处理？请简述理由。

Chapter 2
Knowledge of an L/C
信用证知识

Learning Objectives

◆ 重点掌握常见信用证范例;掌握合同中的单证条款;了解信用证常见条款及短语。

Guide Case

A Case of "No Effect" Clause

The L/C issued by an Italian bank claimed that it could take effect only after receipt of the Italian import license according to the L/C, and this effect was subject to the authorization of the applicant. In addition, the negotiating bank should also prompt the inspection certificate of the applicant. Only after being confirmed by the applicant, the issuing bank could keep money credit on account. This is a typical soft terms L/C. Though it was marked as an irrevocable L/C, it was not different from a revocable L/C in the actual operation. Because the applicant (importer) controlled throughout the entire transaction, and the beneficiary (exporter) was completely located in a passive position.

"暂不生效"条款案

一家意大利银行开出的信用证称,该信用证只有在收到意方进口许可证后方能生效,而这种生效还需经开证申请人的授权。此外,议付行还要提示开证申请人开具检验证书。待由开证申请人确认后,开证银行方可将款项贷记有关账户。这是一张比较典型的带有软条款的信用证。该证虽标有不可撤销信用证的字样,但其在实际运作中与可撤销信用证毫无不同,因为开证申请人(进口商)自始至终都控制着整笔交易,而受益人(出口商)则完完全全地处在被动地位。

2.1　Clauses Concerning Documents in Sales Contracts
　　销售合同中的单证条款

In trade practice, stipulations concerning documents may not be necessary to appear in every contract. In some cases, documents required are stipulated in the contract. They may constitute part or whole of the contents under the column "Remarks" or they may be mentioned in the attachment to a contract. It is not uncommon, however, that there are no such stipulations in the contract at all. In this case, the agreement concerning documents remains an oral one between the buyer and the seller and is binding upon the parties concerned. Still, it is advisable that the relevant stipulations be laid down in the contract in terms of the types, issuing authorities, number of originals or copies, and etc.

While it may not appear in a sales contract, the stipulation "documents required" is always a necessary part of a documentary L/C. Under L/C transactions, sellers are paid against documents presented; buyers pay and receive goods against documents released; and banks deal with the documents instead of the goods. Documents play such an essential role in an L/C transaction that documents to be presented (or to be required) should be clearly stipulated in the relevant L/C.

Examples of clauses of a sales contract are as follows (Sample 2-1):

(1)Signed commercial invoice in triplicate indicating the contract number.

(2)Full set (3/3) plus two copies of clean "on board" marine bill of lading made out to order of ××× company.

(3)Packing list in duplicate, indicating gross weight, net weight, measurement and quantity of the packages.

(4)Insurance policy or certificate in triplicate covering war risk and all risks irrespective of percentage for 110% of the invoice value.

(5)Weight and quality certificate in triplicate indicating the number of bags shipped, total gross and net weight, packing, actual quality analysis report issued by Commodity Inspection Division (CID).

(6)GSP certificate of origin Form A in duplicate issued by CID.

(7)Fumigation/disinfection certificate in triplicate issued by CID.

(8)Phytosanitary certificate in triplicate issued by CID.

(9)Health certificate in triplicate issued by CID for the information into the European Community of peanuts and certain products derived from peanuts originating in or consigned from China.

(10)Beneficiary's statement certifying that...

(11)Shipment details including number of bags shipped, total gross and net weight, packing, B/L date and number, container and seal number, ETD Qingdao, China and ETA Lisbon, Portugal have been sent to applicant by fax (fax No. ××××××××) within 4 days of the shipment date.

(12)One complete set of non-negotiable shipping documents has been sent to the applicant by fax (fax No. ×××××××) within 4 days of the shipment date.

　　在贸易实践中,不是每一份合同都必须标示出与单证相关的条款。在某些情况下,所需单证在合同中被做了明确的规定。它们可能是"备注"中的部分或全部内容,也可能在合同的附件中说明。然而,合同中完全没有规定需要的单证的情况也很常见。在这种情况下,关于单证的规定仍旧是买卖双方之间的口头规定,且这对双方当事人都有约束力。尽管如此,仍然建议在合同中明确规定单证的种类、签发机构、正副本数量等。

　　即使销售合同中无要求,"单证要求"条款仍然是跟单信用证的一个必要组成部分。在信用证交易方式下,卖方凭提交的单证得到货款;买方凭收到的单证付款和提货;银行在办理业务时处理的是单证而不是货物本身。单证在信用证交易中发挥着如此重要的作用,因此需提交(或要求)的单证必须在相关信用证中清楚说明。

　　销售合同中条款样例如下(见样单 2-1):

Sample 2-1　　　　　　　　　　Sales Contract
样单 2-1　　　　　　　　　　销售合同

卖方 SELLER	GUANGDONG FOREIGN TRADE IMP. & EXP. CORP., 15-18F, 351 TIANHE ROAD, GUANGZHOU, CHINA	编号 NO.	SHDS03027
		日期 DATE	APR. 3, 2018
		地点 SIGNED IN	SHANGHAI, CHINA
买方 BUYER	NEO GENERAL TRADING CO., #362 JALAN STREET, TORONTO, CANADA		

买卖双方同意按以下条款达成交易:
This contract is made by and agreed between the BUYER and the SELLER, in accordance with the terms and conditions stipulated below:

1.品名及规格 Name of Commodity & Specification	2.数量 Quantity	3.单价及贸易术语 Unit Price & Trade Terms	4.金额 Amount
		CIFC5 TORONTO	
CHINESE CERAMIC DINNERWARE			
DS1511 30-PIECE DINNERWARE AND TEA SET	542 SETS	USD 23.50	USD 12,737.00
DS2201 20-PIECE DINNERWARE SET	800 SETS	USD 20.40	USD 16,320.00
DS4504 45-PIECE DINNERWARE SET	443 SETS	USD 23.20	USD 10,277.60
DS5120 95-PIECE DINNERWARE SET	254 SETS	USD 30.10	USD 7,645.40
合计 Total	2,039 SETS		USD 46,980.00
允许 With	10%	溢短装,由卖方决定 MORE OR LESS OF SHIPMENT ALLOWED AT SELLER'S OPTION	
5.总值 Total Value	SAY US DOLLARS FORTY SIX THOUSAND NINE HUNDRED AND EIGHTY ONLY.		
6.包装 Packing	DS2201 IN CARTONS OF 2 SETS EACH, DS1511, DS4504 AND DS5120 TO BE PACKED IN CARTONS OF 1 SET EACH ONLY TOTAL: 1,639 CARTONS		

续

7.唛头 Shipping Marks	AT BUYER'S OPTION
8.装运期及运输方式 Time of Shipment & Means of Transportation	TO BE EFFECTED BEFORE THE END OF APRIL 2018 WITH PARTIAL SHIPMENTS ALLOWED AND TRANSSHIPMENT ALLOWED
9.装运港及目的地 Port of Loading & Destination	FROM：GUANGZHOU，CHINA TO：TORONTO，CANADA
10.保险 Insurance	THE SELLER SHALL COVER INSURANCE AGAINST W.P.A., CLASH & BREAKAGE, WAR RISKS FOR 110% OF THE TOTAL INVOICE VALUE
11.付款方式 Terms of Payment	BY IRREVOCABLE SIGHT LETTER OF CREDIT
12.备注 Remarks	
买方 The Buyer NEO GENERAL TRADING CO. Y. BAYER	卖方 The Seller GUANGDONG FOREIGN TRADE IMP. & EXP. CORP. 张立

（1）一式三份已签字、标示合同号码的商业发票。

（2）一整套(3/3)正本及两份副本的凭×××公司指示为抬头的清洁"已装船"海运提单。

（3）一式两份标示毛重、净重、体积和数量的装箱单。

（4）一式三份投保战争险和一切险、投保金额是发票金额110%的保险单或保险凭证。

（5）一式三份标示装运的包裹数量、总毛重、总净重、包装的重量和品质证书及由商品检验司签发的实际质量分析报告。

（6）一式两份由商品检验司签发的普惠制原产地证书格式A。

（7）一式三份由商品检验司签发的熏蒸/消毒证书。

（8）一式三份由商品检验司签发的植物检验检疫证书。

（9）一式三份出口至欧盟的原产于或托运自中国的核桃和核桃产品的由商品检验司签发的卫生证书。

（10）受益人声明证明……

（11）装运包裹数量、总毛重、总净重、包装、提单日期和号码、集装箱号码和封号、预计交货时间(中国青岛)和预计到港时间(葡萄牙里斯本)等装运细节已经在装运后4天内通过传真(传真号码×××××××)发送给开证申请人。

（12）在装运后4天内，一整套不可转让装运单证已经通过传真(传真号码×××××××)发送给开证申请人。

2.2 Sample of an L/C (Table 2-1)
信用证范例(见表2-1)

Table 2-1   Sample of an L/C
表 2-1   信用证范例

APPLICATION HEADER 0700 1840 07130 MRMDUSADXBXXX 1561 893704 070514 1549 N *HSBC BANK USA, N. A. *NEW YORK, NY	银行间互对密押 开证行为汇丰银行纽约分行
SEQUENCE OF TOTAL 27:1/2	本信用证有两页,这是第一页
FORM OF DOC. L / C 40A: IRREVOCABLE DOCUMENTARY	信用证种类:不可撤销跟单信用证
DOC. L/C NUMBER 20: 23395	信用证号码:23395
DATE OF ISSUE 31C:20180130	信用证开证日期:2018年1月30日
APPLICABLE RULES 40E:UCP LATEST VERSION	使用规则:UCP最新版
EXPIRY 31D:DATE 20180515 PLACE CHINA	信用证到期日为2018年5月15日,到期地点为中国
APPLICANT 50:PORT ROYAL SALES,LTD. 95 FROEHLICH FARM BLVD, WOODBURY, NY 11797, USA	开证申请人:PORT ROYAL销售公司 弗勒利希农场大道95号,伍德伯里,纽约州11797,美国
BENEFICIARY 59 :TIDER INDUSTRIAL CO., LTD. NO.310 XINYANG ROAD,GUANGZHOU, CHINA	受益人:泰尔工贸有限责任公司 中国广州新阳路310号
AMOUNT 32B: CURRENCY USD AMOUNT 31,200	信用证总金额:31 200美元
POS./NEG. TOL. (%) 39A: 5/5	信用证金额加减5%
AVAILABLE WITH / BY 41D: ANY BANK BY NEGOTIATION	本信用证为自由议付信用证
DRAFT AT 42C: SIGHT	开立即期汇票
DRAWEE 42D:APPLICANT BANK	汇票的付款人为开证行
PARTIAL SHIPMENTS 43P: PERMITTED	允许分批装运
TRANSSHIPMENT 43T: PERMITTED	允许转运
PORT OF LOADING / AIRPORT OF DEPARTURE 44E: GUANGZHOU,CHINA	装运港/始发航空站是中国广州
PORT OF DISCHARGE/AIRPORT OF DESTINATION 44F: NEW YORK, USA	卸货港/目的航空站是美国纽约

LATEST DATE OF SHIPMENT 44C:20180430	最迟装运日期是 2018 年 4 月 30 日
DESCRIPTION OF GOODS 45A:24/454G PINEAPPLE BROKEN SLICED IN LIGHT SYRUP, 4, 800 CARTONS, ALL OTHER DETAILS ARE AS PER BENEFICIARY'S P/I NO.TDF270102 DATED 18 JANUARY, 2018 PRICE TERMS:FOB GUANGZHOU, CHINA	货物描述:24/454 克糖水菠萝片罐头,4 800 箱,其他细节按照受益人 2018 年 1 月 18 日号码为 TDF270102 的形式发票 价格术语:FOB 广州,中国
SEQUENCE OF TOTAL 27: 2/2	本信用证有两页,这是第二页
DOCUMENTS REQUIRED 46A: (1)SIGNED COMMERCIAL INVOICE, 3-FOLD (2) FULL SET OF CLEAN ON BOARD ORIGINAL MARINE / OCEAN BILL OF LADING, MADE OUT TO ORDER AND BLANK ENDORSED, MARKED FREIGHT COLLECT, NOTIFY APPLICANT INDICATING NAME, ADDRESS, TELEPHONE AND FAX NO. OF THE CARRYING VESSEL'S OF AGENT AT THE PORT OF DISCHARGE (3)PACKING LIST IN 3 COPIES STATING:QUANTITY, DESCRIPTION, MEASUREMENT, GROSS AND NET WEIGHT, BUYERS' PURCHASE ORDER NUMBER AND L/C NO. (4)ORIGINAL CERTIFICATE OF ORIGIN (5) BENEFICIARY'S STATEMENT CERTIFYING THAT THE SHIPMENT UNDER THIS LETTER OF CREDIT CONTAINS NO WOOD PACKAGING	应提交的单据: (1)已签署商业发票一式三份 (2)全套清洁已装船正本海运提单,做成空白抬头、空白背书,标明运费已付,通知开证申请人,标明在卸货港的承运人的代理人名称、地址、电话号码和传真号码 (3)装箱单一式三份,标明数量、货物描述、体积、毛重与净重、买方订单号和信用证号码 (4)原产地证书正本 (5)受益人声明,证明本信用证项下货物没有使用木质包装
ADDITIONAL COND. 47A: (1) ALL DOCUMENTS MUST BEAR OUR L/C NUMBER (2) UNLESS OTHERWISE SPECIFIED HEREIN, DOCUMENTS ISSUED PRIOR TO THE DATE OF THIS DOCUMENTARY L/C ARE NOT ACCEPTABLE (3)THE BILL OF LADING MUST BE CERTIFIED THAT GOODS MUST BE SHIPPED IN THREE 20' CONTAINERS, FCL, ON WHICH CONTAINER NUMBERS AND SEAL NUMBERS MUST BE MARKED. (4) 5 PERCENT MORE OR LESS IN QUANTITY AND AMOUNT ARE ACCEPTABLE (5) EACH CAN MARKED WITH NET SHOULD HAVE LABLES PRINTED WITH NET WEIGHT, DATE OF PACKING AND EXPIRY DATE, 2 YEARS FROM THE DATE OF PRODUCTION IN ENGLISH LANGUAGE	附加条款: (1)所有单据标明本信用证号码 (2)除非另有规定,早于跟单信用证开具的单据不接受 (3)货物必须用 3 个 20 英尺整箱包装,提单对此要做出证明,并且要标明集装箱号和集装箱封号 (4)数量和金额允许 5% 增减 (5)每个罐头要用英文标注标签,内容为净重、包装日期和从生产日期起保质期为两年的到期日

DETAILS OF CHARGES 71B: ALL BANKING CHARGES OUTSIDE COUNTRY OF ISSUE ARE FOR ACCOUNT OF BENEFICIARY	费用细节:进口国以外的所有银行费用由受益人承担
PRESENTATION PERIOD 48: WITHIN 15 DAYS AFTER THE SHIPMENT DATE, AND WITHIN THE VALIDITY OF L/C	交单期:在装运日后15天内并在信用证有效期内
CONFIRMATION 49: WITHOUT	不保兑
SEND TO REC. INFO. 72: UPON RECEIPT OF CREDIT CONFORM DOCUMENTS, WE SHALL COVER YOU ACCORDING TO YOUR INSTRUCTIONS AND AS PER L/C TERMS	银行间的通知:一收到与信用证条款相符的单据,我们将按照你方指示和信用证条款贷记你方账户

2.3 Clauses and Phrases of an L/C（Table 2-2）
信用证条款及短语(见表2-2)

Table 2-2   Clauses and Phrases of an L/C
表2-2   信用证条款及短语

Clauses and Phrases of an L/C	信用证条款及短语
Ⅰ. Kinds of an L/C	一、信用证类别
1. revocable L/C/irrevocable L/C	1.可撤销信用证/不可撤销信用证
2. confirmed L/C/unconfirmed L/C	2.保兑信用证/不保兑信用证
3. sight L/C/usance L/C	3.即期信用证/远期信用证
4. transferable L/C/nontransferable L/C	4.可转让信用证/不可转让信用证
5. revolving L/C	5.循环信用证
6. back to back L/C/reciprocal L/C	6.背对背信用证/对开信用证
7. L/C with T/T reimbursement clause	7.带电汇条款信用证
8. without recourse L/C/with recourse L/C	8.无追索权信用证/有追索权信用证
9. documentary L/C/clean L/C	9.跟单信用证/光票信用证
10.deferred payment L/C/anticipatory L/C	10.延付信用证/预支信用证
Ⅱ.Names of Parties Concerned	二、有关当事人的名称
1. opener	1.开证人
（1）opener	（1）开证人
（2）applicant	（2）开证人（开证申请人）
（3）principal	（3）开证人（委托开证人）
（4）accountee	（4）开证人
（5）accreditor	（5）开证人（委托开证人）
（6）for account of Messrs.	（6）以某人账户支付
（7）at the request of Messrs.	（7）应某人请求
（8）on behalf of Messrs.	（8）代表某人
（9）by order of Messrs.	（9）奉某人之命

Clauses and Phrases of an L/C	信用证条款及短语
（10）from accreditor	（10）根据某人的指示
2.beneficiary	2.受益人
（1）beneficiary	（1）受益人
（2）in favor of	（2）以……为受益人
（3）in one's favor	（3）以……为受益人
（4）favoring yourselves	（4）以你本人为受益人
3.drawee	3.付款人（或称受票人）
（1）to draw on (or upon)	（1）以……为付款人
（2）to value on	（2）以……为付款人
（3）to issue on	（3）以……为付款人
4.drawer	4.出票人
5.advising bank	5.通知行
（1）advising bank	（1）通知行
（2）notifying bank	（2）通知行
（3）advised through ... bank	（3）通过×××银行通知
（4）advised by airmail/cable through ... bank	（4）通过×××银行以航空信/电报的方式通知
6.opening bank/issuing bank/establishing bank	6.开证行
7.negotiation bank/negotiating bank	7.议付行
8.paying bank	8.付款行
9.reimbursing bank	9.偿付行
10.confirming bank	10.保兑行
Ⅲ.Amount of an L/C	三、信用证金额
1.amount RMB ...	1.金额为……人民币
2.up to an aggregate amount of Hong Kong Dollars	2.累计金额最高为……港币
3.for a sum (or: sums) exceeding a total of GBP ...	3.总金额不得超过……英镑
4.to the extern of HKD ...	4.总金额为……港币
5.for the amount of US Dollar ...	5.金额为……美元
6.for an amount not exceeding total of EUR ...	6.金额的总数不得超过……欧元的限度
Ⅳ.Stipulations for the Shipping Documents	四、装运单证的规定
1. available against surrender of the following documents bearing our L/C number and the full name and address of the opener	1.凭交出下列注明本证号码和开证人的全称及地址的单据付款
2.drafts to be accompanied by the documents marked (×) below	2.汇票必须随附下列注有(×)的单据
3.accompanied against to documents hereinafter	3.随附下列单据
4.accompanied by the following documents	4.随附下列单据
5.documents required	5.单据要求
6.accompanied by the following documents marked (×) in duplicate	6.随附下列注有(×)的单据一式两份
7.draft is to be accompanied by	7.汇票要随附(某单据)

Clauses and Phrases of an L/C	信用证条款及短语
V.Draft (Bill of Exchange)	五、汇票
1.kinds of draft	1.汇票种类
（1）available by draft at sight	（1）凭即期汇票付款
（2）draft(s) to be drawn at 30 days sight	（2）汇票开立为见票后30天付款
（3）sight draft	（3）即期汇票
（4）time draft	（4）远期汇票
2.drawn clauses	2.出票条款
（1）all drafts drawn under this L／C must contain clause "Draft drawn under Bank of ... L/C No. ... dated ..."	（1）本证项下开具的汇票须注明"本汇票系凭×××银行××××年××月××日第××号信用证项下开具"
（2）drafts are to be drawn in duplicate to our order bearing the clause "Drawn under United Malaysian Banking Corp. Ltd. irrevocable letter of credit No. ... dated July 12，2018"	（2）汇票一式两份,以我行为抬头,并注明"根据马来西亚联合银行2018年7月12日第××号不可撤销信用证项下开具"
（3）drawn under this L／C to be marked "Drawn under ... Bank L/C No. ... dated ... (issuing date of L/C)"	（3）根据本证开出的汇票须注明"凭××银行××××年××月××日(按开证日期)第××号信用证的名义开具(注明信用证开立日期)"
（4）drafts in duplicate at sight bearing，the clause "Drawn under ... Bank L/C No. ... dated ..."	（4）即期汇票一式两份,注明"根据×××银行第××号信用证于××××年××月××日开具"
（5）drafts drawn must be indicated with number and date of this L/C	（5）开具的汇票必须注上本证的号码和日期
（6）drafts bearing the clause "Drawn under documentary L/C No. ... (shown above) of ... Bank"	（6）汇票注明"根据×××银行跟单信用证××号(如上所示)项下开具"
VI.Invoice	六、发票
1.signed commercial invoice	1.已签署的商业发票
in duplicate	一式二份
in triplicate	一式三份
in quadruplicate	一式四份
in quintuplicate	一式五份
in sextuplicate	一式六份
in septuplicate	一式七份
in octuplicate	一式八份
in nonuplicate	一式九份
in decuplicate	一式十份
2. beneficiary's original signed commercial invoices at least in 8 copies issued in the name of the buyer indicating (showing/evidencing/specifying/declaring) the merchandise，country of origin and any other relevant information	2.以买方的名义开立,注明商品、原产国(地区)及其他有关信息,并经受益人签署的商业发票正本至少一式八份
3. signed attested invoice combined with certificate of value and origin in 6 copies as required for imports into Nigeria	3.输入尼日利亚的进口商品需提供已签署的经过认证的发票、估价和原产地联合证明书,一式六份

续表

Clauses and Phrases of an L/C	信用证条款及短语
4. beneficiary must certify on the invoice "Have been sent ... to the accountee" 5. 4% discount should be deducted from total amount of the commercial invoice 6. invoice must be stowed "Under A/P No. ... dated of expiry 19th Jan., 2019" 7. documents in combined form are not acceptable 8. combined invoice is not acceptable	4. 受益人必须在发票上证明"已将……寄交开证人" 5. 商业发票的总金额应该扣除4%的折扣 6. 发票必须表明"根据第××号的委托购买证,到期日为2019年1月19日" 7. 不接受联合单据 8. 不接受联合发票
Ⅶ.Bill of Lading 1. full set of shipping (×× company's) clean on board bills of lading marked "Freight Prepaid" to order of shipper endorsed to ... bank and notifying buyer 2. bills of lading made out in negotiable form 3. clean shipped on board ocean bills of lading to order and endorsed in blank marked "Freight Prepaid" and notifying importer (opener/accountee) 4. full set of clean "on board" bills of lading / cargo receipt made out to our order / to order and endorsed in blank and notifying buyer M/S ... Co. calling for shipment from China to Hamburg marked "Freight Prepaid" "Freight Payable at Destination" 5. bill of lading issuing in the name of ... 6. bill of lading must be dated not before the date of this L/C and not later than Aug. 15, 2018 7. bill of lading marked notifying buyer "Freight Prepaid", Liner terms "Received for shipment B/L not acceptable" 8. non-negotiable copy of bills of lading	七、提单 1. 全套已装船(××公司的)清洁提单应注明"运费预付",做成以装船人指示为抬头,背书给×××银行,并通知买方 2. 做成可议付提单 3. 清洁且已装船的提单做空白抬头并空白背书,注明"运费预付",并通知进口商(开证人) 4. 全套清洁"已装船"提单或货运收据,做成以我(行)为抬头或空白抬头、空白背书,并通知买方××公司,要求货物自中国运往汉堡,注明"运费预付""运费在目的港付" 5. 提单以××名称为抬头 6. 提单日期不得早于本证的日期,也不得迟于2018年8月15日 7. 提单注明通知买方"运费预付",班轮条件是"备运提单不接受" 8. 不可议付的提单副本
Ⅷ.Insurance Policy (or Certificate) 1. stipulations of insurance (1) marine insurance policy (2) specific insurance policy (3) voyage insurance policy (4) time insurance policy (5) floating policy (or open policy)	八、保险单(或凭证) 1. 保险条款 (1) 海运保险单 (2) 单独保险单 (3) 航程保险单 (4) 期限保险单 (5) 流动保险单

Clauses and Phrases of an L/C	信用证条款及短语
(6)ocean marine cargo insurance clauses	(6)海洋运输货物保险条款
(7)ocean marine cargo insurance clauses (frozen products)	(7)海洋运输冷冻货物保险条款
(8)ocean marine cargo war risk clauses	(8)海洋运输货物战争险条款
(9)ocean marine insurance clauses (wood oil in bulk)	(9)海洋运输散装桐油保险条款
(10) overland transportation cargo insurance clauses (trains, trucks)	(10)陆地运输货物保险条款(火车、汽车)
(11) overland transportation cargo insurance clauses (frozen products)	(11)陆地运输货物冷冻货物保险条款
(12)air transportation cargo insurance clauses	(12)航空运输货物保险条款
(13)air transportation cargo war risk clauses	(13)航空运输货物战争险条款
(14)parcel post insurance clauses	(14)邮包保险条款
(15)parcel post war risk clauses	(15)邮包战争险条款
(16) livestock & poultry insurance clauses (by sea, land or air)	(16)活牲畜、家禽的海洋、陆地、航空保险条款
(17)risks clauses of the PICC subject to CIC	(17)根据中国人民财产保险股份有限公司的保险条款
(18) marine insurance policies or certificates in negotiable form for 110% of full CIF invoice covering the risks of war & W.P.A. as per the People's Insurance Company of China dated Jan. 1, 1981 with extended cover up to Kuala Lumpur with claims payable in (at) Kuala Lumpur in the currency of draft (irrespective of percentage)	(18)做成可议付格式的海运保险单或凭证,投保中国人民财产保险股份有限公司1981年1月1日的战争险和水渍险,保险负责到吉隆坡为止,按照汇票所使用的到岸价的发票金额的110%投保,使用汇票上约定的货币在吉隆坡赔付(不计免赔率)
(19)Name of assured in insurance policy (certificate) to be showed: ABC Co., Ltd.	(19)保险单(凭证)须做成以ABC公司为保险人
(20) insurance policy / certificate covering all risks, war and mines risks	(20)投保一切险、战争险、地雷险的保险单(凭证)
2.risks & coverage	2.险别
(1)free from particular average (FPA)	(1)平安险
(2)with particular average (W.P.A.)	(2)水渍险(基本险)
(3)all risks	(3)一切险(综合险)
(4)total loss only (TLO)	(4)全损险
(5)war risk	(5)战争险
(6)cargo (extended cover) clauses	(6)货物(扩展)条款
(7)additional risk	(7)附加险
(8)from warehouse to warehouse clauses	(8)仓至仓条款
(9)theft, pilferage and non-delivery (T.P.N.D.)	(9)偷窃、提货不着险
(10)rain fresh water damage	(10)淡水雨淋险
(11)risk of shortage	(11)短量险
(12)risk of contamination	(12)玷污险
(13)risk of leakage	(13)渗漏险
(14)risk of clash & breakage	(14)碰损破碎险

Clauses and Phrases of an L/C	信用证条款及短语
(15)risk of odour	(15)串味险
(16)damage caused by sweating and/or heating	(16)受潮/受热险
(17)hook damage	(17)钩损险
(18) loss and / or damage caused by breakage of packing	(18)包装破裂险
(19)risk of rusting	(19)锈损险
(20)risk of mould	(20)发霉险
(21)strike, riots and civil commotion (SRCC)	(21)罢工、暴动和民变险
(22)risk of spontaneous combustion	(22)自燃险
(23)deterioration risk	(23)腐烂变质险
(24)inherent vice risk	(24)内在缺陷险
(25)risk of natural loss (or normal loss)	(25)途耗或自然损耗险
(26)special risk	(26)特别附加险
(27)failure to delivery risk	(27)交货不到险
(28)import duty risk	(28)进口关税险
(29)on deck risk	(29)舱面险
(30)rejection risk	(30)拒收险
(31)aflatoxin risk	(31)黄曲霉素险
(32)survey in customs risk	(32)海关检验险
(33)survey in jetty risk	(33)码头检验险
(34)institute war risk	(34)协会战争险
(35)overland transportation risks	(35)陆运险
(36)overland transportation all risks	(36)陆运综合险
(37)air transportation risk	(37)航空运输险
(38)air transportation all risks	(38)航空运输综合险
(39)air transportation cargo war risks	(39)航空运输战争险
(40)parcel post risk	(40)邮包险
(41)parcel post all risks	(41)邮包综合险
(42)parcel post war risk	(42)邮包战争险
(43)investment insurance (political risk)	(43)投资保险(政治风险)
(44)property insurance	(44)财产保险
(45)erection all risks	(45)安装工程一切险
(46)contractors all risks	(46)建筑工程一切险

Clauses and Phrases of an L/C	信用证条款及短语
IX.Certificate of Origin	九、原产地证书
1.certificate of origin of China showing stating/evidencing/specifying/indicating declaration of	1.中国原产地证书列明/证明/说明/表明……声明
2.certificate of Chinese origin	2.中国原产地证书
3.certificate of origin, shipment of goods of ... origin prohibited	3.原产地证书不允许装运……的产品
4.declaration of origin	4.原产地声明
5.certificate of origin separated	5.单独出具的原产地证书
6.certificate of origin Form A	6.原产地证书格式 A
7.generalized system of preference certificate of Form A	7.普惠制原产地证书格式 A
X.Packing List and Weight List	十、装箱单与重量单
1. packing list packing specification and contents of each package list showing in detail ...	1.载明每件货物之内包装的规格和内容的装箱单
2.packing list detailing	2.详注的装箱单
3.packing list	3.装箱单
4.weight list	4.重量单
5.weight note	5.重量单(磅码单)
6.detailed weight list	6.明细重量单
7.weight and measurement list	7.重量和尺码单
XI.Inspection Certificate	十一、检验证书
1.certificate of weight	1.重量证书
2.certificate of inspection certifying quality & quantity in triplicate issued by CID	2.由商品检验司出具的一式三份的品质和数量检验证书
3.phytosanitary certificate	3.植物检验检疫证书
4.plant quarantine certificate	4.植物检验检疫证书
5.fumigation certificate	5.熏蒸证书
6.certificate stating that the goods are free from live weevil	6.无活虫证书(熏蒸除虫证书)
7.sanitary certificate	7.卫生证书
8.health certificate	8.卫生(健康)证书
9.analysis certificate	9.分析(化验)证书
10.tank inspection certificate	10.油舱检验证书
11.certificate of aflatoxin negative	11.黄曲霉素证书
12.certificate of non-aflatoxin negative	12.无黄曲霉素证书
13.survey report on weight issued by CID	13.商品检验司签发的重量检验证明书

Clauses and Phrases of an L/C	信用证条款及短语
XII.Other Documents	十二、其他单证
1.full set of forwarding agents' cargo receipt	1.全套货代出具之货物承运收据
2.airway bill for goods consigned to ... quoting our L/C number	2.以××为收货人、注明本证号码的航空运单
3.parcel post receipt	3.邮包收据
4.parcel post receipt showing parcel addressed to ... A/C accountee	4.注明收件人通过××转交开证人的邮包收据
5.parcel post receipt evidencing goods consigned to ... and quoting our L/C number	5.以××为收货人并注明本证号码的邮包收据
6.certificate customs invoice on Form 59A combined certificate of value and origin for developing countries	6.适用于发展中国家的包括价值和产地联合证书的格式59A海关发票证明书
7.pure food certificate	7.纯食品证书
8.combined certificate of value and Chinese origin	8.价值和中国原产地联合证书
9.a declaration in terms of Form 5 of New Zealand Forest Produce Import and Export Regulations or a declaration from the exporter to the effect that no timber has been used in the packing of the goods, either declaration may be included on certified customs invoice	9.依照新西兰林木产品进出口法格式5条款的声明或出口人关于货物用非木器包装的声明,该声明也可以在海关发票中做出
10.Canadian customs invoice (revised form) all signed in ink showing fair market value in currency of exporting country	10.笔签的加拿大海关发票(修订格式)并用出口国货币标明本国公平市价
11.Canadian import declaration Form 111 fully signed and completed	11.以格式111完整签署和填写的加拿大进口声明
XIII.Shipping Terms	十三、装运条款
1.combined certificate of value and origin for loading port and destination	1.装运港和目的港价值与原产地联合证书
(1)dispatch/shipment from China port to ...	(1)从中国港口发送/装运往
(2)evidencing shipment from China to ... CFR by steamer in transit Saudi Arabia not later than 15th July, 2018 of the goods specified below	(2)列明下面的货物按成本加运费价格用轮船不得迟于2018年7月15日从中国通过沙特阿拉伯转运到……
2.time of shipment	2.装船期
(1)bills of lading must be dated not later than August 15, 2018	(1)提单日期不得迟于2018年8月15日
(2)shipment must be effected not (or no) later than July 30, 2018	(2)货物不得迟于(或于)2018年7月30日装运
(3)shipment latest date ...	(3)最迟装运日期为……
(4)evidencing shipment/dispatch on (or before)	(4)列明货物在××日或在该日以前装运/发送
(5)from China port to ... not later than 31st August, 2018	(5)不迟于2018年8月31日从中国港口至……

Clauses and Phrases of an L/C	信用证条款及短语
3.partial shipments and transshipment （1）partial shipments are (not) permitted （2）partial shipments are (not) allowed （3）without transshipment （4）transshipment at Hong Kong allowed （5）partial shipments are permissible , transshipment is allowed except at ... （6）partial/prorate shipments are permitted （7）transshipment is permitted at any port against through B/L	3.分批装运与转运 （1）（不）允许分批装运 （2）准许（不准）分批装运 （3）不允许转运 （4）允许在中国香港转运 （5）允许分批装运，除在……外允许转运 （6）允许分批装运/按比例装运 （7）凭联运提单允许在任何港口转运
XIV.Date & Place of Expiry 1.valid in ... for negotiation until ... 2. draft(s) must be presented to the negotiating (or drawee) bank not later than ... 3.expiry date for presentation of document 4.draft(s) must be negotiated not later than ... 5.this L/C is valid for negotiating in China (or your port) until 15th July，2018 6.bills of exchange must be negotiated within 15 days from the date of bills of lading but not later than August 8，2018 7.this L/C remains valid in China until 23rd May，2018 (inclusive) 8.expiry date:August 15，2018 in beneficiary's country for negotiation 9.draft(s) drawn under this L/C must be presented for negotiation in China on or before 30th August，2018 10.this L/C shall cease to be available for negotiation of beneficiary's draft after 15th Aug.，2018	十四、有效日期与地点 1.在……议付至……止 2.汇票不得迟于……交议付行（付款行） 3.交单到期日 4.汇票要不迟于……议付 5.本证于2018年7月15日止在中国（或你方港口）议付有效 6.汇票须自提单日起15天内议付,但不得迟于2018年8月8日 7.本证到2018年5月23日为止（包括当日在内）在中国有效 8.于2018年8月15日在受益人国家议付到期 9.根据本证项下开具的汇票须在2018年8月30日或该日前在中国交单议付 10.本证将在2018年8月15日以后停止议付受益人之汇票
XV.The Guarantee of the Opening Bank 1.We hereby engage with you that all drafts drawn under and in compliance with the terms of this L/C will be duly honored 2.We undertake that drafts drawn and presented in conformity with the terms of this L/C will be duly honored 3.We hereby engage with the drawers，drawn under and in compliance with the terms of the L/C that such draft(s) shall be duly honored on due presentation and	十五、开证行付款保证 1.我行保证及时对所有根据本信用证条款开具的汇票兑付 2.开具并交出的汇票如与本证条款相符,我行保证按时付款 3.凡根据本证开具并与本证条款相符的汇票,并能按时提示和交出本证规定的单据,我行保证对出票人承担付款责任（须在本证有效期内开具汇票并议付）

Clauses and Phrases of an L/C	信用证条款及短语
delivery of documents as specified (if drawn and negotiated within the validity date of this L/C)	
4. Provided such drafts are drawn and presented in accordance with the terms of this L/C, we hereby engage with the drawers, endorsers and bona fide holders that the said drafts shall be duly honored on presentation	4.凡根据本证条款开具并出示汇票,我们担保对其出票人、背书人和善意持有人在交单时承兑付款
5. We hereby undertake to honor all drafts drawn in accordance with the terms of this L/C	5.所有按照本证条款开具的汇票,我行保证兑付
XVI.Special Conditions 1.for special instructions please see overleaf 2.at the time of negotiations you will be paid the draft amount less 5% due to ... 3.which amount the negotiation bank must authorize us to pay 4.if the terms and conditions of this L/C unacceptable, please contact the opener for necessary amendments 5.negotiations unrestricted/restricted to advising bank 6.(the price) including packing charges 7.all documents must be separated 8.beneficiary's drafts are to be made out for 95% of invoice value, being 5% commission payable to L/C opener 9.drafts to be less 5% drawn for full CIF value less 5% commission, invoice to show full CIF value 10.5% commission to be remitted to L/C opener by way of bank drafts in sterling pounds drawn on ... this commission not to be shown on the invoice	十六、特别条款 1.特别事项请看背面 2.议付时汇票金额应少付5%给……(这种条款是开证行对议付行的指示) 3.该项金额须由议付行授权我行支付(指佣金的金额) 4.如你方不接受本证条款,请与开证人联系以做必要修改 5.不限制议付行/限于通知行 6.(价格)包括包装费用 7.各种单据须分开(意即联合单证不接受) 8.受益人的汇票按发票金额的95%开具,5%的佣金付给开证人 9.汇票按CIF总金额减少5%佣金开具,发票须表明CIF总金额 10.5%佣金用英镑开成以……为付款人的银行汇票汇付给开证人,该佣金勿在发票上表明
XVII.In Reimbursement 1.instructions to the negotiation bank (1)the amount and date of negotiation of each draft must be endorsed on reverse hereof by the negotiation bank (2)this copy of the L/C for your own file, please deliver the attached original to the beneficiary (3)without your confirmation thereon (4)documents must be sent by consecutive airmail (5)documents must be sent by successive (or succeeding) airmail (6)all original documents are to be forwarded to us by airmail and duplicate documents by sea mail (7)original documents must be sent by registered airmail, and duplicate by subsequent airmail	十七、索偿文句 1.议付行注意事项 (1)每张汇票的议付金额和日期必须由议付行在本证背面签注 (2)本证副本供你行存档,请将随附之正本递交给受益人 (3)(本证)无须你行保兑 (4)单据须分别由连续航次邮寄 (5)单据要由连续航邮寄送 (6)全部单据的正本须用航邮,副本用海邮寄交我行 (7)单据的正本须用挂号航邮寄送,副本于下一班航邮寄送

Clauses and Phrases of an L/C	信用证条款及短语
（8）please dispatch the first set of documents including three copies of commercial invoices directly to us by registered airmail and the second set by following airmail	（8）请将包括3份商业发票在内的第一套单据用挂号航邮直接寄我行，第二套单据在下一次航邮寄出
（9）all documents made out in English must be sent to our bank in one lot	（9）用英文缮制的所有单据须一次交我行
2.methods of reimbursement	2.索偿办法
（1）in reimbursement, we shall authorize your Bank of China head office in Beijing to debit our head office RMB account with them, upon receipt of relative documents	（1）偿付办法：我行收到有关单据后将授权你北京总行借记我总行在该行开立的人民币账户
（2）in reimbursement, draw your own sight drafts in sterling on ... bank and forward them to our London office, accompanied by your certificate that all terms of this L/C have been complied with	（2）偿付办法：由你行开出英镑即期汇票向××银行支取。在寄送汇票给我行伦敦办事处时，应随附你行的证明，声明已经履行本证的全部条款
（3）available by your draft at sight payable by us in London on basis to sight draft in New York	（3）凭你行开具之即期汇票向我行在伦敦的机构索回票款，票款在纽约即期兑付
（4）in reimbursement, please aim from our RMB account held with your banking department Bank of China head office Beijing with the amount of your negotiation	（4）偿付办法：请在北京总行我行人民币账户中索回你行议付之款项
（5）upon presentation of the documents to us, we shall authorize your head office banking department by airmail to debit the proceeds to our foreign business department account	（5）一旦向我行提交单据，我行将用航邮授权你总行借记我行国外营业部账户
（6）after negotiation, you may reimburse yourselves by debiting our RMB account with you, please forward all relative documents in one lot to us by airmail	（6）议付时，你可以在我行在你行开立的人民币账户议付，并将全部有关单据用航邮一次寄给我行
（7）all bank charges outside UK are for our principal account, but must be claimed at the time of presentation of documents	（7）在英国境外发生的所有银行费用，应由开证人负担，但须在提交单据时索取
（8）negotiating bank may claim reimbursement by TT on the ... bank certifying that the L/C terms have been complied with	（8）议付行须证明本证条款已履行，并按电汇条款向××银行索回货款
（9）negotiating bank is authorized to reimburse themselves to amount of their negotiation by redrawing by airmail at sight on ... bank attaching the reimbursement draft to their certificate stating that all terms of the L/C have been complied with and that the original and duplicate drafts and documents have been forwarded to us by consecutive airmail	（9）授权议付行用航邮向××银行重开一张即期汇票索取议付之货款。索偿汇票须附上证明，声明本证所有条款已履行，汇票及单据的正、副本已由连续航次寄交我行

Training Case 2-1

A Case that Beneficiary Accept a "Soft Terms" L/C

In early 2019, a bank of Hong Kong (hereinafter referred to as the issuing bank) opened an L/C, total amount for $220,000 for 100,000 pcs of woven bags, FOB price. The L/C was a payment L/C and there were the following soft clauses in the L/C at the same time: INSPECTION CERTIFICATE ISSUED BY CID, CONTERSIGNED AND ENDORSED BY APPLICANT WHOSE AUTHORITY AND SIGNATURE MUST BE IN CONFORMITY WITH THE RECORDS BY THE ISSUING BANK. After receipt of the L/C, a foreign trade company in Dalian (hereinafter referred to as the beneficiary), paid RMB 400,000 to the trade intermediary as the quality deposit. At this point, the scam purpose of swindlers has been achieved, who will not ship the goods under the terms of the contract.

However, in order to fulfill the purchase contract signed with manufacturers, the beneficiary chartered and booked shipping space actively to deliver 100,000 woven bags to Hong Kong, China and made payment of freight. In March 2019, without the condition whether the signature of the applicant in the inspection certificate was consistent with the signature of the retained sample in the issuing bank, a bank in Dalian (hereinafter referred to the negotiating bank) made negotiation. After documents arrived in Hong Kong, China, the issuing bank refused to make payment and refund on the ground that the signed inspection certificate did not tally with the specimen signature.

The negotiating bank then recoursed to the beneficiary and the beneficiary refused to refund. The negotiating bank claimed against the beneficiary. The court froze the beneficiary's carrying amount for RMB 300,000 and part of the property.

From the result of execution of this case, the negotiating bank and the beneficiary have suffered serious losses. Most of $220,000 of negotiating bank's amount would not be taken back and RMB 400,000 of the quality deposit was paid by the beneficiary. The goods would be extracted by no one after they arrived in Hong Kong, China, which caused a lot of storage charges, and may be auctioned.

受益人接受"软条款"信用证上当案

2019年年初,中国香港某银行(下称开证行)开出了一笔22万美元的信用证,购买10万条编织袋,FOB价格,信用证系开证行付款信用证。同时,信用证还有如下软条款:"检验证书由商品检验司签发,由申请人会签和背书,申请人的印章和签字必须和开证行预留印鉴一致。"大连市一家外贸公司(下称受益人)收到信用证后,便向贸易中间人支付了40万元人民币的质量保证金。至此,诈骗分子的诈骗目的已经达到,根本不会根据合同条款派船装货。

然而,受益人为了履行与生产厂家签订的购货合同,主动租船订舱,支付运费,将10万条编织袋运往中国香港。2019年3月,大连市某银行(下称议付行)在没有确定检验证书上开证申请人的签字是否与开证行留存的签字样本一致的情况下,叙做了押汇。单据到达中国香港后,开证行以检验证书上的签字与签字样本不符为由拒付并退单。

议付行随后便向受益人追索,而受益人拒绝退款。议付行状告受益人。法院冻结了受益人账面金额30万元人民币和部分财产。

从本案的执行结果看,议付行和受益人都遭受了严重损失。议付行22万美元的押汇款大部分恐难收回,受益人支付了40万元人民币的质量保证金。货物到达中国香港后无人提取,已产生大量的仓储费,可能被拍卖。

Training Case 2-2

Read the "Skin" of Soft Clause of an L/C

On December 25, 2015, bank A in China received an irrevocable L/C at sight from Japanese bank B, the applicant was Japanese company D, the beneficiary was China's food processing enterprise C of a foreign trade company. After the bank received the L/C, they carefully reviewed and found that there was a soft clause "INSPECTION CERTIFICATE ISSUED BY MR. ZHANG FOD, ×× OFFICE IN TWO COPIES". Staffs informed the beneficiary and reminded the beneficiary of that soft clause. The beneficiary didn't raise an objection. Company C delivered the goods in two lots within the L/C validity and submitted the documents required to the bank A for negotiation. The first negotiation for USD 26,800 was on January 29, 2016 and recovered the payment on time. The problem was on the second negotiation.

The second negotiation for USD 107,520 was on February 5, 2016. Because there was a reimbursing bank, the negotiating bank could timely receive the documentary style. But after a few days, the issuing bank telexed the negotiating bank and claimed that there were discrepancies with the documents "signature was forged on the inspection certificate". The issuing bank refused to pay and reclaimed the payment from the reimbursing bank. At the same time, the applicant company D in our country office also came to bank A, said that they had received an empty container with no goods. Bank A was aware of the seriousness of the problem and made a decision by the research: first of all, they must ensure the safety of the funds and the payment received could not be refunded. At the same time, according to the UCP600 regulation "Bank shall not be responsible for any document form, completeness, accuracy, authenticity, falsification or legal effect, or for a document to the general peculiarity and (or) additional conditions", telexed the issuing bank and argued on the basis of reason and overreacted. After negotiation, the issuing bank finally agreed on payment on March 15, 2016.

揭去软条款信用证的"皮"

2015年12月25日,我国A银行收到日本B银行的即期不可撤销的信用证,申请人为日本的D公司,受益人为我国一个外贸公司所属的食品加工企业C。银行收到信用证后认真审查了该证,发现有一软条款"INSPECTION CERTIFICATE ISSUED BY MR. ZHANG FOD, ×× OFFICE IN TWO COPIES"。工作人员在通知受益人时,指出了该软条款,提醒受益人注意。受益人未提出异议。后C公司在信用证有效期内分两次发货,并提交规定单据到A银行议付。第一次议付时间是2016年1月29日,金额为26 800美元,准时收回货款;问题出在第二次议付上。

第二次议付时间是 2016 年 2 月 5 日,议付金额为 107 520 美元。因该证有偿付行,议付行及时收到了押汇款。可时隔几日开证行发电至议付行称该单据有不符点,"检验证书上签字系伪造",拒付并要求退回已收到的偿付行的款项。同时,申请人 D 公司驻我国办事处亦来到 A 银行,称他们收到的为空箱,根本没有货。A 银行意识到问题的严重性,经研究做出决定:首先要保证资金安全,收到的款项不能退回。同时根据 UCP600"银行对于任何单据的形式、完整性、准确性、真实性、伪造或法律效力,或对于单据上规定的或附加的一般性及(或)特殊性条件概不负责"的规定给开证行发电据理力争,毫不退让。经过交涉,开证行最终在 2016 年 3 月 15 日同意付款。

Key Terms

L/C clauses 信用证条款　　clauses concerning documents 单证条款　　soft clauses 软条款

Exercise

◎ *Case Analysis*

L/C Amendment

Bank I opened an irrevocable negotiation L/C to notify the beneficiary through bank A. In addition to the other terms, the L/C required: (1) the certificate of origin in duplicate; (2) signed packing list. Beneficiary delivered the documents to bank A for negotiation. After the bank audited the documents submitted by the beneficiary, which were in conformity with the balance of the L/C, negotiated and sent documents to the bank I. Bank I received the documents and claimed that there were discrepancies after checking the documents. Bank I immediately cabled bank A that they refused to accept the documents because of discrepancies: (1) The date of the certificate of origin was later than the date of shipment; (2) No date on the packing list. Bank I advised bank A that documents was temporarily protected for processing.

After receipt of the refusal notice, bank A telexed reply as follows: We did not accept your refusal, the reasons were as follows: (1) There was no mistake that the date of the certificate of origin was later than the date of shipment. The proof of origin was conducted before the shipment, the certificate of origin was issued later. In addition, your views couldn't find the evidence in the L/C and the UCP600 Art. 4. The issuing date of the certificate of origin was within the validity of the L/C, and was submitted according to the regulations of the UCP600 Art 4. (2) Packing list was not required to indicate the issuing date, and the content of the packing list complied with the terms of the L/C and other documents' requirements.

Please study and analysis of the above example, and answer the following questions:

(1) Was it right for bank I to refuse to pay?

(2) Was there a clause that indicated the date of issuing documents in UCP600?

(3) Was packing list needed to indicate the date of issuing documents?

改证案例

I 银行开立了不可撤销的议付信用证并通过 A 银行通知受益人。除其他条款外,信用证还要求:(1)一式两份原产地证书;(2)有签字的装箱单。受益人将单证提交给 A 银行议付。A 银行审核了受益人提交的单证,认为与信用证余款相符,议付单证后向 I 银行寄单索偿。I 银行收到单证审核后认为单证存在不符点。I 银行立即电告 A 银行因下列不符点拒付单据:(1)原产地证书的日期晚于装船日期;(2)装箱单上没有日期。I 银行通知 A 银行单据暂为保管听候处理。

接到拒付通知后,A 银行电传答复如下:对于你们提出拒付我们不予接受,理由是:(1)原产地证书的日期迟于装船日期并无错误,产地的证实是在装船前进行的,原产地证书是后来出具的。此外,你们的观点在信用证和 UCP600 第 4 条中找不到证据。原产地证书的出具日期在信用证有效期之内,又是根据 UCP600 第 4 条规定提交的。(2)装箱单没有要求表明出单日期,装箱单内容与信用证和其他单证要求一致,因此符合信用证条款。

请分析上述案例,回答下面的问题:

(1)I 银行的拒付正确吗?

(2)UCP600 中有要求原产地证书表明出单日期的条款吗?

(3)装箱单需要注明出单日期吗?

Chapter 3

Examination and Amendment to an L/C

信用证的审核与修改

Learning Objectives

◆ 重点掌握根据合同审核信用证;正确识别信用证的软条款;根据实际需要提出信用证的修改意见;了解信用证的审核方法及修改程序;熟悉信用证的各项条款;了解信用证欺诈的常见方式及防范措施。

Guide Case

Yali Garments Company is an industry and trade enterprise mainly majored in producing all kinds of woolen sweater with import and export rights, the annual exports is more than $5 million. At present, the company's trade scale is expanding, customers are throughout the world, and the company wins the trust of customers at home and abroad with good reputation. In the spring of 2018 Canton Fair, Steven of the British TAD Trade Co., Ltd. showed great interest to the export clothing of Ningbo Yali Garments Company, and had carried on the preliminary discussion with the manager Wang of Yali Garments Company. After several times of communication, both sides reached an agreement on July 20 on sweaters imported and exported and signed a formal contract, then the TAD Trade Co., Ltd. opened an L/C according to the contract's requirement.

SALES CONTRACT

S/C NO.: YC899

Date: JULY 20, 2018

The Seller: YALI GARMENTS COMPANY

Add.: 99 FUJIN ROAD, NINGBO, CHINA

The Buyer: TAD TRADE CO., LTD.

Add: NO. 555 W. N. STREET, LONDON, BRITISH

The seller agrees to sell and the buyer agrees to buy the under mentioned goods according to the terms and conditions as stipulated below:

Name of Commodity, Specification, Packing	Quantity	Unit Price	Total Amount
			CIF LONDON
100% WOOLEN SWEATER ART. 768	2,000 PCS	USD 12.00/PC	USD 24,000.00
100% WOOLEN SWEATER ART. 769	1,600 PCS	USD 10.00/PC	USD 16,000.00
PACKING: ONE PIECE TO A POLY BAG AND 80 PCS TO ONE CARTON.			
Total Value (in words): SAY US DOLLARS FORTY THOUSAND ONLY.			

Shipment: within 45 days of receipt of the L/C and not later than the month of October 2018 with partial shipments and transshipment allowed, from any Chinese port to London, British.

Insurance to be effected by seller for 110% of CIF invoice value covering all risks only as per China Insurance Clause.

Payment: by 100% confirmed irrevocable letter of credit of 45 days after the B/L opened by the buyer.

Confirmed by:

The Seller: YALI GARMENTS COMPANY   The Buyer: TAD TRADE CO., LTD.

陈志伟   Steven

DOCUMENTARY LETTER OF CREDIT

FROM: BRITISH LOYAL BANK, LONDON, BRITISH

SEQUENCE OF TOTAL 27: 1/1

L/C NO. 20: LC222

DATE OF ISSUE 31C: SEP. 10, 2018

EXPIRY DATE AND PLACE 31D: NOV. 15, 2018, LONDON

APPLICANT 50: TAD TRADE CO., LTD.

NO. 555 W. N. STREET, LONDON, BRITISH

BENEFICIARY 59: YALI GARMENTS TRADE COMPANY

99 FUJIN ROAD, NINGBO, CHINA

CURRENCY CODE AMOUNT 32B: USD 40,000.00

AVAILABLE WITH/BY 41D: WITH ANY BANK BY NEGOTIATION IN CHINA

DRAFT AT 42C: AT 45 DAYS AFTER SIGHT

DRAWEE (PAYING BANK) 42D: OURSELVES

PARTIAL SHIPMENTS 43P: NOT ALLOWED

TRANSSHIPMENT 43T: NOT ALLOWED

LOADING AT/FROM 44A: NINGBO

FOR TRANSPORTATION TO 44B: LONDON, BRITISH

THE LATEST DATE OF SHIPMENT 44C: OCT. 1, 2018

TERMS OF DELIVERY: CIF LONDON

DESCRIPTION OF GOODS 45A: 100% WOOLEN SWEATER AS PER S/C NO. YC899 JULY 20, 2018

STYLE 768 2,000 PCS USD 12. 00/PC

STYLE 769 1,600 PCS USD 10.00/PC

DOCUMENTS REQUIRED 46A:

1. SIGNED COMMERCIAL INVOICE IN 4 COPIES CERTIFYING THAT THE QUALITY OF SHIPMENT IS IN ACCORDANCE WITH THE STIPULATIONS OF S/C AND SHOWING FREIGHT CHARGES AND FOB VALUE.

2. PACKING LIST IN 3 COPIES.

3. 2/3 OF CLEAN ON BOARD MARINE BILLS OF LADING MADE OUT TO ORDER AND ENDORED IN BLANK SHOWING FREIGHT PREPAID AND NOTIFYING APPLICANT.

4. FORM A ISSUED BY CHINESE GOVERNMENTAL ORGANIZATION.

5. BENIFICIARY'S CERTIFICATE CERTIFYING THAT 1/3 ORIGINAL B/L AND ONE SET OF NON-NEGOTIABLE DOCUMENTS HAVE BEEN SENT TO APPLICANT AFTER SHIPMENT IMMEDIATELY.

6. INSURANCE POLICY IN DUPLICATE FOR 120% OF INVOICE VALUE COVERING ALL RISKS AND WAR RISK SUBJECT TO CIC DATED JAN. 1ST, 1981.

7. QUALITY INSPECTION CERTIFICATE SIGNED BY REPRESENTATIVE DESIGNED BY BUYER SHOWING SHRINKAGE RATE IS UNDER 6%.

8. SHIPPING ADVICE.

ADDITIONAL CONDITIONS 47A:

+ ALL DOCUMENTS MUST SHOW THIS L/C NO.

+ PLS NOTE IF DOCS. PRESENTED CONTAIN DISCREPANCY, A FEE OF USD 30 WILL BE DEDUCTED.

PERIOD FOR PRESENTATION 48: DOCUMENTS MUST BE PRESENTED WITHIN 15 DAYS AFTER SHIPMENT DATE BUT WITHIN L/C VALIDITY.

CONFIRMATION INSTRUCTIONS 49: WITHOUT

CHARGES 71B: ALL BANKING CHARGES OUTSIDE OF NEW YORK ARE FOR THE BENEFICIARY'S ACCOUNT.

BANK TO BANK INFORMATION 72: THIS L/C IS SUBJECT TO UNIFORM CUSTOMS AND PRACTICE FOR DOCUMENTARY CREDITS, 2007 REVISION, ICC PUBLICATION NO. 600.

雅丽服装公司是一家以生产各类羊毛衫为主、有自营进出口权的工贸企业,年出口额达到500万美元以上。目前公司贸易规模正日益扩大,客户遍及世界各地,以良好的信誉获得了国内外客户的信赖。在2018年春季广交会上,英国TAD贸易有限公司的Steven对宁波雅丽服装公司的出口服装表现出极大的兴趣,并与雅丽服装公司的王经理进行了初步洽谈。后经多次沟通交流后,双方于7月20日就羊毛衫进出口事宜达成协议,并签订了正式合同。随后,英国TAD贸易有限公司按合同要求开出信用证。

问题:

(1)根据上述背景资料,请以雅丽服装公司外贸单证员小王的身份审核信用证。

(2)根据信用证审核结果,提出修改意见。

3.1 Review of an L/C
信用证的审核

In international trade, when using L/C payment, the rights and obligations of all parties concerned under the L/C only based on the terms of the L/C, which is not bound by a trade contract. As a result, the relevant parties of the L/C should audit the terms of the L/C strictly after receipt of the L/C, timely put forward revision after finding the problems. Otherwise it will directly affect the processing of documents under an L/C initiatively and make exchange collection safely in the future. The review of an L/C will be made jointly by foreign trade companies and banks. The followings will be introduced respectively.

在国际贸易中,使用信用证方式结算货款时,信用证的特点决定信用证项下有关各方的权利与义务仅以信用证条款为依据,不受贸易合同的约束。因此,信用证的相关当事人在收到信用证后,应对信用证条款进行严格审核,发现问题后及时提出修改;否则将直接影响处理信用证项下单证的主动权与日后出口货款的安全收汇。信用证的审核由外贸企业和银行共同进行,下面分别加以介绍。

3.1.1 Audit of an L/C by an Advising Bank
通知行对信用证的审核

According to the regulations of UCP600, the advising bank is only responsible for identifying the authenticity of the L/C and notice to the beneficiary timely, and no review of the terms of the L/C and the obligation of content. But domestic advising bank will review some of the important contents of the L/C and will endorse on the L/C correspondingly for the interests of the beneficiary. Beneficiary must pay attention to the endorsement and take corresponding measures. In practice, the advising bank mainly reviews the following several aspects:

(1)Review the authenticity of the L/C;

(2)Review the issuing bank's credit standing.

按照UCP600规定,通知行只负责鉴别信用证的真实性并及时将信用证通知给受益人,并无审核信用证条款和内容的义务。但是国内的通知行为了受益人的利益,仍会对信用证中的一些重要内容进行审核并在信用证上做相应批注。受益人对银行的批注必须重视并采取相应的措施。在实践中,通知行主要审核以下内容:

(1)审核信用证的真实性;

(2)审核开证行的资信。

3.1.2   Audit of an L/C by Beneficiary
受益人对信用证的审核

In practice, the advising bank mainly reviews the following aspects:

1.Review Consistencies of an L/C with an Contract

The followings should be specially paid attention by the beneficiary:

(1)The name of the applicant and the beneficiary.

(2)The description of the goods. In addition to the name of commodity, it should also include the buying and selling contract No., kinds of goods, size and composition, etc.

(3)Shipping port or the destination.

(4)The unit price, quantity, and total amount. Sometimes the number that the price specified in the L/C times the total amount of the L/C is not in conformity with the contract or a certain item does not match the contract, and the beneficiary will be confronted with difficulties in operation. According to the regulations of UCP600, when there is the word "about" before the quantity specified in the L/C, there is 10% more or less quantity amplitude, meanwhile there should be the word "about" of the total amount in the L/C. In turn, when there is the word "about" before the total amount, there should be 10% of more or less amplitude of the total amount in the L/C, meanwhile there should be the word "about" of the quantity in L/C. But for the goods being unable to measure, there is 5% more or less amplitude, meanwhile there should be the total amount amplitude of the L/C.

2.Review Feasibility and Acceptability of Clauses of an L/C

Because some clauses which are difficult to do and some conditions which are difficult to meet appear in the L/C, the beneficiary has no way to meet the conformity of documents with documents and documents with letters of credit. They mainly manifest in the following situations:

(1) Is it an irrevocable L/C? Is the L/C effective? Though a certain L/C is called an irrevocable L/C, it states: "The certificate has not been effective." The beneficiary can make shipment only after the L/C takes effect.

(2) The validity, time of shipment, period for presentation. Sometimes, when the time of receipt of your L/C is too close to the latest date of shipment, the L/C validity and period for presentation, it is difficult to make shipment timely and present documents to the bank. If there is only the latest date of shipment or only the validity of the L/C, the shipping date and validity are considered as the same day, that is "double due", on which the beneficiary should make the shipment ahead to have sufficient time to maneuver. If an L/C states that the date when the beneficiary presents the documents should not be later than the shipping date, we should pay attention to the time limit whether it is reasonable and can be made. It is easier for an issuing bank or a paying bank to be refused to make payment because of overdue presentation caused by documents delivery delayed if we met maturity L/C abroad.

(3) For transportation clauses (including the modes of transportation, means of transport, transport routes, or regulations issued by vessel carrier, or terms that are not allowed to transfer,

etc.), the beneficiary should be clear whether it is feasible or not.

(4) Partial shipment clause. If an L/C states that partial shipment is not allowed, the beneficiary should decide if he can do it according to the different goods. Sometimes, the L/C allows partial shipment but attaches with the clause "shipment of goods must be in a container" restriction.

(5) Price clause. Using FOB and CFR terms, the L/C shall specify "insurance shall take the responsibility of the importer to handle". Among them, transport documents shall be marked "freight collect" under FOB term, transport documents shall be marked "freight prepaid" under the CFR term, and in addition to transport documents, it should also include the insurance documents marked "freight prepaid" under the CIF term.

(6) Whether we can meet the L/C insurance clauses.

(7) Whether the L/C clauses is contradict or ambiguous. Such as: An L/C is required to provide a set of port to port ocean bills of lading from port of shipment Shanghai to the destination Chicago. But the destination Chicago is not harbour, the beneficiary may only provide multimodal transport bill of lading. So this kind of the L/C clause is contradict and should be modified.

(8) Can the L/C documents be provided? For example: some credits of lading require that invoice, certificate of origin and other documents must be presented by the importing country's embassy or consulate, but there is not a local country's embassy or consulate.

(9) Whether freight forwarder designated in the L/C can be accepted. Under the condition of FOB term, freight representative company is usually designated by the importer. If freight representative company's credit is poor, exporters have risk. Exporters shall generally clinch a deal with CIF term, arrange transportation by themselves and should entrust reputable freight agency, mind your own goods, avoid the tragedy of money and goods empty.

(10) Whether the shipping mark specified in the L/C can be accepted. According to international practice, if an L/C regulates shipping mark, but it is not clear to state that such signs can only be accepted, exporters should make the shipping mark with the prescribed mark and also can appropriately increase the other contents, such as container number, package number, and port of destination, etc. If an L/C limits marks, the exporter must completely brush marks on the packaging as stipulated in the L/C and prepare the documents.

(11) Whether there is a "soft clause" in the L/C. "Soft clause" refers to the elastic clause which makes exporters in disadvantage, and which all can't be controlled by the beneficiary in the L/C. The L/C in common "soft clause" listed is as follows:

① The L/C requires an inspection quarantine permit issued by the applicant or the designated, and the signature must be consistent with the signature samples retained in the issuing bank.

② The L/C has not been effective, when the importer gets an import license or other related documents, the issuing bank will notify the L/C or take effect in the form of L/C modification.

③ The vessel and shipment date will be informed by the importer to the issuing bank, and the issuing bank will inform the beneficiary in the form of L/C modification.

④After the goods arrived at the port of destination, the issuing bank will take the payment obligation after the import inspection and quarantine departments make inspection on imported goods and issue the relevant certificate or after notification by importers.

在实践中,通知行主要审核以下内容:

1.审核信用证与合同的一致性

下面的内容是受益人特别应当注意的:

(1)开证申请人、受益人的名称。

(2)货物的描述。除商品名称外,还应包括买卖合同号,货物的种类、尺寸、成分等。

(3)装运港或目的地。

(4)单价、数量和总金额。有时信用证中规定的单价乘以数量与信用证总金额不符或某一项与合同不符,很可能是信用证开错;有时信用证规定的商品数量与总金额不匹配,使受益人在操作时会遇到困难。根据UCP600的规定,当信用证规定的数量前有"大约"字样时,则数量有10%的增减幅度,这时信用证总金额也应有"大约"字样;反过来,如果信用证总金额前有"大约"字样,则总金额有10%的增减幅度,这时数量也应有"大约"字样。但是不能以个数来计量的商品可以有5%的增减幅度,此时信用证总金额也应当有增减幅度。

2.审查信用证条款的可操作性和可接受性

有些信用证中会出现一些受益人难以办到的条款或难以满足的条件,受益人因而无法做到单单相符、单证相符。这主要表现在以下几种情况:

(1)它是否为不可撤销信用证? 信用证是否生效? 有些信用证虽名为不可撤销信用证,但其中声明"本证尚未生效",此时受益人必须等信用证生效后才能办理出运。

(2)到期日、装运期和交单期。有时,受益人收到信用证的时间离最后装运日、信用证到期日和交单日太近,很难做到按期装运货物和向银行交单。如果信用证只有最迟装运期或只有信用证有效期,则视装运期和有效期为同一天,即"双到期",此时受益人应提前办理托运,使装运、制单工作有足够回旋的时间。如果信用证规定"受益人向银行交单的日期不得迟于装运日期后若干天",我们要注意该期限是否合理、能否办到。如果我们遇到在国外到期的信用证,则更易发生因单据传递延误而造成过期交单招致开证行或付款行拒付的情况。

(3)对运输条款(包括运输方式、运输工具、运输路线、承运人出具的规定或不许转运等条款),受益人应明确是否可行。

(4)分批装运条款。如果信用证规定不允许分批装运,受益人应根据不同的商品确认是否能做到。有时,虽然信用证允许分批装运,但又附带"货物出运必须以一个集装箱为单位"的限制条款。

(5)价格条款。如用FOB和CFR价格术语,信用证中应说明"保险由进口商负责办理"。其中,FOB价格术语下运输单证应注明"运费到付",CFR价格术语下运输单证应注明"运费已付",而CIF价格术语下除运输单证应注明"运费已付"外,保险单证也要注明"运费已付"。

(6)信用证的保险条款是否能满足。

(7)信用证的条款是否互相矛盾或意思模棱两可。例如,某信用证要求受益人提供一整套从起运港上海至目的地芝加哥的港至港海运提单,而目的地芝加哥不是海港,受益人只能提供多式联运提单。所以这种信用证条款是自相矛盾的,应予以修改。

（8）信用证要求的单据是否都能提供。譬如：有的信用证中要求发票、原产地证书等单据须由进口国的大使馆或领事馆认证，而当地没有该国大使馆或领事馆。

（9）信用证指定的货运代理公司是否可接受。在 FOB 术语下，通常由进口商指定货运代理公司。如货运代理公司信誉不佳，出口商就有风险。出口商一般应争取以 CIF 术语成交，由自己安排运输并应委托信誉好的货代机构，管好自己的货物，避免造成财货两空的惨剧。

（10）信用证指定的唛头是否可以接受。根据国际惯例，如果信用证规定唛头，但没有明确表明只能接受这样的标志，出口商可以将唛头做成载有该规定标志，还可适当增加其他内容，如箱号、件号、目的港等。如果信用证中限制唛头，则出口商必须完全按照信用证规定将唛头刷在包装上并制作单据。

（11）信用证中是否有"软条款"。"软条款"是指置出口商于不利地位的弹性条款，即信用证中所有无法由受益人自主控制的条款。信用证中常见的"软条款"列举如下：

①信用证要求一份开证申请人或其指定人签发的检验检疫证书，且其签字须和留存开证行的签字样本相符。

②信用证尚未生效，待进口商取得进口许可证或其他相关进口文件后，开证行将以信用证修改形式通知信用证生效。

③所装船只和出运日期由进口商通知开证行，开证行将以信用证修改形式通知受益人。

④货物运抵目的港后，开证行在进口地检验检疫部门对进口商品检验合格并出具相关证书或待进口商通知后才履行付款义务。

3.1.3　*Review of Exchange Collection Security*
审查收汇保障

An issuing bank should make clear about guarantee payment in an L/C. The most common is: "Our bank will guarantee drawers and bona fide holders that we will take the responsibility of making payment as long as drafts opened and negotiated according to the L/C, are strictly in conformity with the clauses of this L/C and the reasonable hint on the maturity date." If there is no L/C guarantee payment clause but clear regulating words that L/C should be opened or bound according to UCP600, beneficiary can also be acceptable, which clearly regulates the responsibilities of confirming bank.

开证行在信用证中应有保证付款的明确表示。最常见的是："凡根据本证开具和议付的汇票，只要严格符合本证条款的规定并经合理提示，我行保证对出票人和善意持票人在到期日时承担付款责任。"如遇信用证无保付条款，但明确规定该证按 UCP600 开立或受其约束的字样，受益人也可接受，UCP600 已对保兑行的责任有明确规定。

3.1.4　*Audit Ownership of Cargo Controlled*
审核货权控制情况

During the exporter's bank submits documents to the issuing bank and the issuing bank makes payment, the exporter should manage to keep control of the goods in order to control the goods when they meet the importer or the issuing bank dishonored to protect their own rights and interests. Exporters must pay attention to the following conditions in receipt of an L/C:

(1)The L/C regulates that the importer should be as the consignee in the B/L.

(2)The L/C requires air waybill or parcel post receipt, and the importer should be as the consignee.

(3)The L/C regulates that exporter should send part of the bills of lading or full set of bills of lading directly to the importer. This is common practice, and there is a greater risk.

在向出口地银行交单至开证行付款以前这段时间,出口商应设法保持对货物的控制权,以便在遇到进口商或开证行拒付时能够控制货物,保护自己的权益。出口商在收到信用证时有下列情况的必须引起注意:

(1)信用证规定提单应以进口商作为收货人。

(2)信用证要求航空运单或邮包收据,并以进口商为收货人。

(3)信用证规定出口商在货物装运后将部分提单或全套提单直接寄给进口商。此种情形在实务中较为常见,而且有较大风险。

3.1.5 *Audit Charges*
审核费用

All bank charges under an L/C are various, divided into two parts: domestic banks expenses and foreign banks expenses. According to the provisions of UCP600: a party which instructs the other party services is responsible for any charges caused by the instructed party for which they supply service, in relation to their instructions, including fees, costs and other expenses.

At the same time it also stipulates that if an L/C states that these expenses shall be borne by the instructed party of one party, and these charges cannot be collected, indicating party finally still have to pay the costs of such responsibility. In L/C business, the applicant is the indicated party, so the bank charges shall be borne by the importer. In practice, fewer credits of lading will regulate that all bank charges shall be borne by the importer, but mostly by the beneficiary and by the both sides commonly, i. e. the importer pays for all issuing bank charges and the exporter covers the expenses of the negotiating bank and the third country bank.

In a word, in the export business, the foreign trade enterprises can immediately make shipment and make documents, according to provisions of a doubtless L/C. For unacceptable terms, the foreign trade enterprises should notify the applicant as soon as possible to make necessary revision to protect their own interests, to avoid problems after the date of shipment and are in a passive situation. What should be paid special attention to is that it takes time to amend the L/C, in order to ensure timely shipment, the amendment should be audited as soon as possible after receipt of the L/C. In addition, the content and the form of the L/C are not identical, and the general trend is getting increasingly complicated, especially the special terms, the types of documents and requirements. This needs relevant personnel have enough patience to audit carefully, word for word, to find out all the problems to be settled as soon as possible. Otherwise, it will not only affect the shipment, but also affect the funds to be collected safely. It is worth mentioning that audit should include all amendments under the L/C because the amendment is a part of the L/C.

To protect their own rights and interests, the beneficiary should audit the L/C comprehensively. If the beneficiary finds anything not in conformity with the contract, the terms and provisions which they can not accept or can't do, they must inform the importer to make the necessary changes.

Main responsibility of audit is to find problems in time and solve problems before the goods are shipped to pave the way for smooth export and security funds in a timely manner. Ignoring audit can make discrepancies which can be avoided originally become a fait accompli, and cause irreparable damage.

This lesson is profound. For example, a bank opened an L/C which regulated that the beneficiary must inform the issuing bank about shipment information in the form of cable by the negotiating bank within 24 hours after shipment. And the cable shall be attached to other documents presented to the issuing bank. It was the negotiating bank that found documents for negotiation were not delivered after shipment because the beneficiary did not audit after receipt of the L/C. At the moment, it was after the time stipulated in the L/C, and documents have been dishonored after presenting to the issuing bank. Finally the beneficiary had to accept the importer's selling requirement.

信用证项下的银行费用种类繁多,可分国内银行费用和国外银行费用两部分。按UCP600的规定:指示另一方服务的一方,有责任负担被指示方为其服务而产生的与其指示有关的任何费用,包括手续费、成本和其他开支。

同时规定:如果信用证规定这些费用由指示方之外的一方负担,而这些费用不能被收取,指示方最终仍须承担支付此类费用的责任。在信用证业务中,开证申请人是被指示方,因此银行费用应由进口商负担。在实务中,有较少的信用证规定所有的银行费用由进口商负担,更多的是规定所有银行费用由受益人负担,由双方共同承担银行费用也比较常见,即进口商承担开证行的费用,出口商承担议付行和第三国银行的费用。

总之,在出口业务中,对于无疑义的信用证条款,外贸企业可立即按其规定办理货运、制单;对于不能接受的条款,则应尽快地通知信用证申请人做必要的修改,从而保护自己的利益,避免在货物装运后发现问题而处于被动的境地。应特别注意的是,修改信用证是需要一定时间的,为了保证及时装运,一般应在收到信用证后尽快审核完毕。此外,信用证的内容、形式各不相同,且总的趋势日趋复杂化,尤其是特别条款、单证的种类和要求等越来越多。这就需要相关人员在审证时有足够的耐心,逐字逐句地审核,找出所有的问题以便尽快解决;否则,不仅会影响货物装运,更影响安全收汇。值得一提的是,审证应包括信用证项下的所有修改书,因为修改书也是信用证的一部分。

为保护自身权益,受益人应对收到的信用证进行全面审查。如发现任何与货物买卖合同不符而又不能接受或无法做到的条款和规定,必须通知进口商进行必要的修改。

审证工作的主要职责是及时发现问题并将问题解决于货物出运之前,为顺利出口和安全、及时收汇铺平道路。忽视审证会使本来可以避免的不符点变为既成事实,而造成无法弥补的损失。

这种教训是深刻的。譬如,某银行开出一张信用证,其中规定:受益人必须在装船后24小时内将装船信息由议付行以电文的形式告知开证行,而且此电文须附在其他单据中一起交开证行。由于受益人收到信用证后没有审证,直至装运完毕将单据交议付行时,议付行才发现没有发送装船通知电文,但此时早已过了信用证规定的时间,单据交开证行后遭到了拒付,最后受益人不得不接受进口商的减价要求。

3.2　Amendment to an L/C
　　信用证的修改

Amendment to an L/C refers to the behavior that some clauses in the L/C opened are to be modified. When auditing, if some clauses can't be accepted, or do not agree with the sales contract, or contain incomplete and impossible terms, the beneficiary must require the applicant to amend the L/C to protect their own interests. Sometimes the applicant may also ask to amend the L/C due to the change of the situation.

修改信用证是指对已开立的信用证中的某些条款进行修改的行为。审证中,如发现信用证某些条款不能接受,或有与销售合同不一致之处,或含有不完整及无法办到的条款,受益人必须要求开证申请人修改信用证,从而保护自己的利益。有时,开证申请人也可能由于形势的变化而要求修改信用证。

3.2.1　Principle of L/C Amendment
　　　修改信用证的原则

In any case, the amendment of an irrevocable letter of credit shall be put forward and modified by the issuing bank which is required by the applicant. Only if it is approved by the issuing bank, the confirming bank (if already confirmed) and the beneficiary, can it take effect.

在任何情况下,不可撤销信用证的修改应由开证申请人要求开证行提出,由开证行修改,并经开证行、保兑行(如已保兑)和受益人的同意,才能生效。

3.2.2　Procedure of L/C Amendment
　　　修改信用证的程序

The general procedure of L/C amendment is: the applicant puts forward-the issuing bank-the advising bank - the beneficiary. If the beneficiary puts forward to modify, firstly it should be approved by the applicant, and then deal with according to the above procedure. Only after the parties agree to accept the amendments, can it be effective.

信用证修改的一般程序是:开证申请人提出—开证行—通知行—受益人。若由受益人提出修改,首先应征得开证申请人的同意,再按上述程序办理。各方都同意接受该修改书后,方能有效。

3.2.3　Attention when Amending an L/C
　　　修改信用证的注意事项

(1)Since amendment, the issuing bank is irrevocably bound by this modification. For the confirming bank, it can confirm to modify and shall be bound by this modification since being informed to make amendment. The confirming bank may choose to notify the beneficiary amendment without confirmation, but it must not delay to inform the issuing bank and the beneficiary.

(2) The previous terms of the L/C for the beneficiary are still valid before the beneficiary informs the advising bank of modified opinions. The beneficiary should make a response to the notice whether accepts or refuses the amendment, but he/she may also make no response. If not, the previous L/C terms are still valid. If the documents submitted by the beneficiary to the nominated bank or the issuing bank are in compliance with the L/C and modification, the beneficiary shall be deemed to accept the notification of modification. There are two kinds of methods to state whether the beneficiary accepts modification. The first is that the beneficiary will make an amendment notice immediately to accept or refuse to accept after receipt of the amendment. The second is presentation. If the documents submitted by the beneficiary are in conformity with the content of the amendment, this will be deemed as he/she accepts the amendment and meanwhile the L/C has been modified. But if the documents submitted by the beneficiary are not in conformity with the content of the amendment, this will not be deemed as he/she accepts the amendment which is invalid to the beneficiary.

(3) The provisions modified are maximum constraint to the issuing bank while they give maximum freedom to the beneficiary. After the beneficiary receives the amendment, he/she will quickly decide to accept if it is an obvious advantage to them, such as to extend the shipment date; or reject if it is an obvious disadvantage to them, such as to change the specifications of goods near the shipment date. But if you can't judge whether it is an obvious advantage for yourself immediately, the beneficiary can choose not to respond and be able to achieve success one way or another because no comment is more active than statements, and when submiting documents in an impregnable position. If the beneficiary does not respond, the issuing bank and the applicant will be in the passive position. Therefore, some issuing banks take measures to fill in "silent acceptance" clause in the amendment, such as: "If this amendment is not refused within five working days, it will be automatically taken effect."

(4) It is not allowed for the beneficiary to accept part of the contents or not to accept when modifying the same part. Even if the parties have agreed to accept partly, it is also invalid unless the issuing bank makes another new revision of amendment.

(5) When the transferred L/C is used, according to the regulations of UCP600, the first beneficiary must irrevocably instruct the transferring bank before the demand of transfer but not be transferred. UCP600 also regulates that the refusal of the L/C modification by one or more second beneficiaries do not affect other second beneficiaries to accept amendment.

(6) A few problems in the L/C which are inconsistent with the contract, are often encountered, and the beneficiary may decide whether to amend the L/C or not according to conditions. For example: the contract number in the L/C is 2018-MX, but the contract number in the contract is 2018/MX. Before the beneficiary ensures that there is no problem in the premise of the customs and commodity inspection, he/she will use the way of making the same mistake to avoid trouble

caused by amendment of L/C.

(1)自发出修改之时起,开证行即不可撤销地受该修改的约束。对保兑行而言,可将其保兑扩展至修改,并应通知自修改之时起不可撤销地受该修改的约束。但是,保兑行可自行选择,仅将修改通知受益人而不对其加具保兑,但其必须毫不延误地将此告知开证行和受益人。

(2)在受益人将接受修改的意见告知通知行之前,原信用证的条款对受益人依然有效。受益人应对接受或拒绝接受该修改的通知做出表态,但也可不表态。如未做表态,信用证原条款仍有效。如果受益人向指定银行或开证行提交的单据符合信用证和修改,即视为受益人接受该修改的通知。受益人是否接受修改可以有两种表示方法:其一是受益人在收到修改书后立即做出接受或拒绝接受修改的通知。其二是用交单表示。如果受益人所交单据与修改书的内容相符,则认为其接受了该修改,并于此时起信用证已被修改;如果受益人所交单据不符合修改书的内容,则视为其不接受修改,修改书对受益人无效。

(3)修改的规定对开证行加以最大限度的约束,而对受益人给予最大限度的自由。受益人接到修改后,如果对自己明显有利,如延长装运期,或对自己明显不利,如临近装运期却要修改货物规格,则会很快判断接受与拒绝。但如果不能马上判断对自己是否有利,则受益人可选择不予表态,因为不表态比表态更主动,交单时可左右逢源,立于不败之地。如受益人对修改不及时表态,开证行和开证申请人将陷于被动境地。为此,一些开证行纷纷采取措施,在修改书中加注"沉默接受"条款,如:"若本修改书自发出后5个工作日未被受益人书面拒绝,则将自动生效。"

(4)受益人对同一修改内容部分接受、部分不接受是不允许的。即便各方都同意部分接受,也属无效,除非开证行另做新的修改。

(5)在转让信用证的使用中,根据UCP600的规定,第一受益人必须在要求转让而未转让前不可撤销地指示转让行,同时规定如果信用证转让给数名第二受益人,其中一名或多名第二受益人对信用证修改的拒绝并不影响其他第二受益人接受修改。

(6)在单据制作中,常常会遇到信用证中的一些小问题有与合同不一致的情况,受益人可以视情况决定是否修改信用证。比如:信用证中的合同编号为2018-MX,而合同上为2018/MX。受益人在确保海关、商检等环节没有问题的前提下,可以采用将错就错的办法,避免修改信用证引起的麻烦。

3.2.4 *Amendment Fees*
修改费

The amendment fees usually depend on the specific situation, in theory, if the amendment is caused by mistake when the issuing bank opens the L/C, all amendment fees are on the issuing bank's account; If the modification is put forward by the beneficiary, the beneficiary will negotiate with the importer; If the L/C modification is caused by the applicant when applying for the issuing of L/C, all fees shall be borne by the applicant.

It is worth that the beneficiary has the right to unilaterally cancel the contract, and refuses to accept the L/C and may claim compensation from the importer if the L/C is inconsistent with the contract, which makes the beneficiary can't accept L/C, after notifying the applicant.

信用证修改费的收取通常视具体情形而定,从理论上讲:若信用证修改是由开证行开证时的失误引起的,则由开证行自负所有修改费;若修改是受益人提出的,则由受益人与进口商协商;若信用证修改是由开证申请人在申请开证时未按照合同填写开证申请书而导致的,则由开证申请人承担所有修改费。

值得一提的是,如果由于信用证与合同不符,受益人不能接受信用证,受益人有权在通知开证申请人后单方面撤销合同,拒绝接受信用证,并可向进口商提出索赔。

3.3 L/C Fraud and Precaution
信用证欺诈与防范

According to the general law, fraud refers to get virtual interests in essentially unfair or abnormal way. In foreign trade practice, L/C fraud cases are increasing. Therefore, it is necessary for us to analyze means, characteristics and nature of L/C fraud to control and prevent the happening of fraud from broader perspectives, deeply understanding in more effective and more scientific methods.

根据一般法律条文,欺诈是指以不公平或不正常的途径获取实质上的利益。在外贸实践中,利用信用证欺诈的案件日趋增多。因此,我们有必要对信用证欺诈进行分析,从更广阔、更深入的视角来认识、分析欺诈的方式、特点、性质,以更有效、更科学的手段去遏制与防范欺诈的发生。

3.3.1 *Counterfeit or Fake Signature Fraud*
假冒或伪造签字诈骗

Counterfeit or fake signature fraud refers that fraudsters counterfeit or fake the opening bank's personnel seal (signature) typed with a typewriter and sent by mail in order to cheat beneficiary (exporter) to make blind shipment, and finally achieve the purpose of defrauding export goods. Generally there are the following characteristics of this kind of fraud:

(1) The L/C is sent directly to the beneficiary without further notice, there is not the sender's address in detail and the postmark is vague.

(2) The L/C format is obsolete or out of date.

(3) The signature stroke of the L/C is not smooth or use block letters.

(4) The terms of the L/C are contradict or contrary to convention.

(5) The L/C requires airfreight, or the applicant (importer) is required to be consignee in bill of lading.

For example, a foreign trade company has received a documentary letter of credit in the name of the British Standard Chartered Bank Birmingham Branch, total amount for $65,000. The advising bank was National Westminster Bank in London. The L/C was not audited as usual by local bank professional staffs. There are several suspicious points:

(1) The format of the L/C was very old, there was no return address on the envelope and the

postmark was blurry, unable to identify whether sent from local.

(2)The L/C confined the advising bank, National Westminster Bank in London. This was contrary to convention.

(3)Details of the bank were not checked in the bank yearbook.

(4)The signature of the L/C was a printing style instead of the handwritten form, and couldn't be checked.

(5)The L/C required that the goods should be shipped to Nigeria where fraud always took place.

The bank initially determined that the L/C was forged according to the points above. After examination and contact by the issuing bank head office, indeed it was true, hence avoided a forge L/C fraud.

假冒或伪造签字诈骗是指诈骗分子在以打字机打出并将通过邮寄方式传递的信用证上,假冒或伪造开证行有权对信用证签字人员的印鉴(签字),企图以假冒信用证欺骗受益人(出口商)盲目发货,最终达到骗取出口货物的目的。这种诈骗一般有如下特征:

(1)信用证不经通知,而直达受益人手中,且信封无寄件人详细地址,邮戳模糊。

(2)所用信用证格式是陈旧的或过时的。

(3)信用证签字笔画不流畅,或采用印刷体签字。

(4)信用证条款自相矛盾,或违背常规。

(5)信用证要求货物空运,或提单做成申请人(进口商)为受货人。

例如,某外贸公司曾收到一份以英国渣打银行伯明翰分行名义开立的跟单信用证,金额为6.5万美元,通知行为伦敦国民西敏寺银行。因该证没有像往常一样经受益人当地银行专业人员审核,有如下几点可疑之处:

(1)信用证的格式很陈旧,信封无寄件人地址,且邮戳模糊不清,无法辨认是否从当地寄出。

(2)信用证限制通知行——伦敦国民西敏寺银行议付,有违常规。

(3)该行的详情在银行年鉴上查不到。

(4)信用证的签字为印刷体而非手签,且无法核对。

(5)信用证要求货物运至尼日利亚,而该国为诈骗案多发地。

根据以上几点,银行初步判定该证为伪造信用证。后经开证行总行联系查实,确实如此,从而避免了一起伪造信用证诈骗。

3.3.2   *Embezzle or Use Bank Test Key (Password) Fraud*
盗用或借用他行密押(密码)诈骗

It refers that fraudsters pretend to use the third bank to open a cable L/C, while the third bank's confirmation is not added and confirmed, try to deceive everybody to defraud export goods. The followings are characteristics of this kind of fraud:

(1)The L/C has no test key, claimed by the third bank to confirm.

(2)The shipment date or validity of the L/C is shorter, to induce the beneficiary rush delivery.

(3)The L/C stipulates that the beneficiary should send a copy of the original B/L to the applicant after shipment.

(4)To open a time L/C, and offer competitive rates.

(5)The applicant and the consignee of the L/C are in different countries or regions.

盗用或借用他行密押(密码)诈骗是指诈骗分子在电开信用证中伪称使用第三家银行密押,而该第三家银行的确认书却无加押证实,企图瞒天过海,骗取出口货物。这种诈骗通常有如下特征:

(1)来证无密押,而声称由第三家银行来电证实。

(2)来证装运期或有效期较短,以诱使受益人仓促发货。

(3)来证规定装船后由受益人寄交一份正本提单给申请人。

(4)开立远期付款信用证,并许以优惠费率。

(5)来证中申请人与收货人分别在不同的国家或地区。

3.3.3 "Soft Clauses"(Trap Terms)Fraud
"软条款"(陷阱条款)诈骗

Frauds using "soft clauses" (trap terms) basically have the following characteristics:

(1)The amount of the L/C is larger, often more than \$500,000.

(2)The L/C contains "soft clauses" restricting the beneficiary's rights, such as stipulates that the inspection certificate should be issued by the applicant or its designated representatives, or specifies the name of vessel, date of shipment, sailing routes by the applicant or claims that the certificate is invalid etc. Swindlers require that export enterprises should pay 5%~15% of the contract amount or the issuing amount in advance, and commission to the representative or the agent designated by the buyer.

After the buyer gets performance payments commission or quality retention money, he/she will make pass or refuse to issue the inspection certificate or will not make shipment, which makes enterprises unable to get a full set of documents for negotiation, and suffers in vain.

For example, a certain Bank of China has received an L/C from Hong Kong KP Bank in China, of which the amount is \$180,000 and the beneficiary is a certain Zhejiang import and export company. The L/C has the following "soft clause": "THIS L/C IS NON-OPERATIVE UNLESS THE NAME OF CARRYING VESSEL HAS BEEN APPROVED BY APPLICANT AND TO BE ADVISED BY L/C OPENING BANK A L/C AMENDMENT TO BENEFICIARY."

The Bank of China informed the beneficiary to remind its attention to the "soft clause", suggested to amend the L/C and pay attention to the possible risks. Later, after consultations, the applicant cancelled the L/C, and pay another L/C by the Hong Kong IB Bank in China with the same amount, the same goods and the same beneficiary, but the L/C still stipulated a "soft clause": "SHIPMENT CAN ONLY BE EFFECTED ON RECEIPT OF AN AMENDMENT OF THIS L/C ADVISING NAME OF CARRYING VESSEL AND SHIPMENT DATE." The initiative was in the hands of the applicant. The beneficiary would face the risk unable to submit a full set of documents to the negotiation bank if the applicant refused to send shipping notice. Meanwhile the Bank of China realized that a certain foreign trade company associated with the import and export company had remitted RMB 400,000 quality retention money to the representative of the applicant in our side. And the import and export company was planning to make packaged loans of RMB 2,000,000 for order to a certain applicant. So the bank made decisive measures, on the one hand, paused its credit, on the other hand, urged it to try to assist the foreign trade company to take back quality retention money. Only the two sides cooperated with each other, could they avoid loss.

利用"软条款"(陷阱条款)进行诈骗主要有以下特征：

(1)来证金额较大，往往在50万美元以上。

(2)来证含有制约受益人权利的"软条款"，如规定申请人或其指定代表签发检验证书，或由申请人指定运输船名、装运日期、航行路线或声称"本证无效"等。诈骗分子要求出口企业按合同金额或开证金额的5%~15%预付履约金；佣金给买方指定代表或中介人。

买方获得佣金或质量保证金后，其会同意或拒绝出具其检验证书或者不装运货物，这会使企业无法获得全套单据议付，徒劳无功。

例如，某家中国银行收到一张来自中国香港KP银行的信用证，信用证金额是180 000美元，受益人是某浙江进出口公司。信用证的"软条款"如下："除非运输船舶的名称已经被申请人接受并且通过开证行以修改证书的形式通知了受益人，此证书才有效。"

中行在将来证通知受益人时提醒其注意这一"软条款"，并建议其修改信用证，注意可能出现的风险。后来，经磋商，申请人撤销该信用证，另由中国香港IB银行开出同一金额、同一货物、同一受益人的信用证，但证中仍有这样的"软条款"：装运只有在收到本证修证书所指定的运输船名和装运日期时，才能实施。"主动权掌握在申请人手中，受益人却面临若申请人拒发装船通知，则无法提交全套单据给银行议付的风险。此时，中行了解到与该进出口公司联营的某外贸公司已将40万元人民币质保金汇往申请人在我方的代表，而且该进出口公司正计划向某申请人打包贷款200万元人民币做订货之用。于是，该行果断地采取措施，一方面暂停向其贷款，另一方面敦促其设法协助外贸公司追回质保金。双方配合，才免遭损失。

3.3.4 Use Forged Amendment to Fraud
利用伪造修改书诈骗

The fraud mainly includes the following characteristics:

(1) The original L/C is real, legitimate, but contains some clauses which restrict the beneficiary's rights and need to be modified.

(2) The amendment is issued by cable or telex, and embezzles test key or uses the original L/C password.

(3) The amendment is not opened by the issuing bank, but is directly sent to the advising bank or the beneficiary.

(4) The L/C specifies that a copy of the original B/L shall be sent to the applicant by mail after shipment.

(5) The date of shipment or validity of the L/C is too shorter to force the beneficiary to make rush delivery.

For example, there was an L/C amount for $10,920,000 and the beneficiary was a certain

Ningbo foreign trade company. It contained such a "soft clause" : "Only when you received the telex amendment which notified the buyer of the shipping instructions, name of vessel, date of shipment could you make shipment and the amendment must be negotiated in each set of documents." Also it stipulated that the original bill of lading must be sent to the applicant by express mail after shipment. The Bank of China drew their attention to these terms and conditions and the prevention when the Bank of China notified the beneficiary. Later the Bank of China received a fax under the original L/C amendment which specified the name of vessel and the date of shipment, and also regulated that the original L/C "partial shipments and transshipment allowed" should be changed into "partial shipments are prohibited", but the test key continued to use the original password. The Bank of China was immediately nervous, and quickly queried the issuing bank and immediately informed the beneficiary to stop shipments after they identified the fax to be a forged amendment. While the beneficiary was ready to export goods, the risk was self-evident.

这种诈骗主要有以下特征：

（1）原信用证虽是真实、合法的,但含有某些制约受益人权利的条款,亟待修改。

（2）修改书以电报或电传方式发出,且盗用密押或借用原信用证密码。

（3）修改书不通过开证行开出,而直接发给通知行或受益人。

（4）来证规定装运后邮寄一份正本提单给申请人。

（5）来证装运期或有效期较短,以迫使受益人仓促发货。

例如,有一份金额为1 092万美元的信用证,受益人为宁波某外贸公司。来证含有这样一个"软条款"："你方只有在收到我行加押电报修改书,通知买方装运指示、指定船名、装运日期时才可装货,而且该修改书必须在每套单据中议付。"同时信用证规定正本提单在装船后用特快方式邮寄给申请人。中行在来证通知受益人时,提请其关注这些条款,并做好防范工作。稍后,该中行又收到原证项下电文修改书一份,修改书指定船名、船期,并将原证"允许分批装运和转运"改为"禁止分批装运",但其密押是沿用原来的密码。该中行马上警惕起来,并迅速查询开证行,在确认该电文为伪造修改书后立即通知受益人停止发货,而此时受益人的出口货物正整装待发,其风险不言而喻。

3.3.5　*False Inspection Certificate Fraud*
假检验证书诈骗

False inspection certificate fraud refers that fraudsters issued inspection certificate on behalf of the applicant's representative in the place of shipment, the beneficiary's documents are refused to be paid and the goods were taken away because fraudsters' signature is not in conformity with the issuing bank's seal. This kind of fraud often has the following features:

（1）The L/C contains "soft clause" with an inspection certificate signed by the applicant.

（2）The L/C stipulates that the signature of the representative of the applicant must be consistent with the seal of the opening bank.

（3）The L/C requires a copy of the original bill of lading to be sent to the applicant.

（4）The applicant gives a large cheque to the beneficiary for mortgage or guarantee.

（5）The applicant manipulates the whole transaction process by designating a representative.

For example, a certain Bank of China received an L/C opened by a certain Hong Kong financial company in China, a clothing foreign trade company in Ningbo as the beneficiary, amount for $150,000 and export goods were 60,000 pieces of clothes. The L/C required that the applicant should issue the goods inspection certificate by representative designated before shipment, the signature must be confirmed by the issuing bank, and 1/2 original clean on board bills of lading should be given to the applicant after shipment. During shipment, the representative of the applicant came to the shipping place, provided an inspection certificate, and took one of the original bill of lading from the hand of the exporter with a large cheque for mortgage. Later, the beneficiary entrusted the check to the local bank for negotiation, but were told: "The check is a blank check, the signature of the inspection certificate issued by the applicant's representative is purely forged." However, all the goods have been taken away and missing. The beneficiary suffered major losses.

假检验证书诈骗是指诈骗分子以申请人代表名义在受益人发货地签发检验证书,因其签字与开证行预留印鉴式样不符,致使受益人单据遭到拒付,而货物却被骗走。这种诈骗通常有以下特征:

(1)来证含有"软条款",申请人签署检验证书。

(2)来证规定申请人代表签字必须与开证行预留印鉴式样相符。

(3)来证要求一份正本提单交给申请人。

(4)申请人将大额支票给受益人做抵押或担保。

(5)申请人通过指定代表操纵整个交易过程。

例如,中国银行某分行收到中国香港某金融公司开出的以宁波某服装外贸公司为受益人的信用证,金额为15万美元,出口货物是6万件衣服。信用证要求发货前由申请人指定代表出具货物检验证书,其签字必须由开证行证实,且规定1/2的正本清洁已装船提单在装运后交予申请人。在装运时申请人代表来到出货地,提供检验证书,并以一张大额支票作为抵押从出口商手中拿走了其中一份正本提单。后来,受益人将支票委托当地银行议付,但被告知:"托收支票为空头支票,而申请人代表出具的检验证书签字纯属伪造。"可是,货物已被全部提走,下落不明。受益人蒙受重大损失。

3.3.6 *Fraud which Alters an L/C*
涂 改 信 用 证 诈 骗

Fraud which alters an L/C refers that fraudsters will deliberately alter an invalid L/C's amount, shipping date and beneficiary's name, and mail directly or send to the beneficiary to defraud export goods, or lure exporter to require a bank to open the reciprocal L/C to defraud bank financing. This kind of fraud often has the following features:

(1)The original L/C is opened by letter in order to be altered.

(2)The contents altered are the amount of the L/C, shipment date, and beneficiary's name.

(3)The place altered in the L/C is without signature confirmation of the issuing bank.

(4)The L/C is directly sent to the beneficiary without further notice by advising bank.

(5)The amount is huge for huge profits swindled.

涂改信用证诈骗是指诈骗分子将过期失效的信用证刻意涂改,变更金额、装运期和受益人名称,并直接邮寄或面交受益人,以骗取出口货物,或诱使出口商要求银行开出对开信用证,骗取银行融资。这种诈骗往往有以下特征:

(1)原信用证为信开方式,以便于涂改。

(2)涂改内容为信用证金额、装运期及受益人名称。

(3)信用证涂改之处无开证行签章证实。

(4)信用证不经通知行通知,而直接交受益人。

(5)金额巨大,以骗取暴利。

3.3.7 *Forged Confirmed L/C Fraud*
伪造保兑信用证诈骗

Forged confirmed L/C fraud refers that fraudsters deliberately falsify international large bank confirmation letter to achieve the goal of diddling our export goods on the basis of the false L/C. This fraud often has the following characteristics:

(1)The issuing bank of the L/C is counterfeit or cannot be verified.

(2)The confirming bank is international famous bank in order to increase fraudulence.

(3)The confirming letter is sent separately and its signature is counterfeit.

(4)Both parties don't know each other in advance, only through intermediaries.

(5)The amount of the L/C is larger, and the shipment time is shorter.

伪造保兑信用证诈骗是指诈骗分子在提供假信用证的基础上,为获得我方的信任,蓄意伪造国际大银行的保兑函,以达到骗取我方出口货物的目的。这种诈骗常常有以下特征:

(1)信用证的开证行为假冒或根本无法查实之银行。

(2)保兑行为国际著名银行,以增加欺骗性。

(3)保兑函另寄来,其签字为伪冒签字。

(4)贸易双方事先并不了解,仅通过中介人相识。

(5)来证金额较大,且装运期较短。

3.4 Prevention of L/C Fraud
信用证诈骗的防范

3.4.1 *Preventive Countermeasures of L/C Fraud*
信用证诈骗的防范对策

From the various conditions of L/C fraud above, the main targets of fraudsters are our export enterprises, the victims also involve the exporter bank and industrial and trading company, and all parties should cooperate closely and take concrete and effective measures in order to avoid or reduce the happening of the fraud. The following preventive countermeasures can be taken concretely:

（1）The exporter bank (advising bank) must be responsible to check the authenticity of the L/C, and master the issuing bank's credit standing. For the L/C opened by letter, the signature or seal should be checked whether they are in conformity with each other thoroughly and carefully. The large amount L/C should require the issuing bank to add and confirm. For the L/C opened by telex and amendment, we should timely check whether test key is consistent or not in case of fake and forged. At the same time, we should also compare the issuing bank's name and address and credit situation with the yearbook in order to find suspects and immediately contact the issuing bank to ensure authenticity, legitimacy of the L/C and the issuing bank's reliability.

（2）Export enterprises must choose trade partners carefully. When looking for a trading partner and trade opportunities, we should contact and understand the customer through formal channels as far as possible (such as to attend the Canton Fair and field trips) and don't do business with customers whose credit is unknown or bad. Before signing a contract, we should try to entrust relevant consultancy to investigate customer credit in order to know fairly well to make the right choice in order to avoid loss caused by incorrect trading partner.

（3）Banks and export enterprises shall examine and verify an L/C carefully. L/C examination by bank focuses on the effectiveness and risks. Once we find "soft clause" in the L/C which is not in their hands to the clause (trap) and other unfavorable terms, we must determine to contact customers to change quickly or take appropriate preventive measures in order to nip in the bud.

（4）When export enterprises or trade companies make contracts with foreigners, they should establish the terms of the contract equallies, rationally and carefully. On national and collective interests, thoroughly eliminate all detriment to the interests of the state and the collective inequality, unreasonable clauses, such as payment in advance, quality retention money, fees and commission terms, etc., so as not to miss each other in the trap.

　　从上述信用证诈骗的各种情况来看,诈骗分子的行骗对象主要是我方出口企业,受害者还涉及出口方银行和工贸公司。各方均应密切配合,采取切实有效的措施,以避免或减少上述诈骗案的发生。具体可实施以下防范对策:

　　(1)出口方银行(指通知行)必须认真负责地核验信用证的真实性,并掌握开证行的资信情况。对于信开信用证,应全面细致核对印鉴是否相符,大额来证还应要求开证行加押证实;对于电开信用证及其修改书,应及时审核密押是否相符,以防假冒和伪造。同时,我们应对开证行的名称、地址和资信情况与银行年鉴进行比较分析,发现疑点,立即向开证行查询,以确保来证的真实性、合法性和开证行的可靠性。

　　(2)出口企业必须慎重选择贸易伙伴。我们在寻找贸易伙伴和贸易机会时,应尽可能通过正式途径(如参加广交会和实地考察)来接触和了解客户,不要与资信不明或资信不好的客户做生意。在签订合同前,我们应设法委托有关咨询机构对客户进行资信调查,以便心中有数,做出正确的选择,以避免错选贸易伙伴,自食苦果。

　　(3)银行和出口企业均须对信用证进行认真审核。银行审证侧重来证的有效性和风险性。一经发现来证含有主动权不在自己手中的"软条款"(陷阱条款)及其他不利条款,我们必须坚决和迅速地与客商联系修改,或采取相应的防范措施,以防患于未然。

（4）出口企业或贸易公司在与外商签约时,应平等、合理、谨慎地确立合同条款。以国家和集体利益为重,杜绝一切有损国家和集体利益的不平等、不合理条款,如预付货款、质保金、手续费和佣金条款等,以免误中对方圈套。

3.4.2 *Demonstration of L/C Examination*
审证示范

The first step: according to the requirements of the task, the beneficiary reviews the L/C carefully. The results of the review are as follows:

Results of L/C Audit	Analysis List of an L/C	
1.Text format of an L/C	☐BY LETTER	☑SWIFT
2.L/C No.	LC222	☑NOT SPECIFIED
3.Notifying bank No.		
4.Date of issuing an L/C	SEP. 10,2018	
5.Date of validity	NOV. 15,2018	
6.Place of validity	LONDON	☐NOT SPECIFIED
7.Means of payment	☐PAYMENT	☐ACCEPTANCE
	☐NEGOTIATION	
8.Currency	DOLLARS	
9.Amount in detail	$40,000	
10.Maximum amount	☐NOT SPECIFIED	
11.Amount more or less allowed	☐NOT SPECIFIED	
12.Presentation period (in Chinese)	15 DAYS	
13.Applicant (name)	TAD TRADE CO.,LTD.	
14.Beneficiary (name)	YALI GARMENTS TRADE COMPANY	
15.Issuing bank (name)	BRITISH LOYAL BANK,LONDON,BRITISH	
16.Advising bank (name)	☑NOT SPECIFIED	
17.Negotiating bank (name)	ANY BANK	☑NOT SPECIFIED
18.Payment/reimbursement bank (name)	ISSUING BANK	☑NOT SPECIFIED
19.Name of commodity	100% PURE WOOL SWEATER	
20.Contract/order/proforma invoice number	YG899	☐NOT SPECIFIED
21.Contract/order/proforma invoice date	JULY 20,2018	☐NOT SPECIFIED
22.Price/delivery/trade term	CIF	☐NOT SPECIFIED
23.Latest date of shipment	OCT. 1,2018	
24.Loading port	NINGBO	
25.Destination	LONDON	
26.Partial shipments	☐ALLOWED	☑NOT ALLOWED
27.Transshipment	☐ALLOWED	☑NOT ALLOWED
28.Shipping marks	☑NOT SPECIFIED	
29.Transport party	☑SEA ☐AIR ☐LAND TRANSPORTATION	

30.Document list submitted to the bank (in Arabic numbers) (Table 3−1)。

Table 3−1   Document List Submitted to the Bank

Name	Draft	Invoice	Packing List	Weight List	Measurement List	Carrier Certificate	Shipping Company Certificate	Voyage Certificate	Beneficiary's Certificate	Dispatching Documents	Shipping Note
Copy	2	4	3	×	×	×	×	×	1	×	1
Name	B/L	Air Waybill	Certificate of Origin	CCPIT Certificate of Origin	GSP Certificate of Origin	Inspection Certificate	Official Inspection Certificate	CCPIT Inspection Certificate	Insurance Policy	Insured Notice	Express Receipt
Copy	2	×	×	×	1	1	×	×	2	×	×

The second step: according to the requirements of the task, Xiao Wang made some suggestions for the revision according to the results of the review, details as Table 3−2.

Table 3−2   L/C Amendments

No.	Contract Stipulations	L/C Clauses (Discrepancies)	L/C Amendments
1	Seller: YALI GARMENTS COMPANY	Beneficiary: YALI GARMENTS TRADE COMPANY	Beneficiary: YALI GARMENTS COMPANY
2	Destination: LONDON	Destination: CHINA	Destination: LONDON
3	Payment:45 DAYS AFTER B/L	Payment: 45 DAYS AFTER SIGHT	Payment:45 DAYS AFTER B/L
4	Partial shipments: ALLOWED	Partial shipments: NOT ALLOWED	Partial shipments: ALLOWED
5	Transshipment: ALLOWED	Transshipment: NOT ALLOWED	Transshipment: ALLOWED
6	Loading port: ANY CHINESE PORT	Loading port: NINGBO	Loading port: ANY CHINESE PORT
7	Latest date of shipment: NOT LATER THAN THE MONTH OF OCTOBER 2018	Latest date of shipment: OCT. 1, 2018	Latest date of shipment: OCT. 31, 2018
8	Insured amount: 110% OF CIF INVOICE VALUE	Insured amount: 120% OF INVOICE VALUE	Insured amount: 110% OF INVOICE VALUE
9	Quality inspection certificate	SIGNED BY REPRESENTATIVE DESIGNATED BY BUYER	SIGNED BY GOVERNMENTAL ORGANIZATION
10	Require to open CONFIRMED L/C	UNCONFIRMED L/C	CONFIRMED L/C
11	B/L pay to the bank for negotiation	2/3 OF CLEAN ON BOARD MARINE BILLS OF LADING	FULL SET OF CLEAN ON BOARD MARINE BILLS OF LADING

第一步:根据任务的要求,受益人对信用证进行了认真的审核。审核结果如下:

信用证审核结果	信用证分析单	
1.信用证文本格式	□信开	☑电开
2.信用证号码	LC222	☑未注明
3.通知银行编号		
4.开证日	2018年9月10日	
5.到期日	2018年11月15日	
6.到期地点	伦敦	□未注明
7.付款方式	□付款	□承兑 □议付
8.货币	美元	
9.具体金额	4万美元	
10.最高限额	□未注明	
11.金额允许增减幅度	□未注明	
12.交单期(中文)	15天	
13.开证人(名称)	TAD TRADE CO., LTD.	
14.受益人(名称)	雅丽服装贸易公司	
15.开证银行(名称)	BRITISH LOYAL BANK,LONDON,BRITISH	
16.通知银行(名称)	☑未注明	
17.议付银行(名称)	任何银行	☑未注明
18.付款/偿付银行(名称)	开证行	☑未注明
19.货物名称	100%纯羊毛衫	
20.合同/订单/形式发票号码	YG899	□未注明
21.合同/订单/形式发票日期	2018年7月20日	□未注明
22.价格/交货/贸易术语	CIF	□未注明
23.最迟装运期	2018年10月1日	
24.装运港	宁波	
25.目的港	伦敦	
26.分批装运	□允许	☑不允许
27.转运	□允许	☑不允许
28.唛头	☑未注明	
29.运输方	☑海运	□空运 □陆运

30.向银行提交的单据清单(用阿拉伯数字表示)(见表3-1)。

表3-1　　　　　　　　　向银行提交的单据清单

名称	汇票	发票	装箱单	重量单	尺码单	承运人证明	船公司证明	航程证明	受益人证明	寄单证明	装船通知
份数	2	4	3	无	无	无	无	无	1	无	1
名称	海运提单	航空运单	原产地证书	中国贸促会原产地证书	普惠制原产地证书	检验证书	官方检验证书	中国贸促会检验证书	保险单	投保通知	寄单快件收据
份数	2	无	无	无	1	1	无	无	2	无	无

第二步:按照任务的要求,小王根据审核结果提出了修改意见(见表3-2)。

表3-2 信用证修改

序号	合同规定	信用证条款(信用证不符点)	信用证修改
1	卖方:雅丽服装公司	受益人:雅丽服装贸易公司	受益人:雅丽服装公司
2	目的地:伦敦	目的地:中国	目的地:伦敦
3	付款:提单日后45天	付款:见票后45天	付款:提单日后45天
4	分批装运:允许	分批装运:不允许	分批装运:允许
5	转运:允许	转运:不允许	转运:允许
6	装运港:任何中国港口	装运港:宁波	装运港:任何中国港口
7	最迟装船期:不晚于2018年10月	最迟装船期:2018年10月1日	最迟装船期:2018年10月31日
8	保险金额:CIF发票值的110%	保险金额:发票值的120%	保险金额:发票值的110%
9	品质检验证书	由买方指定代表签	由政府机构签
10	保兑信用证	非保兑信用证	保兑信用证
11	提交银行议付的提单	2/3清洁已装船提单	全套清洁已装船提单

3.5　Processing of Discrepant Documents under an L/C with Relief 信用证项下不符单据的处理与救济

The issuing bank to contain the discrepant documents shall have the right to refuse to pay. Some inexperienced companies upon receiving notice from the issuing bank dishonored often panic and accept the price requirements of their clients in a hurry, which led to the economic losses directly. In fact, documents dishonored under an L/C, does not mean that the payment for goods under export was sentenced to death penalty, the price also is not the only way to solve the problem. Facing the discrepancies put forward by the issuing bank, the exporter shall take the following measures:

1. Review whether the Premise Condition of the Discrepancies Put forward by the Issuing Bank is Established

The premise conditions of the discrepancies put forward by the issuing bank include:

(1) Within a reasonable time discrepancies are put forward to the documents reminder by the issuing bank, i.e. commenced from the date following the receipt of documents within five working days.

(2) Without delay in a telecommunication way the discrepancies shall be informed to the reminder.

(3) Discrepancies must be one-time put forward, that is, such as first mentioned discrepancies,

even if there are substantial discrepancies of documents, the issuing bank has no right to put forward again.

(4) When discrepancies are noticed, safekeeping disposal or refund of documents must be shown.

The above conditions must meet at the same time; otherwise, the issuing bank is not entitled to claim documents discrepancies and refuse to pay.

2. Audit whether the Discrepancies from the Issuing Bank are Established

Trade documents member should examine and verify the discrepancies from the issuing bank carefully according to the terms of the L/C, the UCP and ISBP to judge whether they are set up. If not, he should argue with the issuing bank by the negotiating bank until the issuing bank makes payment.

(1) If discrepancies are set up and conditions allow, documents can be resubmitted. Relief of discrepant documents under an L/C is that when documents are refused to be paid by the issuing bank due to discrepancies, the beneficiary may resubmit the documents replaced or corrected back to the issuing bank within the prescribed period of time in a timely manner.

According to the regulations of UCP600, the bank decides to refuse to pay when there are discrepancies after audit, then the issuing bank can exempt from responsibility to make payment of the L/C; but when the beneficiary fills the documents conform to the stipulations of the L/C within the allotted time, the issuing bank must be liable for the payment. If the beneficiary wastes a lot of time in the early stage of the operation, he/she will lose time to resubmit the documents.

(2) If discrepancies are set up and documents can not be resubmitted, positive negotiation with the applicant should be made. The issuing bank dishonored does not mean that the applicant refuses to pay, if the applicant gives up the discrepancies in the end, in spite that the issuing bank is not bound by the decision of the applicant, but it will cooperate with the applicant to make payment typically. So after the issuing bank refuses to pay, if discrepancies do set up, and the consistent documents can't be resubmitted, the relationship between the applicant and the actual situation of the deal should be analyzed to determine how to negotiate with and persuade the applicant to accept discrepancies and make payment. As long as the quality of goods passes and commodity market price is better, generally the applicant does not refuse to accept the documents as an excuse. Additionally, the way of reducing the price also can be taken to enable the applicant to make payment.

(3) If discrepancies are established, and the applicant refuses to accept the documents, another buyer can be found in the country of import. After all, the beneficiary has the discretion of the documents. But the premise is that the L/C requires to submit a full set of original bills of lading, if 1/3 original bills of lading have been sent to the applicant, 2/3 original bills of lading are submitted to the bank, this is likely to face the lost plight of goods and money.

(4) Return the documents and goods. If the beneficiary fails to find another buyer in the

country of import, he/she can only return the documents and goods. Before making this decision, however, whether the cost of the goods and the value is profitable must be closely calculated.

开证行对于包含不符点的单据有权拒付。一些经验不足的公司在接到开证行的拒付通知时往往惊慌失措,匆匆忙忙接受客户的降价要求,直接导致了经济损失。其实,当信用证项下的单据被拒付时,并不意味着出口项下的货款被判了死刑,降价也不是解决问题的唯一办法。面对开证行提出的不符点,出口商应当采取以下措施:

1.审核开证行提出不符点的前提条件是否成立

开证行提出不符点的前提条件包括:

(1)在合理的时间内提出不符点,即在开证行收到单据次日起算的5个工作日之内向单据的提示者提出不符点。

(2)无延迟地以电讯方式将不符点通知提示者。

(3)不符点必须一次性提出,即如果第一次所提不符点不成立,那么即使单据还存在实质性的不符点,开证行也无权再次提出。

(4)通知不符点的同时,必须说明单据代为保管听候处理,或退交单者。

以上条件必须同时满足;否则,开证行便无权声称单据不符点而拒付。

2.审核开证行所提的不符点是否成立

外贸单证员应根据信用证、UCP和ISBP条款认真审核开证行所提的不符点,判断其是否成立。若不成立,他应通过议付行与开证行据理力争,直至开证行付款。

(1)若不符点成立,条件允许,可补交相符单据。信用证项下不符点单据的救济是指当单据由于不符而遭开证行拒付之后,受益人可在规定的时间内及时将替代或更正后的相符单据补交给开证行。

根据UCP600的规定,单据经审核存在不符点,且银行决定拒付时,则开证行所承担的信用证项下的付款责任得以免除;但当受益人在规定时间内补交了符合信用证规定的单据时,开证行必须承担其付款责任。如果受益人在前期操作过程中浪费了大量时间,就会丧失补交单据的时间。

(2)若不符点成立,且无法补交相符单据,此时要积极与开证申请人洽谈。开证行拒付并不意味着开证申请人拒付,如果开证申请人最终放弃不符点,尽管开证行并不受开证申请人决定的约束,但一般会配合开证申请人付款。所以开证行拒付后,如果不符点确实成立,且无法补交相符单据,应分析与开证申请人之间的关系以及此笔交易的实际情况,以决定怎样与其交涉,说服开证申请人接受不符点并付款。只要货物质量过关,商品市场价格较好,开证申请人一般不会以此为借口拒绝接受单据。另外,也可以采取降价的方式,使开证申请人能付款赎单。

(3)若不符点成立,且开证申请人拒绝接受单据,则可在进口国另寻买主。毕竟受益人拥有对单据的处理权。但其前提是信用证要求递交全套正本提单,若1/3正本提单已寄给开证申请人,2/3正本提单提交给银行,则可能会面临钱、货两失的困境。

(4)退单退货。如果受益人无法在进口国另寻买主,就只能退单退货了。不过在做出此决定之前,受益人一定要仔细核算运回货物所需的费用和货值之间是否有利可图。

Training Case 3-1

A Dispute Case of Discrepant Documents

A certain mineral export company (company A) exported a batch of phosphate rock to a Southeast Asian company (company B). The description of goods of the L/C was 50,000 MT PHOSPHATE ROCK, FOB FANGCHENGGANG, CHINA, AS PER PROFORMA INVOICE NO.NV03H-1.

Documents' terms specified as follows:

(1)COMMERCIAL INVOICE IN TRIPLICATE.

(2)CERTIFICATE OF ORIGIN ISSUED BY CID.

(3)3/3 SET OF CLEAN ON BOARD BILLS OF LADING CONSIGNED TO THE ORDER OF ISSUING BANK.

(4) BENEFICIARY'S CERTIFY REQUIRED IN TRIPLICATE STATING THAT THE APPLICANT HAS BEEN ADVISED OF THE COMPLETE DETAILS OF SHIPMENT BY TELEX / FAX NO. 505759 AND COPY OF TELEX / FAX ADVICE IS REQUIRED FOR NEGOTIATION.

After receiving the documents, the issuing bank refused and put forward the following discrepancies:

(1) The goods' description in the invoice does not show "AS PER PROFORMA INVOICE …".

(2) The consignee of the certificate of origin differs from the B/L's.

(3) The B/L does not show the name of master.

(4) The beneficiary's "CERTIFICATE" mistyped "CERTIFY".

(5) Shipping advice: No evidence of the shipping details has been actually faxed.

Company A studied the documents against the discrepancies put forward by the issuing bank immediately and consulted with company B. Because company A was an old customer, and the product quality was better, company B quickly agreed to accept the discrepancies, and made payment settlement soon.

不符点单据异议案

我方某矿产出口公司(A公司)向东南亚的某公司(B公司)出口一批磷矿石,信用证上的货物描述为50 000公吨磷矿石,FOB中国防城港,形式发票NV03H-1。

单证条款规定如下:

(1)商业发票一式三份。

(2)由商品检验司签发的原产地证书。

(3)3份凭开证行指示、已装船的清洁提单。

(4)受益人证明一式三份,申明开证申请人通过电传号505759已经得到了完全的装船信息,并且凭电传装船通知复印件议付。

开证行在收到单据后表示拒付,并提出如下不符点:

(1)发票中的货物描述没有显示"按照形式发票……"。

（2）原产地证书上的收货人与提单上的不一致。

（3）提单没有显示船长名。

（4）将受益人证明中的"CERTIFICATE"，错误地拼写成"CERTIFY"。

（5）装船通知：没有任何证据表明实际已传真过装船的详细信息。

A公司针对开证行所提出的单据不符点，立即对单据进行研究并与B公司磋商。由于A公司是老客户，加之产品质量较好，B公司很快同意接受不符点，不久付款赎单结案。

Training Case 3-2

An L/C "Soft Clause" Fraud Case

A certain city branch of Bank of China of received an L/C issued by telex from a certain Singapore bank, for $1,000,000.00, 50,000 tons of granite rocks; the destination port was Karachi, Pakistan. There were the following terms in the L/C: (1) Inspection certificate issued and signed by the authorized signatory of the applicant before shipment and the signature must be inspected by the issuing bank; (2) The goods could be shipped only after the applicant nominated the vessel and the issuing bank added electrical amendment for the advising bank, which must be presented for negotiation with the original documents. Q: Can you accept this L/C?

"软条款"信用证欺诈案

中国银行某市分行收到新加坡某银行电开信用证一份，金额为100万美元，购5万吨花岗岩石块，目的港为巴基斯坦卡拉奇。信用证中有下述条款：（1）检验证书于货物装运前开立并由开证申请人授权的签字人签字，该签字必须由开证行检验；（2）货物只能待开证申请人指定船只并由开证行给通知行加押电修改后装运，而该加押电修改必须随同正本单据提交议付。请问：该接受该信用证吗？

Key Terms

discrepancy 不符点

Exercise

◎ *Case Analysis*

Case 1

A company received an irrevocable L/C from abroad. The L/C stipulated that the shipment date should not be later than August 30, 2018; the expiry date was on September 15, 2018. But due to the transportation problem, we couldn't make shipment on schedule. On Aug. 25 our business personnel faxed importer to extend shipment date to September 30 and also the validity of the L/C to a month.

On August 29, the company got a reply: "Agree to your fax on Aug. 25. Please extend the shipment date to not later than September 30, 2018, the expiry date of the L/C also extend a month." After contact, our business personnel organized quickly to make shipment and finished shipment on September 16. On October 10, a full set of documents were prepared for negotiation, but the bank refused to accept. Q:

(1)After we showed our cable which the importer agreed to extend, could the bank agree to make negotiation? Why?

(2)What were the problems when our business personnel operated?

某公司收到国外开来的一份不可撤销信用证。该证规定装运期不得迟于 2018 年 8 月 30 日,议付有效期为 2018 年 9 月 15 日。但因运输问题,我方无法如期装运。我方业务人员遂于 8 月 25 日电请进口商将船期延至 9 月 30 日,信用证有效期同样延展一个月。

8 月 29 日接对方复电称:"同意你方 8 月 25 日电,请将装运期改为不得迟于 2018 年 9 月 30 日,信用证议付有效期同样延展一个月。"接电后,我方业务人员迅速组织出运,于 9 月 16 日装运完毕;10 月 10 日备齐全套单据向银行交单议付,但银行拒绝收单。请问:

(1)我方出示进口商同意展期的电报后,银行是否可同意议付?为什么?

(2)我方业务人员在操作上存在哪些问题?

Case 2

A company clinched a deal with a foreign businessman on CIF Rotterdam basis. Insurance was covered for 110% of the invoice value against all risks and war risks. In the sales contract, payment terms were regulated as "Payment by L/C". There was the following question in the L/C clauses: "Payment under this L/C will be made by us only after arrival of goods at Rotterdam", which the beneficiary did not find when examining the L/C. Therefore, our company did not require amending the L/C. When our company made settlement, the negotiating bank also did not lodge a complaint. Unfortunately, 60% of goods were destroyed by fire on the way, and the issuing bank refused to pay all payments for goods after the ship arrived in the port of destination. Q: Did the issuing bank dishonor reasonably? Why?

某公司以 CIF 鹿特丹与外商成交一批货物,按发票金额 110% 投保一切险及战争险。销售合同中的支付条款规定为"信用证支付"。国外来证条款中有如下问题:"该证项下的款项在货到鹿特丹后由我行支付。"受益人在审证时未发现,因此未请对方修改。在我方公司交单结汇时,议付行也未提出异议。不幸的是,60% 的货物在途中被大火烧毁,船到目的港后开证行拒付全部货款。请问:开证行拒付是否合理?为什么?

◎ *Practice*

Practice 1

根据以下销售合同审核国外开来的信用证,指出信用证中存在的问题并说明应如何修改。

SALES CONTRACT

NO:0003916   DATE:SEP. 30, 2018

SELLER:NINGBO HUADU TEXTILE INTERNATIONAL TRADE CORP.

BUYER:SUNNY MKN CORPORATION

COMMODITY AND SPECIFICATION:POLO BRAND FULL COTTON MEN'S SHIRT 15,000

PCS,5% MORE OR LESS AT SELLER'S OPTION

PACKING:IN CARTONS OF 20 PCS EACH,CONTAINERIZED

UNIT PRICE:USD 2.40 PER PIECE CFR TORONTO

TOTAL VALUE:USD 36,000.00 (US DOLLARS THIRTY-SIX THOUSAND ONLY)

TIME OF SHIPMENT:DURING NOV./DEC. 2018 IN TWO EQUAL MONTHLY LOTS, FROM CHINA TO TORONTO,ALLOWING TRANSSHIPMENT.

INSURANCE:TO BE COVERED BY THE BUYER

TERMS OF PAYMENT:BY IRREVOCABLE SIGHT LETTER OF CREDIT TO REACH THE SELLER 15 DAYS BEFORE THE MONTH OF SHIPMENT AND REMAIN VALID FOR NEGOTIATION IN CHINA UNTIL THE 15TH DAYS AFTER DATE OF SHIPMENT.

IRREVOCABLE DOCUMENTARY L/C

L/C NO.: 180086   DATE:OCT. 12,2018

FROM:ROYAL BANK OF CANADA

TO:BANK OK CHINA,NINGBO,CHINA

WE OPEN IRREVOCABLE DOCUMENTARY L/C NO.180086

BENEFICIARY:NINGBO HUADU TEXTILE IMP. AND EXP. CO., LTD.
        JIEFANG SOUTH ROAD 111,NINGBO,CHINA

APPLICANT:SUNNY MKN CORPORATION
        P.O. BOX NO. 6789,TORONTO,CANADA

AMOUNT:USD 36,000. 00 (US DOLLARS THIRTY-SIX THOUSAND ONLY)

THIS L/C IS AVAILABLE BY BENEFICIARY'S DRAFT AT 30 DAYS AFTER SIGHT FOR 100% OF INVOICE VALUE DRAWN ON ROYAL BANK OF CANADA.

ACCOMPANIED BY THE FOLLOWING DOCUMENTS:

SIGNED COMMERCIAL INVOICE IN 3 COPIES.

FULL SET OF CLEAN ON BOARD BILLS OF LADING MADE OUT TO ORDER AND BLANK ENDORSED MARKED FREIGHT PREPAID AND NOTIFY APPLICANT.

INSURANCE POLICY IN DUPLICATE COPIES FOR 110% OF INVOICE VALUE COVERING ALL RISKS AND WAR RISK SUBJECT TO CIC DATED JAN. 1ST, 1981.

CERTIFICATE OF ORIGIN IN DUPLICATE ISSUED BY CHINA INTERNATIONAL CHAMBER OF COMMERCE OR OTHER GOVERMENT AUTHORITIES.

INSPECTION CERTIFICATE OF QUALITY ISSUED BY APPLICANT.

COVERING:

POLO BRAND FULL COTTON MEN'S SHIRT 15,000 PCS AT USD 2.40 PER PIECE CFRC3% TORONTO AS PER S/C NO. 0003916 DATED SEP. 30, 2018.

LATEST SHIPMENT:NOV. 30,2018 FROM NINGBO TO TORONTO.

PARTIAL SHIPMENTS:ALLOWED.

TRANSSHIPMENT:PROHIBITED.

THE GOODS SHALL BE CONTAINERIZED.

DOCUMENTS MUST BE PRESENTED WITHIN 8 DAYS AFTER THE DATE OF THE B/L, BUT WITHIN THE VALIDITY OF THE L/C.

ROYAL BANK OF CANADA

Practice 2

根据销售合同审核国外开来的信用证,并回答题后问题。

SALES CONTRACT

1.S/C NO.: HOSH3178B

2.DATE: MAY 27, 2018

3.SELLER: NINGBO XINGSHIJIE IMP. AND EXP. CORP.

ADDRESS: 58 YAOAI ROAD, NINGBO, CHINA

TEL: 86-574-×××××××   FAX: 86-574-××××××××

E-MAIL: LZHONGCHEN@163.COM

4.BUYER: CLOTHES CARE CO., LTD.

ADDRESS: 290 BOTANY ROAD, ALEXANDRIA NSW, AUSTRALIA

E-MAIL: JACKY@ HOTMAIL.COM

THE SELLER AGREES TO SELL AND THE BUYER AGREES TO BUY THE UNDERMENTIONED GOODS ACCORDING TO THE TERMS AND CONDITIONS AS STIPULATED BELOW:

28,000 PCS 210 GRAM/M2, POID BRAND POLY COTTON SHIRT IN ROYAL BLUE

SIZE	S	M	L	XL	XXL
RATIO	1 PC	2 PCS	5 PCS	5 PCS	1 PC
UNIT PRICE	USD 1.2/PC	USD 1.2/PC	USD 1.2/PC	USD 1.3/PC	USD 1.3/PC

5.PACKING: PACKED IN CARTONS OF 40 PCS

6.SHIPPING MARKS: C. C. C.

XSHI2018

SYDNEY

NO.1-UP

7.PORT OF SHIPMENT: ANY CHINESE PORT

8.PORT OF DESTINATION: SYDNEY, AUSTRALIA

9.TIME OF SHIPMENT: NOT LATER THAN OCT. 31, 2018

10. TERMS OF PAYMENT: L/C AT 30 DAYS AFTER SIGHT WITH ACCEPTANCE

11. FORCE MAJEURE: The Seller shall not be held responsible if it, owing to Force Majeure causes, fails to make delivery within the time stipulated in the contract or can't deliver the goods. However, in such a case the Seller shall inform the Buyer immediately by cable. The Seller shall send to the Buyer by registered letter at the request of the Buyer a certificate attesting the existence of such a cause or causes issued by China Council for the Promotion of International Trade or by a competent authority.

12. DISCREPANCY AND CLAIM: In case discrepancy on the quality of the goods is found by the Buyer after arrival of the goods at the port of destination, claim may be lodged within 30 days after arrival of the goods at the port of destination, while for quantity discrepancy, claim may be lodged within 15 days after arrival of the goods at the port of destination, being supported by Inspection Certificate issued by a public survey or agreed upon by both parties. The Seller shall consider the claim in the light of actual circumstances. For the losses due to natural cause or causes falling within the responsibilities of the Shipowner or the Underwriter, the Seller shall not consider any claim for compensation. In case the Letter of Credit does not reach the Seller within the time stipulated in the Contract, or under FOB price term the Buyer does not send vessel to the appointed port or the Letter of Credit opened by the Buyer does not correspond to the Contract terms and the Buyer fails to amend thereafter its terms by telegraph within the time limit alter receipt of notification by the Seller, the Seller shall have the right to cancel the contract or to delay the delivery of the goods and shall have also the right to lodge claims for compensation of losses.

13. ARBITRATION: All disputes in connection with this contract or the execution there of, shall be settled amicable by negotiation. In case no settlement can be reached, the case under dispute may then be submitted to the China International Economic and Trade Arbitration Commission for arbitration. The arbitration shall take place in China and shall be executed in accordance with the provisional rules of procedure of the said Commission and the decision made by the Commission shall be accepted as final and binding upon both parties for setting the disputes. The fees for the arbitration shall be borne by the losing party unless otherwise awarded.

THE SELLER:	THE BUYER:
NINGBO XINGSHIJIE IMP. AND EXP. CORP.	CLOTHES CARE CO., LTD.
陈林中	JACKY

DOCUMENTARY LETTER OF CREDIT

FROM: OVERSEAS CHINESE BANKING CORPORATION, SINGAPORE

ADVISING BANK: CHINA EVERBRIGHT BANK, SHANGHAI

IRREVOCABLE DOCUMENTARY L/C NO.: 666888

DATE: MAY 26TH, 2018

DATE AND PLACE OF EXPIRY: JULY 10TH, 2018, IN BENEFICIARY'S COUNTRY

BENEFICIARY: SHANGHAI JINHAI IMP. & EXP. GROUP GARMENTS BRANCH, NO. 50 LANE 424 YAOHUA ROAD, SHANGHAI, CHINA

APPLICANT: ANTAK DEVELOPMENT PTE LTD.

　　101 KIT CHENER ROAD, JALAN PLAZA, SINGAPORE

TEL NO.: 3423457　　　FAX NO.: 4723456

AMOUNT: USD 56,300.00 CIF SINGAPORE (UNITED STATES DOLLARS FIFTY-SIX THOUSAND AND THREE HUNDRED ONLY)

PARTIAL SHIPMENTS: NOT ALLOWED

TRANSSHIPMENT: NOT ALLOWED

SHIPMENT FROM CHINESE PORT TO SINGAPORE

LATEST SHIPMENT DATE: 26TH JUNE, 2018

THIS L/C IS AVAILABLE WITH THE ADVISING BANK BY NEGOTIATION AGAINST PRESENTATION OF THE DOCUMENTS DETAILED HEREIN AND BENEFICIARY'S DRAFT(S) AT SIGHT DRAWN ON ISSUING BANK FOR FULL INVOICE VALUE.

DOCUMENTS REQUIRED (IN TWO-FOLD UNLESS OTHERWISE STIPULATED):

+SIGNED COMMERCIAL INVOICE

+SIGNED WEIGHT/PACKING LIST

+CERTIFICATE OF CHINESE ORIGIN

+ INSURANCE POLICY / CERTIFICATE ENDORSED IN BLANK FOR 110% OF CIF VALUE COVERING: WAR RISK AND ALL RISKS

FULL SET PLUS ONE PHOTOCOPY OF CLEAN ON BOARD OCEAN BILLS OF LADING MADE OUT TO ORDER OF BANK OF CHINA. SINAPORE MARKED FREIGHT PREPAID AND NOTIFY APPLICANT EVIDENCING SHIPMENT OF:

1094L: 700 DOZEN MEN'S COTTON WOVEN LABOURER SHIRTS (USD 19,180.00)

286G: 800 DOZEN MEN'S COTTON WOVEN SHIRTS (USD 31,680.00)

678X-J: 60 DOZEN MEN'S COTTON WOVEN SHIRTS (USD 15,440.00)

S/C NO. HOSH3178B

CIF SINGAPORE

SHIPPING MARKS: ANTAK

              HOSH3178B

              SINGAPORE

              NO.1-190

OTHER TERMS AND CONDITIONS:

ALL BANK CHARGES, INCLUDING REIMBURSEMENT CHARGES, OUTSIDE SINGAPORE ARE FOR ACCOUNT OF BENEFICIARY. THE NUMBER AND DATE OF THIS L/C, AND THE NAME OF ISSUING BANK MUST BE QUOTED ON ALL DOCUMENTS.

A FEE OF USD 40.00 OR ITS EQUIVALENT TO BE DEDUCTED FROM THE PROCEEDS UPON EACH PRESENTATION OF DISCREPANT DOCUMENTS EVEN IF THE L / C INDICATES THAT ALL BANKING CHARGES ARE FOR THE ACCOUNT OF APPLICANT AND ACCEPTANCE OF SUCH DOCUMENTS DOES NOT IN ANY WAY AFTER THE OTHER TERMS AND CONDITIONS OF THIS L/C.

THE WHOLE CONSIGNMENT TO BE UNDER ONE BILL OF LADING.

BENEFICIARY'S CERTIFICATE TO CERTIFY THE FOLLOWINGS ARE REQUIRED:

INVOICE WEIGHT/PACKING LIST AND NON-NEGOTIABLE BILL OF LADING MUST BE AIRMAILED TO THE APPLICANT IMMEDIATELY AFTER SHIPMENT.

COPIES OF INVOICE AND BILLS OF LADING HAVE BEEN FAXED TO APPLICANT IMMEDIATELY AFTER SHIPMENT.

INSURANCE POLICY OR CERTIFICATE MUST SHOW CLAIMS SETTLING AGENT AS: "CHINA INSURANCE CO., LTD. SINGAPORE."

BILLS OF LADING TO EVIDENCE THE FOLLOWINGS:

SHIPMENT EFFECTED INTO 20 FEET CONTAINER LOAD (CY-CY).

SHIPMENT EFFECTED BY CONTAINERISED VESSEL ONLY.

SHOWING APPLICANT'S ADDRESS, TELEPHONE NO. AND FAX NO.

SHOWING CARRIER/CARRIERS AGENT AS: "CHINA OCEAN SHIPPING (GROUP) CO."

SHOWING CONTAINER NUMBER.

SHIPMENT OF THE WHOLE CONSIGNMENT EFFECTED INTO LOOSE CARGO LOAD IS NOT ACCEPTABLE.

PACKING: GOODS MUST BE PACKED IN STRONG CARTONS AND STRAPPED WEIGHT STRONG NYLON STRAPS. WEIGHT/PACKING LIST TO SHOW THIS PACKING IS REQUIRED.

ALLOWED TO INCREASE OR DECREASE THE QUANTITY AND AMOUNT BY 5%.

INSTRUCTIONS TO THE NEGOTIATING BANK:

THE AMOUNT AND DATE OF EACH NEGOTIATION DRAFT MUST BE ENDORSED ON THE REVERSE OF THE ORIGINAL L/C BY THE NEGOTIATING BANK.

ALL DOCUMENTS ARE TO BE SENT TO THE ISSUING BANK IN ONE LOT.

UPON RECEIPT OF DOCUMENTS IN CONFORMITY WITH THE TERMS AND CONDITIONS OF THIS L/C, WE SHALL CREDIT OUR HEAD OFFICE ACCOUNT WITH US.

THIS L/C IS SUBJECT TO UNIFORM CUSTOMS AND PRACTICE FOR DOCUMENTARY CREDITS (2007 REVISION) ICC PUBLICATION NO. 600, BANK OF CHINA, SINGAPORE AUTHORIZED SIGNATURE.

请回答以下问题:

(1)这份信用证是什么类型的信用证?

(2)这份信用证的兑付方式是什么? 是否需要汇票? 若需要汇票,要求提供什么汇票?

(3)这份信用证的开证日期、到期日、到期地点、最迟装船日期、交单期各是何时?

(4)这份信用证的申请人、受益人、开证行、通知行、保兑行、付款行各是谁?

(5)这份信用证要求提供哪些单据? 各几份?

(6)这份信用证的价格条款是什么? 保险应由谁办理?

(7)若将来受益人提交的单据有3个不符点,开证行将收取多少不符点处理费?

(8)这份信用证的特殊条款中要求受益人在所有单据中显示什么内容?

(9)这份信用证是否允许分批装运与转运? 装运港与目的港分别是什么地方?

(10)这份信用证有没有软条款? 若有,应如何修改?

Chapter 4

Transaction Documents
交易单证

Learning Objectives

◆ 重点掌握商业发票的制作;掌握销售合同和形式发票的制作;了解询盘函、报盘函、递价/递盘/报价/报盘。

> ### Guide Case
> #### A Damage Case Caused by Error Invoice and Draft Made Out
>
> A certain export company (company A) in our country clinched a deal with a certain Kuwait middleman, terms of trade for CFRC5%, value of RMB 52,500. The total amount of the L/C from abroad was RMB 49,875, which indicated "to deduct 5% commission for negotiation of payment to a firm". But company A ignored in checking the L/C amount, when they made both invoice and draft, the bank deducted 5% of contract value RMB 52,500 for negotiation, and RMB 49,875 to the debit of the issuing bank account in Beijing. After the issuing bank accepted the order, they cabled to refuse payment; the reason was that the invoice value exceeded the amount of the L/C. After repeated negotiations with the issuing bank and middleman which were invalid, company A rushed to make new invoice and draft in the period of validity, which amounted to RMB 49,875 deducted to commission. In the end, company A had lost 5% of their income amount 2,493.75 yuan.
>
> The company business personnel in this case are lack of experience, and lax attitude toward reviewing documents, therefore setting a trap in the foreign businessman. The lessons of this case are as follows:
>
> (1) Ignore to review whether the amount of the L/C is consistent with the contract's amount. The case to the total amount is RMB 49,875 the L/C, but company A failed to find whether the amount listed in the L/C was not in conformity with the contract. According to the contract, the

total amount shall be RMB 52,500, not RMB 49,875. Business personnel put the "to deduct 5% commission for negotiation ..." wrong understanding for the net amount RMB 49,875, to which the total contract amount of RMB 52,500 is deducted 5% commission, so made the invoice and bill of exchange according to the contract provisions. It is inevitable that the issuing bank will refuse to make payment when it finds that the documents do not conform to the L/C. This error could have been avoided, only because company A is lax for reviewing documents. Therefore, company A set a trap in the foreign businessman and lost 5% commission equal to RMB 2,493.75.

(2) Examining an L/C and making documents must have comprehensive professional knowledge and strong sense of responsibility. Examining an L/C is a careful and professional work; the staff on a slight negligence will bring irreparable damage. As documents staff, they should not only have good professional knowledge, familiar with the terms of the contract and operation methods, but also have the consciousness of risk prevention and rich experience; otherwise, they will give the foreign fraud opportunity and cause unnecessary loss.

发票和汇票缮制错误致损案

我方某出口公司(A公司)与科威特某中间商成交货物一批,贸易术语为CFRC5%,货值为52 500元人民币。国外开来总金额为49 875元人民币的信用证,并注明"议付时扣5%佣金给某商号"。但A公司在制单中忽视核对信用证金额,在缮制发票和汇票时均按照合同金额52 500元人民币,议付时银行扣除5%,按49 875元人民币借记开证行北京账户。开证行接单后来电拒付,理由是发票金额超过来证金额。A公司经多次与开证行及中间商交涉均无效,只好在有效期内另赶制新发票和汇票,即金额改为49 875元人民币,再扣去佣金,白白损失了5%的合计2 493.75元人民币的收入。

本案例中的公司业务人员因缺乏经验,并对缮制单据复核把关不严,以致中了国外商人设下的圈套。本案的教训如下:

(1)忽视审查金额与合同金额是否相符。本案来证总金额为49 875元人民币,A公司审证时未能发现信用证所列金额与合同不符。按照合同,总金额应是52 500元人民币,而不49 875元人民币。业务人员对于信用证上"议付时扣5%佣金……"错误理解为:信用证上金额是合同总金额52 500元扣5%佣金后的净额49 875元,于是在缮制发票、汇票时均按合同规定办理。开证行发现单证不符予以拒付是必然的。这个错误本来可以避免,只是由于A公司审证制单把关不严,才误入了国外商人设下的圈套,等于白送了5%的佣金,即人民币2 493.75元。

(2)审证制单要有全面的专业知识和较强的责任心。审证是一项既细致又专业性很强的工作,工作人员稍有疏忽就会带来不可弥补的损失。外贸单证工作人员不仅要具备良好的专业知识,熟悉合同的条款及操作方法,而且要有风险防范意识和丰富的经验;否则,就会给外方欺诈机会,给自己造成不必要的损失。

Transaction documents are issued by the buyer and the seller to define their business relationship and provide an accounting record of individual transactions. These documents range from a simple letter of inquiry to a contract for the sale of goods and a commercial invoice. This category does not include specific export, transport, import, or bank documents.

In the most straightforward sale, the buyer might call or fax the seller and order a quantity of goods, and the seller simply issues an invoice. At the other end of the spectrum, the process can be much more formal with an importer/buyer submitting a request for proposal for bids on a product with 100 pages of detailed specifications, engineering charts and the like.

Most business personnel are already familiar with basic transaction documents because these are virtually the same as the ones used in domestic business.

交易单证是确定买卖双方业务关系的个体交易会计凭证,包括简单的询盘、销售合同和商业发票,但并不包括特殊出口单证、运输单证、进口单证和银行单证。

最简单的销售方式是,买方通过电话或传真告知卖方需要订购一定量货物,卖方开具发票。相反,较正式的是进口商/买方需提交长达100页关于产品的详细说明和工程图表等的报价函。

由于外贸单证与国内业务的大部分单证相似,因此大部分的业务人员都熟悉基本交易单证。

4.1 Keys on Transaction Documents
交易单证的要点

The quantity and formality of transaction documents are influenced by the relationship of the buyer and the seller, the countries of export and import, as well as the goods sold. For example, if the buyer and the seller know each other, the preliminaries may be handled by telephone and the only transaction document issued will be the commercial invoice.

The key document in this category is the commercial invoice. Copies of this document will be retained by the exporter and presented to the export authorities, the freight carrier, the import authorities, the importer and the bank (if a documentary collection or letter of credit is used).

Transaction documents may need to have additional information and/or be in the language of the country of export or import.

交易单证的数量和形式受到买方和卖方、进口国和出口国之间的关系,以及所销售货物的影响。例如,如果买方和卖方相互认识,首先可通过电话进行沟通,唯一需要开具的交易单证是商业发票。

交易单证中最重要的是商业发票。商业发票的副本由出口商保存,呈递给出口国当局、货运公司、进口国当局、进口商和银行(如果使用跟单托收或信用证)。

交易单证可能还需要其他信息,以及/或者以进口国或出口国语言表示。

4.2 Flow of Transaction Documents
交易单证的制作流程

A typical exchange of documents between the buyer and the seller proceeds in the following patterns:

(1)The importer/buyer sends a letter of inquiry to the exporter/seller asking if the company either has certain products available or would like to bid on a project.

(2) The seller sends a reply letter stating an interest in bidding perhaps including a capabilities statement.

(3) The buyer sends a request for quotation generally if the goods have to be designed or manufactured to the buyer's specification as outlined in the request for propsoal. The seller prepares and sends the buyer a formal proposal including product specifications, quantities, prices, terms, conditions.

(4) The buyer and the seller negotiate specifications, quantities, prices, terms and conditions.

(5) The buyer issues a letter of acceptance or signs an order form.

(6) The buyer and the seller prepare and sign a purchase contract (Sample 4-1) or a contract for the sale of goods (Sample 2-1).

(7) The seller prepares a commercial invoice.

典型的买方与卖方交换交易单证的流程如下:

(1)进口商/买方向出口商/卖方发出询盘函,探询该公司是否有某种货物出售或是否愿意对某一项目进行投标。

(2)卖方发出回复信表明递盘的兴趣,可能还包括一份资质声明。

(3)一般来说,如果货物需要根据买方在报价函中规定的规格进行设计或生产,买方需发送报盘函。卖方准备并发给买方正式的报盘,包括产品规格、数量、价格、条款和条件。

(4)买方和卖方就产品规格、数量、价格、条款和条件进行谈判。

(5)买方发出接受函或签订单。

(6)买方和卖方签订购货合同(见样单4-1)或销售合同(见样单2-1)。

(7)卖方备好商业发票。

Sample 4-1　　　　　　　　　　　**Purchase Contract**

样单4-1　　　　　　　　　　　　　　**购货合同**

合同编号: Contract No.: OA180602	签订日期: Date: JUNE 2ND, 2018	签订地点: Signed in: SHENZHEN, CHINA
1.买方: Buyer: SHENZHEN OCDA FOOD CO., LTD. 地址: Address: 7F, OCDA BLDG, KEYUAN RD., SHENZHEN, CHINA 电话(Tel): 86-755-82626268　　　　　　　传真(Fax): 86-755-82626269		
2.卖方: Seller: ARELLA CO., ARELLA SPACO. 地址: Address: PLAZA COLLEGIO CAIROLIN, 327100 PAVIA, ITALY 电话(Tel): 81-307-282828　　　　　　　传真(Fax): 81-307-282829		
经买卖双方确认,根据下列条款订立本合同: The undersigned Seller and Buyer have confirmed this contract is in accordance with the terms and conditions stipulated below:		

续

3.商品名称及规格 Name of Commodity & Specification	4.数量 Quantity	5.单价 Unit Price	6.金额 Amount
CANNED MUSHROOMS 24 TINS×425 GRAMS	1,700 CARTONS/FCL	CFRC2% DAMMAM PORT USD 7.80/CTN	USD13,260.00
		合计: Totally:	USD13,260.00

7.总值(大写):

　　Total Value (in words): SAY US DOLLARS THIRTEEN THOUSAND TWO HUNDRED AND SIXTY ONLY.

8.允许溢短＿＿＿＿%

　　 5 %　more or less in quantity and value allowed.

9.价格术语:

　　Terms:

　　□FOB　　　　☑CFR　　　　□CIF　　　　□DAP

10.包装

　　Packing: EXPORT CARTON

11.唛头:

　　Shipping Marks: N/M

12.运输起讫:由＿＿＿＿＿＿＿＿(装运港)到＿＿＿＿＿＿＿＿(目的港)。

　　Shipment from　PAVIA, ITALY　(Port of Shipment) to　SHENZHEN, CHINA　(Port of Destination).

13.转运:　　　　　　□允许　　☑不允许

　　Transshipment:　　□allowed　☑not allowed

　　分批装运:　　　　□允许　　☑不允许

　　Partial Shipments:　□allowed　☑not allowed

　　运输时间:

　　Shipment Time: WITHIN 20 DAYS AFTER RECEIPT OF IRREVOCABLE SIGHT L/C.

14.保险:由＿＿＿＿方按发票金额的＿＿＿＿%投保＿＿＿＿,加保＿＿＿＿从＿＿＿＿到＿＿＿＿。

　　Insurance: to be covered by the SELLER　for　110　% of the invoice value covering Institute Cargo Clauses (A)

　　1/1/82 , additional Institute War and Strikes Clauses-Cargo 1/1/82 from PAVIA, ITALY to SHENZHEN,CHINA.

15.付款条件:

　　Terms of Payment:

　　□买方应不迟于＿＿＿＿年＿＿月＿＿日前将100%货款用即期汇票/电汇方式支付给卖方。

　　　The buyer shall pay 100% of the sales proceeds through sight (demand) draft/by T/T remittance to the

　　　seller not later than＿＿＿＿＿＿/＿＿＿＿＿＿.

　　☑买方应于＿＿＿＿年＿＿月＿＿日前通过＿＿＿＿＿＿＿＿银行开立以卖方为受益人的＿＿＿天

　　　不可撤销信用证,有效期至装运后＿＿＿天在中国议付,并注明合同号。

　　　The buyer shall issue an irrevocable L/C at 90 days sight through a ＿＿＿＿＿＿＿＿＿BANK in favour

　　　of the seller prior to　JUNE 6TH, 2018　indicating L/C shall be valid in　PAVIA, ITALY　through

　　　negotiation within 10 days after the shipment effected, the L/C must mention the Contract Number.

　　□付款交单:买方应凭卖方开立给买方的＿＿＿期跟单汇票付款,付款时交单。

　　　Documents against payment (D/P): the buyer shall dully make payment against documentary draft made out

续

to the buyer at_____/_____sight by the seller.

□承兑交单:买方应凭卖方开立给买方的____期跟单汇票付款,承兑时交单。

Documents against acceptance (D/A): the buyer shall dully accept the documentary draft made out to the buyer at_____/_____days by the seller.

16.装船通知:一旦装运完毕,卖方应立即电告买方合同号、品名、已装载数量、发票总金额、毛重、运输工具名称及起运日期等。

Shipping Advice: Upon the completion of the loading of the goods, the seller shall immediately advise the buyer of the contract No., names of commodity, loaded quantity, invoice value, gross weight, names of vessel and shipment date by TLX/FAX.

17.检验与索赔:

Inspection and Claims:

①卖方在发货前由_____检验机构对货物的品质、规格和数量进行检验,并出具检验证书。

The seller shall have the quality, specifications, quantities of the goods carefully inspected by the _____Inspection Authority, which shall issue Inspection Certificate before shipment.

②货物到达目的口岸后,买方可委托当地的商品检验机构对货物进行复验。如果发现货物有损坏、残缺或规格、数量与合同规定不符,买方需于货物到达目的口岸的____天内凭_____检验机构出具的检验证书向卖方索赔。

The buyer has the right to have the goods inspected by the local commodity inspection authority after the arrival of the goods at the port of destination. If the goods are found damaged/short/their specifications or quantities not in compliance with that specified in the contract, the buyer shall lodge claims against the seller based on the Inspection Certificate issued by the _____ Inspection Authority within_____days after the goods arrival at the destination port.

③如买方提出索赔,凡属品质异议需于货物到达目的口岸之日起____天内提出;凡属数量异议需于货物到达目的口岸之日起____天内提出。对所装货物所提任何异议应由保险公司、运输公司或邮政机构负责的,卖方不负任何责任。

The claims, if any regarding to the quality of the goods, shall be lodged within____days after arrival of the goods at the destination port, if any regarding to the quantities of the goods, shall be lodged within____days after arrival of the goods at the destination port. The seller shall not take any responsibility if any claims concerning the shipping goods in up to the responsibility of Insurance Company/Transportation Company/Post Office.

18.不可抗力:如因不可抗力造成本合同全部或部分不能履行,卖方概不负责,但卖方应将发生的上述情况及时通知买方。

Force Majeure: the seller shall not hold any responsibility for partial or total non-performance of this contract due to Force Majeure, but the seller shall advise the buyer on time of such occurrence.

19.争议的解决方式:任何因本合同而发生的或与本合同有关的争议,应提交中国国际经济贸易仲裁委员会,按该委员会的规则进行仲裁。仲裁裁决是终局性的,对双方均有约束力。

Disputes Settlement: all disputes arising out of the contract or in connection with the contract, shall be submitted to the China International Economic and Trade Arbitration Commission for arbitration in accordance with its Rules of Arbitration. The arbitral award is final and binding upon both parties.

20.法律适用:本合同的签订地或发生争议时的货物所在地在中华人民共和国境内或被诉人为中国法人的,适用于中华人民共和国法律;除此规定外,适用于《联合国国际货物销售合同公约》。

Law Applications: it will be governed by the law of the People's Republic of China under the circumstances that the contract is signed or the goods while the disputes arising are in the People's Republic of China or the defendant is Chinese legal person, otherwise it is governed by The United Nations Convention on Contracts for the International Sale of Goods.

本合同使用的术语源自国际商会的《2010年国际贸易术语解释通则》。

The terms in the contract based on INCOTERMS 2010 of the International Chamber of Commerce.

21.文字:本合同中、英文两种文字具有同等法律效力;在文字解释上若有异议,以中文解释为准。

Versions: this contract is made out in both Chinese and English of which version is equally effective. Conflicts between these two languages arising there from, if any, shall be subject to Chinese version.

22.附加条款:本合同上述条款与本附加条款有抵触时,以本附加条款为准。

Additional Clause: conflicts between contract clauses here above and this additional clause, if any, it is subject to this additional clause.

23.本合同共_____份,自双方代表签字/盖章之日起生效。

This contract is in __2 (Two)__ copies, effective since being signed/sealed by both parties.

买方代表:

Representative of the Buyer:

签字:

Authorized Signature:

卖方代表:

Representative of the Seller:

签字:

Authorized Signature:

4.3 Kinds of Transaction Documents
交易单证的种类

International transaction documents include letter of inquiry, request for quotation, proposal/bid / quotation / offer, proforma invoice, sales contract, request for proposal, commercial invoice, and so on.

国际交易单证包括询盘函、递价/递盘/报价/报盘、报盘函、报价函、销售合同、形式发票和商业发票等。

4.3.1 Letter of Inquiry
询 盘 函

This is a simple letter written by the buyer asking the seller if a product is available or if the seller will bid on the supply of a product. This letter is generally short and does not include detailed specifications.

询盘函是一封由买方撰写询问卖方是否有产品出售或卖方是否会对某种商品的供给进行递盘的简单电函。函电一般比较简短,不包括详细说明。

4.3.2 Proposal/Bid/Quotation/Offer
递价/递盘/报价/报盘

This is the seller's written offer to sell specified products under specified terms and conditions. It can be as simple as a one page letter listing stock number, quantities, price per unit and sales terms, or it can be a 1,000 pages proposal complete with engineering drawings, and complicated terms and conditions. A limited term of validity of the proposal is given so that if business conditions change, the seller has the option to modify the terms and conditions of the proposal.

该函是由卖方撰写的在特定条款和条件下出售某类商品的信函。该函可以简单到只用一页纸的篇幅简单罗列出产品货号、数量、单价和销售条款,也可以用1 000页纸的篇幅说明包括工程图纸、复杂条款和条件在内的建议。发盘函应该限定有效期间,从而在某些业务条件改变的情况下,卖方有权更改发盘函中的条款和条件。

4.3.3 Request for Quotation
报盘函

Request for quotation (RFQ) is a letter written by the buyer asking the seller to submit a formal price quotation for a specified product and quantity. RFQ is generally used for a one time sale of an existing product from the seller's inventory or product line, or a fungible product.

报盘函是由买方撰写的要求卖方对指定商品和数量做正式报价的信函。报盘函一般针对卖方库存或生产线上的既有产品或可替代产品的一次性销售。

4.3.4 Request for Proposal (RFP)
报价函

RFP is a request for a formal proposal for the sale, supply or manufacture of products. It includes the following elements: name and address of importer/buyer (as on a letterhead), name and address of proposed exporter/seller, date, statement of the request for a formal proposal and product specification.

The key element is the product specification list. This can be a simple statement of a known item (such as a commodity known by international standards) or as complex as book-length listing of engineering drawings, raw material specifications, delivery schedules, packaging and shipping instructions, documents complied with inspection requirements and so on.

报价函是一份针对产品销售、供给或生产拟定的正式要约的邀请。它包括以下要素:进口商/买方的名字和地址(与信头上的相同)、潜在出口商/卖方的名字和地址、日期、正式报价声明、产品详细说明。

关键是产品详细说明表。它可以对知名商品进行简单说明(例如受国际标准认可的货物),或是长达一本书厚度的复杂列表,包括工程图纸、原材料详细说明、交货时间表、包装和运输说明及符合检验要求的单证等。

4.3.5 Sales Contract
销售合同

This is a formal, legal agreement between the exporter and the importer stating products and prices, responsibilities and rights, terms and conditions. It is issued by either the seller or the buyer, with the drafter having the advantage of claiming greater influence on contract terms, but the disadvantage of being subject to strict interpretation of the terms should there be a dispute.

Regardless of whether you draft the terms of the contract by yourself, or hire an attorney, you need to be aware of the key contract provisions. It is up to you to insist on the protection of your own interests. The best course of action is to define all of the provisions of your agreement in writing at the tie you enter into it.

1.Complete International Contract for Sale of Goods

Not every provision is applicable to every transaction.

(1) Contract date.

(2) Identification of parties.

(3) Goods-description, quantity, and price.

(4) Payment-method of payment, medium of exchange, and exchange rate.

(5) Costs and charges-duties and taxes, insurance, handling and transport.

(6) Packaging arrangements.

(7) Delivery-date, place, and transfer of title.

(8) Transportation-carrier, storage, notice provisions, shipping time, and insurance.

(9) Import/export documents.

(10) Invoice preparation and delivery.

(11) Reexportation prohibition.

(12) Inspection rights.

(13) Indemnities.

(14) Intellectual property rights.

(15) Warranties.

(16) Enforcement and remedies.

(17) Arbitration provisions.

(18) Time is of the essence.

(19) Modification of contract.

(20) Cancellation.

(21) Liquidated damages.

(22) Attorneys' fees.

(23) Force majeure.

(24) Increment and assignment.

(25) Conditions precedent.

(26) Governing law.

(27) Choice of forum.

(28) Severability of provisions.

(29) Integration of provisions.

(30) Notices.

(31) Authority to bind.

(32) Independent counsel.

(33) Acceptance and execution.

2.Key Elements of Sales Contract

(1) Names of commodity(ies) and specification(s).

(2) Quality of goods.

(3) Quantity of goods.

(4) Packing of goods.

(5) Unit price.

(6) Amount.

(7) Port of loading.

(8) Port of destination.

(9) Shipping mark.

(10) Time of shipment.

(11) Terms of payment.

(12) Insurance.

(13) L/C clauses.

(14) Documents.

(15) Quality/Quantity discrepancy.

(16) Arbitration.

(17) Other conditions.

销售合同是出口商与进口商订立的确定产品、价格、责任与权利、条款与条件的正式的、合法的契约。销售合同可由卖方或买方拟定,拟定人可根据自身利益对合同的条款施加更大的影响力,但如有争端则必须服从于条款的严格的解释。

不管合约条款是由自己还是律师起草,都需要注意关键的合同条款。保护自身利益的最好方式是以书面方式明确合约中与自己相关联的所有书面规定。

1.完整的国际货物销售合同

不是所有的条款都适合于每一次的交易。

(1)合同日期。

(2)合同当事人。

(3)货物——描述、数量和价格。

(4)付款——付款方式、货币币种、外汇汇率。

(5)成本和费用——税费、保险费、搬运费。

(6)包装安排。

(7)交货——日期、地点、所有权转移。

(8)运输——承运人、储存、通知条款、装运时间、保险。

(9)进口/出口单证。

(10)发票准备和交货。

(11)禁止复出口条款。

(12)检验权。

(13)免责。

(14)知识产权。

(15)保证。

(16)执行和救济。

(17)仲裁条款。

(18)时间是至关重要的。

(19)合同的修改。

(20)取消。

(21)违约赔偿金。

(22)律师费。

(23)不可抗力。

(24)增量和分配。

(25)先决条件。

(26)管辖法律。

(27)管辖权选择。

(28)终止条款。

(29)完整协议条款。

(30)注意事项。

(31)约束力。

(32)独立检察官。

(33)接受和执行。

2.销售合同的要点

(1)货物名称和规格。

(2)货物质量。

(3)货物数量。

(4)货物包装。

(5)货物单价。

(6)金额。

(7)装运港。

(8)目的港。

(9)唛头。

(10)装运时间。

(11)付款条件。

(12)保险。

(13)信用证条款。

(14)单证。

(15)质量/数量异议。

(16)仲裁。

(17)其他条款。

4.3.6　*Proforma Invoice*
形式发票

This is a preliminary invoice made up by the exporter at the importer's request prior to shipment of merchandise (Sample 4-2). It identifies the parties to the transaction and includes the kinds and quantities of goods to be sent, their value, specifications and shipping costs. The proforma invoice is used by the importer to see what the purchase will cost, to obtain any necessary import licenses and international exchange approval, and to apply for a letter of credit.

A proforma invoice is issued by the seller as a response to an inquiry from the potential buyer. It is a document similar to a commercial invoice and it contains the same information as those in the commercial invoice. It is a statement of sales, issued before a transaction has been concluded rather than a record of sales already effected.

A proforma invoice is needed in the following circumstances. If an irrevocable letter of credit is required by the exporter, the importer will use the proforma invoice to substantiate the need for a letter of credit to his bank. Sometimes it is needed by the importer to apply for the import licenses and international exchange. A proforma invoice, in some other circumstances, may be required by the importer to help him apply for the relevant letter of credit. Therefore, a proforma invoice has no legal status and serves only as a means to facilitate the buyer to accomplish the above-mentioned tasks.

形式发票是在货物装运之前,出口商应进口商的要求发出的一份初步的发票(见样单4-2)。它明确双方交易主体,并包括发运货物的种类、数量、价值、规格和运输成本。形式发票被进口商用于了解购买商品所需成本、获得必要的进口许可证和外汇证明,以及申请信用证。

Sample 4-2　　　　　　　　Proforma Invoice
样单4-2　　　　　　　　　　形式发票

TO:
NEO GENERAL TRADING CO.
P.O. BOX 99552, RIYADH 22766, KSA

INVOICE NO.: 2018SDT001
INVOICE DATE: MAR. 20TH, 2018
S/C NO.: NEO2018026
S/C DATE: FEB. 28TH, 2018

TERM OF PAYMENT: L/C AT SIGHT
PORT OF LOADING: TIANJIN, CHINA
PORT OF DESTINATION: DAMMAM PORT, KSA
TIME OF DELIVERY: APR. 20TH, 2018
INSURANCE: TO BE COVERED BY THE BUYER
VALIDITY: MAY 10TH, 2018

续

Marks and Numbers	Number and Kind of Package; Description of Goods	Quantity	Unit Price	Amount
ROSE BRAND 178/2018 RIYADH	ABOUT 1,700 CARTONS CANNED MUSHROOMS PIECES & STEMS 24 TINS×425 GRAMS NET WEIGHT (D.W.227 GRAMS) ROSE BRAND	1,700 CARTONS	**CFR DAMMAM PORT** USD 7.80	USD 13,260.00
Total:		1,700 CARTONS		USD 13,260.00

SAY TOTAL:

US DOLLARS THIRTEEN THOUSAND TWO HUNDRED AND SIXTY ONLY.

BENEFICIARY:

TIFERT TRADING CO., LTD.

NO.86 ZHUJIANG ROAD, GUANGZHOU, CHINA

ADVISING BANK:

BANK OF CHINA, GUANGZHOU BRANCH

HEAD OFFICE 148 ZHONGSHAN SOUTH ROAD, GUANGZHOU

TELEX: 34226/34327 BOCJS CN

NEGOTIATING BANK:

BANK OF CHINA, TIANJIN BRANCH

JIEFANGBEI ROAD, PEACE ZONE, TIANJIN

TELEX: 67356/68523 BOCJS CN

TIFERT TRADING CO., LTD.
张立

形式发票由卖方开具以回应潜在买方的询盘。形式发票非常近似于商业发票,并且包含了与商业发票相同的信息。形式发票是一份销售声明,是在正式履行完合同之前所开出的一种销售单据,而不是一份已经执行了的销售记录。

在以下情况下需提供形式发票:(1)如果出口商要求将不可撤销信用证作为结算方式,那么进口商将使用形式发票向银行证实其开证要求。(2)形式发票有时被进口商用来申请进口许可证和外汇。(3)在其他情况下,进口商要求卖方出具形式发票来帮助其申请相关信用证。因此,形式发票不具有法律效力,只相当于一种可促使买方完成以上所提及工作的工具。

4.3.7 Commercial Invoice
商业发票

When manufacture is complete and the products are ready for shipment, ordinarily the seller will prepare a commercial invoice which is the formal statement for payment to be sent directly to the buyer or submitted through banking channels for payment by the buyer

(Sample 4-3). Such invoices may also contain the detailed terms or conditions of sale on the front or back of the form.

When the export goods are shipped, the exporter must prepare a commercial invoice which is a statement to the buyer for payment. Usually English is sufficient but some countries require the seller's invoice to be in their languages. Multiple copies of a commercial invoice are usually required, some of which are sent with the bills of lading and other transport documents. The original of a commercial invoice is forwarded through banking channels for payment (except on open account sales, where it is sent directly to the buyer). On letter of credit transactions, the commercial invoice must be issued by the beneficiary of the letter of credit and addressed to the applicant for the letter of credit. Putting the commercial invoice number on the other shipping documents helps to tie the documents together. The customs laws of most countries require that a commercial invoice be presented by the buyer (or the seller if the seller is responsible for clearing customs), and the price listed on it be used as the value for the assessment of customs duties where the customs duties are based upon a percentage of the value (ad valorem rates). (Brazil, Egypt, Colombia, Guatemala, Senegal, Bahrain, Sri Lanka, Dominican Republic, Myanmar, and other countries may assess duties on fair market value rather than invoice price.)

Perhaps the most important thing to note here is that many countries, like the United States, have special requirements for the information that, depending upon the product involved, must be contained in commercial invoice. It is extremely important that, before shipping the products and preparing the commercial invoice, the exporter should check either through an attorney, the buyer, or the freight forwarder to determine exactly what information must be included in the commercial invoice in order to clear international customs. In addition, certain items, such as inland shipping expenses, packing charges, installation and service charges, financing charges, international transportation charges, insurance, royalties, or license fees, may have to be shown separately because some of these items may be deducted from or added to the price in calculating the customs value and the payment of duties. Many countries in the Middle East and Latin America require that commercial invoices covering shipments to their countries be "legalized". This means the export country's embassy or consulate must stamp the invoice. When an export control license is needed for the shipment (and on some other types of shipments), a destination control statement must be put on the commercial invoice.

1.Contents of Commercial Invoice

The commercial invoice is the exporting firm's invoice, addressed to the foreign importer, describing key transaction details particularly the total value and claiming for payment. It is one of the most important documents used in international trade. It is used as the foundation for keeping accounts and making declarations to the customs. It is often one of the documents required for payment settlement. The commercial invoice serves as a record of the essential details of a transaction. Usually, it includes the basic information:

(1)Buyer's reference (order number/indent number).

(2)Invoice number and date.

（3）Export or import license number.

（4）Method of dispatch.

（5）Shipment terms.

（6）Names and addresses of the seller and the buyer.

（7）Country from which the shipment is made.

（8）Description of the goods-quantity, weight or measurement of the goods, unit price, total amount payable (including price of goods, freight, insurance and so on).

（9）Rebate or similar incentives.

（10）Signature of the exporter.

2.Key Elements

（1）Name and address of seller or buyer. Unless otherwise stipulated in the letter of credit, the commercial invoice must be made out in the name of the applicant (buyer). But in a transferable documentary L/C the invoice may be made out to the third party.

（2）Date of issuance.

（3）Invoice number.

（4）Order or contract number.

（5）Quantity and description of the goods. It is virtually important that the description of the goods and the terms listed in the commercial invoice corresponds precisely with the description of the goods in the contract of sale and with a documentary letter of credit (if that form of payment is used).

（6）Any other information as required by the seller (e.g. country of origin). The buyer, the seller, and the banks should all carefully check for discrepancies in the invoice. The details specified herein should not be inconsistent with those of any other documents and should exactly conform to the specifications of the L/C.

（7）Shipping details include weight of the goods, number of packages, and shipping marks.

（8）Terms of delivery and payment.

（9）Unit price, total price, other agreed upon charges, and total invoice amount. The invoice amount should match exactly or at least should not exceed the amount specified in the letter of credit. The banks and the buyer have the right to refuse invoices issued for amount in excess of the amount stated in the L/C. The exception is when a documentary L/C specifies "about" in relation to the currency amount and quantity of merchandise, in which case the invoice may specify an amount equal to plus or minus 10 percent of the stipulated amount of the L/C. The invoice should be made out in the same currency as the letter of credit.

3.Checklist for Commercial Invoice

（1）Is the commercial invoice in the name of the beneficiary?

（2）Is the commercial invoice addressed to the applicant named in the letter of credit?

（3）Do you sign the commercial invoice if required?

（4）Is the commercial invoice countersigned by any other party if required in the letter of credit?

(5)Does the commercial invoice conform to the letter of credit's terms relative to the following items:

① Total amount,unit price, and computations.

② Description of merchandise and terms (FOB,CFR,CIF,and so on).

③ Description of packing (if required).

④ Declarations clauses properly worded.

⑤ Shipping marks on the commercial invoice agreed with that appearing on the bill of lading.

⑥ Are all merchandise shipped if partial shipments are prohibited? Or, does the commercial invoice conform to the value of the merchandise shipped if partial shipments are permitted? Or, does the commercial invoice conform to the value of the merchandise invoiced in proportion to the quantity of the shipment when the letter of credit does not specify unit price, if partial shipments are permitted?

⑦ Does foreign language used for the merchandise description conform to that used in the letter of credit?

4.Functions of Commercial Invoice

(1)It is the importer's and the exporter's evidence of keeping accounts and verifying.

(2)It is the basis on which applying for the customs entry and paying duties in places of exporting and importing.

(3)It is one of documents offered to handle insurance with the insurance company and to handle exchange settlement with the bank.

(4)It facilitates the importer to check and accept the goods and make payment.

5.Samples of Commercial Invoice Clauses

(1)The invoice should certify that the goods shipped and other details are as per S/C No.888 dated March 3rd, 2018.

(2)The beneficiary's original signed commercial invoices at least in 8 copies issued in the name of the buyer indicating (showing/evidencing/specifying/declaring) the merchandise, country of origin and any other relevant information.

(3)All invoices must show FOB,freight and insurance costs separately.

(4)Combined invoice is not acceptable.

(5)5% commission invoice is not acceptable.

(6)The invoice to certify that the goods shipped are exactly equal to the samples presented to the buyer.

(7)4% discount should be deducted from total amount of the commercial invoice.

(8)All invoices must show break down value: FOB value, freight prepaid, insurance premium prepaid.

(9)Your declaration that no wood container has been used in packing of the goods listed on the invoice is required.

(10)The commercial invoice must indicate the following: a. That each item is labeled "Made in China";b. That one set of non-negotiable shipping documents has been airmailed in advance to the buyer.

6.Special Provisions of Commercial Invoice in Some Countries

（1）South Asian countries including India, Nepal and Sri Lanka: manually signed invoice is requested and the customs tariff number of the commodity should be indicated.

（2）Latin American countries including Mexico, Peru, Panama, Chile and Venezuela: a name of commodity should be in Spanish. If based on CIF term, the freight, insurance premium and FOB should be showed separately on the manually signed invoice which should be certificated by the importer's consular. If there is no diplomatic and consular mission here, the invoice can be certified by CCPIT agent, but in a clear express, e.g. "There is ×××country's consulate here".

（3）Arab countries such as Kuwait, Bahrain and Iran: manufacturers' name and address should be shown on the invoice or certificate of origin, indicating the customs tariff number of the commodity, and the manually signed invoice should be certificated by the importer's consular. If there is no diplomatic and consular mission here, the invoice can be certified by CCPIT agent, but in a clear express, e.g. "There is ×××country's consulate here".

（4）Lebanon: real confirmed words and sentences should be filled on the invoice. "We hereby certify that this Invoice is authentic, that it is the only one issued by us for the goods herein, that the value and price of the goods are correct without any deduction of payment in advance and its origin is exclusively China."

在货物生产出来准备装运时,通常卖方会准备好商业发票。商业发票是一种直接向买方开具或通过银行渠道递交的由买方付款的正式单据(见样单4-3)。商业发票在发票的正面或背面可能会包含具体的销售条款或条件。

在装运出口货物时,出口商必须出具商业发票,作为买方的支付凭证。通常情况下,英文单证是通用的,但有些国家要求卖方用买方国家的语言来开具发票。通常要求开具多份发票,其中的一些会连同提单或其他运输单证一起寄送。商业发票的原件通过银行渠道转寄作为付款单据(除了赊账销售时,商业发票的原件将直接寄给买方)。在使用信用证的交易中,商业发票必须由信用证规定的受益人出具,信用证的申请人为抬头人。在其他单证上标示商业发票号码有助于把全套单证联系起来。多数国家的海关法要求在清关时由买方递交商业发票(如果由卖方负责清关,应由卖方递交),而且要求用商业发票上列示的价格来计算海关关税,计税的方法是基于商品价值一定百分比来计算(从价税)。(巴西、埃及、哥伦比亚、危地马拉、塞内加尔、巴林、斯里兰卡、多米尼加共和国、缅甸和其他国家通过公平市价而不是发票价格来评估关税。)

也许在这里要重点提及的是在大部分国家,比如美国,对商业发票必须包含的信息有专门的要求,取决于所涉及的产品。最为重要的是出口商要在装运货物及准备商业发票之前,通过律师、买方或货运代理行查询,以确定为顺利清关必须包含在商业发票中的信息都有哪些。除此之外,通常某些项目,如内陆的装运费、包装费、安装及服务费、财务费用、国际运输费、保险费、版税、许可证费也必须分别罗列出来,因为这些项目当中的某些可能要在计算关税价值及支付税费时从价格中扣除或加到价格上。中东和拉美的许多国家要求装运到这些国家的货物的商业发票必须是得到法律认可的。这就意味着出口国在这些国家的大使馆或领事馆必须在发票上盖章。当装运(以及一些其他类型的装运)需要出口限制许可证时,目的地国的控制声明也必须在商业发票中标示。

Sample 4-3   **Commercial Invoice**
样单4-3   **商业发票**

To:			Invoice No.	2018SDT001
NEO GENERAL TRADING CO.			Invoice Date	APR. 16TH, 2018
P.O.BOX 99552, RIYADH 22766, KSA			S/C No.	NEO2018026
TEL: 00966-1-4659220 FAX: 00966-1-4659213			S/C Date	FEB. 28TH, 2018
From	TIANJIN, CHINA	To	DAMMAM, KSA	
Letter of Credit No.	0011LC123756	Issued by	APR. 16TH, 2018	
Marks and Numbers	Number and Kind of Package; Description of Goods	Quantity	Unit Price	Amount
ROSE BRAND 178/2018 RIYADH	ABOUT 1,700 CARTONS CANNED MUSHROOMS PIECES & STEMS 24 TINS × 425 GRAMS NET WEIGHT (D.W. 227 GRAMS) ROSE BRAND	1,700 CARTONS	CFR DAMMAM PORT USD 7.80	USD 13,260.00
Total:		1,700 CARTONS		USD 13,260.00
SAY TOTAL: US DOLLARS THIRTEEN THOUSAND TWO HUNDRED AND SIXTY ONLY.				
			TIFERT TRADING CO., LTD. 张立	

1. 商业发票的内容

商业发票是出口商公司写给国外进口商的发票,发票上说明交易的主要信息(尤其是商品的总值)并提示买方付款。这是国际贸易中最重要的单证之一,不仅是做账和向海关申报的基础,也经常是结算时必需的单证之一。商业发票还可以记录交易的基本资料。一般来说,一张商业发票应标示以下基本内容:

(1)买方参考(订单号码)。

(2)发票号码和日期。

(3)出口或进口许可证号码。

(4)发货方式。

(5)装运条款。

(6)买卖双方的名称和地址。

(7)货物起运国。

(8)货物描述,包括货物数量、重量或体积、单价、应付总金额(包括商品的价格、运费、保险费等)。

(9)折扣或类似激励。

(10)出口商的签字。

2. 主要内容

(1)卖方或买方的名称和地址。除非信用证另有约定,商业发票必须以申请人(买方)为抬头开具,但可转让跟单信用证中发票可以第三方为抬头开具。

（2）出票日期。

（3）发票号码。

（4）订单或合同号码。

（5）货物的数量和描述。事实上尤为重要的是商业发票中的货物描述和条款要与销售合同中的货物描述相一致,同时要与跟单信用证相一致(如果采用的是这种付款方式)。

（6）卖方要求的其他任何信息(如原产国)。买方、卖方和银行都应该认真核实发票的分歧点。所有细节都应该与其他单证、信用证的规定相符。

（7）装运细节包括货物重量、包装数量和唛头。

（8）交货和付款条款。

（9）单价、总价、其他协商一致的费用和发票总额。发票总额应该与信用证总额完全一致或至少不应该超出信用证指定的总额。银行和买方有权利拒绝总额超出信用证规定的总额的发票。例外情况是,当跟单信用证在涉及金额、商品数量时注明"约"字样,发票总额可以等于信用证规定总额加减10%。发票应使用与信用证相同的货币。

3.商业发票的审核内容

（1）商业发票的抬头是受益人吗?

（2）商业发票的抬头是否与信用证申请人的名称相一致?

（3）如果需要的话,你是否在商业发票上签字了?

（4）如果信用证有要求,商业发票由第三方会签了吗?

（5）商业发票是否与信用证的如下条款相一致:

①总金额、单价和估算。

②货物和条款的描述(FOB、CFR、CIF等)。

③包装的描述(如果需要)。

④报关条款准确表述。

⑤商业发票中的唛头与提单相一致。

⑥如果不允许分批装运,所有装运的货物是否都装运? 或者,如果允许分批装运,商业发票是否与装运货物的价值相一致? 或者,如果允许分批装运,当信用证没有明确注明单价时,商业发票金额是否与发票中所注明的商品价值相一致,而商品价值与装运商品数量是对应的。

⑦如果在信用证中有商业发票条款,其使用的外语是否与货物描述使用的外语一致?

4.商业发票的作用

（1）商业发票是进出口商记账和通关检验的凭证。

（2）商业发票是申请通关和在进出口地缴税的基础。

（3）商业发票是与保险公司办理保险以及与银行进行结汇的单证之一。

（4）商业发票便于进口商验收货物和付款。

5.商业发票条款样例

（1）发票应证明装运货物和其他有关细节与2018年3月3日第888号销售合同相符。

（2）正本至少一式八份的受益人签署的商业发票,以买方为抬头,标明商品名称、原产国和其他相关信息。

（3）所有发票均应分别列出FOB价、运费和保险费。

（4）不接受联合发票。

（5）不接受从发票金额中扣除5%的佣金。

（6）发票应证明装运货物与已交付买方的样品相符。

（7）应从商业发票总金额中扣除4%的折扣。

（8）所有发票应标明分类价格：FOB价、预付运费、预付保费。

（9）发票上需声明所列货物未使用木制容器包装。

（10）商业发票必须标示以下内容：①每件商品标明"中国制造"；②一套非议付装运单证已预先航空邮寄给买方。

6.某些国家对商业发票的特殊规定

（1）印度、尼泊尔和斯里兰卡等南亚国家：发票要求手签，要注明商品的海关税则号。

（2）墨西哥、秘鲁、巴拿马、智利和委内瑞拉等拉丁美洲国家：商品名称用西班牙文表示。如果是CIF术语的，则要在发票上分别显示运费、保险费和FOB价，发票手签并要求进口国领事认证。如果出口地没有使馆、领事馆，可以由中国贸促会代理认证，但要在发票上明示，如"本地无某国领事馆"。

（3）科威特、巴林和伊朗等阿拉伯国家：发票或原产地证书上应显示厂商的名称与地址，注明商品的海关税则号，发票手签并要求进口国领事认证。如果出口地没有使馆、领事馆，可以由中国贸促会代理认证，但要在发票上明示，如"本地无某国领事馆"。

（4）黎巴嫩：发票上加注真实性证实词句。"我们特此证明：本发票是我们为本合同商品出具的经过认证的唯一发票，商品的价值和价格准确无误，不扣除任何预付款，商品的唯一原产地是中国。"

4.3.8　Special Customs Invoices
特别海关发票

In addition to the commercial invoice, some countries require special customs invoice designed to facilitate clearance of the goods and the assessment of customs duties in that country. Such invoices list specific information required under the customs regulations of that country. It is similar in some ways to the consular invoice, except that it is prepared by the exporter and does not need to be signed or certified by the consulate.

除了商业发票之外，一些国家要求提供特别海关发票。设计这些特别海关发票的目的是为货物清关与评估海关关税提供便利。这样的发票包含了那个国家海关法规之下的专门信息。其除了是由出口商开具的并且不需要领事馆在发票上签字或证明之外，其他方面都与领事发票相似。

Training Case 4-1

A Case that Invoice Number can't be Shown in Documents

China PH import and export company exported a batch of goods to Singapore. An L/C was opened by N.H.M. Bank on March 5, 2016, the date of shipment was on March 23, which was valid for April 3. The clause of the L/C was required as follows: "FULL SET OF CLEAN ON BOARD OCEAN BILLS OF LADING AND ONE COPY OF NON - NEGOTIABLE B/L AND GENERALIZED SYSTEM OF PREFERENCE CERTIFICATE OF ORIGIN FORM A." "ALL DOCUMENTS EXCEPT DRAFT AND

INVOICE MUST NOT SHOW L/C NUMBER AND INVOICE NUMBER."

When documentation specialist in PH import and export company made out the GSP certificate of origin before shipment, he found that invoice number in all documents could not be shown in the L/C, but GSP certificate of origin Form A was required to fill in the invoice number and date. PH import and export company immediately contacted with the local commodity inspection authority, the commodity inspection authority resolutely didn't agree to issue the invoice number blank in the GSP certificate of origin because UNCTAD regulates that this section may not be blank when the relevant provisions of the GSP certificate of origin Form A are filled in.

PH import and export company immediately faxed to Singapore importer and put forward: "Your L/C required invoice number and the L/C number could not be shown in all documents except invoices and the drafts, but you required us to provide the GSP certificate of origin which was demanded to fill in the invoice number in the certificate in accordance with the regulations of UNCTAD, so your L/C was inconsistent with the above regulations, and our local authorities didn't agree to accept the terms and conditions. Please amend the L/C as follows: 'ALL DOCUMENTS EXCEPT DRAFT, INVOICE AND GENERALIZED SYSTEM OF PREFERENCE CERTIFICATE OF ORIGIN FORM A MUST NOT SHOW L/C NUMBER AND INVOICE NUMBER.'"

Singapore importer replied: please immediately make shipment, the L/C is applying for modification.

PH import and export company then arranged shipment on March 22. One week after the shipment, the L/C amendment was still not opened, and the validity was coming. Contacting Singapore importer, he said he had dealt with the L/C modification. On April 3, PH import and export company had to issue a letter of guarantee to assure China Everbright Bank for negotiation. The ship's name in the bill of lading submitted to the China Everbright Bank by PH import and export company marked: "INTENDED VESSEL FREESEA", but should fill in the actual carrier, the date of shipment in the "on board" notation and the carrier signature.

After documents were sent abroad, the issuing bank proposed that the documents were not consistent with each other and it substituted the documents. There were two discrepancies: "First of all, the invoice number shown in column 10 of the GSP certificate of origin Form A did not conform to the stipulation in the L/C; secondly, carrier filled in the actual date of shipment and the name of the ship in the original bill of lading, but without the remark in the copy of the bill of lading, the applicant did not agree to accept."

PH import and export company was surprised after receiving the refusal notice by the issuing bank from China Everbright Bank. The invoice number of the GSP certificate of origin has been put forward to Singapore importer, which the other party not only agreed to, but also dealt with the L/C amendment. Why did he suggest documents discrepancy?

PH import and export company immediately put forward the followings through China Everbright Bank to the issuing bank for documents discrepancies under the L/C No. ×××:

（1）The invoice number shown in the GSP certificate of origin was according to the regulation of UNCTAD. As long as a little common sense in this regard, you should not argue. At the same time, the applicant not only agreed to the discrepancies, but also amended the L/C. How did discrepant documents exist?

（2）For "intended vessel" in the bill of lading, the carrier has notated the actual shipment and the name of the ship in the bill of lading and the carrier shall be signed. According to UCP600 regulation: "If the bill of lading contains the indication 'intended vessel' or similar qualification in relation to the name of the vessel, an on board notation indicating the date of shipment and the name of the actual vessel is required." Therefore the bill of lading has been complied with the UCP600, constituting a "shipped" requirement, original B/L was a valid file. As for the copy of the bill of lading, it was uneffective reference documents, and the carrier couldn't fill in and sign on a copy of bill of lading. Therefore, the bill of lading I provided already constituted a "shipped" bill of lading, which was consistent with the documents. According to the above situation, you should accept the documents, make payment on time.

The issuing bank contradicted later after receiving argument from PH import and export company:

For clauses problem which the GSP certificate of origin did not represent the invoice number, our bank did not amend the L/C, the applicant did not apply for a change after checking. According to the UCP600 regulation, the only standard of bank documents audit is whether documents on the surface are in conformity with the terms of the L/C, not considering the rules of UNCTAD. The invoice number was indicated on the certificate of origin, which was the documents discrepancy with the L/C.

There was notation for the original bill of lading by the carrier, so as for a copy of bill of lading. Although the carrier could make no signature on the bill of lading, its each side contents shall be completely and exactly the same as the original bill of lading. The original has, while the copy has not, which forms documents inconsistence with each other.

According to the above situation, the applicant could not accept the documents. Please inform the documents processing opinion.

In the end, after the buyer and the seller repeated representations, and because the goods' price was higher, the buyer decided to make payment. It was 3 months later for the payment than normal. PH import and export company lost interest of $14,000.

单证不能表示发票号码的案例

我方PH进出口公司对新加坡出口一批货物。2016年3月5日由N.H.M.银行开来装船期为3月23日、有效期为4月3日的信用证。在信用证条款中要求提供："整套清洁已装船提单，一份非议付副本提单和普惠制原产地证书格式A。""除汇票和发票外，其他所有单证必须不要显示信用证号码和发票号码。"

　　PH进出口公司的制单员在装船前缮制普惠制原产地证书时，发现信用证要求所有单据不能表示发票号码，而普惠制原产地证书格式A却要求填写"发票号码和日期"。PH进出口公司立即与当地商检机构联系，商检机构坚决不同意出具发票号码留空不填的普惠制原产地证书，其理由是根据联合国贸发会对于填写普惠制原产地证书格式A的有关规定，此栏目不得留空不填。

　　PH进出口公司立即发传真给新加坡进口商，提出："你方信用证要求一切单据除发票和汇票外，不得表示发票号码和信用证号码，但是你方又要求我方提供普惠制原产地证书，该证书按照联合国贸发会规定必须填写发票号码，故你方信用证与上述规定有抵触，而且我地出证当局也不同意接受此条款。请你方修改信用证为：'除汇票、发票和普惠制原产地证书格式A外，其他所有单证必须不要显示信用证号码和发票号码。'"

　　新加坡进口商电复：请立即装船，信用证正在申请办理修改中。

　　PH进出口公司随即安排3月22日装船，装船后一周仍未见其修改信用证开到，有效期将至。PH进出口公司联系新加坡进口商，对方却称已经办理信用证修改。4月3日，PH进出口公司只好出具保函向中国光大银行办理担保议付。PH进出口公司向中国光大银行提交的提单中船名标注"INTENDED VESSEL FREESEA"，但是在"已装船"批注中填实际已装船的船名和装船日期，并有承运人签章。

　　单据寄到国外后，开证行提出单证不符，暂代保管单据。不符点有二："其一，普惠制原产地证书格式A第10栏表示的发票号，与我方信用证的规定不符；其二，正本提单上承运人加注了实际装船的船名和日期，但是在副本提单上却无此批注，开证申请人不同意接受。"

　　PH进出口公司接到中国光大银行送来的开证行拒付通知后感到奇怪，对于普惠制原产地证书的发票号一事，早已向新加坡进口商提出，对方不但同意，而且办理了信用证修改，为何还提出单证不符？

　　PH进出口公司立即通过中国光大银行向开证行提出对于×××号信用证项下单据的不符点一事：

　　（1）普惠制原产地证书表示的发票号是根据联合国贸发会的规定。只要稍有这方面的常识，就不应该提出异议。同时，开证申请人不但同意此不符点，而且已经修改了信用证，怎么还会单证不符？

　　（2）对于提单的"预期船名"，我方在提单上已经由承运人批注了实际装船的船名和装船日期，并由承运人签章。根据UCP600规定："如果提单包含'预期船'字样或类似有关限定船只的词语，装上具名船只必须由注明装运日期以及实际装运船只名称的装船批注来证实。"故我方所提供的提单已符合UCP600规定，构成"装上船"的要求，提单正本是有效文件。至于提单副本，它属于不生效的参考文件，承运人不可能在副本提单上加注和签章。因此，我方提供的提单已构成"装上船"的提单，已经单证相符。根据上述情况，你方应该接受单据，按时付款。

开证行收到PH进出口公司的申辩后又提出反驳意见：

对于GSP原产地证书不表示发票号的条款问题，我行并未修改信用证，经查对，我方申请人也未有申请过修改的情况。根据UCP600的规定，银行对单据审核的唯一标准就是单据表面上是否与信用证条款相符，并不考虑联合国贸发会的规定。原产地证书上标明了发票号，就是表面上单证不符。

正本提单上有承运人批注内容，而副本也应该有该批注的内容。虽然承运人可以对提单副本不进行签章，但其各面内容均应与提单正本内容完全一样齐全。正本有，而副本没有，即构成单单不符。

根据上述情况，申请人无法接受该单据。请速告对单据处理意见。

最后，买卖双方经过反复交涉，又由于当时货物价格趋涨，买方才决定付款。付款时间比正常收汇拖延了3个月，PH进出口公司损失利息14 000美元。

Training Case 4-2
A Dispute Case Caused by the Invoice without Specification Clause

A certain export company (company A) received an L/C from the advising bank. The provisions of the relevant goods were: 50 M/T frozen snapper sea bream, fresh, quick frozen, weight per fish: 2-3 kg. After company A got the goods ready for shipment and completed shipment on July 21, the confirmation of the issuing bank was turned from the advising bank on July 23. After the documentation specialist mailed the documents to the negotiating bank on July 24, the issuing bank put forward objection on August 2: "Your documents No. ... after audit, were found that specifications in the invoice were not shown, whole fish ungutted (whole internal organs). Documents are still preserved in our bank, at your disposal."

After documentation specialists of company A received the above cable from the issuing bank, they compared documents counterfoil and the L/C clauses and found that clauses regarding specifications did not regulate "whole internal organs" or similar terms, how can it be said that specifications were leak of "whole internal organs"? After contacting the related salesman, company A knew that the issuing bank had sent the confirmation by mail, which regulated "whole internal organs". The related salesman thought at that time that there was such regulation in the contract, the actual goods were of the specifications of the "whole not to internal organs", and the shipped goods were complete, so they did not pass the confirmation to documentation specialists. Then company A studied with the negotiating bank at once, who claimed that specifications can be not shown and made the argument on August 3: "Your cable on August 2 about our documents number ×××, your L/C on July 16 does not regulate 'whole internal organs' or the similar terms, therefore our documents are in conformity with the L/C. According to the regulations of the UCP600: if the issuing bank uses telecommunications relay or amendment proven, the telecommunication is regarded as effective L/C documents or effective amendment. If the confirmation is still mailed, then the mail confirmation is invalid. The advising bank also has no obligation to check the mail confirmation and the effective L/C documents in telecommunications way to transfer files or effective amendment. Therefore, according to the above stipulations, you issue and audit documents. As for the confirmation you mailed on July 23 which said it belongs to an invalid file. The specification in the confirmation 'whole internal organs' shall be regarded as no such regulations. So the documents discrepancy is not established, make payment on time."

On August 10, the issuing bank finally told the payment for goods had been put into account and it made settlement.

发票未表示规格条款引起的纠纷案

某出口公司收到通知行转来一张信用证。有关商品条款规定:50公吨冻加吉鱼,新鲜,速冻,每条鱼重2~3千克。A公司备妥货物准备装运后于7月21日装运完毕,7月23日又接到通知行转来开证行的邮寄证实书。7月24日单证人员向议付行交单议付后,8月2日开证行来电提出异议:"你方……号单据经审核后发现其中发票规格漏表示,整条不去内脏。单据仍在我行代保存,听候你方处理意见。"

A公司单证人员接到开证行上述来电后即对照留底单据与L/C条款,发现关于规格条款并未规定"整条不去内脏"的类似条款,怎能说规格漏表示"整条不去内脏"? 经联系有关业务员,A公司获悉才知开证行曾寄来证实书,证实书确有规定"整条不去内脏"规格的规定。该有关业务员当时认为合同确有这样的规定,而且实际货物已是"整条不去内脏"的规格,货又已装运完备,所以未将该证实书交给单证人员。A公司随即与议付行研究,议付行称可以不用表示该规格,即于8月3日做出如下反驳:"你8月2日电关于我第×××号单据事,你行7月16日的电开L/C中并未规定'整条不去内脏'的类似条款,故我单证相符。根据UCP600规定:如开证行使用经证实的电讯传递或修改书,该电讯即被视为有效信用证文件或有效修改书,不应邮寄证实书;如仍邮寄证实书,则该邮寄证实书无效。通知行亦无义务将该邮寄证实书与所收到的以电讯方式传递的有效信用证文件或有效修改书进行核对。因此,按上述条文规定,你电开出具单据和审核单据。至于你于7月23日又邮寄来证实书应属于无效的文件。你在证实书上规定'整条不去内脏'的规格应视为无此规定。故你行所谓单证不符是不成立的,应按时付款。"

8月10日开证行终于告知该票货款已转入账下而结案。

Key Terms

commercial invoice 商业发票

Exercise

◎ *Practice*

Practice 1

2018年6月25日,英国Goodlucky有限公司根据合同规定开出了以浙江省福鑫对外贸易有限公司为受益人的第DCLUT180954号信用证。2018年7月23日,该公司单证员开始安排了订舱、报检、投保等工作,根据下列信用证以及其他相关资料缮制商业发票。

信用证中有关发票缮制的内容为:

SEQUENCE OF TOTAL 27：1/1

FORM OF DOC. 40A：IRREVOCABLE L/C

DOC. L/C NUMBER 20：DCLUT180954

DATE OF ISSUE 31C：20180625

EXPIRY 31D：DATE 20180824 PLACE IN CHINA

APPLICANT 50：GOODLUCKY CO., LTD., 96 HIGHWAYS LUTON, BEDFORDSHIRE LU1 1XL, UNITED KINGDOM

APPLICANT BANK 51A：HSBC BANK PLC, LONDON

BENEFICIARY 59：FUXIN FOREIGN TRADE CORP. OF ZHEJIANG, LTD.
288 WEST SECOND RING ROAD, ZHUJI, ZHEJIANG, CHINA

DESCRIPTION OF GOODS 45A：MEN'S SOCKS AND BABIES' HOSIERY AS PER S/C NO. ZF18E0620 AND APPLICANTS ORDER NO. 599/2018

TRADE TERMS：CIF FELIXSTOWE

DOCUMENTS REQUIRED 46A：

+ ORIGINAL SIGNED COMMERCIAL INVOICE PLUS THREE COPIES

ADDITIONAL COND. 47A：

+ APPLICANTS ORDER NO. 599/2018 MUST BE SHOWN ON ALL DOCUMENTS

其他相关资料：

发票编号：ZFA0723-Q

短袜4 800打　　　12.00英镑/打

毛重：25千克/箱

唛头：GOODLUCKY
　　　MEN'S SOCKS
　　　C/NO. 599/2018
　　　FELIXSTOWE
　　　NO.1-400

婴儿袜2 000打　　　　9.00英镑/打

毛重：9千克/箱

唛头：GOODLUCKY
　　　BABIES' HOSIERY
　　　C/NO. 599/2018
　　　FELIXSTOWE
　　　NO. 401-600

合同号：ZF18E0620

发票日期：2018年7月23日

合同日期：2018年6月20日

Practice 2

根据下列信用证以及其他相关资料缮制商业发票。

TO：BANK OF CHINA，JIAXING BRANCH

FM：UNION BANK OF CALIFORNIA N. A.，LOS ANGELES

MT：700

SEQUENCE OF TOTAL 27：1/1

FORM OF DOC. 40A：IRREVOCABLE L/C

DOC. L/C NUMBER 20：T-117641

DATE OF ISSUE 31C：20181201

EXPIRY 31D：DATE 20190215 PLACE IN THE PEOPLE REP. OF CHINA

APPLICANT 50：POWER PLAY INC.

        2ND FLOOR，NO.137E 33RD STREET，LOS ANGLES，CA.90011，U. S. A.

BENEFICIARY 59：ZHEJIANG JIAXING WENSANG GARMENT CO. ，LTD.

        NO. 120 SOUTH FURUN ROAD，NANHU DISTRICT，JIAXING，CHINA

AMOUNT 32B：CURRENCY USD AMOUNT 39，600.00

POS/NEG TOL (%) 39A：5/5

AVAILABLE WITH/BY 41D：ANY BANK IN CHINA BY NEGOTIATION

DRAFTS AT 42C：AT 30 DAYS AFTER SIGHT FOR FULL INVOICE VALUE

DRAWEE 42D：UNION BANK OF CALIFORNIA N. A. ALL OFFICE IN U. S. A.

PARTIAL SHIPMENTS 43P：NOT ALLOWED

TRANSSHIPMENT 43T：NOT ALLOWED

PORT OF LOADING 44K：SHANGHAI

PORT OF DISCHARGE 44F：LOS ANGELES

LATEST DATE OF SHIPMENT 44C：20190131

SHIPMENT OF GOODS 45A：

DYED MEN'S SHIRTS COTTON 80 PCT POLYESTER 20 PCT OTIIKK DETAILS AS PER S/C NO.11JW1106

PACKING：ONE PC IN A POLYBAG AND 12 PCS INTO AN EXPORT CARTON. TOTAL INTO ONE 20′ FULL CONTAINER CIF LOS ANGELES

DOCUMENTS REQUIRED 46A：

+ COMMERCIAL INVOICE IN QUADRUPLICATE SHOWING FREIGHT CHARGE AND PREMIUM SEPARATELY.

+ FULL SET CLEAN ON BOARD BILLS OF LADING MADE OUT TO OUR ORDER MARKED FREIGHT PREPAID NOTIFY APPLICANT SHOWING FULL NAME AND ADDRESS.

+ INSURANCE POLICY OR CERTIFICATE IN DUPLICATE ISSUED BY PEOPLE'S INSURANCE COMPANY OF CHINA INCORPORATING THEIR OCEAN MARINE CARGO CLAUSES FREE FROM PARTICULAR AVERAGE DATED 01/01/2010 FOR 110 PERCENT OF CIF INVOICE VALUE INDICATING THE PREMIUM PAID.

+ DETAILED PACKING LIST IN TRIPLICATE.

+ CERTIFICATE OF ORIGIN IN DUPLICATE.

ADDITIONAL COND. 47A：

1.THE NUMBER AND THE DATE OF THIS L/C AND THE NAME OF OUR BANK MUST BE QUOTED ON ALL DRAFTS REQUIRED.

2.AN ADDITIONAL FEE OF USD 100.00 WILL BE DEDUCTED FROM THE PROCEED AND PAID UNDER ANY DRAWING WHERE DOCUMENTS PRESENTED ARE FOUND NOT TO BE IN STRICTLY CONFORMITY WITH THE TERMS OF THIS L/C 3.5 PCT MORE OR LESS BOTH IN AMOUNT AND QUANTITY ARE ALLOWED.

DETAILS OF CHARGES 71B：ALL BANKING CHARGES OUTSIDE THE ISSUING BANK INCLUDING ADVISING COMMISSION ARE FOR ACCOUNT OF BENEFICIARY AND MUST BE CLAIMED AT THE TIME OF ADVISING.

PRESENTATION PERIOD 48：NOT LATER THAN 15 DAYS AFTER THE DATE OF ISSUANCE OF THE SHIPPING DOCUMENTS BUT WITHIN THE VALIDITY OF THE L/C.

CONFIRMATION 49：WITHOUT.

INSTRUCTIONS 78：UPON OUR RECEIPT OF THE DOCUMENTS IN ORDER，WE WILL REMIT IN ACCORDANCE WITH NEGOTIATING BANK'S INSTRUCTIONS AT MATURITY.

其他相关资料：

数量：10 000件

单价：7.80美元/件

发票号码：ABC160116

毛重：14千克/箱

海运费：1 500美元

实际出运时，货物没有增减，完全按照合同所述出口。

唛头：POWER PLAY

    11JW1106

    LOS ANGELES

    NO.1-220

发票日期：2019年1月16日

发票签署：梁东

保险费：66美元

Chapter 5

Shipping Documents
装运单证

Learning Objectives

◆ 重点掌握海运提单的制作；掌握包装单的制作；了解各种形式的提单、包装单、装船通知。

Guide Case

Does it Constitute the Bad Notation of the Bill of Lading

A letter of credit opened by company A regulated: "Full set clean on board marine bills of lading ..." The goods of the beneficiary were shipped by container, and the filling in the bill of lading provided was: "Shipper's load and count, said to contain." But the documents sent to the issuing bank have been proposed " The L/C do not accept unclean bill of lading, and the bill of lading you provided is unclean bill of lading, so we can't accept it. Documents are temporarily taken care, at your disposal."

The beneficiary studied with the negotiating bank and agreed that the issuing bank's opinion was not in conformity with international practice. UCP600 regulates: "A clean transport document is one bearing no clause or notation expressly declaring a defective condition of the goods or their packaging. The word 'clean' need not appear on a transport document, even if a credit has a requirement for that transport document to be 'clean on board'." According to the above rules, the so-called unclean bill of lading was filling defect of goods itself or on the package. Our bill of lading was filled with "Shipper's load and count, content is according to the reports by consignor". So, it is not an unclean bill of lading.

Through contradiction of the negotiating bank, the issuing bank accepted the documents and paid interest of delay at last.

是否构成提单的不良批注

　　A公司开来一张信用证规定"全套清洁已装船海运提单……"。受益人的货装集装箱运输,提供的提单加注:"内容标明托运人装载和统计数。"但单据寄到开证行后被提出:"信用证不接受不清洁提单,而你方所提供的提单是不清洁提单,故不能接受。单据暂代保管,听候你方处理意见。"

　　受益人和议付行共同研究,一致认为开证行的意见不符合国际惯例。UCP600规定:清洁运输单据指未载有明确宣称货物或包装有缺陷的条款或批注的运输单据。"清洁"一词并不需要在运输单据上出现,即使信用证要求运输单据为"清洁已装船"的。按上述规定,所谓不清洁提单是加注商品本身或包装上存在缺陷情况的。我们提单注有"发货人装载及计数,内容据发货人报称",所以根本构成不了不清洁提单。

　　经过议付行反驳,开证行终于接受单据,并支付延误付款的利息。

International shipments of goods can be made by ocean going vessel, airplane, rail, truck, and barge on inland waterways, carrier or any combination of modes (multimodal). An individual shipment may be placed or packed in an ocean container, airfreight container (unit load device or ULD), in less than container load (LCL) shipments, in dry or wet bulk (such as grain, iron ore or crude oil) or in drums, sacks, or crates.

There are various shipping documents used in international shipments. They are bill of lading (in various form), packing list, shipping instructions, forwarder's instructions, stowage instructions, hazardous materials instructions/declaration, dock receipt, mate's receipt and captain's (or master's) protest. Among all the documents issued by different transport modes and packing means, the bill of lading is the most important.

The followings are the various documents used in international shipments. It's rarely seen that all of these documents are used in a single shipment, but we should understand each exists conceptually as requirements.

　　国际货物运输可以通过海洋运输、航空运输、铁路运输、公路运输、内河运输、邮政运输以及多种运输方式的组合(多式联运)等方式实现。货物可装在海运集装箱、空运集装箱(成组装运设备)中运输,或通过拼箱以及大宗货物运输的方式(如谷物、铁矿石或原油)进行。另外,其他的运输包装如桶、麻袋和板条箱等也是常用的方式。

　　国际运输有各种各样的装运单证,有提单(各种形式)、装箱单、装船指示、货运代理的通知、装载通知、有害物质声明、码头收据、大副收据和船长声明。在各种运输方式和包装方式下所签发的单证中,提单是最重要的一种单证。

　　以下将介绍国际货物运输中使用的各种单证。在一次单独运输中使用所有种类的单证并不常见,但是我们应该知道,每种规定的单证都有其独特性。

5.1 Bill of Lading
提　单

5.1.1 Definition of Bill of Lading
提单的定义

A bill of lading (B/L) is a key transport document that identifies the consignor, the consignee, the carrier, the mode of transport and other facts about the shipment (Sample 5-1).

A bill of lading is a document issued by a carrier to a shipper (exporter/seller/consignor), signed by a captain, agent, or owner of a vessel, furnishing written evidence regarding receipt of the goods (cargo), the conditions of transportation (based on contract of carriage), and the engagement to deliver goods at the prescribed port of destination to the lawful holder of the bill of lading.

A bill of lading is, therefore, both a receipt for merchandise and a contract to deliver it as freight. There are a number of different types of bills of lading and a number of issuers that related to them as a group of documents.

Negotiable document - a written document that can be transferred merely by endorsement (signing). Checks, bills of exchange, bills of lading, and warehouse receipts (if marked negotiable), and promissory notes are examples of negotiable instruments which can be bought and sold. Endorsement of such a document transfers the right to use money or goods described in the negotiable instrument to the holder of the document.

提单(B/L)是证明发货人、收货人、承运人、运输方式和其他运输事项的重要单据(见样单5-1)。

提单是由承运人签发给托运人(出口商/卖方/发货人)、由船长或其代理人或运输工具的所有人签发的单据,是签发人收讫货物和履行运输条件(根据运输合同要求)的书面证明。另外,提单还是提单签发人将货物送达约定目的港并交给提单合法持有人的书面承诺。

因此,海运提单既是一项收货凭证,又是一份运货合同。提单的种类很多,签发人也因实际情况有所不同。

可转让单据是仅可以通过背书(签字)的方式转让的书面文件。支票、汇票、提单、仓库收据(在标明可转让的情况下)和本票都是可以转让的支付工具,这些可转让的单据可以被购买、销售。被背书后,这些单据上的金额或货物的使用权就被转让给单据的持有人。

5.1.2 Types of Bills of Lading
提单的种类

In documentary letter of credit transactions, if multiple modes of transport are permitted, or partial shipments are allowed and part of the goods will be shipped by one mode of transport and part by another, it is necessary to put "or" or "and/or" between the names of the required transport

Sample 5-1
样单 5-1

Ocean Bill of Lading
海运提单

Shipper ABC COMPANY NO.128 ZHONGSHANXI ROAD, SHANDONG	B/L No.
Consignee TO ORDER OF UFJ BANK,TOKYO	**SINOTRANS** 中国外运广东公司 **SINOTRANS GUANGDONG COMPANY** **OCEAN BILL OF LADING**

SHIPPED on board in apparent good order and condition (unless otherwise indicated) the goods or packages specified herein and to be discharged at the mentioned port of discharge or as near thereto as the vessel may safely get and be always afloat.

The weight, measurement, marks and numbers, quality and value, being particulars furnished by the Shipper, are not checked by the Carrier on loading.

The Shipper, Consignee and the Holder of this Bill of Lading hereby expressly accept and agree to all printed, written or stamped provisions, exceptions and conditions of this Bill of Lading, including those on the back hereof.

IN WITNESS WHEREOF the number of original Bills of Lading stated below have been signed, one of which being accomplished the other(s) to be void.

Notify party		
XYZ COMPANY 6-2 OHTEMACHI, 1-CHOME CHIYADA-KU, TOKYO		
Pre-carriage by	Port of loading QINGDAO,CHINA	
Vessel VICTORY V.666	Port of transshipment	
Port of discharge TOKYO, JAPAN	Final destination	

Container No./seal No./ marks & Nos.	Number and kind of package	Description of goods	Gross weight (KGS)	Measurement (CBM)
XYZ TOKYO 04GD002 1-88 CTNS CONTAINER NO.PLU1234567 SEAL NO.006789 1×20′ CY/CY	PACKED IN 88 CTNS SHIPPEND IN ONE CONTAINER ON BOARD JAN. 18TH, 2019	HOSPITAL UNIFORM 5,250 PCS	1,232.00 KGS	4.20 CBM

Freight and charges	REGARDING TRANSSHIPMENT INFORMATION PLEASE CONTACT

Ex. rate	Prepaid at	Freight payable at	Place and date of issue QINGDAO, CHINA　　JAN. 17TH, 2019
	Total prepaid	No. of original B(s)/L 3(THREE)	Signed for or on behalf of the master 李好　　　　　　As Agent

documents. For example, if the goods are to be shipped by both sea and air, the letter of credit might specify "marine bill of lading and/or air waybill".

在跟单信用证项下,如果允许多式联运和分批装运,而且货物的不同批次由不同的运输工具装运,那么在信用证的运输单据要求中应使用"或"或者"和/或"字样。例如,如果货物通过海运和空运两种方式装运,那么信用证应注明"海运提单和/或航空运单"。

5.1.2.1　Straight Bill of Lading (Non-Negotiable)
　　　　　记名提单(不可流通转让)

1.Definition

A straight bill of lading indicates that the name of consignee in the consignee item. In this case, the goods will be delivered to the consignee only. To claim the goods, the consignee only needs to present identification. A straight bill of lading is often used when payment for the goods has already been made in advance or when the goods are shipped on open account. A straight bill of lading, therefore, cannot be negotiated or transferred by endorsement.

2.Key Elements

(1) Name of carrier with a signature identified as that of the carrier, ship master, or agent for the carrier or ship's master.

(2) An indication or notation that the goods have been loaded "on board" or shipped on a named vessel, also, the date of issuance or date of loading.

(3) An indication of the port of loading and the port of discharge.

(4) A sole original, or if issued in multiple originals, the full set of originals.

(5) The terms and conditions of carriage or a reference to the terms and conditions of carriage in another source or document.

(6) No indication that the document is subject to a charter party and no indication that the named vessel is propelled by sail only.

(7) Meets any other stipulations of the letter of credit (when applicable).

3.Notes

Because a non-negotiable bill of lading is not a title document, it eliminates many of the inconveniences of a bill of lading and offers advantages in situations where the rigid security of a bill of lading is not required. It reduces the opportunity for fraud and it removes the problems of goods arriving ahead of documents.

1.定义

记名提单的"收货人"一栏明确标示收货人的姓名。在这种情况下,货物只能交付给该收货人。收货人只要出示身份证件即可提货。在预付货款和赊销方式下可使用记名提单。记名提单不可流通,也不可通过背书的方式转让。

2.主要内容

(1)承运人名称和签字。其中,承运人、船长或两者的代理人均有签字权。

(2)货物已装船或已装指定船只的说明、签发日期或装船日期。

(3)装运港和卸货港名称。

(4)一套单独正本提单或一整套一式几份正本提单。

（5）运输条款和条件或对另外来源或单证的运输条款和条件的参考。

（6）无"本单据受制于某一个租船合同"等内容，也无"该指名船只是推动帆船"等内容。

（7）符合信用证的任何其他规定（在适用本提单的情况下）。

3.注释

不可流通提单并非契约文件，因此该类提单删除了许多普通提单的烦琐之处。当一份提单不需要严格的安全保障时，这是很便利的。这种方式降低了利用提单进行欺诈的机会，也解决了货物早于提单到达的问题。

5.1.2.2　Shipper's Order Bill of Lading (Negotiable)
　　　　托运人指示提单（可流通转让）

A shipper's order bill of lading is a title document to the goods, issued "to the order of" a party, usually the shipper, whose endorsement is required to effect in negotiation. Because it is negotiable, a shipper's order bill of lading can be bought, sold while the goods are in transit. These are highly favored for documentary letter of credit transactions. The buyer usually needs the original or a signed copy as proof of ownership to take possession of the goods.

托运人指示提单是一份契约文件。在这类提单中，收货人一栏应注明"由……指示"，通常为托运人。这时，托运人往往需要对提单进行背书以使之流通转让。因其流通转让的特性，这类提单可以在货物运输过程中被购买、销售。在跟单信用证交易中，这类提单被普遍使用。买方通常需要提单的正本或有签名的副本作为提货和拥有货物所有权的凭证。

5.1.2.3　Blank Endorsed Negotiable Bill of Lading
　　　　空白背书可转让提单

1.Definition

A blank endorsed negotiable bill of lading is one that has been endorsed without naming an endorsee. In simple terms, any person in possession of a blank endorsed negotiable bill of lading may claim possession of the goods. Possession of this document equals rights to possession of the shipment.

2.Key Elements

（1）Name of carrier with a signature identified as that of the carrier, ship master, or agent for the carrier or ship's master.

（2）An indication or notation that the goods have been loaded "on board" or shipped on a named vessel, also, the date of issuance or date of loading.

（3）An indication of the port of loading and the port of discharge.

（4）A sole original, or if issued in multiple originals, the full set of originals.

（5）The terms and conditions of carriage or a reference to the terms and conditions of carriage in another source or document.

（6）No indication that "the document is subject to a charter party" and no indication that "the named vessel is propelled by sail only".

（7）Meets any other stipulations of the letter of credit (when applicable).

3.Notes

(1) Vessel name. If a bill of lading includes the notation "intended vessel", it must also contain an "on board" notation of a named vessel along with the date of loading, even if the named vessel is the same as the intended vessel.

(2) Port of loading. If an L/C only specifies a general loading port or destination port, such as Chinese ports, or European ports, the specific port name should be filled according to the actual situation. If the document indicates a place where the goods are received by the carrier different from the port of loading, the document must also contain an "on board" notation indicating the port of loading as named in the letter of credit and the named vessel, along with the date.

(3) Transport documents. If a documentary letter of credit calls for a port-to-port shipment but does not call specifically for a marine bill of lading, the banks will accept a transport document, however named, that contains the above information. Banks will normally accept the following transport documents under this title: ocean bill of lading, combined transport bill of lading, provided it carries the notation "on board".

(4) Endorsement. If the documents are drawn up "the order of" the exporter or "to order", they must be endorsed. About means of endorsement: ① blank endorsement: only fill in the endorser's name and address. ② special endorsement: fill in both endorser's name and address, and the endorsee's (transfer objects of ocean marine bill of lading) name and address. ③ registered indicating endorsement: fill in both the endorser's name and address and the name and address of "TO ORDER OF + the endorsee's (ocean marine bill of lading transfer objects)".

(5) Transshipment. If a letter of credit prohibits transshipment, this document will be rejected if it specifically states that the goods will be transshipped.

(6) Transfer in transit. Since this is a negotiable instrument, it may be endorsed and transferred to the third party while the goods are in transit.

(7) Signature.

① Signed by a carrier. If the carrier is COSCO, signature of a bill of lading should be COSCO (the signature of carrier on behalf of) as carrier.

② Signed by a carrier agent. If the carrier is COSCO, the agent is ABC Shipping Co., signature of a bill of lading should be ABC Shipping Co. (the signature of agent on behalf of) as agent for the carrier COSCO.

③ Signed by a captain. If the carrier is COSCO, signature of a bill of lading should be COSCO (captain's signature) as the master.

④ Signed by the master agent. If the captain's name is XYZ, the agent is ABC Shipping Co., signature of a bill of lading should be ABC Shipping Co. (the signature of agent on behalf of) as agent for the master.

1.定义

空白背书提单即在背书时不注明被背书人的提单。简而言之,任何持有空白背书提单的人都可以提货。得到提单就意味着得到货物。

2.主要内容

(1)承运人名称和签字。其中,承运人、船长或两者的代理人均有签字权。

(2)货物已装船或已装指名船只的说明、签发日期或装船日期。

(3)装运港和卸货港名称。

(4)一套单独正本提单或一整套一式几份正本提单。

(5)运输条款和条件或对另外来源或单证的运输条款和条件的参考。

(6)无"本单据受制于某一个租船合同"等内容,也无"该指名船只是推动帆船"等内容。

(7)符合信用证的任何其他规定(在适用本提单的情况下)。

3.注释

(1)船名。如果提单中含有"预期船只"字样,即使该指定船只与预期船只是同一条船,那么该提单必须同时标示某指名船只"已装船"字样及装运日期。

(2)装运港。如果信用证中只笼统规定装运港或目的港名称,如中国港口或欧洲港口,应根据实际情况填写具体港口名称。如果提单中有承运人接货的地点,且该地点与装运港不同,那么提单在标明船名、装船日期以及信用证中规定的装运港时必须同时注明"已装船"字样。

(3)运输单证。如果跟单信用证中仅要求港至港运输,而并未要求必须提交海运提单,只要提交能体现以上信息的运输单证,银行即可接受。银行将接受以下类型的运输单证:海运提单、联合运输提单,只要这些单据注明"已装船"字样。

(4)背书。如果单据中注明"凭出口人指示"或"凭指示",那么该单据应被背书。关于背书方式:①空白背书(不记名背书),只书写背书人名称及地址;②记名背书,既书写背书人名称及地址,也书写被背书人(海运提单转让对象)名称及地址;③记名指示背书,既书写背书人的名称及地址,又要书写"TO ORDER OF +被背书人(海运提单转让对象)"的名称及地址。

(5)转运。如果信用证禁止转运,而单据标示货物将被转运,单据将被拒收。

(6)运输途中转让。因为这是可转让支付工具,因此货物在运输途中时该单据即可背书和转让给第三方。

(7)签署。

①承运人签署提单。如果承运人为COSCO,则提单签署应为作为承运人的COSCO(承运人代表签字)。

②承运人的代理人签署提单。如果承运人为COSCO,代理人为ABC船务公司,则提单签署应为作为承运人COSCO代理的ABC船务公司(承运人的代理人代表签名)。

③船长签署提单。如果承运人为COSCO,则提单签署应为COSCO的船长(船长代表签字)。

④船长的代理人签署提单。如果船长姓名为XYZ,代理人为ABC船务公司,则提单签署应为作为代理人的ABC船务公司(船长的代理人代表签字)。

5.1.2.4　Air Waybill
航空运单

An air waybill is a form of bill of lading used for the air transport of goods and is not negotiable (Sample 5-2).

Notes:

(1)In a letter of credit payment situation an air waybill should not be required to be issued "to order" or "to be endorsed" (since it is not a negotiable instrument). Also, since it is not negotiable, and it does not evidence title to the goods, in order to maintain some control of goods not paid for by cash in advance, sellers often consign air shipments to their sales agents or freight forwarders' agents in the buyer's countries.

(2) About the shipper. When direct shipping, the shipper is the owner. When collective shipping, the shipper is the freight agent. Under the payment by the L/C, the shipper is the beneficiary. When consigning dangerous goods, the shipper must be actual shipper, airlines don't accept freight agent checked.

(3) About the consignee. The air waybill must name a consignee (who can be the buyer). When direct shipping, the consignee is the actual consignee. When collective shipping, the consignee is the freight agent or overseas agent. The carrier generally will not accept two or more than two consignees in one lot. In fact, if there are more than two consignees, the consignee is the first consignee and the notify party is the second consignee.

(4) When loading airport or destination airport is not clear, the name of the city can be filled in.

航空运单是专用于航空运输货物的提单,该单据不可转让(见样单5-2)。

注释:

(1)在信用证支付方式下,航空运单不需要注明"凭指示"或"背书"(因为它不是可转让票据)。因其不可转让性,航空运单不具备物权凭证的性质。在非预付货款的情况下,卖方通常将空运货物的收货人填写为自己的销售代理或位于买方国家的货运代理,以便能在一定程度上对货物进行有效控制。

(2)关于托运人。直接托运时,托运人是货主;集中托运时,托运人是货运代理人。在信用证支付方式下,托运人是信用证受益人。托运危险货物时,托运人必须是实际托运人,航空公司不接受货运代理人托运。

(3)关于收货人。航空运单必须填写收货人名称(买方)。直接托运时,收货人是实际收货人;集中托运时,收货人是货运代理人或海外代理人。承运人一般不接受一票货物有两个或两个以上收货人。如果实际上有两个以上收货人,收货人是第一收货人,通知方是第二收货人。

(4)在始发站机场或目的站机场不明确时,可填写城市名称。

5.1.2.5　Courier Receipt
快件收据

A courier receipt is a document issued by a courier or delivery service evidencing receipt of goods for delivery to a named consignee and is not negotiable.

快件收据是由快件公司或送货机构签发的证明签发人收到货物并送至指定收货人的不可流通单据。

5.1.2.6　Post Receipt
邮政收据

A post receipt is a document issued by the postal service of a country evidencing receipt of goods for delivery to a named consignee.

邮政收据是由邮政公司签发的证明其收到货物并送至指定收货人的单据。

Sample 5-2

样单5-2

Air Waybill

航空运单

999			999-					
Shipper's Name and Address	Shipper's Account Number		Not Negotiable Air Waybill Issued by		中国国际航空公司 **AIR CHINA** BEIJING CHINA			
JIANGSU TEXTILE GARMENT CO., LTD. HUARONG MANSION RM2901 NO.85 GUANJIAQIAO,NANJING 210005, CHINA			Copies 1, 2 and 3 of this Air Waybill are originals and have the same validity.					
Consignee's Name and Address	Consignee's Account Number		It is agreed that the goods described herein are accepted for carriage in apparent good order and condition (except as noted) and SUBJECT TO THE CONDITIONS OF CONTRACT ON THE REVERSE HEREOF. ALL GOODS MAY BE CARRIED BY AND OTHER MEANS INCLUDING ROAD OR ANY OTHER CARRIER UNLESS SPECIFIC CONTRARY INSTRUCTIONS ARE GIVEN HEREON BY THE SHIPPER. THE SHIPPER'S ATTENTION IS DRAWN TO THE NOTICE CONCERNING CARRIER'S LIMITATION OF LIABILITY. Shipper may increase such limitation of liability by declaring a higher value for carriage and paying a supplemental charge if required.					
FASHION FORCE CO., LTD. P.O.BOX 8935 NEW TERMINAL, ALTA, VISTA OTTAWA, CANADA								
Issuing Carrier's Agent Name and City								
Agent's IATA Code	Account No.							
Airport of Departure (Addr. of First Carrier) and Requested Routing NANJING, CHINA			Accounting Information FREIGHT PREPAID					

To	By First Carrier	To	By	To	By	Currency	CHGS Code	WT/VAL		Other		Declared Value for Carriage	Declared Value for Customs
						USD		PPD	COLL	PPD	COLL		
								×		×			

Airport of Destination MONTREAL, CANADA	Flight No./Date for Carrier Use Only FX0910 APRIL 7, 2018	Amount of Insurance	INSURANCE-If Carrier offers insurance, and such insurance is requested in accordance with the conditions thereof, indicate amount to be insured in figures in box marked "Amount of Insurance".

Handling Information

(For USA only) These commodities licensed by U.S. for ultimate destination....................Diversion contrary to U.S. law is prohibited

No. of Pieces	Gross Weight	Kg lb	Rate Class	Commodity Item No.	Chargeable Weight	Rate Charge	Total	Nature and Quantity of Goods (incl. Dimensions or Volume)
1,700 CTNS	19,074.44	K	N		19,074.44	20.61	393,124.21	CANNED MUSHROOM PIECES & STEMS 24 TINS × 425 GRAMS

Prepaid Weight Charge 393,124.21	Collect	Other Charges AWC: 50.00
Valuation Charge		Shipper certifies that the particulars on the face hereof are correct and that insofar as any part of the consignment contains dangerous goods, such part is properly described by name and is in proper condition for carriage by air according to the applicable Dangerous Goods Regulations.
Tax		
Total other Charges due Agent		
Total other Charges due Carrier 50.00		Signature of Shipper or his Agent
Total Prepaid 393,174.21	Total Collect	7/APRIL/2018 NANJING,CHINA JIANGSU TEXTILE GARMENT CO., LTD.
Currency Conversion Rates	CC Charges in Dest. Currency	Executed on (date) at (place) Signature of Issuing Carrier or its Agent
For Carrier's Use only at Destination	Charges at Destination	Total Collect Charges	Air Waybill Number 999-

5.1.2.7 Multimodal Transport Bill of Lading
多式联运提单

1.Definition

A multimodal/combined transport bill of lading (Sample 5-3) is a single bill of lading covering a single shipment by more than one mode of transport (for example, by truck, then by rail and then by ship to its final destination). It is issued by a freight forwarder, logistics company, or carrier. In some instances the document may be filled in by the exporter consignor, and then signed by an agent of the carrier.

2.Notes

Even if a letter of credit prohibits transshipment, banks will accept a multimodal transport document that indicates that transshipment will or may take place, provided that the entire carriage is covered by one transport document.

A multimodal transport B/L issued by a freight forwarder is acceptable to banks in a letter of credit unless the credit stipulates specifically calls for a "marine bill of lading". The issuing freight forwarder accepts carrier responsibility for performance of the entire contract of carriage and liability for loss or damage wherever and however it occurs. As a rule, multimodal transport documents are not negotiable.

1.定义

多式联运提单(见样单5-3)是指一批货物经由一种以上的运输方式运输而签发的单据(例如,货物先由卡车运输,然后通过铁路运输,再由海运运至最终目的地)。多式联运提单可以由货运代理、物流公司或承运人签发。在某些情况下,可以先由出口托运人填好提单,然后由承运人代理签字。

2.注释

即使信用证禁止转运,只要是同一份包括全程运输的运输单证,银行也会接受注明货物将被转运或可被转运的多式联运提单。

在信用证下,银行接受由货运代理签发的联合运输提单,除非信用证规定必须使用"海运提单"。签发提单的货运代理承担运输合同中的全部承运人责任,并对在任何地点和任何情况下货物发生的损失或损害承担赔偿责任。按照惯例,多式联运单据是不可流通转让的。

5.1.2.8 Clean Bill of Lading
清洁提单

A clean bill of lading is one where the carrier has noted that the merchandise has been received in apparent good condition (no apparent damage loss, etc.) and that does not bear such notations as "shipper's load and count", etc. Most forms of documentary payments require a "clean" bill of lading in order for the seller to obtain payment.

清洁提单是指货物在装船时外表状况良好(无明显损伤等),承运人未加任何货损、包装不良等批注的提单,提单上无"由托运人装货和清点数量"等字样。在多数跟单支付情况下,卖方需提交"清洁"提单作为收付的条件。

5.1.2.9 Claused Bill of Lading
非清洁提单

Opposite of clean bill of lading, a claused bill of lading is one that contains notations that specify a shortfall in quantity or deficient condition of the goods and/or packaging. There are some

Sample 5-3
样单 5-3

Combined Transport Bill of Lading
联合运输提单

Shipper SHANGHAI FOREIGN TRADE IMP. AND EXP. CORP.	**PIL** B/L NO. PACIFIC INTERNATIONAL LINES (PTE) LTD. (Incorporated in Singapore) COMBINED TRANSPORT BILL OF LADING
Consignee TO ORDER	Received in apparent good order and condition except as otherwise noted the total number of containers or other packages or units enumerated below for transportation from the place of receipt to the place of delivery subject to the terms hereof. One of the signed Bills of Lading must be surrendered duly endorsed in exchange for the Goods or delivery order. On presentation of this document (duly) Endorsed to the Carrier by or on behalf of the Holder, the rights and liabilities arising in accordance with the terms hereof shall (without prejudice to any rule of common law or statute rendering them binding on the Merchant) become binding in all respects between the Carrier and the Holder as though the contract evidenced hereby had been made between them. SEE TERMS ON ORIGINAL B/L
Notify Party EAST AGENT COMPANY 126 ROOM STREET, ANTWERPEN, BELGIUM	

Vessel and Voyage Number DAFENG E002	Port of Loading NANJING, CHINA	Port of Discharge LONDON, UK
Place of Receipt	Place of Delivery ANTWERPEN, BELGIUM	Number of Original Bs/L 1(ONE)

PARTICULARS AS DECLARED BY SHIPPER-CARRIER NOT RESPONSIBLE

Container Nos./Seal Nos. Marks and/Numbers	No. of Containers/Packages/ Description of Goods	Gross Weight (KGS)	Measurement (CBM)
CBD LONDON NOS1-200	LADIES LYCRA LONG PANT	2,000 KGS	6 CBM

	Number of Containers/Packages (in words) ONE HUNDRED CARTONS ONLY.
FREIGHT & CHARGES FREIGHT PREPAID	Shipped on Board Date: OCT. 18, 2018
	Place and Date of Issue: NANJING,CHINA OCT. 20, 2018
	In Witness Whereof this number of Original Bills of Lading stated Above all of the tenor and date one of which being accomplished the others to stand void for PACIFIC INTERNATIONAL LINES (PTE) LTD. as Carrier.

circumstances in which transport documents with clauses are acceptable. For example, in the steel trade, such notations are the rule rather than the exception. If this is the case, the letter of credit should explicitly state which clauses will be deemed acceptable.

　　与清洁提单相反,非清洁提单是加有货物和/或包装存在短量、缺陷等问题的批注的提单。在某些情况下,附带有这些批注的提单是可以接受的。例如,在钢材贸易中,以上批注可以使用。在这种情况下,信用证应明确说明以上哪个条款是可以接受的。

5.1.2.10   Charter Party Bill of Lading
租船提单

A charter party bill of lading (Sample 5-4) is a transport document covering port to port shipments of goods issued by a party chartering a vessel. It is issued by the party chartering a vessel, specifically not a carrier.

Notes: the charter party bill of lading may have preprinted wording indicating that the shipment has been loaded "on board" the "named vessel", but the document must still be signed by the ship's master or owner, or an agent for the ship's master or owner.

If preprinted wording is used, the date of issuance is deemed to be the date of loading on board. In all other cases the document must contain an "on board" the "named vessel" notation along with the date the shipment is loaded on board.

租船提单（见样单5-4）是由租船方开立的港到港运输的运输单证。租船提单由租船方开立，特别注意的是租船方不是承运人。

Sample 5-4   Charter Party Bill of Lading
样单5-4   租船提单

Code Name: "CONGENBILL" EDITION 1978		BILL OF LADING B/L NO. TO BE USED WITH CHARTER PARTIES
Shipper SHANGHAI CHEMICAL IMP. & EXP. CORP. LTD. ROOM 610 NO.27, CHUNGSHAN ROAD E.1. SHANGHAI, 200001, CHINA		Reference No. SHIPCRAFT TRANSPORT INC. General Agents: SHIPCRAFT A/S
Consignee TO ORDER		P.O. B. 142 DK-2970 HOENSHOLM, DENMARK Phone:4-245781
Notify address ABCDIS CO. ASMBERSTRAAT 90, ANTWERPEN		Telex:37845 SHPCR DK Fax:4-258745 Agent for Switzerland: MAT TRANSPORT AG
Vessel CONIT. JORK V. YCJ009	Port of loading SHANGHAI, CHINA	ERLENSTRASSES 95 P.O.BOX CH40222 BASEL, SWITZERLAND
Port of discharge AQABA PORT, JORDAN		Phone:00616866000 Fax:0616666001
Shipper's description of goods 400 DRUMS NITROCELLULOSE FOR LACQUER		Gross weight 22,000 KGS
ORIGINAL		
(of which-0-(none) on deck at Shipper's risk; the carrier not being responsible for loss or damage however arising)		
Freight payable as per	SHIPPED at the Port of Loading in apparent good order and condition on board the vessel for carriage to the Port of Discharge or so near thereto as she may safely get the goods specified above. Weight, measure quality, quantity, condition, contents and value Unknown. IN WITNESS WHEREOF the Master or Agent of the said Vessel has signed the number of Bills of Lading indicated below all of this tenor and date. Any one of which being accomplish the others shall be void. FOR CONDITIONS OF CARRIAGE SEE OVERLEAF	
Charter-party dated JAN. 20TH, 2019		
Freight advance		
Received on account of freight		
Time used for loading___days___hours.		
Freight payable at	Place and date of issued SHANGHAI, CHINA JAN. 18TH, 2019	
Number of original B(s)/L THREE(3)	Signature	

注释:租船提单可能有如货物"已装上×××船(指定船只)"的内容,但是该提单必须由船长或船舶所有人或他们各自的代理人签字。

如果租船提单上有如上内容,那么提单的签发日即视为装船日期。在无如上内容的情况下,单据有货物"已装上×××船(指定船只)"字样时,必须同时标明装船日期。

5.1.2.11　Courier Receipt
快递收据

A courier receipt is a document issued by a courier or expedited delivery service evidencing receipt of goods for delivery to a named consignee. Courier receipts should include the following elements: the name of issuer, stamp, sign or authentication by the service, name and address of the shipper/consignor (seller), name and address of the consignee, the date of pick-up or receipt of the goods by the service.

快递收据是由快递员或加快送货服务公司出具的收到货物并交付给指定收货人证明的单证。快递收据应包括下列内容:开单人、邮戳、印章或服务标志的认证、(卖方)托运人/发货人名字和地址、收货人的名称和地址、邮寄或收货日期。

5.1.2.12　Post Receipt
邮政收据

A post receipt is a document issued by the postal service of a country evidencing receipt of goods for delivery to a named consignee. It is typically filled out by the exporter/seller/consignor, but then signed by an agent of the postal authority.

邮政收据是由国家的邮政公司开立的,证明送往指定收货人并收到货物的单证。一般由出口商/卖方/发货人填写,之后邮政公司代理人签署。

5.1.3　*Checklist for a B/L*
提单核对内容

(1) Are bills of lading in negotiable form if required in the letter of credit?

(2) Are all originals being presented to the bank or accounted for?

(3) Are all originals properly endorsed when consigned "to the order" of the shipper?

(4) Are bills of lading clean (no notation showing defective goods or packaging)?

(5) Do bills of lading indicate that merchandise is loaded on board and loaded within the time specified in the letter of credit? If this provision is not part of the text but in the form of a notation, is the notation dated and signed (initiated) by the carrier or its agent?

(6) Are the bills of lading made out as prescribed in the letter of credit (in other words, with names and addresses of beneficiary, applicant, notify parties, and flag, if any)?

(7) If freight was prepaid, is this payment clearly indicated by either "FREIGHT PREPAID" or "FREIGHT PAID"?

(8) If charter party, sailing vessel, on deck, forwarders, or consolidator's bills of lading is presented, does the credit specifically allow for them?

(9) Do marks and numbers, quantities, and the general description of goods agree with the commercial invoice and letter of credit, with no excess merchandise shipped?

（10）Does the bill of lading show transshipment if prohibited in the letter of credit?

（11）Is the document signed by the carrier or its agent? Are corrections, if any, signed or initiated by the carrier or agent?

（1）如果信用证要求提交可转让提单,提单是否已经满足信用证要求?

（2）是不是所有的正本提单都提交给银行或向银行说明了?

（3）当收货人栏填写"凭发货人指示"时,是不是所有的正本提单已被正确地背书?

（4）提单是否清洁(无货物或包装有缺陷的批注)?

（5）提单是否标明货物已装运并且在信用证规定的时间内装运? 如果这个内容不是提单的条款而是以批注的形式标示,那么这个批注是否附带装船期并由承运人或其代理人签字(姓名首字母)?

（6）提单内容是否符合信用证要求(换言之,如果有的话,是否标明受益人、开证申请人、通知人的名称和地址及标志)?

（7）如果运费已预付,那么提单上是否标示"运费预付"或"运费已付"?

（8）如果提交的是租船提单、帆船提单、甲板提单、货代提单或拼箱运输提单,信用证是否允许?

（9）提单上的运输标志和标识号、数量和商品描述是否与商业发票和信用证规定的一致? 货物是否多装?

（10）如果信用证禁止转运,提单上是否有转运的信息?

（11）提单是否由承运人或其代理人签字? 如果已签,签字是否正确? 是否签全名或姓名字首?

Training Case 5-1

A Damage Case Caused by Wrong Filling in "to Orderer" in a B/L

An export company A clinched a deal with Swiss businessman B. In the L/C opened abroad, the documents clause of Bill of Lading is specified as below: "Full set of clean on board ocean Bill of Lading made out to orderer marked freight prepaid." Company A made shipment according to the L/C and offered a Marine Bill of Lading according to the above requirement. The column of consignee in the bill of lading is filled "to orderer" according to the L/C. Ocean shipping agency proposed that they had never seen such filling in the consignee, whether it was "to order" without "er". The handling personnel in the company checked the L/C and told ocean shipping agency that the L/C was regulated like this and the bill of lading was exactly right. Otherwise it was unable to make settlement of exchange. When company A presented shipping documents to go through the formalities for negotiation, the negotiating bank put forward the objection of filling method of the consignee column in the bill of lading. The handling personnel in the company insisted that the filling method of in the bill of lading was no difference to that stipulation in the L/C. The L/C regulated "to the orderer", we also made out "to the orderer", and the bill of lading was issued by the captain in person. Besides the sailing ship already left port, it was difficult to change. Finally company A sent documents in a way of guarantee negotiation.

After documents were sent abroad, the issuing bank refused payment, the reason was that the filling method of the consignee in bill of lading was wrong, was not in conformity with the provisions of the requirements, and so can't be accepted. Documents were temporarily taken care of, at seller's disposal.

The negotiating bank notified company A the above condition which the issuing bank refused to pay. After company A finally negotiated with businessman B many times, it has been delayed for more than four months to recover the payment for goods, loss of more than $5,400.

提单错填"to Orderer"致损案

某出口公司A与瑞士商人B成交一笔交易。在国外开来的信用证中,其单据条款对提单做如下规定:"全套已装船清洁海运提单凭指示抬头,标明运费已付。"A公司即按证装船并提供了上述要求的海运提单。该提单的收货人栏按信用证说法填"to orderer"。外轮代理公司提出从未见过这样填制收货人,是否系"to order"之误,多了"er"。公司经办人员又核对了信用证并告诉外轮代理公司,信用证就是如此规定,提单制法完全正确,否则无法结汇。A公司向议付行交单办理议付手续时,议付行对提单收货人栏的填法又提出异议。A公司经办人员坚持认为该提单的填法与信用证规定丝毫不差,信用证规定"to orderer",我们也是"to orderer",并且该提单系船长亲自签发,何况船早已开航离港,难以更改。最后A公司以担保议付方式寄单。

单据寄达国外后,开证行提出拒付货款,其理由是提单的收货人填法有误,不符合规定的要求,故无法接受。单据暂代保管,听候卖方处理意见。

议付行即将上述开证行拒付货款的情况通知A公司。A公司最后通过驻外机构与B商洽商多次,拖延了4个多月才收回货款,损失5 400多美元。

Training Case 5-2

Company A exported goods and booked shipping space through the forwarder company B to a foreign shipping company C. After shipment, company C signed triplicate straight bill of lading issued by company A. After the goods reached the port of destination, the consignee on the straight bill of lading carried off all the goods from the hand of the company C without original bill of lading. Company A sued company C in the country with the reason that the carrier for shipment released goods without collection of bill of lading. (The bill of lading marked on applicable law in the United States. In the United States, when the carrier of registered makes delivery to the consignee of the original bill of lading, he/she is not responsible for the obligation that the registered consignee is required to present or submit original bill of lading.)

Please analyze and answer according to the theme:

(1) Which country's law is applicable for the case? Why?

(2) Is the carrier liable for shipment released without collection of bill of lading? Why? (Please state respectively according to the maritime law of the People's Republic of China and the United States.)

A贸易公司出口货物,并通过B货代公司向某国外班轮公司C订舱出运货物。货装船后,C公司向A公司签发一式三份记名提单。货到目的港,记名提单上的收货人在未取得正本提单的情况下,从C公司手中提走全部货物。A公司以承运人无单放货为由,在国内起诉C公司。(提单上注明适用美国法律。在美国,承运人向记名提单的记名收货人交付货物时,不负有要求记名收货人出示或提交记名提单的义务。)

　　请根据题意分析并回答:

　　(1)本案适用何国法律? 为什么?

　　(2)承运人是否承担无单放货责任? 为什么?(请根据《中华人民共和国海商法》和美国法分别阐述。)

5.2　Packing List
装箱单

A packing list (Sample 5-5) is a document made out by the seller stating the detailed contents of each individual shipment. It is a supplementary document to the commercial invoice used to make up the deficiency of an invoice by giving all the necessary particulars of the goods. A packing list is one of the documents required for mandatory inspection, export and import customs formalities and negotiation of payment. It is also used to facilitate the general checking of goods the before shipment by the seller. The buyer also needs a packing list to check the goods on their arrival at the destination. In addition, It can facilitate insurance claims and claims settlements in case of loss or damage.

A packing list is utilized to describe the way in which the goods are packed for shipment, such as number of packages, the types of packaging used, the weight of each package, the size of each package, and any marks that may be on the packages. Forms for packing lists are available through packing companies who prepare export shipments. Sometimes packing lists are required by the customs laws of foreign countries, but even if they are not, an important use of packing lists are for filing insurance claims if there are some damages or casualty to the shipment during transportation.

1.Contents of a Packing List

A packing list usually contains the following details:

(1)Invoice number.

(2)Buyer and consignee.

(3)Country of origin.

(4)Vessel or flight date.

(5)Port or airport of loading and discharge.

(6)Place of delivery.

(7)Shipping marks.

(8)Container number.

(9)Weight and/or volume of goods.

(10)Full details of goods.

2.Types of Packing Lists

(1)Packing list.

(2)Specification list.

(3)Weight list/weight memo.

(4)Measurement list.

(5)Neutral packing list.

(6)Packing declaration.

(7)Packing specification.

(8)Packing summary.

(9)Weight certificate.

(10)Assortment list.

3.Key Elements

(1)Name and address of seller (consignor)：name should correspond with the stipulations of the L/C.

(2)Name and address of buyer (consignee)：name should correspond with stipulations of the L/C.

(3)Date of issuance：should correspond with the invoice's.

(4)P/L number：should correspond with the invoice's.

(5)Order or contract number.

(6)Quantity and description of the goods.

(7)Weight of the goods：the gross weight, net weight, total gross and net weight should be listed and the numbers should correspond with other documents.

(8)Number of packages.

(9)Shipping marks.

(10)Quantity and description of contents of each package, carton, crate or container.

(11)Any other information as required in the shipper's instruction：generally, the unit price and the total amount are not stated.

4.Checklist for a Packing List

(1)Does the packing type shown agree with the commercial invoice?

(2)Does the quantity, or do the units, match the commercial invoice?

(3)Is the exact breakdown of merchandise per individual package shown, if required?

5.Main Points of Making out a Packing List

(1)Names should correspond with the stipulations of the L/C.

(2)The gross weight, net weight, total gross and net weight should be listed and the numbers should correspond with other documents.

(3)Generally, the unit price and the total amount are not stated and the number and issuing date should correspond with the invoice's.

装箱单(见样单5-5)是由出口商缮制,说明装运细节的单证,是商业发票的补充单证。在强制检验、进出口报关和议付货款时,装箱单是必备单证之一。对出口商来说,装箱单有助于货物装运前进行总体清点。买方也需要装箱单来检查货物抵达目的地的情况。此外,一旦损失或损坏发生,装箱单可使保险的索赔和理赔方便解决。

Sample 5-5

样单 5-5

Packing List

装箱单

To	NEO GENERAL TRADING CO. P.O.BOX 99552, RIYADH, 22766, KSA TEL: 00966-1-4659220 FAX: 00966-1-4659213			Invoice No.	2018SDT001	
				Invoice Date	APR. 16TH, 2018	
				S/C No.	NEO2018026	
				S/C Date	FEB. 28TH, 2018	
From	SHANGHAI, CHINA		To	DAMMAM, KSA		
Letter of Credit No.	0011LC123756		Date of Shipment	APR. 25TH, 2018		
Marks and Numbers	Number and Kind of Package/ Description of Goods	Quantity	Package	G.W	N.W	Meas.
ROSE BRAND 178/2018 RIYADH	ABOUT 1,700 CARTONS CANNED MUSHROOMS PIECES & STEMS 24 TINS × 425 GRAMS NET WEIGHT (D.W.227 GRAMS) ROSE BRAND	1,700 CTNS	1,700 CTNS	19,074 KGS	17,340 KGS	22.80 CBM
TOTAL		1,700 CTNS	1,700 CTNS	19,074 KGS	17,340 KGS	22.80 CBM
SAY TOTAL	ONE THOUSAND SEVEN HUNDRED CARTONS ONLY.					
				ABC CO. 张欢		

装箱单是描述货物装运方式的单据,如装运的包装数量,包装方式,每个包装的重量、尺寸以及包装上可能出现的任何标志。装箱单的表格由负责准备出口装运的包装公司提供。有些外国海关法中会规定提供装箱单,但即使无此规定,装箱单也有一个很重要的用途:当货物在运输途中受到损害或灭失时,装箱单是提出保险索赔的依据。

1.装箱单内容

装箱单通常包括以下内容:

(1)发票号码。

(2)买方和收货人。

(3)原产国。

(4)船舶或航班日期。

(5)装运和卸货的港口或机场。

(6)交货地点。

(7)运输标志(又称唛头)。

(8)集装箱号码。

(9)货物的重量和/或体积。

(10)货物的详细信息。

2.包装单种类

(1)装箱单/包装单。

(2)规格单。

(3)重量单/磅码单。

(4)尺码单。

(5)中性包装单。

(6)包装声明。

(7)包装说明。

(8)包装提要。

(9)重量证书。

(10)花色搭配单。

3.主要内容

(1)卖方(托运人)的名称地址:名称必须与信用证规定一致。

(2)买方(收货人)的名称地址:名称必须与信用证规定一致。

(3)签发日期:必须与商业发票日期一致。

(4)装箱单号码:必须与商业发票号码一致。

(5)订单或合同号码。

(6)商品描述和数量。

(7)货物重量:必须明确列出各类商品的毛重、净重以及毛重和净重的总值,装箱单上的重量必须与其他单据中的重量一致。

(8)包装数量。

(9)唛头。

(10)每个包装、纸箱、板条箱或集装箱所装商品的数量和描述。

（11）托运人指示要求的其他信息：一般来说，商品的单价和总值不标示在装箱单上。

4.装箱单核对内容

（1）包装方式是否与商业发票标示的一致？

（2）数量或单位是否与商业发票标示的一致？

（3）如果有规定，是否每个包装单位内所装商品的详细目录都根据要求标示？

5.缮制装箱单的要点

（1）装箱单上标示的名称应与信用证规定的一致。

（2）必须明确列出各类商品的毛重、净重以及毛重和净重的总值，装箱单上的重量必须与其他单据中的重量一致。

（3）一般来说，装箱单上不标示单价和总金额；装箱单号码和签发日期应与商业发票一致。

5.3　Other Certificates
　　其他证明

（1）Certificate of shipping company.

（2）Certificate of ship's nationality.

（3）Certificate of vessel's age.

（4）Certificate of classification.

（5）Black list certificate.

（6）Master/Captain's receipt.

（7）Beneficiary's certificate.

（8）Beneficiary's certificate for dispatch of documents.

（1）船公司证明。

（2）船籍证明。

（3）船龄证明。

（4）船级证明。

（5）黑名单证明。

（6）船长收据。

（7）出口公司(受益人)证明。

（8）出口公司(受益人)寄单证明。

Training Case 5-3

　　Businessman A signed a sales contract with American Businessman B, which regulated that canned pineapples should be packed into cartons, 40 tins each carton. Seller A shipped and delivered the goods according to the requirement of the contract, but 40 tins of canned goods were lack of inventory, with 30 tins in a small carton instead. After the goods reached the port of destination, the buyer rejected the whole batch of goods on the grounds that the packaging was not in conformity with the provisions of the contract, the seller insisted that the buyer should accept all the goods because the buyer at the location confirmed that the price of canned pineapple, 30 tins or 40 tins each carton, was the same. Was it reasonable that the buyer refused to accept the whole goods? Why?

A商与美商B签订销售合同,合同规定菠萝罐头装入箱内,每箱40听。卖方A商按合同的要求发运并交付货物,但其中一部分因40听装货物库存不足,就以30听的小箱来代替。货到目的港后,买方以包装不符合合同规定为由拒收整批货物,卖方则坚持买方应接受全部货物,理由是在买方所在地证实了,不论是每箱30听装或者40听装的菠萝罐头,它们的市场价格是完全相同的。买方拒收整批货物是否合理? 为什么?

Training Case 5-4

Businessman B in our country signed a contract with French businessman C, which regulated that payment should be made by the L/C. We shipped the goods on time, made out a full set of documents as required, and submitted documents to the issuing bank for payment, but the issuing bank dishonored. The reason was that the name of the packing list in the L/C requirement was "Detailed Packing List", and the name of the packing list we made was "Packing List". Documents were not in conformity with the L/C, therefore they refused to pay. Now please answer: Was it reasonable that the issuing bank refused to pay? Why?

我国B商与法国C商签订出口合同,合同规定以信用证支付,我方按时发运货物,制作信用证要求的全套单据,向开证行交单并要求付款,但遭到开证行的拒付,理由是在信用证中装箱单的名称要求是"Detailed Packing List",而我方制作的装箱单的名称只是"Packing List",单证不符,因此拒付。请问:开证行的拒付是否合理? 为什么?

Key Terms

bill of lading提单   packing list装箱单

Exercise

◎ *Case Analysis*

An owner shipped a batch of goods through a NVOCC and issued a H-B/L. The NVOCC delivered the goods to a shipping company. And a CIF contract of daily articles regulated "shipment in September", that is, the validity of the L/C was on October 15. And the documents submitted to the bank for negotiation on October 6 included clean on board bill of lading issued on September 29. Upon examination and approval by the bank, the bank accepted the documents and made payment for goods. But after the buyer received the goods, they found that the goods were badly damaged, and a shortage of 50 cartons. Therefore the buyer refused to accept the goods and required to refund payment. Q:

(1)Did the buyer have the right to refuse to accept the goods and demand a refund? Why?

(2)How the buyer should deal with in the case reasonably?

一货主将一批货交由无船承运人运输,并签发H-B/L,无船承运人将货物交给船公司。买卖日用品的CIF合同规定"9月份装运",即期信用证的有效期为10月15日。卖方10月6

日向银行办理议付所提交的单据,包括9月29日签发的已装船清洁提单。经银行审核,银行接受单据并支付了货款。但买方收到货物后,货物受损严重,且短少50箱。买方因此拒绝收货,并要求卖方退回货款。问题:

(1)买方有无拒收货物并要求退款的权利,为什么?

(2)此案中的买方应如何合理处理此事?

◎ *Practice*

Practice 1

请根据下述信用证条款及其他资料,以货运代理人身份填制海运提单。

(1)信用证条款:

ISSUING BANK:METITA BANK LTD. FIN-00020 METITA,FINLAND

TERM OF DOC. L/C:IRREVOCABLE

CREDIT NUMBER:KHL12-22457

DATE OF ISSUE:20180505

EXPIRY DATE AND PLACE:20180716, CHINA

APPLICANT:FFK CORP. AKEKSANTERINK AUTO P. O. BOX 9,FINLAND

BENEFICIARY:GUANGDONG RONGHUA TRADE CO. ,LTD.

　　　　　　　168 DEZHENG ROAD SOUTH,GUANGZHOU,CHINA

AMOUNT: CURRENCY USD 38,400. 00

POS./NEG. Tol.(%):5/5

AVAILABLE WITH/BY:ANY BANK IN ADVISING COUNTRY BY NEGOTIATION

PARTIAL SHIPMENTS:NOT ALLOWED

TRANSSHIPMENT:ALLOWED

LOADING IN CHARGE:GUANGZHOU

FOR TRANSPORT TO:HELSINKI

SHIPMENT PERIOD:AT THE LATEST JULY 16,2018

DESCRIPTION OF GOODS:9,600 PCS OF WOMEN'S SWEATERS

UNIT PRICE: USD 4. 00/PC,OTHER DETAILS AS PER S/C NO. 98GQ468001

PACKING: 12 PCS/CTN CFR HELSINKI (INCOTERMS 2010)

DOCUMENTS REQUIRED:FULL SET OF CLEAN ON BOARD MARINE BILLS OF LADING,
　　　　　　　　　　MADE OUT TO ORDER OF THE ISSUING BANK,MARKED
　　　　　　　　　　"FREIGHT PREPAID" AND DOC. COLLECT, SHOWING
　　　　　　　　　　INSURANCE PREMIUM, SURCHARGE AND TRADE TERMS
　　　　　　　　　　NOTIFY APPLICANT

ADDITIONAL CONDITION:

a. T. T. REIMBURSEMENT IS PROHIBITED.

b. ALL DOCUMENTS MUST BE MARKED THE S/C NO. AND THE L/C NO.

(2)其他资料:

提单号码:KTT1245678　　　　　　　货物总毛重:6,500 KGS

货物总尺码:25 CBMS　　　　　　　唛头:ABC/HELSINKI/NO. 1-800

船名:第一程:DONGFANG　　　第二程:MAKIS V. 002

转运港:中国香港　　　　　　集装箱号码:SIHUSSSASYDQCD

SEAL NO.123456 CY/CY　　　附加费:USD 300.00

提单签发地点:广州　　　　　承运人代理人:XYZ SHIPPING CO.

保险费:USD 100.00　　　　　提单签发日期:2018年7月10日

承运人:ABC SHIPPING CCX　　提单签发人:李溪

提单装船批注日期:2018年7月11日

货物由托运人负责装箱、计数及封箱,整箱装,由集装箱堆场至集装箱堆场。

Shipper		B/L NO.
	≡≡PIL	
	PACIFIC INTERNATIONAL LINES (PTE) LTD.	
	(Incorporated in Singapore)	
	COMBINED TRANSPORT BILL OF LADING	
Consignee	Received in apparent good order and condition except as otherwise noted the total number of containers or other packages or units enumerated below for transportation from the place of receipt to the place of delivery subject to the terms hereof. One of the signed Bills of Lading must be surrendered duly endorsed in exchange for the Goods or delivery order. On presentation of this document (duly) Endorsed to the Carrier by or on behalf of the Holder, the rights and liabilities arising in accordance with the terms hereof shall (without prejudice to any rule of	
Notify Party	common law or statute rendering them binding on the Merchant) become binding in all respects between the Carrier and the Holder as though the contract evidenced hereby had been made between them.　SEE TERMS ON ORIGINAL B/L	
Vessel and Voyage Number	Port of Loading	Port of Discharge
Place of Receipt	Place of Delivery	Number of Original B(s)/L

PARTICULARS AS DECLARED BY SHIPPER-CARRIER NOT RESPONSIBLE

Container Nos./Seal Nos. Marks and Numbers	No. of Containers/Packages/ Description of Goods	Gross Weight (KGS)	Measurement (CBM)
Freight & Charges	Number of Containers/Packages (in words)		
	Shipped on Board Date:		
	Place and Date of Issue:		
	In witness whereof this number of original bills of lading stated above all of the tenor and date one of which being accomplished the others to stand void for PACIFIC INTERNATIONAL LINES (PTE) LTD. as carrier		

Practice 2

广东省荣华贸易有限公司与芬兰ABC公司成交一笔出口交易。ABC公司按期开来信用证,荣华公司按期出运,并填制好海运提单,请根据下面信用证提供的内容审核海运提单编号①至⑧的内容,对单证不符的内容进行修改。

ISSUING BANK: METITA BANK LTD. FIN-00020 METITA, FINLAND

TERM OF DOC. L/C: IRREVOCABLE

L/C NUMBER: LRT9802457

DATE OF ISSUE: 20180505

EXPIRY DATE AND PLACE: 20180716, CHINA ABC CORP.

APPLICANT: AKEKSANTERINK AUTO P. O. BOX 9, FINLAND

BENEFICIARY: GUANGDONG RONGHUA TRADE CO., LTD.

        168 DEZHENG ROAD SOUTH, GUANGZHOU, CHINA

AMOUNT: CURRENCY USD 36,480. 00 (SAY US DOLLARS THIRTY-SIX THOUSAND FOUR HUNDRED AND EIGHTY ONLY.)

POS./NEG. TOL. (%): 5/5

AVAILABLE WITH/BY: ANY BANK IN ADVISING COUNTRY BY NEGOTIATION

PARTIAL SHIPMENTS: NOT ALLOWED

TRANSSHIPMENT: ALLOWED

LOADING IN CHARGE: GUANGZHOU

FOR TRANSPORT TO: HELSINKI

SHIPMENT PERIOD: AT THE LATEST JULY 16, 2018

DESCRIPTION OF GOODS: 9,600 PCS OF WOMEN'S SWEATERS

UNIT PRICE: USD 3. 80/PC, OTHER DETAILS AS PER S/C NCX 98GQ468001

PACKING: 12 PCS/CTN TOTAL 800 CTNS CFR HELSINKI (INCOTERMS 2010)

DOCUMENTS REQUIRED: FULL SET OF CLEAN ON BOARD MARINE BILLS OF
                  LADING, MADE OUT TO ORDER OF METITA BANK LTD.,
                  FINLAND, MARKED "FREIGHT PREPAID" AND NOTIFY
                  APPLICANT (AS INDICATE ABOVE)

ADDITIONAL COND.:

T.T. REIMBURSEMENT IS PROHIBITED.

ALL DOCUMENTS MUST BE MARKED THE S/C NO. AND L/C NO.

SHIPPING MARKS: ABC
        HELSINKI
        NO. 1-800

1. Shipper Insert Name, Address and Phone GUANGDONG RONGHUA TRADE CO., LTD. 168 DEZHENG ROAD SOUTH, GUANGZHOU, CHINA ①		B/L No. Port-to-Port or Combined Transport **BILL OF LADING** RECEIVED in external apparent good order and condition except as otherwise noted. The total number of packages or unites stuffed in the container, the description of the goods and the weights shown in this Bill of Lading are finished by
2. Consignee Insert Name, Address and Phone ABC CORP. AKEKSANTERINK AUTO P. O. BOX 9, FINLAND ②		the Merchants, and which the carrier has no reasonable means of checking and is not a part of this Bill of Lading contract. The carrier has issued the number of Bills of
3. Notify Party Insert Name, Address and Phone METITA BANK LTD. FIN-00020 METITA, FINLAND ③		Lading stated below, all of this tenor and date. One of the original Bills of Lading must be surrendered and endorsed or signed against the delivery of the shipment and
4. Combined Transport Pre-carriage by	5.Combined Transport Place of Receipt	whereupon any other original Bills of Lading shall be void. The Merchants agree to be bound by the terms and conditions of this Bill of Lading as if each had personally signed this Bill of Lading.
6. Ocean Vessel Voy. No. SUISUN 103	7. Port of Loading GUANGZHOU	SEE clause 4 on the back of this Bill of Lading (Terms
8. Port of Discharge HELSINKI VIA HONG KONG	9. Combined Transport Place of Delivery	continued on the back hereof, please read carefully). Applicable Only When Document Used as a Combined Transport Bill of Lading.

Marks & Nos; Container/ Seal No.	No. of Containers or Packages; Description of Goods (If Dangerous Goods, See Clause 20)	Gross Weight (KGS)	Measurement (CBM)
N/M ④	9,600 PCS WOMEN'S SWEATERS ⑤ TOTAL: EIGHT HUNDRED CARTONS ONLY. ⑥ S/C NO. LRT9802457 ⑦	13,600.00 KGS FREIGHT COLLECT ⑧	25 CBM

Description of Contents for Shipper's Use Only (Not Part of This B/L Contract)

10. Total Number of Containers and/or Packages (in words)

Subject to Clause 7 Limitation						
11. Freight & Charges		Revenue Tons	Rate	Per	Prepaid	Collect
Declared Value Charge						

Ex. Rate	Prepaid at	Payable at	Place and Date of Issue GUANGZHOU, MAY 5, 2018
	Total Prepaid	No. of Original B(s)/L THREE(3)	

Laden on Board the Vessel	
Date	By

Practice 3

根据给出的资料填制航空运单。

Applicant：YYY TRADING CO.，LTD.

220 SIGMUND STR 80035 NOLA (ITALY)

Beneficiary：GUANGDONG ABC IMPORT & EXPORT COMPANY LTD.

NO. 188 XIAOGANG ROAD，GUANGZHOU

Loading in Charge：GUANGZHOU

For Transport to：MILAN，ITALY

Description of Goods：1,700 PCS OF LADIES' 55% RAMIE 36% WOOL 9% NYLON KNITTED SWEATER CFR MILAN AIRPORT AS PER SALES CONFIRMATION NO. 2018MCGS02007 DD8. 3. 2018

TOTAL AMOUNT：USD 12,614. 00

Documents Required：CLEAN AIR WAYBILL FOR GOODS AIRFREIGHTED TO YYY TRADING CO., LTD. 220 SIGMUND STR 80035 NOLA (ITALY) MARKED FREIGHT PREPAID AND EVIDENCING THAT ORIGINAL INVOICE AND PACKING LIST ACCOMPANY THE GOODS NOTIFY APPLICANT

航空运单填开日期：MAY 25, 2018

始发站：GUANGZHOU

航班号及日期：CA1234/26，MAY 2018

唛头：YYY/MILAN/NOS. 1-40

航空运单填开地点：GUANGZHOU

货物装箱情况：1,700 PCS/40 CTNS

总毛重：420 KGS

计费重量：400 KGS

计费货币：USD

航空运单号码：03030030509

填开货运单的代理人名称：XYZ CARGO

尺码：30×40×20 CM

航空运单注明没有声明价值和没有商业价值。

Shipper's name and address	Not Negotiable
	Air Waybill
	中国国际航空公司
Consignee's name and address	Issued by AIR CHINA
	It is agreed that the goods described herein are accepted for carriage in apparent good order and condition (except as noted) and SUBJECT TO THE CONDITIONS OF CONTRACT ON THE REVERSE HEREOF. ALL GOODS MAY BE CARRIED BY ANY OTHER MEANS INCLUDING ROAD OR ANY OTHER CARRIER UNLESS SPECIFIC CONTRARY INSTRUCTIONS ARE GIVEN HEREON BY THE SHIPPER. THE SHIPPER'S ATTENTION IS DRAWN TO THE NOTICE CONCERNING CARRIER'S LIMITATION OF LIABILITY.
Issuing Carrier's Agent Name and City	
Agent's IATA Code　　Account No.	Shipper may increase such limitation of liability by declaring a higher value of carriage and paying a supplemental charge if required.

Airport of Departure (Add. of First Carrier) and Requested Routing	Accounting Information

To	By first carrier	To	By	To	By	Currency	WT/VAL	Declared Value for Carriage	Declared Value for Customs
							PP CC		

Airport of Destination	Flight No.	Flight Date	Amount of Insurance	INSURANCE - If carrier offers insurance and such insurance is requested in accordance with the conditions thereof indicate amount to be insured in figures in box marked "Amount of Insurance"

Handling Information
(For USA only) These commodities licensed by US for ultimate destination.................Diversion contrary to US law is prohibited.

No. of Pieces	Gross Weight	Kg Lb	Rate Class	Chargeable Weight	Rate Charge	Total	Nature and Quantity of Goods

Prepaid Weight Charge	Collect	Other Charges
Valuation Charge		Shipper certifies that the particulars on the face hereof are correct and that insofar as any part of the consignment contains dangerous goods, such part is properly described by name and is in proper condition for carriage by air according to the applicable Dangerous Goods Regulations.
Tax		
Total other Charges due Agent		
Total other Charges due Carrier		--
		Signature of Shipper or His Agent
Total Prepaid	Total Collect	
Currency Conversion Rates	CC Charges in Dest. Currency	--
		Executed on　　　at　　　　Signature of Issuing Carrier or Its Agent
For Carrier's Use Only at Destination	Charges at Destination	Total Collect Charges	Air Waybill Number
			999-80693231

Chapter 6
Export Documents
出口单证

Learning Objectives

◆ 重点掌握一般原产地证书和海关发票;掌握出口许可证、货物报检单、出口货物报关单、装船通知、保险单、汇票和加拿大海关发票;了解订舱单。

Guide Case

A certain company received an L/C from abroad, which regulated "ship on or about May 15". The company made shipment on May 8 and submitted a bill of lading issued on May 8 to the bank. But it was refused to pay. Question: why?

某公司接到国外开来的信用证,规定"于或约于5月15日装船"。该公司于5月8日装船,并向银行提交了一份5月8日签发的提单,但遭到银行拒付款。请问:这是为什么?

The successful completion of a single transaction may involve many documents. They may include government granted documents such as export license and quota, commercial documents such as commercial invoice and packing list, transport documents such as bill of lading and shipping advice, insurance documents such as insurance policy or insurance certificate, and financial documents such as letter of credit. Some documents are used for very specific reasons and then only required at certain stage, others such as commercial invoice and packing list are of more general uses, appearing at most of the stages throughout the performance of a transaction.

To fully illustrate the sophistication of export documents, the next part will develop an extensive discussion about the various kinds of documents, following the fulfillment of a CIF contract which requires payment by the L/C. The reason to choose such a contract is two folded. On one hand, transactions of this type are very common in practice; On the other hand, such contract requires the use of documents of the greatest number and variety when comparing with others. It can provide a full picture of the documents practice with consideration satisfaction.

一笔交易的成功可能会涉及许多种单证,如出口许可证和配额等政府授予的单证、商业发票和装箱单等商业单证、提单和装船通知等运输单证、保险凭证和保险单等保险单证以及信用证等资金单证。有些单证由于特殊原因只在特定环节中运用,而商业发票和装箱单等单证则被普遍使用,贯穿整个交易的全过程。

为了将复杂的出口单证全面翔实地介绍给大家,本章的以下内容将对不同类型的单证进行广泛的讨论,随后将介绍一份以信用证为支付方式的 CIF 合同的填写方法。选择介绍这类合同有两个方面的原因:一方面,这类交易在实践中应用得非常广泛;另一方面,相对于其他合同,这类合同要求的单证数量和种类都是最多的。通过介绍,可以最大程度了解到制单的全部过程。

6.1　Documents Required before or at Contract Negotiations 合同谈判之前或之中所需的单证

Before the negotiation of the contract, the seller is expected to apply for export license or at least make sure that he is able to obtain it if the commodity he is to sell falls under the export control. During the negotiation of the terms and conditions of a contract, sometimes offers are made on a Proforma Invoice (details as section 4.3.4), which in this case should only be seen as a form of quotation. After acceptance is made at the end of the negotiation, the seller and the buyer will draft a sales contract which can be referred back to chapter 1.

Export license is issued by the export authority or government agency with regulatory authority of a country of export. They are often required for the export of certain natural resources, cultural relics, drugs, technology, live animals, food products, strategic commodities, and arms and armaments.

Export license is the first document a seller has to prepare when he intends to export commodities that are under export control of his country. Export license is issued by the government or its authorized institutions and required at the time of customs clearance. The goods under export control normally include the main raw materials, machinery or equipment in short supply, military or other goods relating to national security, and works of art and antiques which are of national, cultural or historical importance. In some cases the licensing system is used to implement government policy such as economic sanctions against certain countries.

1.Definition

Export license is a document granting an individual or business entity the general right to export or the right to export a specific shipment of a commodity or good to a named country (Sample 6-1).

2.Certain Elements Are Likely to Be Included in All Export Licenses

(1)Name and address of seller, name and address of buyer.

（2）Date of issuance, validity date.

（3）Description of goods.

（4）Name of country of origin.

（5）Name of country of ultimate destination.

（6）Statement that the goods will not be diverted to another country contrary to the laws of the exporting country.

3.Notes

The license is a means of control, taxation and statistical reporting. In some cases the lack of export license can be cited as a reason why goods cannot be shipped, even though payment has been made. Buyers should be especially careful about buying sensitive goods from countries with a demonstrated lack of rule by law.

Export license is typically the seller's responsibility. However, a buyer who is dealing in sensitive goods should research the need for export license beforehand. Failure to secure such a license can delay or prevent shipment and can jeopardize the validity of a payment such as a documentary letter of credit.

如果预售的商品受到国家出口管制，那么在合同谈判开始前，卖方应已经申请到或至少保证能申请到出口许可证。在合同条件和条款的谈判中，有时候发盘会做成形式发票（详见4.3.4部分），这时它的作用仅是报价单而已。在谈判临近结束，双方都接受对方的条件时，买卖双方将起草一份销售合同，相关内容可以参考第1章。

出口许可证是由出口监管机构或政府代理机构开立的。出口某些自然资源、文物、药物、技术、活的动物、食品、战略物资、武器及军备通常要求提供出口许可证。

如果卖方计划销售本国出口管制的商品，那么出口许可证将是第一个需要准备的单证。出口许可证由政府或其授权部门签发，并需在办理清关手续时出示。受到出口管制的商品一般包括主要的原材料、短缺的机器设备、军用物资或其他涉及国家安全的商品，以及对国家、文化和历史都有重要意义的艺术品和文物。有时候许可制度是国家执行政策的一种方式，如一国对某些特定国家实行经济制裁时，许可制度就是一个有效的方式。

1.定义

出口许可证是授予某个人或企业一般出口权或有权出口某特定商品到指定国家的单证（见样单6-1）。

2.出口许可证包括的内容

（1）卖方的名称和地址、买方的名称和地址。

（2）签发日期和有效期。

（3）商品说明书。

（4）原产地名称。

（5）最终目的地的国家名称。

（6）货物不会转移到另一国而违反出口国法律的声明。

Sample 6-1　　　　**Export License of the People's Republic of China (A)**

样单6-1　　　　　　　　**中华人民共和国出口许可证(A类)**

申领许可证单位 Exporter	编码　195762654 福州毛织品进出口贸易公司	出口许可证编号 License No.	2019122433
发货单位 Consignee	195762654 福州毛织品进出口贸易公司	许可证有效期 Validity	2019-12-31
贸易方式 Terms of trade	一般贸易	输往国家(地区) Country of destination	加拿大
合同号 Contract No.	ST303	付款方式 Terms of payment	信用证
出运口岸 Port of shipment	福州	运输方式 Means of transport	江海

唛头/包装件数 Marks & numbers/number of packages	无唛头　98箱

商品名称 Description of commodity	全棉抹布	商品编码 Commodity code	888.666

商品规格、型号 Specification	单位 Unit	数量 Quantity	单价(美元) Unit price	总值(人民币) Amount	总值折美元 Amount in USD
10"×10"	打	16,000	1.31	136,240.00	20,960.00
20"×20"	打	6,000	2.51	97,890.00	15,060.00
30"×30"	打	11,350	4.73	348,955.75	53,685.50
总计 Total	打	33,350		583,085.75	89,705.50

备注 Supplementary details	发证机关盖章 Issuing authority's stamp 发证日期 Signature date

商务部监制　　　　　　　　　　　　　　　　　　　　本证不得涂改,不得转让

3.注意事项

许可证是一种管制、税收和统计手段。在某些情况下,即使付款了,但缺乏出口许可证,也可成为货物不能装运的原因。买家应特别小心从缺乏法律规范的国家购买敏感货物。

出具出口许可证通常是卖方的责任。然而,购买敏感货物的买家应该事先研究是否需要出口许可证。无许可证会延迟或妨碍装运并且影响跟单信用证的付款有效期。

6.2 Documents Involved in Goods Preparations
备货时涉及的单证

After the seller has got the goods prepared and packed, he will then issue a commercial invoice (details as section 4.3.7) and a packing list (details as section 5.2). Both documents are very important and required in all main stages of an export procedure.

当出口商将货物准备和包装好之后,他将会签发一份商业发票(详见4.3.7部分)和一份装箱单(详见5.2部分)。这两份单证都很重要,而且它们的应用将贯穿整个出口的主要过程。

6.3 Documents Concerning Mandatory Inspections
与强制检验有关的单证

If the goods need to go through mandatory inspection required by the stipulations of the government or the contract, the seller has to apply for it by filling out an inspection application form. After inspection, if the goods are up to the required standard, the seller will receive the relevant inspection certificate from the inspection body.

如果根据国家规定或合同的要求,货物必须进行强制检验的话,那么卖方应填写检验申请表。经检验,如果货物符合检验标准,那么卖方将收到一份由检验机构签发的相关检验证书。

6.3.1 *Export Commodity Inspection Application*
出口商品检验申请书

Export commodity inspection application is one of the essential domestic documents for the export of many commodities in China. The state administration for commodity inspection, in the light of the needs in the development of international trade, makes, adjusts and publishes a list of import and export commodities subject to inspection by the commodity inspection authorities. The export of commodities on this list is not allowed until they have been inspected. Therefore, if the goods of the seller are on this list, he is required to fill out an application form to apply for inspection.

Upon submission, he will also be asked to present other documents such as the sales contract, the letter of credit, the commercial invoice, and the packing list. In some cases, only the inspection report supplied by the manufacturer is required.

出口商品检验申请书是众多中国出口商品必备的国内单证之一。国家商检机构根据国际贸易发展的需要制定、调整和发布必须由商品检验机构检验的进出口商品目录。在此目录上的商品未经检验不允许出口。因此,如果出口商预售的商品属于目录内商品,那么出口商必须填写申请表,申请检验。

提交表格时,出口商同时还需出示销售合同、信用证、商业发票和装箱单等单证;但在一些情况下只需提交制造商提供的检验报告即可。

6.3.2　*Inspection Certificate*

检验证书

1.Definition

Inspection certificate is a document indicating the results of the inspection of the goods in terms of quality, quantity or any other element that has been specified. Inspection certificate may be issued by a government institution, surveyors of chamber of commerce or an independent service company. Inspection certificates are required when the goods are cleared for export and import and when the seller negotiates payment at the bank.

Its primary function is to ensure that the goods are meeting the relevant requirements stipulated by certain authorities.

The types of inspection and quarantine organs are shown as Table 6-1.

Table 6-1　　　　　　　Types of Inspection and Quarantine Organs

Types of Inspection and Quarantine Organs	Implication	For Example
Official inspection and quarantine institution	Administrative institutions set up and invested directly by the sovereign state or the local government, in accordance with the relevant state laws and regulations' legal implement for import and export commodity inspection and quarantine, supervision and administration	CID
Semi-official inspection and quarantine institution	The notary inspection organizations approved by the state and authorized by the government, carry out commodity inspection and appraisal work and part of the management	China Import and Export Commodity Inspection Corporation
Folk inspection agency	Non-governmental civil commodity inspection organizations, such as chamber of commerce and industry association of professional inspection appraisal technical ability surveyor or company	SGS IITS UL

2.Kinds of Entry-Exit Inspection and Quarantine Documents

(1)Entry application form for inspection (Sample 6-2).

(2)Entry customs clearance bill.

(3)Entry notification of inspection and quarantine.

(4)Export application form for inspection (Sample 6-3).

(5)Export customs clearance bill.

(6)Export receipt of exchange.

(7)Inspection certificate.

(8)Certificate of sanitary.

（9）Inspection certificate of veterinary.

（10）Inspection certificate of animals and plants.

（11）Inspection certificate of means of transport.

3.Application Procedure and Regulations of Entry-Exit Inspection and Quarantine

（1）Qualification of applicant.

（2）The range and the procedure.

（3）The period and locations.

（4）Documents attached.

4.Regulations of Filling in Export Application for Inspection

Export inspection application should be made by the inspection declarant who should fill in export inspection application form in accordance with the contract and related documents within 7 days before the customs declaration or shipment.

Inspection application form is made out for one batch of exports (one classification or one B/L). The form should be filled out completely and the "/" is used for the blank content. Any alteration is forbidden.

1.定义

检验证书是说明货物的质量检验、数量检验或其他专项检验结果的单证。检验证书可由政府机构、商会检验员或独立服务公司签发。检验证书在货物进出口通关时以及出口商向银行议付货款时使用。

检验证书的基本职能是保证货物达到特定机构所制定的相关标准。

检验检疫机构的类型如表6-1所示。

表6-1　　　　　　　　　　　　　检验检疫机构的类型

检验检疫机构的类型	含　义	举　例
官方检验检疫机构	由主权国家或地方政府投资并直接设立的行政机构，按照国家有关法律法规对进出口商品实施法定检验检疫和监督管理	商品检验司
半官方检验检疫机构	由国家批准设立的公证检验机构，获得政府授权，行使商品检验鉴定工作和部分管理工作	中国进出口商品检验总公司
民间检验机构	非政府的民间商品检验机构，如商会、行业协会等具有专业检验鉴定技术能力的公证行或检验公司	SGS集团 英之杰检验集团 美国保险商试验所

2.出入境检验检疫单证种类

（1）入境货物报检单（见样单6-2）。

（2）入境货物通关单。

（3）入境货物检验检疫情况通知单。

（4）出境货物报检单（见样单6-3）。

（5）出境货物通关单。

（6）出境货物换证凭单。

（7）检验证书。

（8）卫生证书。

（9）兽医卫生证书。

（10）动植物检验检疫证书。

（11）运输工具检验检疫证书。

Sample 6-2　　　　　　　　　　Entry Application Form for Inspection

样单6-2　　　　　　　　　　　　　　入境货物报检单

报检单位(加盖公章)		上海朗明商贸有限公司			*编　号		
报检单位登记号:52304125596　联系人:王明　电话:021-58693215					报检日期:2018年8月12日		
收货人	(中文)	上海朗明商贸有限公司		企业性质(划"√")	☑合资　□合作　□外资		
	(外文)	SHANGHAI LANGMING TRADING CO., LTD.					
发货人	(中文)	东方代理公司					
	(外文)	EAST AGENT COMPANY					
货物名称(中/外文)		H.S.编码	原产国(地区)	数/重量	货物总值		包装种类及数量
高尔夫球帽 H6-59940BS GOLF CAPS		59019091	日本	1 800打	USD 14 580.00		36箱
运输工具名称、号码		VOLENDAM VOY. 8080			合同号		18TG28711
贸易方式	一般贸易	贸易国别(地区)	日本	提单/运单号	SOCO02596		
到货日期	2018-08-09	起运国家(地区)	日本	许可证/审批号	CT88661125839		
卸货日期	2018-08-13	起运口岸	大阪	入境口岸	上海		
索赔有效期至	两年	经停口岸		目的地	上海		
集装箱规格、数量及号码		20英尺×1					
合同、信用证订立的检验检疫条款或特殊要求				货物存放地点	上海市康元街119号		
				用途	外贸自营内销		

随附单据(划"√"或补填)		标记及号码	*外商投资资产(划"√")	□是　□否
☑合同	□到货通知	V.H SHANGHAI C/NO.1-360 MADE IN JAPAN	*检验检疫费	
☑发票	☑装箱单			
☑提/运单	□质保书		总金额 (人民币元)	
□兽医卫生证书	□理货清单			
□植物检验检疫证书	□磅码单		计费人	
□动物检验检疫证书	□验收报告			
□卫生证书	□			
□原产地证书	□		收费人	
☑许可/审批文件	□			
报检人郑重声明:			领取证单	
1.本人被授权报检。			日期	
2.上列填写内容正确属实。				
签字:　　　王明			签字	

注:有"*"号栏目由出入境检验检疫机关填写　　　　　　　　◆中华人民共和国海关总署制

Sample 6-3   Export Application Form for Inspection

样单 6-3   出境货物报检单

报检单位(加盖公章):   *编号＿＿＿＿＿＿

报检单位登记号   联系人:张立   电话:13877782512   报检日期: 2018 年 8 月 12 日

发货人	(中文)	江西蓝星有限公司
	(外文)	JIANGXI LANXING CO., LTD.
收货人	(中文)	东方代理公司
	(外文)	EAST AGENT COMPANY

货物名称(中/外文)	H.S.编码	产地	数/重量	货物总值	包装种类及数量
高尔夫球帽 H6-59940BS GOLF CAPS	59019091	南昌	1 800 打	14 580.00 美元	90 箱

运输工具名称、号码		昌海 802		贸易方式	一般贸易	货物存放地点	工厂仓库
合同号		03TG28711		信用证号	LTR0505457	用途	外销
发货日期	2018-08-12		输往国家(地区)	日本	许可证/审批号		
起运地	南昌		到达口岸	秋田	生产单位注册号		

集装箱规格、数量及号码	20英尺×1

合同、信用证订立的检验检疫条款或特殊要求	标记及号码	随附单据(划"√"或补填)		
	V.H LAS PLAMS C/NO.	☑合同 ☑信用证 ☑发票	□换证凭单 □厂检单 ☑装箱单	□包装性能结果单 □许可/审批文件 □

需要证单名称(划"√"或补填)				*检验检疫费
☑品质证书	＿正＿副	□植物检验检疫证书	＿正＿副	总金额 (人民币元)
□重量证书	＿正＿副	□熏蒸/消毒证书	＿正＿副	
□数量证书	＿正＿副	☑出境货物换证凭单	＿正＿副	
□兽医卫生证书	＿正＿副			计费人
□健康证书	＿正＿副	□		
□卫生证书	＿正＿副	□		收费人
□动物卫生证书	＿正＿副			

报检人郑重声明:	领取证单
1.本人被授权报检。	
2.上列填写内容正确属实,货物无伪造或冒用他人的厂名、标志、认证标志,并承担货物质量责任。	日期
签字:＿＿＿张立＿＿＿	签字

注:有"*"号栏由出入境检验检疫机关填写   ◆中华人民共和国海关总署制

3.进出口检验检疫的申请程序和规定

(1)申请人资格。

(2)范围和程序。

(3)时间和地点。

(4)附带单证。

4.填写出境货物报检单的规定

检验申请人应在出口报关或装运前7天内申请出口检验,同时根据合同和相关单证填写检验申请表格。

检验申请表仅用于一批出口货物(一类或一份提单)。表格内容应全部填满,在空白处使用"/"。填写的内容禁止修改。

6.4　Documents Involved in Transportations
运输单证

For booking shipping space or chartering vessel, the seller is required to fill out a booking note. In return, the seller will receive a shipping order from the carrier or the agent.

1.Booking Note (B/N) (Sample 6-4)

A booking note is a form which is to be filled out by the exporter providing the carrier or the shipping agent all the necessary particulars about the shipment when an exporter intends to book shipping space on a liner or charter a ship for the carriage of export goods. When shipping space is booked or a ship is chartered, the carrier or the agent will inform the exporter of the particulars by means of a shipping order.

2.Shipping Order (Sample 6-5)

A shipping order is a notice to the shipper (exporter) from the carrier or the agent, indicating that goods are received for loading. Thus a shipping order contains detailed information concerning the sailing, goods, place of loading, etc. When the carrier or the agent is in receipt of the goods, he will mark and sign the shipping order properly so that the goods can be ready for export clearance. After the customs clearance, the Customs will stencil on the face of the shipping order evidencing that goods are cleared for export. This shipping order will be presented to the carrier at the time of loading. Without a shipping order, goods are not allowed to be loaded.

为了订舱位或租船,卖方需填写一份订舱单,卖方会收到一份承运人或其代理人签发的装货单。

1.订舱单(见样单6-4)

订舱单是出口商计划预订班轮舱位或租船装运出口货物时,填写的向承运人或海运代理提供装运货物所有必要信息的单证。如果订舱成功或租船成功,承运人或其代理人将通过装货单通知出口商相关的细节。

Sample 6-4

Booking Note

样单 6-4

订舱单

日期：2018年3月11日

1.发货人		4.信用证号码	63211020049		
JIANGXI TEXTILES IMP. & EXP. CORPORATION 8/F, JIANGXI TEXTILES MANSION,168 XIAOBEI ROAD, NANCHANG, CHINA		5.开证银行	BNP PARIBAS (CANADA)		
		6.合同号码	F01LCB05127	7.成交金额	USD 32,640.00
		8.装运口岸	SHANGHAI	9.目的港	MONTREAL
		10.转运	ALLOWED	11.分批装运	NOT ALLOWED
2.收货人		12.信用证有效期	2018-04-10	13.装船期限	2018-03-25
TO ORDER OF BNP PARIBAS (CANADA)		14.运费	PREPAID	15.成交条件	CIF
		16.公司联系人	李好	17.电话/传真	0791-58818844
3.通知人		18.公司开户行	中国银行	19.银行账号	58625935148
DADAI CORPORATION P.O.BOX 8935, NEW TERMINAL, ALTA, VISTA OTTAWA, CANADA		20.特别要求			
21.标记唛码	22.货号规格	23.包装件数	24.毛重	25.净重	26.数量	27.单价	28.总价
DADAI F01LCB05127 CTN NO. MONTREAL MADE IN CHINA	LADIES COTTON BLAZER (100% COTTON, 40×20/140×60)	85 CARTONS	19 KGS	17 KGS	2,550 PCS	USD 12.80	USD 32,640.00
	29.总件数	30.总毛重	31.总净重	32.总尺码	33.总金额
	85 CARTONS	19 KGS	17 KGS	21.583 CBM	USD 32,640.00

34.备注

2.装货单(见样单6-5)

　　装货单是承运人或其代理人给托运人(出口商)发送的,说明货物已收到待装运的通知。装货单包含航行、货物和装运地等内容的详细信息。承运人或其代理人收到货物后,就在装货单上做正确的标记和签字,以备通关之用。通关后,海关将在装货单上盖放行章证明货物已办理海关手续。这份装货单在货物装运时需向承运人出示。没有装货单货物不可装运。

Sample 6-5　　　　　　　　　　　Shipping Order
样单6-5　　　　　　　　　　　　　装货单

EXPORTER:	No.: YSM2018901
GUANGDONG MACHINERY IMPORT AND	DATE: NOV.11, 2018
EXPORT CORP. (GROUP)	LOADING PORT: GUANGZHOU, CHINA
	DESTINATION: MELBOURNE, AUSTRALIA
	B/L NO.: MANE962/25
CONSIGNEE:	NOTIFY:
TO ORDER OF K-MART AUSTRALIA LIMITED	K-MART AUSTRALIA LIMITED
800 TORONGA VIC 3416 AUSTRALIA	800 TORONGA VIC 3416 AUSTRALIA

SHIPPING MARKS	QUANTITY	DESCRIPTION OF GOODS	NET WEIGHT	GROSS WEIGHT	MEASUREMENT
K-MART CTN NO.1-20	120 BAGS	EDGING KNIFE WITH METAL HANDLE	10,800.00 KGS	12,000.00 KGS	3.672 CBM
TOTAL: 120 BAGS			10,800.00 KGS	12,000.00 KGS	3.672 CBM

PARTIAL SHIPMENTS: NOT ALLOWED	ORIGINAL B/L: 2
TRANSSHIPMENT: NOT ALLOWED	COPY B/L: 3
LATEST SHIPMENT DATE: NOV.11, 2018	GOODS IN : DASONGGANG
EXPIRY DATE: DEC.11, 2018	AMOUNT: USD 6,000.00
MEANS OF FREIGHT PAYMENT : FREIGHT PREPAID	L/C NO.: T/T
INVOICE NO.: YSM52165	CONTRACT NO.: VX562445636
DOCUMENTS REQUIRED:	
MEANS OF TRANSPORTATION: BY SEA	
TRAFFIC TON:	
FREIGHT RATE:	
SPECIAL CONDITIONS:	GUANGDONG MACHINERY IMPORT AND EXPORT CORP. (GROUP) 张立

6.5　Documents Needed for Export Customs Clearances
出口清关需要的单证

　　The export goods can not be loaded for shipment until they are cleared for export. To clear goods for export, exporters should declare the export goods to the customs by filling the relevant customs forms such as the customs declaration for export commodity (used in China). After customs clearance, the customs or the authorized institution will either stamp on the face of the shipping order or issue a customs clearance for export commodity to the seller, evidencing that goods are cleared for export.

出口货物获得放行前不可装船。为了办理放行手续,出口商应填写出口货物报关单(仅在中国使用)等报关表格以便向海关办理出口报关手续。通关后,海关或其授权机构将在装货单上盖放行章或向卖方签发一份出口货物结关证书,证明货物已办结海关手续。

6.5.1 *Customs Declaration for Export Commodity*
出口货物报关单

To clear the export commodity for export customs, the seller should fill out a customs declaration for export commodity (Sample 6-6), which will be submitted to the customs or the relative authorized institutions. In addition, some supporting documents may need to be submitted as well such as a commercial invoice, packing documents (a packing list and certificate of weight etc.), transport documents (ocean bill of lading, bill of lading, air waybill, cargo manifest, railway bill, etc.). Also some special documents need to submit an export license (if required), processing and trade of electronic manual and electronic account, specific tax reduction or exemption certificate, certificate of origin, customs form, a copy of the sales contract and an inspection certificate (in case of, mandatory inspection) and a shipping order.

1.Definition of Customs Declaration

An exporter has to apply to the customs for declaration of the commodity before the shipment. The customs officer will sign on the customs declaration form and release the goods if the goods are up to the requirement.

According to Customs law, customs declaration and duty paying procedures of import/export goods shall be handled by customs declaration enterprises approved by and registered with the customs office or by enterprises entitled to do import/export business.

2.Objects of Customs Declaration

(1)Exit & entry conveyance.

(2)Exit & entry cargos.

(3)Articles of international consignment.

3.Main Contents and Notes of Customs Declaration Form

(1)No. of pre-record. It is given by the customs while the exporter is applying to customs. It is given by computers automatically.

(2)No. of customs. It is given by the computer system automatically or given by the customs officer.

(3)Port of export. It refers to the name and code of the customs at final port of export.

(4)Record No. for checking. It refers to the number of "Register Manual" or the number of "Certificate of Paid or Free Tax".

(5)Date of export. It refers to the date of shipment. It is the applied date of departure of the vessel.

(6) Date of application. It is the date that the exporter applies for declaration.

(7) Executive company. Fill in the company's name who signs and executes the S/C in Chinese (generally refers to the exporter), and the customs code of the company.

(8) Mode of transportation. It refers to the final departure mode of transportation, such as sea, road, railway and air, etc.

(9) Name of transportation Tool. It refers to the name of departure tool of transportation (for example, sea for vessel and number of voyage, railway for the number of train and air for the number of flight).

(10) Delivery numbers. It refers to all kinds of transport documents numbers, such as sea for B/L No., air for flight bill No. and road for receipt No.

(11) Entrusting company. It refers to the manufacturer or exporter.

(12) Mode of trade. Fill in the mode of trade stipulated in "Customs Modes of Trade Numbers" in brief style (Table 6-2, Table 6-3).

Table 6-2　　　　　　　　　　　　　TRANSAC

Code	Name	Code	Name
1	CIF	4	C&I
2	CFR	5	Market Price
3	FOB	6	Ex Warehouse

Table 6-3　　　Corresponding Table of Modes of Trade and INCOTERMS 2010

Groups	Group E	Group F			Group C				Group D		
Terms	EXW	FCA	FAS	FOB	CFR	CPT	CIF	CIP	DAT	DAP	DDP
Mode of Trade		FOB			CFR				CIF		

(13) Kind of tax. Fill in the kind of tax in brief style stipulated in "the Customs Tax Kinds", such as general tax or free of tax.

(14) Payment style. It refers to the payment styles of L/C, D/P, D/A, T/T, etc.

(15) License No. If the export license is required, fill in the license number.

(16) Name of destination country (region). It is the final destination, generally the import country.

(17) Designated destination port. It is the destination of port.

(18) Original place of delivered goods.

(19) Number of approved documents. Fill in the approved documents and numbers except the export license (if there is no other approved documents, it does not need to fill).

(20) Trade Terms. Fill in according to the code of price terms stipulated in "Customs Trade Terms Codes", for example, FOB, CFR, and CIF.

(21) Freight. They are the charges paid to the shipping company for transportation. Indicate type of the international currency.

(22) Insurance Premium. The premium is paid for the goods' insurance on CIF or CIP terms. Indicate type of the international currency.

(23) Additional Expenses. It refers to the other charges except the freight and insurance premium. Fill in with RMB.

(24) Contract No.

(25) No. of Packages.

(26) Type of Package. Fill in carton, bale, drum, case, etc.

(27) Gross Weight. It refers to the gross weight with packing weight. The unit is kg.

(28) Net Weight. It refers to the net weight without packing weight, the unit is kg.

(29) Container No.

(30) Attached Documents. They are the other documents except customs declaration form, such as copy S/C, invoice, packing list, etc.

(31) Manufacturer. It is the final firm that produces the goods for export. It may be filled in the exporter if it is unknown.

(32) Marks' Nos. and Remarks. Fill in the shipping marks printed on packing. "N/M" is made out if there are no marks.

(33) Item No. and No. of Commodity. Item No. refers to the order of this type of commodity in this customs declaration form. The No. of commodity is made out according to commodity classification for China Customs Statistics.

(34) Quantity and Unit. Fill in the quantity of package and unit of measurement. For example 200 dozen, 10,000 kilograms, etc.

(35) Final Destination Country (Region). It refers to the country (region) that consumes, uses and processes the delivered goods.

(36) Unit Price. It is made out according to the terms of price, such as USD 600.00/MT CIF Rotterdam.

(37) Tax Paid or Not. This column is made out by the customs officer.

(38) Applying Company (Seal). Sign with seal. The seal is specially used only for customs.

4.Customs Declarer

A customs declarer is a person who controls the aircraft or sea-going ship, or the ship agent. Documents to be submitted by a customs declarer shall include:

(1) A customs declaration.

(2) Detailed lists of goods.

(3) A written request of the customs declarer.

(4) A copy of bill of lading.

5.Notes on Customs Declaration

（1）The customs declarer shall be responsible before the law for using the temporarily imported components and spare parts in accordance with the declaration.

（2）An exporter has to apply to the customs for declaration of the commodity before the shipment. The customs officer will sign on the customs declaration form and release the goods if the goods are up to the requirement.

（3）The person who asks for declaration is required to be qualified, that is to say, he/she should have the certificate of customs declaration. The examination is held by the General Administration of Customs of China.

（4）The customs declaration form is in different colors, for example: the white one is made out for general trade and the pink one is used for processing trade. The contents of these documents are similar. We take the specification of an export customs declaration form for general trade as an example to show the method of making out the document.

要办理出口报关手续,卖方需填写出口货物报关单(见样单6-6)并交给海关或相关的授权机构。另外,还需提交的基本单证包括商业发票,包装单据(装箱单、重量证书等),装运单据(海运提单、提货单、装货单、航空运单、载货清单、铁路运单等)。还需提交的特殊单证包括出口许可证(如果需要)、加工贸易电子化手册和电子账册、特定减免税证明、原产地证书、通关单、销售合同副本、检验证书(若是法定检验商品)和装货单等。

1.报关的定义

出口商必须在货物装运之前申请报关。如果货物符合要求,海关官员会在报关单上签字,货物将予以通关。

根据海关法,报关和进出口货物付税的程序应由海关当局认可的报关企业或登记在案的报关企业或有权从事进出口业务的公司来办理。

2.报关的标的物

(1)出入境交通工具。

(2)出入境货物。

(3)国际托运协议。

3.报关单的主要内容和注意事项

(1)预先登记号码:当出口商申请报关时,由海关的计算机系统自动给出。

(2)海关号码:由计算机系统自动给出或由海关官员提供。

(3)出口港:指最终出口港海关的名称和代码。

(4)商检号码:指"人工登记"的号码或"付款凭证或免税"号码。

(5)出口日期:指装运日期,是船启程的生效日期。

(6)申请日期:指出口商报关日期。

(7)执行公司:用中文填写签署和执行销售合同的公司的名称(一般为出口商),以及公司的海关代码。

(8)运输方式:指最终离岸的交通方式,例如海运、陆运、铁路运输和空运等。

(9)交通工具名称:指离岸交通工具的名称(例如:海运船只及航号、铁路运输的列车车次、空运的航班号)。

Sample 6-6   **Customs Declaration for Export Commodity**

样单 6-6   **出口货物报关单**

预录入编号：DS9110002   海关编号：

出口口岸 上海浦江海关（2202）	备案号 ×××	出口日期 2018-03-28	申报日期 2018-03-18
经营单位 南京纺织有限公司（3201004261）	运输方式 江海（2）	运输工具名称 SU YUE V.981	提运单号 CSLMJ180180
发货单位 南京纺织有限公司	贸易方式 一般贸易（0110）	征免性质 一般征免（1）	结汇方式 信用证（6）
许可证号 ×××	运抵国（地区） 加拿大（501）	指运港 蒙特利尔（CAMTL）	境内货源地 南京（CNNJG）
批准文号 35/0591540	成交方式 CIF（1）	运费 502/1 260/3	保险费 502/1 250/3	杂费 ×××
合同协议号 F01LCB05127	件数 2 550	包装种类 纸箱	毛重（千克） 3 015.00KGS	净重（千克） 2 010.00KGS
集装箱号 CCLU1000752*3（5）	随附单据		生产厂家 南京纺织有限公司

标记唛码及备注
FASHION FORCE
F01LCB05127
CTN NO.
MONTREAL
MADE IN CHINA

项号	商品编号	商品名称及 规格型号	数量及单位	最终目的国 （地区）	单价	总价	币制	征免
1	62043200.90	100%棉女式运动衣 40×20/140×60	2 550件	加拿大	12.80	32 640.00	美元	照章 （1）
		总计：	2 550件			32 640.00美元		

FREIGHT: USD 1,000.00
FOB VALUE: USD 31,640.00

税费征收情况

税务登记号码　320102134773852

录入员　　录入单位	兹声明以上申报无讹 并承担法律责任	海关审单批注及放行日期（签章）
		审单　　　　　审价
		征税　　　　　统计
单位地址　南京市管桥85号，华荣大厦 　　　　　　2901室 邮编 210005　电话 025-84715004	报关员 申报单位（签章） 南京纺织有限公司 填制日期 2018-03-18	查验　　　　　放行

(10)交货号码:指多种运输单证的号码,如海运提单号码、航空运单号码以及铁路运单号码。

(11)委托公司:指生产厂商或出口商。

(12)成交方式:按照合约规定以简洁明了的方式来填写成交方式(见表6-2和表6-3)。

表6-2　　　　　　　　　　　　　　　　　**成交方式代码表**

成交方式代码	成交方式名称	成交方式代码	成交方式名称
1	CIF	4	C&I
2	CFR	5	市场价
3	FOB	6	垫仓

表6-3　　　　　　　　　　　　**成交方式与INCOTERMS 2010对应表**

组别	E组	F组			C组				D组		
术语	EXW	FCA	FAS	FOB	CFR	CPT	CIF	CIP	DAT	DAP	DDP
成交方式		FOB			CFR		CIF				

(13)税收种类:以简洁明了的方式按照合约规定填写"海关税收种类",如一般税或免税。

(14)付款方式:这是指信用证、即期汇票、承兑交单和电汇等付款方式。

(15)许可证号码:如果需要出口许可证,须填写许可证号码。

(16)目的地国家(地区)名称:指的是最终目的地,一般来说是进口国。

(17)指定目的港:指的是目的地港口。

(18)装运货物的原产地。

(19)被认可单证的号码:除了出口许可证之外,填写被认可的许可证号码(如果没有其他的被认定的单证,则不需要填写)。

(20)贸易术语:根据"海关贸易术语代码"中的价格术语的代码来填写,如FOB、CFR和CIF。

(21)运费:指的是付给运输公司的费用。注明外币的类型。

(22)保险费:指的是支付货物到岸价格的货物保险。注明外币的类型。

(23)额外的费用:指的是除了运费和保险费之外的其他费用。以人民币填写。

(24)合同号码。

(25)包装号码。

(26)包装类型:以箱、捆、卷和盒等为单位填写。

(27)毛重:指的是包括包装在内的重量,单位为千克。

(28)净重:指的是除去包装后的重量,单位为千克。

(29)集装箱号码。

(30)附加单证:指除了报关单之外的其他单证,如合约副本、发票和装箱单等。

(31)生产商:生产出口货物的最终企业。如果不知道生产商,填写出口商。

(32)唛头、备注:填写印在外包装上的唛头。如果没有唛头,需要在运输唛头栏目填写"无唛头"字样。

（33）条款号码和货物号码：条款号码指的是该类型货物在报关单上的号码。货物号码是指中国海关统计货物分类号码。

（34）数量和单位：填写包装数量和计量单位，如200打、10 000千克等。

（35）最终目的地国家（地区）：指的是客户消费、使用和加工运输货物的国家（地区）。

（36）单价：根据价格条款定出单价，如每公吨600美元鹿特丹CIF价。

（37）税费征收情况：这一栏由海关官员来填写。

（38）申请公司（盖章）：签字、盖章。此章为海关专用章。

4.报关员

报关员是空运或海运的运输代理人。报关员需要递交的单证包括：

（1）报关单。

（2）详细的货物单。

（3）一份报关员的书面要求。

（4）提单的副本。

5.报关的注意事项

（1）报关员应依法负责临时出口的零部件与报关相一致。

（2）出口商必须在货物装运之前申请货物报关。如果货物符合要求，海关官员会在报关单上签字并予以货物通关。

（3）报关员必须要有报关资格证书。报关员资格考试由海关总署主办。

（4）报关单有不同的颜色。例如，白色报关单用于一般的贸易，粉色报关单用于加工贸易。这些单证的内容相似。我们以一般贸易出口报关单为例来说明报关单的缮制方法。

Training Case 6-1

海南三环公司（4601137432）签订合同从海口海关报关出口一批雨伞（法定计量单位：把）到印度尼西亚泗水（苏腊巴亚）。该批货物由海南文昌宝宜公司（4690160359）生产，于2018年9月18日备妥并用汽车运抵海口港海关监管区，三环公司已办理相关托运和投保手续，并支付国际运杂费共4 000美元，运输保险费共500美元，该批货物计划于9月21日装运离境。三环公司将相关单据交由永佳报关行代理报关。

海南三环进出口贸易有限公司

HAINAN SANHUAN IMP. & EXP. TRADING CO.,LTD

Room 605, No. 397, Longkun Road, Haikou City, Hainan Province, China

TEL：86-898-66745678

COMMERCIAL INVOICE

SOLD TO：   INVOICE NO. ：SHI109001

CV UNIVERSAL ACTIF   S/C NO.：SHI1230

JL GUBERNUR SLFR YO B-34 GBESIK, INDONESIA   DATE：SEP. 18,2018

PAYMENT TERM:T/T

SHIPPED PER：

FROM HAIKOU，CHINA TO SURABAYA，INDONESIA

Marks & Nos.	Description of Goods	Size	Quantity	Unit Price	Amount
N/M				CIF SURABAYA	
	UMBRELLA 直骨伞	2V	30,000 PCS	USD 9.10	USD 27,300.00
	UMBRELLA 折叠伞		35,928 PCS	USD 1.70	USD 61,077.60
				TOTAL	USD 88,377.60

HAINAN SANHUAN IMP. & EXP. TRADING CO., LTD.(公章)

海南三环进出口贸易有限公司

HAINAN SANHUAN IMP. & EXP. TRADING CO., LTD.

Room 605, No. 397, Longkun Road, Haikou City, Hainan Province, China

TEL: 86-898-66745678

PACKING LIST

NO.:SHI109001

CONSIGNEE:

CV UNIVERSAL ACTIF

SHIPPING MARKS:N/M

FROM HAIKOU, CHINA TO SURABAYA, INDONESIA

Carton No.	Packing No.	Description of Goods	Quantity	Net Weight	Gross Weight	Measurement
1-682	682 CTNS	UMBRELLA 直骨伞	30,000 PCS	16,152.50 KGS	16,834.50 KGS	
683-1176	494 CTNS	UMBRELLA 折叠伞	35,928 PCS	8,812.30 KGS	9,306.30 KGS	
TOTAL:	1,176 CTNS			24,964.80 KGS	26,140.80 KGS	52.00 CBM
				HAINAN SANHUAN IMP. & EXP. TRADING CO., LTD. (公章)		

Shipper(发货人) HAINAN SANHUAN IMP. & EXP. TRADING CO.,LTD. ROOM 605, NO.397, LONGKUN ROAD, HAIKOU CITY, HAINAN PROVINCE, CHINA	D/R No.(编号) APLU050741869
Consignee (收货人) CV UNIVERSAL ACTIF JL GUBERNUR SLFR YO B-34 GBESIK,INDONESIA	装货单 场站收据副本 (第五联)
Notify Party(通知人) SAME AS CONSIGNEE	
Pre-Carriage by(前程运输)　　　Place of Receipt(收货地点) HAIKOU, CHINA	
Ocean Vessel(船名) Voy. No.(航次) Port of Loading(装货港) APL REBY　　　　V. 031　　　　HAIKOU, CHINA	

续

Marks & No. (标记与号码)	Container No. (集装箱号) Seal No.(封志号)	Containers or Description of Goods; Kind of Packages (箱数或件数、包装种类与货名)	Gross Weight (毛重/千克)	Measurement (尺码/立方米)
N/M	TGLU3635199/40 GP Seal No. : 9422074	1,176 CTNS UMBRELLA 伞	26,140.80 KGS	52.00 CBM

Total Number of Containers or Packages (in words) 集装箱数或件数合计(大写)	SAY TOTAL: ONE FORTY FT. GP CONTAINER ONLY.

Freight & Charges (运费与附加费)	Revenue Tons (运费吨)	Rate(运费率)	Per(每)	Prepaid(运费预付)	Collect (运费到付)
				FREIGHT PREPAID	

Ex. Rate (兑换率)	Prepaid at(预付地点) HAIKOU, CHINA	Payable at (到付地点)	Place of Issue (签发地点) HAIKOU, CHINA
	Total Prepaid(预付总额)	No. of Original B(s)/L (正本提单份数) THREE(3)	

Service Type on Receiving □-CY □-CFS □-DOOR	Service Type on Delivery □-CY □-CFS □-DOOR	Reefer Temperature Required (冷藏温度)　　　°F　　°C

Type of Goods (种类)
□ Ordinary（普通）　□ Reefer（冷藏）　□ Dangerous（危险品）　□Auto.（裸装车辆）
□ Liquid（液体）　□ Live Animal（活动物）　□ Bulk（散货）

Dangerous（危险品）　Class:　Property:　IMDG Code Page:　UN No.:

Transshipment(可否转运) ALLOWED	Partial Shipment(可否分批装运) ALLOWED

Shipment Date(装船日期)	Validity(有效期)

Amount(金额)	Date(制单日期)

永佳报关行根据以上资料填写出口货物报关单，请选择下列栏目的正确选项：

1."备案号"栏填（　　）。
A.此栏为空　　B. 4601137432　　C.4690160359　　D.SHI109001

2."出口日期"栏填（　　）。
A. 20180918　　B. 20180921　　C.180921　　D. 此栏为空

3."运输方式"栏填（　　）。
A.公路运输　　B. 铁路运输　　C.水路运输　　D.其他运输

4. "经营单位" 栏填（　　　）。

A.海南三环公司（4601137432）　　　　B.海南三环公司

C.文昌宝宜公司（4690160359）　　　　D.永佳报关行

5. "发货单位" 栏填（　　　）。

A.海南三环公司（4601137432）　　　　B.海南三环公司

C.文昌宝宜公司（4690160359）　　　　D.文昌宝宜公司

6. "结汇方式" 栏填（　　　）。

A.D/P　　　　　B.D/A　　　　　　C.T/T　　　　　D.L/C

7. "成交方式" 栏填（　　　）。

A.1　　　　　　B.2　　　　　　　C.3　　　　　　D.4

8. "运抵国(地区)" 栏填（　　　）。

A.中国　　　　B.印度尼西亚　　　C.印度尼西亚泗水　D.中国海口

9. "运费" 栏填（　　　）。

A.502/4,000/3　B.4,000　　　　　C.502/4,000/2　　D.此栏为空

10. "件数" 栏填（　　　）。

A.38,928　　　B.1,176　　　　　C.71,928　　　　D.1

11. "包装种类" 栏填（　　　）。

A.纸箱　　　　B.集装箱　　　　　C.其他　　　　　D.此栏为空

12. "集装箱号" 栏填（　　　）。

A.TGLU3635199　　　　　　　　　B.9422074/40×××××

C.TGLU3635199/40/××××　　　　　D.0

13. "随附单据" 栏填（　　　）。

A.发票、装箱单、提货单　　　　　B.SHI109001

C.APLU050741869　　　　　　　　D.此栏为空

14. "数量及单位" 栏填（　　　）。

A.第一项：36 000 把（第一行），3 000 打（第三行）　第二项：35 928 把

B.第一项：3 000 打　第二项：35 928 把

C.第一项：36 000 把　第二项：35 928 把

D.第一项：3 000 打　第二项：2 994 打

15. "征免性质" 栏填（　　　）。

A.一般征税　　B.全免　　　　　　C.全额退税　　　D.照章征税

6.5.2　Customs Clearance for Export Commodity
出口货物结关证明

A customs clearance is issued by the customs or the authorized institution evidencing the customs clearance for the export commodity. It usually shows customs clearance number, the information of the goods, the contract number, and the voyage. In some cases, a shipping order with the signature by the customs or their agents can serve the same purpose. A customs clearance is required when the goods are to be loaded.

出口货物结关证明是由海关或其授权机构签发的证明出口货物已清关的文件。该文件

通常标示清关号码、货物信息、合同号码和航次。在某些情况下,由海关或其代理机构签字的装货单也具有相同的效力。出口货物结关证明是装运货物前必需的文件。

6.6 Documents Received after Shipment
装运后收到的单证

After they are cleared for export and the customs clearance is obtained, the goods can be arranged to be loaded on the vessel. For his goods to be loaded, the seller shall present the shipping order and/or the customs clearance to the carrier. To ensure the effective notice about the shipment, a shipping time of loading shall be forwarded to the importer by the seller without delay. Upon completion of the shipment, the exporter will get a bill of lading (details as section 5.1) issued by the carrier.

办妥出口货物报关手续并清关后就可以安排装船了。装船前,卖方应向托运人出示托运单和/或出口货物结关证明。为了保证装船通知的有效性,出口商应毫不延迟地将装运时间通知进口商。装运完成后,出口商将收到承运人签发的提单(详见5.1部分)。

6.6.1 Mate's Receipt
大副收据

A mate's receipt is a document issued and signed by the mate of the shipping vessel indicating that the goods have been received by the vessel for loading or that the goods have been loaded on board the vessel. The seller can exchange the mate's receipt for the on board bill of lading at a later time.

大副收据是船舶大副签发的,注明货物已收到待装运或货物已装船的单证。之后,卖方可以将大副收据换成已装船提单。

6.6.2 Shipping Advice
装船通知

A shipping advice (Sample 6-7) is a notice of the shipment details which is issued by the carrier when goods are loaded on board the vessel and given by the seller (shipper) to the buyer (consignee). The purpose of the shipping advice is to notify the buyer that goods are loaded and that he can proceed to prepare for making payment and for receiving the goods at the destination. If the contract is concluded under FOB, FCA, CFR or CPT, the seller also has to pass the shipping advice to the buyer so as to facilitate the buyer to arrange insurance.

A shipping advice should be delivered to the buyer with no delay, within the period stipulated in the sales contract or letter of credit. Occasionally, a copy of the shipping advice may be required for the purpose of payment. A shipping advice usually covers the information as follows:

(1)The number of packages shipped.

(2)The total gross and net weight.

(3)The packing.

(4)The date and number of the B/L.

(5)The container number and seal number (if container is used).

（6）ETD (estimated time of departure).

（7）ETA (estimated time of arrival).

（8）The name of the port of shipment and port of destination.

装船通知（见样单6-7）是货物装船后,由卖方(托运人)缮制并发给买方(收货人),说明装船细节的通知。装船通知的目的是通知买方货物已装船,以便于其进行下一步工作,如准备付款和提货。如果合同采用FOB、FCA、CFR或CPT贸易术语成交,卖方也需向买方发送装船通知以便买方安排保险事宜。

Sample 6-7   Shipping Advice

样单6-7   装船通知

SHIPPING ADVICE

ISSUE DATE: MAR. 21, 2018

OUR REF. DATE:

TO:

FASHION FORCE CO., LTD.

P.O. BOX 8935 NEW TERMINAL, ALTA, VISTA OTTAWA, CANADA

Dear Sir or Madam:

We are pleased to advice you that the following mentioned goods have been shipped out. Full details were shown as follows:

Invoice Number: NT001FF004

Bill of Lading Number: COS6314203208

Ocean Vessel: HUA CHANG V.09981

Port of Loading: BEIHAI, CHINA

Date of Shipment: MAR. 20, 2018

Port of Destination: MONTREAL, CANADA

Estimated Date of Arrival: APR. 25, 2018

Containers/Seals Number: MSKU2612114/1681316

Description of Goods: SALES CONDITIONS: CIF MONTREAL/CANADA

SALES CONTRACT NO. F01LCB05127

LADIES COTTON BLAZER (100% COTTON, 40×20/140×60)

STYLE NO.	PO NO.	QTY/PCS	USD/PC
46-301A	10337	2,550	12.80

Shipping Marks: FASHION FORCE

F01LCB05127

CTN NO.

MONTREAL

MADE IN CHINA

Quantity: 201 CARTONS

Gross Weight: 3,015.00 KGS

Net Weight: 2,010.00 KGS

Total Value: USD 32,640.00

Thank you for your patronage. We look forward to the pleasure of receiving your valuable repeat orders.

Sincerely yours,

GUANGXI TEXTILE
GARMENT CO., LTD.
张立

装船通知必须毫不延迟地在合同或信用证规定的期限内发送给买方。在少数情况下，在结汇时也需提供装船通知。一份装船通知通常包括以下内容：

(1)已装船的包装数量。

(2)总毛重和总净重。

(3)包装。

(4)提单日期和号码。

(5)集装箱号码和封条号(使用集装箱的情况下)。

(6)预计开航时间。

(7)预计到达时间。

(8)装运港和目的港名称。

6.7 Insurance Documents
保险单证

Under a CIF contract, it is the exporter's obligation to cover insurance for the export goods. Insurance is normally obtained after the completion of the loading at the port of shipment. To take out insurance, an insurance application form, also known as the proposal form has to be filled out and submitted to an insurance company for the purchase of cargo insurance. When the application is accepted, an insurance policy or certificate will be issued by the insurer.

在 CIF 合同项下，出口商有义务对出口货物投保。保险通常是货物在装运港被装运后才生效。为货物购买保险，需要填写保险申请表，也称投保单，并向保险公司提出申请。申请表被接受之后，保险人将给申请人签发一份保险单或保险凭证。

6.7.1 *Insurance Application Form*
投保单

Insurance application form (Sample 6-8) is to be filled out by the insured, providing all information about the parties concerned and the shipment involved. The specific information may cover the name of the insured party, the description of the cargoes insured, the voyage insured, the insurance amount, the insurance coverage, etc. Documents needed for submission are the commercial invoice, the packing list, etc. After all necessary formalities concerning insurance is completed, an insurance policy is to be issued by the insurance company or their agents.

投保单(见样单6-8)是提供有关保险当事人和被保险货物详细信息的单证，应由被保险人填写。投保单上的信息应包括被保险人的名称、被保险货物的描述、航次、保险金额、保险范围等。投保时需要的单证包括商业发票和装箱单等。投保手续办妥后，保险公司或其代理人将签发一份保险单。

Sample 6-8   Insurance Application Form
样单 6-8   投保单

发票号码	NT001FF004		投保条款和险别	
被保险人	客户抬头 NANJING TANG TEXTILE GARMENT CO., LTD.		(✓)	PICC CLAUSE
			( )	ICC CLAUSE
			(✓)	ALL RISKS
			( )	W.P.A./W.A.
			( )	F.P.A.
			(✓)	WAR RISKS
	过户 FASHION FORCE CO., LTD		( )	S.R.C.C.
			(✓)	STRIKE
			( )	ICC CLAUSE A
			( )	ICC CLAUSE B
			( )	ICC CLAUSE C
保险金额	USD (35,904.00)		( )	AIR TPT ALL RISKS
	HKD ( )		( )	AIR TPT RISKS
	( ) ( )		( )	O/L TPT ALL RISKS
起运港	BEIHAI		( )	O/L TPT RISKS
目的港	MONTREAL		( )	TRANSSHIPMENT RISKS
转内陆			( )	W TO W
开航日期	MAR. 20, 2018		( )	T.P.N.D.
船名航次	HUA CHANG V.09981		( )	F.R.E.C.
赔款地点	CANADA		( )	R.F.W.D.
赔付币别	USD		( )	RISKS OF BREAKAGE
正本份数	1份正本,1份副本		( )	I.O.P.
其他特别条款	COVERING INSTITUTE CIVIL COMMOTIONS CLAUSES			

以下由保险公司填写			
保单号码		费 率	
签单日期		保 费	

投保日期:2018年3月16日   投保人签章:

6.7.2 *Insurance Policy*
保险单

An insurance policy (Sample 6-9) is a contract made between the insurer and the insured, which is issued by the insurer and confirmed by the insured. In an international trade transaction, insurance policy or certificate forms are part of the chief documents for transactions on a CIF or CIP basis. In addition, in case of loss or damage, the insurance policy or certificate forms are the essential bases for claim and settlement.

Marine (or ocean) or air insurance is important on export shipments. Under the Carriage of Goods by Sea Act, ocean carriers are responsible for the seaworthiness of the vessel, properly manning the vessel, and making the vessel safe for carriage of the cargoes. The ocean carrier is not responsible for negligence of the master in navigating the vessel, fires, perils, dangers, accidents of the sea, acts of God, acts of war, acts of public enemies, detentions or seizures, acts or omissions of shippers, strikes or lockouts, riots and civil commotions, saving or attempting to save a life or property at sea, inherent defects, quality or vice of the goods, insufficiency of packing, quarantine restrictions, insufficiency or inadequacy of marks, latent defects not discoverable by due diligence, and any other causes arising without the actual fault of the ocean carrier.

Without insurance, even when the carrier can be proved liable, responsibility is limited to $500 per "package" on ocean shipments and $20 per kilogram on air shipments unless a higher value is declared in advance and a higher transportation charge paid. Although abbreviated trade terms, such as FOB port of shipment, are supposedly designed to clarify which parties are responsible for arranging and paying for various aspects of an export shipment, often confusion and misunderstandings occur. It is extremely important to clearly determine who will pay for such insurance and who will arrange for it. It is necessary for a seller or buyer to have an "insurable interest" in the merchandise in order to obtain insurance coverage. Depending on the terms of sale, the seller may have an ownership interest up to a particular point or a financial interest in the safe arrival of the shipment up until the time it is paid.

A company can buy an open or blanket cargo marine or air insurance policy that has continuous effect for its shipments, or a special onetime cargo policy that insures a single shipment. Alternatively, it can utilize its freight forwarder's blanket policy. There are many advantages for a company to have its own open cargo policy, but the quantity of exports must justify it, otherwise, it is probably more appropriate to utilize the freight forwarder's blanket policy. Some insurance brokers recommend that a company has its own policy when exports and / or imports reach $500,000 to $1 million. When a blanket policy is used, a separate certificate is issued by the insurance company or the holder of the policy to evidence coverage for each shipment.

Familiarizing oneself with such insurance policies is also important in the event that a casualty occurs and a claim needs to be filed. Generally, it is best to obtain "all risks" (rather than "named peril") and "warehouse-to-warehouse" (or "marine extension") coverage.

Even "all risks" coverage does not include war risk or "strike, riot and civil commotion" coverage and the seller should specifically determine whether these risks and others, such as delay in arrival and change in customs duties, should be covered by rider. Under the INCOTERMS 2010 it is necessary to insure the shipment at 110 percent of the invoice value; in the case of some letters of credit sales, payment cannot be obtained unless insurance in that amount has been obtained.

In order to get paid under letters of credit or documentary collections through banking channels, it may be necessary for the seller to furnish a certificate to the bank evidencing that insurance coverage exists.

Marine insurance companies and insurance brokers can advise on the different types of coverage available and comparative premiums. The premium will depend on the type of merchandise, its value (risk of pilferage), its packing, the type of coverage (including riders), the method of transportation, the country of destination and routing, the loss history of the insured, the carriers used, whether transshipment will occur, etc.

保险单(见样单6-9)是保险人和被保险人间订立的,由保险人签发、被保险人确认的合同。在国际贸易中,保险单或保险凭证是CIF或CIP合同交易的主要单证之一。另外,在发生灭失或损害时,保险单或保险凭证是索赔和理赔的基础。

海运保险或空运保险对出口货物非常重要。根据《海上运输法》,在海运方式下,海运承运人应对船舶的适航性负责,应正确操作船只以保证运输船只的安全。但是,海运承运人不对以下情况负责:由于船长的过失、火灾、海上危险、海上意外事故、不可抗力、海上战争、海上公敌的扣押和掠夺行为、托运人的过失、罢工、暴动、骚乱,以及在海上抢救或试图抢救生命财产、商品内在缺陷、包装不良、检验检疫机构限制入境、运输标志不全或不正确、尽职调查后仍无法发现的潜在缺陷或其他非海运承运人的实际过失造成的损失。

如果不办理保险,即使是承运人的责任,他们的赔偿也是有限额的。比如承运人对每个单位包装的海运货物最高赔偿500美元,对空运货物每千克最高赔偿20美元,但托运人事先申报更高的货物价值并支付了更高的运费除外。即使如FOB装运港等贸易术语已经将各当事人在出口装运各方面的责任义务划分得很清楚,还是经常发生混淆和误解的情况。明确说明由谁负责安排保险和支付保险费是非常重要的。对买卖双方来说,要得到保险的赔付,必须拥有货物的"保险利益"。根据销售条款,卖方对货物的所有者权益可能于某个点终止,或者卖方在货物平安到达目的地之后仍拥有经济利益,直到买方付款为止。

在海运或空运方式下,被保险人可以为货物购买预约货物保险单,这类保险单可以为货物提供持续的保险服务,或专门为某一批货物购买一份保险。另外,也可以使用货运代理商的统保单。使用本公司的预约货物保险单有很多好处,但是装船后需更改货物实际装船的数量,而使用货运代理商的统保单时,单上的数字很可能更准确。有些保险经纪人推荐,如果一家公司的出口和/或进口数量达到50万美元到100万美元,就应该为本公司单独购买保险单。若选择统保单方式,保险公司或保单的持有人将另外签发一份保险凭证,证明每次投保的承保范围。

Sample 6-9   Marine Cargo Transportation Insurance Policy

样单 6-9   **海洋货物运输保险单**

<table>
<tr><td colspan="5" align="center">中国人民财产保险股份有限公司
The People's Insurance (Property) Company of China, Ltd.</td></tr>
<tr><td colspan="3">发票号码
Invoice No.:INV52148</td><td colspan="2">保险单号次
Policy No.</td></tr>
<tr><td colspan="5" align="center">海洋货物运输保险单

MARINE CARGO TRANSPORTATION INSURANCE POLICY</td></tr>
<tr><td colspan="5">被保险人：
Insured:SHANGHAI FOREIGN TRADE IMP. AND EXP. CORP.
中国人民财产保险股份有限公司(以下简称本公司)根据被保险人的要求及其所缴付约定的保险费,按照本保险单承担险别和背面所载条款与下列特别条款承保下列货物运输保险,特签发本保险单。
This policy of Insurance witnesses that the People's Insurance (Property) Company of China, Ltd. (hereinafter called the "Company"), at the request of the Insured and in consideration of the agreed premium paid by the Insured, undertakes to insure the under mentioned goods in transportation subject to the conditions of the Policy as per the Clauses printed overleaf and other special clauses attached hereon.</td></tr>
<tr><td>保险货物项目
Description of Goods</td><td>包装
Packing</td><td>单位
Unit</td><td>数量
Quantity</td><td>保险金额
Amount Insured</td></tr>
<tr><td>LADIES LYCRA LONG PANT</td><td></td><td>200 CTNS</td><td>2,400 PCS</td><td>USD 52,800.00</td></tr>
<tr><td colspan="3">承保险别
Conditions</td><td colspan="2">货物标记
Marks of Goods</td></tr>
<tr><td colspan="3">COVERING RISKS AS PER "INSTITUTE CARGO CLAUSES (A)", AND INSTITUTE WAR CLAUSES (CARGO).</td><td colspan="2">CBD
LONDON
NOS1-200</td></tr>
<tr><td colspan="2">总保险金额
Total Amount Insured</td><td colspan="3">US DOLLARS FIFTY TWO THOUSAND EIGHT HUNDRED ONLY.</td></tr>
<tr><td>保费
Premium</td><td>AS ARRANGED</td><td>装载运输工具
Per Conveyance S.S.</td><td>DAFENG</td><td>开航日期
Slg. on or abt. OCT. 20, 2018</td></tr>
<tr><td>起运港
From</td><td colspan="2">SHANGHAI, CHINA</td><td>目的港
To</td><td>LONDON, UK</td></tr>
<tr><td colspan="5">所有货物,如发生本保险单项下可能引起索赔的损失或损坏,应立即通知本公司下述代理人查勘。如有索赔,应向本公司提交保险单正本(本保险单共有____份正本)及有关文件。如一份正本已用于索赔,其余正本则自动失效。
In the event of loss or damage which may result in a claim under this Policy, immediate notice must be given to the Company's Agent as mentioned hereunder. Claims, if any, one of the Original Policies which has been issued in_____original(s) together with the relevant documents shall be surrendered to the Company. If one of the Original Policies has been accomplished, the others to be void.</td></tr>
<tr><td colspan="2">赔款偿付地点
Claim payable at</td><td colspan="3">LONDON, UK</td></tr>
<tr><td>日期
Date</td><td>OCT. 20, 2018</td><td>在
At</td><td colspan="2">SHANGHAI, CHINA</td></tr>
<tr><td colspan="2">地址
Address</td><td colspan="3"></td></tr>
</table>

　　熟悉保险单很重要,尤其是在货物发生了损失后需要办理索赔手续的情况下。通常来说,最好选择"一切险"(而不是"指定险别")和"仓至仓"条款(或"海运扩展条款")。但即使是"一切险"也不承保战争险,或"罢工、暴动和民变"险,因此卖方还需另外决定这些风险以及其他如到达延迟、关税改变等风险是否需要以附加险的形式投保。根据 INCOTERMS 2010 的规定,应投保发票金额的110%;在信用证方式下,如果保险金额没有达到发票金额的110%,将会遭到银行拒付。

　　在信用证或跟单托收方式下,要得到银行的付款,卖方需向银行提交保险凭证,证明保险的实际承保责任和范围。

　　海运保险公司和保险经纪人可以为投保人建议不同类型的保险范围和相应的保险费用。保险费根据商品的类型、价值(偷窃风险)、包装、险别(包括附加险)、运输方式、目的国和运输路线、被保险人的损失记录、承运人、是否转运等内容的差异而有所区别。

6.7.3　*Checklist for Insurance Policy*
　　保险单审核内容

（1）Are you presenting an insurance policy or a certificate? (Acknowledgements or a broker's cover are acceptable only if expressly allowed in the letter of credit)

（2）Is the insured amount sufficient?

（3）Is the insurance coverage complete and in conformity with the letter of credit as it relates to:

①Special risks when required?

② Coverage of destination and time (in other words, carried through to proper point or covering the entire period of shipment).

③Proper warehouse clauses.

④Has the insurance document been countersigned when required?

（4）Was the insurance document endorsed in blank if payable to the shipper?

（5）Are shipping marks identical to those on the commercial invoice and bill of lading?

（6）The insurer may not agree to issue Acknowledge of Insurance Declaration, so if there are this requirement in the arrival L/C, it should be required to ask to change.

　　（1）出示的是保险单还是保险凭证?(只有信用证明确规定可以接受时,确认书或保险经纪人的暂保单方可使用)

　　（2）保险金额是否充足?

　　（3）承保范围是否完整,是否与信用证规定的一致,应注意以下几个方面的问题:

　　①如有要求,是否已投保特别风险?

　　②承保的最终地点和时间(换句话说,是到某个时间地点还是包括运输的全程)。

　　③仓至仓条款。

　　④如需要,保险单证是否已被会签?

　　（4）如果保险单证的抬头是托运人,它们是否已空白背书?

　　（5）商业发票和提单上的运输唛头是否与实际的唛头完全一致?

　　（6）保险人不一定同意出具投保回执,故如来证有此要求,应要求对方改证。

Training Case 6-2

A certain foreign trade company in our country signed a contract for leather gloves with a Dutch importer. The price term was CIF Rotterdam, and all risks were insured against the People's Insurance (Property) Company of China, Ltd. The temperature of gloves were reduced to the lowest degree by manufacturers at the end of the production process, and they were wrapped in kraft paper into cartons, then in 20ft container. After the goods arrived at the Rotterdam, container seals were in good condition, consistent with the bill of lading numbers marked. But when unpacking the case, all the goods were found wet, mildew, defiled and color changed, loss of $80,000. According to the analysis: the place of export was not abnormally hot, the place of import Rotterdam was not abnormally cold, transit without exception, all belong to the normal transportation. Questions:

(1) Should the insurance company compensate for the batch of loss? Why?

(2) Should the importer pay for the damage of the goods? Why?

(3)In your opinion, how should exporters deal with this matter?

我某外贸公司与荷兰进口商签订一份皮手套合同,价格条件为 CIF 鹿特丹,向中国人民财产保险股份有限公司投保一切险。生产厂家在生产的最后一道工序将手套的温度降低到了最低程度,然后用牛皮纸包好装入纸箱,再装入 20 英尺集装箱。货物到达鹿特丹后,集装箱铅封完好、号码与提单标注的一致,但开箱后发现全部货物潮湿、发霉、污损、变色,损失价值达 8 万美元。据分析:该批货物的出口地不异常热,进口地鹿特丹不异常冷,运输途中无异常,完全属于正常运输。试问:

(1)保险公司对该批损失是否应赔偿? 为什么?

(2)进口商对受损货物是否应支付货款? 为什么?

(3)你认为出口商应如何处理此事?

6.8　Documents for Bank Negotiations
　　银行议付单证

The last and the most important thing the seller has to do is to collect and check all documents specified in the L/C and present them within period required to the negotiating bank for payment settlement. While doing so, he should also fill out a bill of exchange (a draft). The documents needed for submission generally include the commercial invoice, the packing list, the bill of lading, the insurance policy, etc. Apart from these documents, there are also other types of documents required by the buyer and submitted to the bank for negotiation. Among them, the certificate of origin, consular invoice and customs invoice are worth mentioning.

对于卖方来说,最后也是最重要的一件事就是收集和核对所有信用证上规定的单证并在有效期内交给议付行办理议付手续。同时,还需填写汇票。需要提交的单证通常包括商业发票、装箱单、提单、保险单等。除此之外,有时买方要求其他单证,议付时也需要提交,这其中,原产地证书、领事发票和海关发票最值得注意。

6.8.1　*Bill of Exchange (B/E) or Draft*
汇 票

A bill of exchange (B/E) or draft (Sample 6-10 and Sample 6-11) is an unconditional order in writing signed by one party (drawer) requesting the second party (drawee/payer) to make payment in lawful money immediately or at a determined future time to the third party (payee).

Usually, a draft is drawn and presented by the seller to the buyer or its bank as the payment instrument. Strictly speaking, a draft drawn under an L/C is a payment instrument rather than a kind of the documents, though in practice it is accepted as one of the documents required for payment.

It should be noted that a draft drawn under an L/C is usually required to indicate the relevant L/C No. in the drawn clause and the B/E amount should in no case exceed the L/C amount.

1.Drafts for Payment

If payment for the sale is going to be made under a letter of credit or by documentary collection, such as documents against payment ("D / P" or sight draft) or documents against acceptance ("D/A" or time draft), the exporter will draw a draft on the buyer's bank in a letter of credit transaction or the buyer in a documentary collection transaction payable to itself (sometimes it will be payable to the seller's bank on a confirmed letter of credit) in the amount of the sale.

This draft will be sent to the seller's bank along with the instructions for collection, or sometimes the seller will send it directly to the buyer's bank (direct collection). If the payment agreement between the seller and buyer is at sight, the buyer will pay the draft when it is received, or if under a letter of credit, the buyer's bank will pay the draft when it is received. If the agreement between the seller and the buyer is that the buyer will have a grace period before making payment, the amount of the delay, called the usance, will be written on the draft (time draft), and the buyer will usually be responsible for payment of interest to the seller during the usance period unless the parties agree otherwise. The time period may also be specified as some period of time after a fixed date, such as 90 days after the bill of lading or commercial invoice date, or payment simply may be due on a fixed date.

2.Clauses of a Draft

For example:

(1) We hereby issue our irrevocable letter of credit No. 194956 available with any bank in China, at 90 days after bill of lading date by draft.

(2) Credit available with any bank in China, by negotiation, against presentation of beneficiary's drafts at sight, drawn on applicant in duplicate.

(3) All drafts should be marked "Drawn under the Citibank, New York L/C No. 1956717 dated 2018-03-10".

(4) This credit is available with Shanghai Banking Corporation Ltd., Shanghai by negotiation against beneficiary's drafts drawn under this L/C at sight basis.

(5) This letter of credit is to be negotiated against the documents detailed herein a beneficiary's drafts at 60 days after sight with Standard Chartered Bank Shanghai.

（6）The drafts at 90 days sight drawn on Bank of Tokyo, Tokyo branch. Usance drafts drawn under this L/C are to be negotiated at sight basis. Discount charges and acceptance commissions are for account of accountee.

3.Contents of Bills of Exchange

（1）Indicating the word "draft" or "exchange".

（2）An unconditioned order in writing.

（3）Certain amount.

（4）Payer's (drawee's) name, usually the buyer or its nominated bank.

（5）Payee's name, usually the seller or its nominated bank.

（6）Date and place of issue.

（7）Signature of the drawer, usually the seller.

汇票（见样单6-10和样单6-11）是由一个人（出票人）向另一个（受票人/付款人）签发的、要求其立刻或在将来某个时间向第三方（受款人）支付法定货币的书面无条件支付命令。

Sample 6-10   Bill of Exchange (on L/C)

样单6-10   信用证汇票

NO.T03617	Date: OCT. 24，2018

FOR USD 89,705.50

At ×××××× Sight of THIS SECOND BILL of EXCHANGE (First of the same tenor and date being unpaid)

Pay to BANK OF CHINA, GUANGZHOU BRANCH or order the sum of

SAY US DOLLARS EIGHTY-NINE THOUSAND SEVEN HUNDRED AND FIVE POINT FIVE ONLY.

Drawn under NATIONAL PARIS BANK (CANADA) MONTREAL

L/C NO. TH2003   Dated OCT. 06, 2018

TO：

NATIONAL PARIS BANK

24 MARSHALL VEDONCASTER, MONTREAL, CANADA

GUANGZHOU KNITWEAR AND MANUFACTURED
GOODS IMPORT & EXPORT TRADE CORPORATION
张欢

通常来说，汇票作为一种支付工具，由卖方向买方或买方指定的银行出具。严格来说，在信用证项下汇票是一种支付工具而不是一份单证，即使在实际中汇票通常以单证的形式被接受。

需要注意的是，信用证项下的汇票通常需要在汇票条款中标示相关信用证号码。另外，汇票金额绝不能超过信用证金额。

1.汇票付款

如果采用信用证或跟单托收等付款方式，如付款交单（D/P或即期汇票）或承兑交单（D/A或远期汇票），那么，在信用证方式下，出口商应向进口商指定的银行提交与销售金额相等的、以自己为受款人的汇票（有时在承兑信用证项下也可以卖方指定的银行为受款人）；在跟单托收方式下，以上汇票应直接交给进口商。

Sample 6-11　　　　　　　　　　Bill of Exchange (on Collection)
样单6-11　　　　　　　　　　　　　托收汇票

NO. ST007 Exchange for USD 15,000.00 D/P at ××××××× sight this First of Exchange (Second being unpaid)

Pay to the order of Shanghai Banking Corporation, Qingdao

The sum of US Dollars Fifteen Thousand Only

Value received for Shipment of 100 Cartons Shoes as per Invoice No.005

To M/S Hamka Trading Co. Ltd.

378 Gold Rd., Hong Kong

China National Metals Corp.
张欢

　　汇票将根据托收指示交给托收行,有时卖方直接将汇票寄给进口商指定的银行(直接托收)。如果买卖双方间签订的是即期协议,那么买方应在收到汇票后立刻付款;如果使用信用证方式,那么买方指定的银行应在收到汇票后立刻付款。如果买卖双方的协议允许买方在一定时间后付款,那么付款延迟的期限,也称票据期限,应在汇票(远期汇票)上标示。同时,除非双方另有协定,买方通常应按票据期限向卖方支付远期付款的利息。付款期限一般被指定为某个日期后的一段时间,如提单日期或商业发票日期后90天,或直接简单规定为某个日期。

　　2.汇票条款

　　例如:

　　(1)我方在此开具194956号不可撤销信用证,此证可在中国的任何银行议付,同时应出具提单日期后90天的汇票。

　　(2)若受益人提交以开证申请人为付款人的一式两份即期汇票,信用证可在中国的任何银行议付。

　　(3)所有的汇票都应标记"由纽约花旗银行开立,信用证号码1956717,日期2018年3月10日"。

　　(4)本信用证在上海银行议付,随附受益人即期汇票。

　　(5)这份信用证可议付,以60天远期汇票的付款人为上海渣打银行为条件。

　　(6)开立以东京银行东京分行为付款人的90天远期汇票。以本信用证为基础开立的远期汇票可即期议付。贴现费用和承兑手续费由开证申请人支付。

　　3.汇票内容

　　(1)标示"draft"或"exchange"字样。

　　(2)无条件书面命令。

　　(3)确定的金额。

　　(4)付款人(受票人)名称,通常是买方或其指定银行。

　　(5)受款人名称,通常是卖方或其指定银行。

（6）开票日期和地点。

（7）出票人（通常是卖方）签字。

Training Case 6-3

Company ABC in China signed an import contract with a Japanese company to import wood from Canada to China, using the L/C payment. The L/C stipulated "AVAILABLE WITH ISSUING BANK BY ACCEPTANCE, DRAFTS AT 90 DAYS AFTER SIGHT DRAWN ON THE ISSUING BANK". The issuing bank received the documents on May 17, 2018 and made acceptance on the same day. On May 31, 2018, the issuing bank received stop payment order against the L/C business item from the court. The reason was that there was fraud in the export company. Question：（1）Was the stop payment order issued by the court appropriate？（2）In such a case, could the issuing bank be remitted responsibility of making payment？ Why？

我国ABC公司与一家日本公司签订进口合同，从加拿大进口木材到中国，使用信用证方式结算货款。信用证中规定"汇票由开证行承兑，见票90天后向开证行承兑"。开证行收到单据日为2018年5月17日，并于当天对汇票承兑。2018年5月31日，开证行收到法院发出的针对该信用证业务项下的止付令，理由是出口公司存在欺诈行为。请问：（1）法院签发的止付令是否恰当？（2）在此种情况下，开证行是否可以免除其付款责任？为什么？

Training Case 6-4

Company D in China signed an export contract with the British company E to export clothing from China to the country on collection basis. Time limit for the draft was "D/A AT 30 DAYS AFTER SIGHT". At the request of company D, the collecting bank confirmed the draft, noted the "AVALISED" on the bill of exchange and notified the due date was on June 22, 2018. After the draft accepted, the collecting bank sent the draft to company D. However, company D did not get payment on the due date. It was understood through the collecting bank that the drawee company E was made liquidation for bankruptcy. Hence company D required collecting bank to fulfill its responsibility to pay, but was refused by the collecting bank. The reason was that collection business belonged to commercial credit, non-bank credit. Question: In this case, could the collecting bank be removed from the responsibility of payment? Why?

我国D公司与英国E公司签订出口合同，从中国出口服装到该国，使用托收方式结算货款，汇票期限为"D/A AT 30 DAYS AFTER SIGHT"（见票30天后）。代收行应D公司要求，对汇票进行了保证，在汇票上注明"AVALISED"（保付），并通知到期日为2018年6月22日。汇票经承兑后，代收行将汇票寄给D公司。但是，D公司在到期日未获得货款。经向代收行了解，付款人E公司因破产被清盘。D公司于是要求代收行履行付款责任，遭到代收行拒绝，理由是托收业务属于商业信用而非银行信用。请问：在本案中，代收行是否可以免除其付款责任？ 为什么？

6.8.2   *Certificate of Origin*
原产地证书

A certificate of origin (Sample 6-12) is a document certifying the origin of the goods or the place/country of manufacture. It should state the nature, quantity, value, and the place of manufacture. In many countries the certificate of origin is usually prepared by the exporter, signed in the presence of a notary public institution and certified by a non-governmental commercial organization acceptable to the destination country. In China the certificate of origin is generally issued by two governmental authorities: one is the General Administration of Customs of the People's Republic of China, the other is the China Council for the Promotion of International Trade.

There are normally two types of certificates of origin: one is the certificate of origin; the other is the generalized system of preferences certificate of origin (GSP C/O). The GSP certificate of origin is a special type of certificate of origin, and it is used to obtain the preferential customs duty treatment imposed by some developed countries on import commodities from some developing countries.

Different types of certificates of origin may be made at different stage of the export procedure. In normal cases, the seller can start to prepare the certificate of origin when the commercial invoice is ready. However, in some cases, for example GSP Form E, the issuance of a certificate of origin is made based on the submission of both the commercial invoice and the bill of lading. In this case, the preparation of the certificate of origin may be deferred to a time after the seller obtains the B/L. Whenever it is available, the certificate of origin is normally only used when the seller presents documents for negotiation of the payment.

The main purpose of the certificate of origin is to prove the origin of the goods based on which the import customs can set import duties and implement the applicable import controls such as sanctions, quotas, anti-dumping duties or favorable treatments.

Certificates of origin must be distinguished from country of origin marking. Many countries require that the products themselves and the labels on the packages specify the country of origin. A certificate of origin may be in addition to or in lieu of that requirement. A certificate of origin is the one required under the North American Free Trade Agreement (NAFTA).

NAFTA contains product-specific country of origin criteria which must be met to qualify for reduced duty treatment on exports to or imports from Canada or Mexico. In general, in order to be eligible for the duty-free or reduced duty rates under NAFTA, all items imported from outside of North America must have undergone the "tariff shift" during the manufacturing process for that product. In addition, some products must contain a specified "regional value content" usually 50 or 60 percent. Finished goods and sometimes raw materials purchased from others often must be traced backward to establish their countries of origin.

1.Duty-Free and Reduced Duty Programs

Before importing, the importer should ascertain whether or not the product is eligible for one of the special duty-free or reduced duty programs which congress has allowed. The largest program is known as the Generalized System of Preferences (GSP). This program was designed to encourage the economic development of less - developed countries by permitting the importation of those countries' products duty-free. Under the NAFTA, Mexico was eliminated as a beneficiary country as of January 1, 1994. The fact that a product will be imported from one of the GSP beneficiary countries, however, does not guarantee duty-free treatment. Some specific products even from eligible countries have been excluded, and it is necessary for the importer to identify whether the particular product is on the exclusion list. In addition, at least 35 percent of the final appraised value must be added in that country. The importer must claim the duty-free status by putting an "A" in the entry summary and, if requested by customs, obtain a GSP declaration from the exporter.

For imports from the twenty-four countries located in the Caribbean Basin, a similar duty-free program is available, along with imports from Israel under the Israel Free Trade Agreement; imports from Bolivia, Colombia, Peru, and Ecuador under the Andean Trade Preference Act, and imports from thirty-five countries under the African Growth and Opportunity Act.

The final program is a duty - free and reduced duty program, the NAFTA, which was implemented on January 1, 1994. Under the NAFTA, products of Canadian and Mexican origin eventually can be imported duty - free to the United States if various requirements are met. Usually, this means that the product must be of Canadian or Mexican origin under one of six eligibility rules and the exporter must provide the importer with a certificate of origin. Many items were granted duty-free status immediately, but other items will be eligible for duty - free status over a phase-out period of five to fifteen years. Nevertheless, if the importer can comply with the requirements, the duty will be less than on ordinary imports from Canada or Mexico.

2.Country of Origin

Determination of the proper country of origin can affect the duty rate payable on imported goods or whether they are subject to quotas. In addition, Section 304 of the Tariff Act of 1930 requires that imported merchandise be clearly and conspicuously marked in a permanent manner with the English name of the international country of origin. Some types of merchandise are exempt from the marking requirement, but, in such cases, usually the outermost container that will go to the end user must be marked. This is an important preliminary planning consideration, because the customs regulations specify that certain types of products must be marked in certain ways, such as die - stamping, cast - in - the - mold lettering, or etching, during the manufacturing process.

The importer should check the country of origin regulations prior to purchasing products to ascertain whether or not it must advise the supplier or seller of any special marking methods prior to the manufacture of the products. Sometimes off-the-shelf inventory manufactured in an international country can not be modified after manufacture to comply with the U.S. country of origin marking requirements. Merchandise which is not properly marked may be seized by the U.S. Customs. In some cases, the products can be marked after such seizure, but only upon payment of a marking penalty, which increases the cost of importing the products. More seriously, sometimes the U.S. Customs will release the merchandise to the importer, and the importer may resell it. Then, the U.S. Customs may issue a notice of redelivery of the products. If the importer is unable to redeliver the products, a substantial customs penalty may be payable. The marking must remain on the product (including after any repacking) until it reaches the ultimate purchaser, which is usually the retail customer.

3.Checklist for Certificate of Origin

(1)Are names and addresses as per commercial invoice and letter of credit?

(2)Is country of origin, if required, as per commercial invoice and letter of credit?

(3)Have they been issued by proper party and signed?

(4)Do they show a description relative to commercial invoice and letter of credit?

(5)Are they in exact compliance with letter of credit and dated with a reasonably current date?

(6)About the standard of origin:

a.Completely origin, fill in "P".

b.For imported ingredients, but conform to the standards of country of origin, to the following countries, fill in the following:

①The European Union, Norway, Switzerland, Liechtenstein, Japan, Turkey: fill in "W", then fill in the four-digit tariff number of export products, such as "W"96.18; part of imported raw materials which belong to benefit country can be regarded as its raw materials of its country, therefore, if the imported ingredients of the products which carry imported components completely, the standard of origin still should be filled out "P".

②Canada: imported components accounted for below 40% of the ex-factory price of the products,"F" should be filled out.

③Russia, Belarus, Ukraine, Kazakhstan: imported components shall not exceed 50% of the products FOB price, fill in "Y", then fill in the percentage the value of the imported raw materials and components accounted for in the export products FOB price, such as "Y" 35%.

④Australia and New Zealand: if its raw material and labor service's cost is less than 50% of the products' cost, the origin of the product standard should be blank.

4.Kinds of Certificates of Origin

(1)Certificate of origin.

(2)Generalized system of preference certificate of origin Form A (Sample 6-13).

(3)Certificate of manufacturer's origin.

(4)The Asia-Pacific Trade Agreement certificate of origin is applicable to exports of India, Korea, Bangladesh, and Sri Lanka and conform to the provisions of the product.

(5)The China-Asean Free Trade Agreement certificate of origin Form E is applicable to exports of Indonesia, Thailand, Malaysia, Vietnam, Philippines, Singapore, Brunei, Cambodia, Burma, Laos and other countries and comply with relevant regulations.

(6)China-Pakistan Free Trade Agreement certificate of origin: China's export preferential products with this certificate to Pakistan can be obtained preferential duty treatment under the framework by Pakistan.

(7)China-Chile Free Trade Agreement certificate of origin Form F: Since October 1, 2006, China's exports to Chile under the free trade agreement between China and Chile enjoy treatment of Chile tariff reductions.

(8)China-New Zealand Free Trade Agreement certificate of origin: Since October 1, 2008, China's exports to New Zealand in China-New Zealand FTA rules of origin of products enjoy giving preferential duty treatment.

(9)China-Singapore Free Trade Agreement certificate of origin: Since January 1, 2009, China's exports to Singapore in China-Singapore FTA rules of origin of products enjoy giving preferential duty treatment.

(10)China-Peru Free Trade Agreement certificate of origin: Since March 1, 2010, China's exports to Peru in China-Peru FTA rules of origin of products enjoy preferential duty treatment given by Peru.

(11)The Cross-Strait Economic Cooperation Framework Agreement certificate of origin: Since January 1, 2011, Chinese Mainland's exports to Taiwan, China in the Cross-Strait Economic Cooperation Framework Agreement rules of origin products enjoy treatment of tariff reductions in Taiwan, China.

(12)China-Costa Rica Free Trade Agreement certificate of origin: Since August 1, 2011, China's exports in China-Costa Rica FTA rules of origin of products enjoy treatment of tariff reductions in Costa Rica.

5.Clauses of Certificates of Origin

(1)Certificate of origin separated.

(2)Generalized system of preference certificate of origin Form A.

(3)Shipment of goods of origin prohibited in certificate of origin.

(4)Photocopy of original certificate of Chinese or GSP certificate of origin Form A required and such certificate combined with or referred to other documents is not acceptable.

(5)Certificate of origin incorporated in the invoice is acceptable.

(6)For imports from the People's Republic of China a separated certificate of origin is required along with the advising therein of names and addresses of the manufacturers. This certificate must be legalized by China Countil for the Promotion of International Trade.

原产地证书(见样单6-12)是证明商品原产地/国的文件。该证书应标示商品的性质、数量、价值和产地等内容。在很多国家,原产地证书通常由出口商在公证机构在场的情况下填制和签字,由目的国承认的非政府商业机构出证。原产地证书在中国一般由两个政府机关签发:中华人民共和国海关总署和中国国际贸易促进委员会。

原产地证书一般有两种:一般原产地证书和普惠制原产地证书(GSP C/O)。普惠制原产地证书比较特殊,对某些发展中国家来说,向某些发达国家出口商品时使用这种证书可以获得优惠关税待遇。

Sample 6-12　　　　　　　　　　　Certificate of Origin

样单6-12　　　　　　　　　　　　　原产地证书

1.Exporter FUJIAN INTERNATIONAL IMPORT & EXPORT CORP. 8TH FLOOR, 200 ZHANQIAN ROAD, FUZHOU, CHINA	Certificate No. . CERTIFICATE OF ORIGIN OF THE PEOPLE'S REPUBLIC OF CHINA			
2.Consignee NEO GENERAL TRADING CO. P.O.BOX 99552, RIYADH 22766, KSA TEL: 00966-1-4659220　FAX: 00966-1-4659213				
3.Means of transport and route SHIPMENT FROM SHANGHAI, CHINA TO DAMMAM, KSA BY SEA	5.For certifying authority use only			
4.Country/region of destination SAUDI ARABIA				
6.Marks and numbers	7.Number and kind of packages; description of goods	8.H.S. Code	9.Quantity	10.Number and date of invoices
ROSE BRAND 178/2018 RIYADH	ABOUT 1,700 CARTONS CANNED MUSHROOMS PIECES & STEMS 24 TINS × 425 GRAMS NET WEIGHT (D.W. 227 GRAMS) ROSE BRAND	2018.1011	1,700 CTNS	2018SDT001 APR. 25, 2018

SAY TOTAL: ONE THOUSAND SEVEN HUNDRED CARTONS ONLY.

THE NAME OF THE MANUFACTURER:

XUZHOU SHENGTONG FOODSTUFFS CO., LTD.

NO.15 HEPING ROAD, XUZHOU 221009, CHINA

TEL: 86-0516-3402323　FAX: 86-0516-3402330

WE HEREBY CERTIFY THAT GOODS EXPORTED ARE WHOLLY OF CHINESE ORIGIN.

11.Declaration by the exporter The undersigned hereby declares that the above details and statements are correct, that all the goods were produced in China and that they comply with the Rules of Origin of the People's Republic of China. FUZHOU, CHINA APR. 25, 2018 张欢	12.Certification It is hereby certified that the declaration by the exporter is correct. FUZHOU, CHINA　APR. 25, 2018
Place and date, signature and stamp of authorized signatory	Place and date, signature and stamp of certifying authority

不同类型的原产地证书在出口的不同阶段制作。在正常情况下,出口商准备好商业发票后就开始着手一般原产地证书的办理工作。但是,在某些情况下,原产地证书只能在出口商提交了商业发票和提单之后才能出证,例如普惠制《中国-东盟自由贸易协定》原产地证书。这样的话,原产地证书的准备工作就有可能拖延到出口商获得提单之后的某个时间。不管是什么情况,出口商只在交单议付货款时才使用原产地证书。

使用原产地证书的主要目的是在进口国海关征收进口关税时和实施制裁、配额、反倾销税或优惠待遇等进口管制措施时证明货物的原产地。

必须将原产地证书和原产国标志区别开来。很多国家规定在产品上和包装的标签上标明原产国。原产地证书有可能是这些标志的补充或者可以代替它们。在《北美自由贸易协定》中,原产地证书是必需的。

《北美自由贸易协定》中有特定产品的原产地标准,出口至或进口自加拿大或墨西哥的产品要达到这些标准才能享受减免关税的待遇。一般来说,从北美地区外进口的所有商品要得到《北美自由贸易协定》中关税减免的资格,必须在生产的过程中满足"关税税则变更"要求。另外,一些商品必须包含特定的"区域价值成分",一般要达到50%~60%。对成品和有些从外部地区购买的原材料必须追溯来源,以确定原产国。

1.关税减免项目

进口前,进口商应明确这类产品是否能获得国会允许的关税减免。其中最大的关税减免项目是普惠制(GSP)。这个项目的目标是通过免除自不发达国家进口商品的关税来促进这些国家的经济发展。根据《北美自由贸易协定》的规定,墨西哥于1994年1月1日被取消了受益国资格。但事实上,即使是来自普惠制受益国的进口商品,也不一定能获得免税的待遇。某些特定的商品被排除在外,所以进口商必须先确定要进口的商品是否在排除之列。另外,该商品必须有35%以上的价值来自本国成分。如要申请免税,进口商必须在进口汇总申报单上填"A",另外,如果海关有要求,还需提交一份由出口商提供的普惠制原产地证书。

加勒比海盆地24个国家,《以色列自由贸易协定》中的以色列,《安第斯贸易优惠法案》中的玻利维亚、哥伦比亚、秘鲁、厄瓜多尔,以及《非洲增长与机遇法案》中的35个国家进口商品可以享受类似的免税政策。

1994年1月1日开始执行的《北美自由贸易协定》中的最后一个项目是关税减免。在该协定下,原产于加拿大和墨西哥的商品出口至美国时,只要满足一定的条件即可享受免税待遇。这就意味着6条资格条款中的商品必须是加拿大原产或墨西哥原产,同时出口商必须向进口商提供原产地证书。许多商品的免税待遇是只要申请即得,但是有一些商品的审核需要5~15年的时间。尽管如此,只要进口商按要求办理,从加拿大或墨西哥进口的关税始终是比一般关税低的。

2.原产国

对原产国的选择会直接影响进口商品的关税率以及对配额的适用性。另外,《1930年关税法案》304部分规定,进口商品上必须有清晰和明显的原产国英文名称的永久性标记。一些种类的商品不需要在商品上做这个标记,但必须在商品最外层包装上标明原产国。这是很重要的初步规划设想,因为海关规定,某些特定商品必须以某种方式标记,如在商品的生产过程中采用模压印花、模具刻字或铜板刻画等方式。

　　进口商在进口商品前应了解有关原产国标准的规定,以便确定是否需要在货物生产前建议供货商或卖方使用特定的标记方法。有些产于国外的货物在生产工序完成后是无法根据美国原产地标记的要求更改的。无正确标记的商品有可能会被美国海关没收。有时候商品被没收后还可以补上标记,但是需要缴纳一笔标记罚金,这会增加进口成本。更严重的是,有时海关会把商品交给进口商,而有些不知情的进口商会把商品转售。然后,美国海关会签发一份货物再交付通知书。如果进口商无法再交付货物,就要支付一笔金额很大的海关罚款。标记必须保留在商品上(即使重新包装)直到商品到达最终的购买者手里,这些购买者通常是零售消费者。

3.原产地证书审核内容

(1)名称和地址与商业发票和信用证上的是否一致?

(2)如果有规定,原产国与商业发票和信用证规定的是否一致?

(3)证书是否由正确的当事人出具和签字?

(4)商品描述与商业发票和信用证标示的内容是否相关?

(5)证书与信用证是否严格相符,签发日期是不是合理的和近期的日期?

(6)关于原产地标准:

a.完全原产的,填写"P"。

b.含有进口成分,但符合原产地标准,输往下列国家时,填写如下:

①欧盟成员国、挪威、瑞士、列支敦士登、日本、土耳其:填写"W",其后填明出口产品的四位数税则号,如"W"96.18;属于给惠国成分的进口原料部分可视作本国原料,因此,如果产品的进口成分完全采用给惠国成分,则该产品的原产地标准仍填写"P"。

②加拿大:进口成分占产品出厂价的40%以下,填"F"。

③俄罗斯、白俄罗斯、乌克兰、哈萨克斯坦:进口成分不得超过产品FOB价的50%,填"Y",其后填明进口原料和部件的价值在出口产品FOB价中所占百分比,如"Y"35%。

④澳大利亚和新西兰:本国原材料和劳务的成本不低于产品出厂成本的50%,则该产品的原产地标准留空。

4.原产地证书的种类

(1)一般原产地证书。

(2)普惠制原产地证书格式A(见样单6-13)。

(3)厂商产地证明。

(4)《亚太贸易协定》原产地证书:目前适用于印度、韩国、孟加拉国和斯里兰卡出口并符合规定的产品。

(5)《中国-东盟自由贸易协定》原产地证书格式E:目前适用于印度尼西亚、泰国、马来西亚、越南、菲律宾、新加坡、文莱、柬埔寨、缅甸、老挝等国出口并符合相关规定的产品。

(6)《中国-巴基斯坦自由贸易协定》原产地证书:我国出口到巴基斯坦的该优惠框架项下的产品凭此证书可获得巴基斯坦给予的关税优惠待遇。

(7)《中国-智利自由贸易协定》原产地证书格式F:自2006年10月1日起,我国出口到智利的《中国-智利自由贸易协定》项下的产品享受智利给予的关税优惠待遇。

Sample 6-13　　Genèralized System of Preference Certificate of Origin Form A

样单6-13　　　　　普惠制原产地证书格式A

1. Goods consigned from (Exporter's business name, address, country) BEIJING TEXTILE GARMENT CO., LTD. HUARONG MANSION RM2901，NO.85 CHANGAN ROAD, BEIJING, CHINA	Reference No. GENERALIZED SYSTEM OF PREFERENCE CERTIFICATE OF ORIGIN (Combined Declaration and Certificate) FORM A Issued in THE PEOPLE'S REPUBLIC OF CHINA (Country)
2.Goods consigned to (Consignee's name, address, country) FASHION FORCE CO., LTD P.O.BOX 8935, NEW TERMINAL, ALTA, VISTA OTTAWA, CANADA	See Notes Overleaf
3.Means of transport and route (as far as known) SHIPMENT FROM BEIJING, CHINA TO MONTREAL, CANADA BY VESSEL	4.For official use

5. Item number	6.Marks and numbers of packages	7.Number and kind of packages; description of goods	8. Origin criterion (see notes overleaf)	9. Gross weight or other quantity	10.Number and date of invoice
1	FASHION FORCE F01LCB05127 CTN NO. MONTREAL MADE IN CHINA	SALES CONDITIONS: CIF MONTREAL/CANADA SALES CONTRACT NO. F01LCB05127 LADIES COTTON BLAZER (100% COTTON, 40×20/140×60) STYLE NO.　PO NO.　QTY/PCS　USD/PC 46-301A　　10337　　2,550　　12.80 *********************************	"P"	2,550 PCS	NT001FF004
			TOTAL:	2,550 PCS	MAR. 20, 2018

11.Certification It is hereby certified, on the basis of control carried out, that the declaration by the exporter is correct. 　　　BEIJING, CHINA MAR. 22, 2018	12.Declaration by the exporter The undersigned hereby declares that the above details and statements are correct, that all the goods were produced in 　　　CHINA ----------------------------------- 　　　(country) and that they comply with the origin requirements specified for those goods in the Generalized System of Preferences for goods exported to 　　　CANADA ----------------------------------- 　　(importing country) 　　BEIJING, CHINA MAR. 21, 2018 　　　　　张欢
Place and date, signature and stamp of certifying authority	Place and date, signature and stamp of authorized signatory

（8）《中国-新西兰自由贸易协定》原产地证书：自2008年10月1日起，我国出口到新西兰的符合《中国-新西兰自由贸易协定》原产地规则的产品享受新西兰给予的关税优惠待遇。

（9）《中国-新加坡自由贸易协定》原产地证书：自2009年1月1日起，我国出口到新加坡的符合《中国-新加坡自由贸易协定》原产地规则的产品享受新加坡给予的关税优惠待遇。

（10）《中国-秘鲁自由贸易协定》原产地证书：自2010年3月1日起，我国出口到秘鲁的符合《中国-秘鲁自由贸易协定》原产地规则的产品享受秘鲁给予的关税优惠待遇。

（11）《海峡两岸经济合作框架协议》原产地证书：自2011年1月1日起，中国大陆出口到中国台湾地区的符合《海峡两岸经济合作框架协议》原产地规则的产品享受中国台湾地区给予的关税优惠待遇。

（12）《中国-哥斯达黎加自由贸易协定》原产地证书：自2011年8月1日起，我国出口到哥斯达黎加的符合《中国-哥斯达黎加自由贸易协定》原产地规则的产品享受哥斯达黎加给予的关税优惠待遇。

5.原产地证书条款

（1）单独出具的原产地证书。

（2）普惠制原产地证书格式A。

（3）原产地证书不允许装运的产品。

（4）提供中国原产地证书或普惠制原产地证书格式A的复印件，该原产地证书是独立的，不依附于其他单证格式。

（5）与发票联合的原产地证书可以接受。

（6）从中国进口货物应单独缮制原产地证书，并注明厂家名称、地址，由中国国际贸易促进委员会签发。

Training Case 6-5

A Dispute Case which the Date of the Certificate of Origin Issued was Later than the Date of B/L

A certain China export company A exported a batch of goods to a foreign trade company B. Some provisions of L/C shipment and documents were stipulated as following: "SHIPMENT FROM CHINESE PORT TO HAMBURG NOT LATER THAN 20TH JUNE, ×××× ... FULL SET OF CLEAN ON BOARD MARINE BILLS OF LADING MADE OUT TO ORDER OF SHIPPER AND ENDORSED IN BLANK MARKED 'FREIGHT PREPAID' NOTIFYING BUYERS. CERTIFICATE OF ORIGIN..."

After company A made shipment according to regulations, the documents were presented to the negotiating bank for negotiation. After the negotiating bank examined the documents and regarded that documents were in conformity with the L/C, it sent the documents to the issuing bank. However, after the documents reached the foreign country, the issuing bank has challenged: "About your documents No.×××, after auditing it is found that the date of the certificate of origin issued is later than the date of B/L. The issuing date of the certificate of origin was on June 17, but the issuing date of your B/L was on June 15. According to the situation of the above documents inconsistent with the L / C, the documents can not be accepted after researching, and are temporarily taken care of. Please reply immediately how to deal with."

After receiving the notification that the issuing bank refused to pay, company A regarded that the issuing bank was unreasonable. After studying with the negotiating bank, company A argued as the following: "Your fax dated ×× has received. About alleged discrepancies of our documents No.×××, we think that it does not constitute a document discrepancy that certificate of origin issued on the date later than the issuing date of the B / L. Only when you have special provisions on the issuing date of certificate of origin, which shall not be later than the issuing date of B/L,our issuing date of certificate of origin is later than the issuing date of the B/L can constitute document discrepancy. Otherwise you are unable to illustrate our document discrepancy. Above all, our documents are completely consistent with the L/C and you must pay on time."

After company A issued the rebuttals, unexpectedly the issuing bank put forward once again: "Your fax dated ×× about documents No.××× problem, our bank thinks, about the issuing date of the certificate of origin, though there is no restrictions and regulations in our L / C, evidence documents of such a certificate issued by the public surveyor shall be issued before shipment of the goods. Only when the relevant department has tested and checked the actual goods before shipment can make proof. If the goods have been shipped, how can the public surveyor inspect or check the actual goods? So our bank still can't accept the documents and please inform how to deal with as soon as possible."

After company A discussed with the negotiating bank repeatedly, it finally sent the fax as follows:

"About the problem that the certificate of origin issued on the date later than the date of B/L, the issuing date of the certificate of origin and the issuing date of the B/L are unrelated date, besides our issuing date of the certificate of origin is no later than the validity of documents presentation you regulated.

"According to the regulations of UCP600: If a credit requires presentation of a document other than a transport document, insurance document or commercial invoice, without stipulating by whom the document is to be issued or its data content, banks will accept the document as presented if its content appears to fulfil the function of the required document and otherwise complies with sub-article 14 (d). According to the above stipulation, that is to say, if you have special requests for the issuing date of the certificate of origin, you must make the corresponding rules in the L/C, otherwise as long as the data content of the submitted documents and other required documents submitted are not contradictory, your bank should accept our data content in the submitted documents.

"Your view in your fax states that the certificate of origin seems not true if issuing date of the certificate of origin is later than the issuing date of B/L, and which means that the public surveyor can't check the goods. This is only your guess. Actually our goods were applied for on June 13, audited its country of origin on June 14 by the commodity inspection agencies, and shipped on June 15. June 15 and June 16 are our double cease days, so the certificate of origin was issued on June 17.

"From the role of the issuing date of certificate of origin in the project, it does not affect this certificate of origin to prove the goods, and does not constitute a discrepancy with your L/C.

"Above all, there are no so - called discrepancies you have put forward. Please make payment on time."

After company A and the negotiating bank put forward the above rebuttals, the issuing bank's reply could not be seen. But through the negotiating bank, it was informed that the payment had been transferred to the company's account and the case ended.

原产地证书签发日期晚于提单日期争议案

我方出口公司 A 向国外贸易公司 B 出口一批货物。信用证关于装运和单据部分条款规定如下:"最迟于某年 6 月 20 日从中国港口装运至汉堡……全套清洁已装船海运提单,做成以发货人指示抬头,空白背书,注明'运费预付',通知买方。原产地证书……"

A 公司按规定装运后,向议付行交单议付。议付行审单后认为单证相符,即向开证行寄单。但单证寄到国外后,开证行却提出异议:"你方第×××号单据经审核发现,原产地证书的签发日期晚于提单签发日期。原产地证书签发日期为 6 月 17 日,而你方提单签发日期为 6 月 15 日。根据以上单证不符的情况,经研究无法接受,单据暂代保管,速复如何处理。"

A 公司接到上述开证行拒付通知后,认为开证行的异议不合理。经与议付行研究,其做如下反驳:"你方××日电悉。关于我方×××号单据所谓不符点一事,我们认为:原产地证书的签发日期晚于提单签发日期并不构成单证不符。只有在你方对原产地证书的签发日期有特别规定不得晚于提单签发日期,而我方原产地证书的签发日期晚于提单签发日期时,才能构成单证不符,否则无法说明我方单证不符。综上所述,我方单证完全与信用证相符,你行必须按时付款。"

A 公司发出上述反驳意见后,未料到开证行又提出:"你××日电关于第×××号单证问题,我行认为:关于原产地证书的签发日期,虽然我方信用证没有做有关的限制和规定,但类似这样由公证机构出具的证明文件均应在货物装运前出具。有关部门在货物装运前对实际货物进行检验、核对,才能做出证明。如果货物已经装运完毕,公证机构怎能对实际的货物进行检验或核对? 所以我行仍然不能接受单证,速告如何处理。"

A 公司经过与议付行反复探讨,最后又发出如下电文:

"对于原产地证书的签发日期晚于提单签发日期问题,该证书签发日期与提单签发日期是两个互不相干的日期,况且我方原产地证书的签发日期也没有晚于你方规定的交单有效期。

"根据 UCP600 的规定:如果信用证要求提示除运输单据、保险单据或商业发票之外的单据,但未规定该单据由何人出具或单据的内容,只要所提交单据的内容看来满足其功能需要且其他方面与第 14 条 d 款相符,银行将对提示的单据予以接受。按上述条文规定,也就是说,如果你方对原产地证书签发日期有特别要求时,必须在信用证中做出相应的规定,否则只要我方所提交的原产地证书的各项内容不与其他单据同项的内容互相矛盾,你方银行就应该接受我方所提交单据中的各项数据内容。

"你行前电所申述的观点认为,原产地证书的签发日期如晚于提单签发日期,就说明公证机构无法核对货物。这仅是你方的一种猜测。实际上我方该批货物于6月13日即已申请,6月14日经商品检验机构查核落实其原产地,6月15日装运。因6月15日和16日是我地双休日,故6月17日签发原产地证书。

"从原产地证书的签发日期在该项目中的作用看来,它并不影响本证书对该批货物的原产地的情况证明,也不构成与你方信用证不符的条件。

"综上所述,你方所提出的所谓不符点是不存在的。请按时付款。"

A公司和议付行提出上述反驳意见后,再未见开证行的答复,但该争议最终通过议付行通知该货款已转入公司账户而告结。

6.8.3 *Consular Invoice*
领事发票

A consular invoice is a form, usually only obtainable from the importing country's consulate in the exporting country, on which the seller or its agent must enter a detailed description of the goods being shipped. Such a form is required by certain countries in order to compile statistics, control imports, collect import duties and check the origin of goods and the credit of the exporter.

A consular invoice shall carry such information as the name of the goods, the number of the items, their weight, the value and origin of the goods and a declaration that the information given is correct. Most of the consular invoices are in the language of the country to which the goods are shipped, so it is usually considered as the most difficult document of all and must be filled in with special care.

领事发票是一份通常由出口国所在地的进口国领事馆出具的表格,卖方或其代理人须在此表上详细描述已经装船的货物。某些国家要求提供这种单证,为了进行统计、控制进口、征收进口关税和检查货物原产地和出口商的信用。

领事发票应该包括以下内容:货物名称、数量、重量、价值、商品原产地以及所提供的内容正确性的声明。大部分的领事发票使用货物运往国的语言,所以它通常也被认为是最难的单证,必须特别认真填写。

6.8.4 *Customs Invoice*
海关发票

A customs invoice is one of the documents made out on a special form prescribed by the customs authorities of the importing country. Generally, the invoice may include information required by the import customs that is not stated on an ordinary commercial invoice.

This invoice is usually required by some importing countries such as USA, Canada, New

Zealand, Australia and some African countries. It is used to clear customs, to verify the country of origin for import duty and tax purposes, to compare export prices and domestic prices and to fix anti-dumping duties.

Types of customs invoice:

(1)Canada customs invoice (Sample 6-14).

(2)America customs invoice.

(3)Certificate of origin for exports to New Zealand Form 59A.

(4)Combined certificate of value and of origin and invoice of goods for exportation to West Africa Form C. It applies to Sierra Leone, Liberia, etc.

(5)Invoice and declaration of value required for shipment to Jamaica Form C23. It applies to Jamaica, Honduras, etc.

(6)Carioca/Caribbean Common Market customs invoice. It applies to the members of Carioca/Caribbean Common Market: Jamaica, Dominican, Guyana, etc.

(7) Uncertain format customs invoice. There is no name of customs invoice and a designated name in this format. It applies to Malta, Mauritius, etc.

The content and format of West Africa customs invoice format is basically the same content. Words of origin and value can be filled to certify the commodities exported to the countries. If an L/C does not require supplying customs invoice, it can be avoided. Australian customs invoice in has stopped using. A statement can be filled in the commercial invoice in the developing countries. For example:"I declare that the final process of manufacture of the goods for which special rates are claimed has been performed in China and that not less than one half of the factory cost of the goods is represented by the value of labor and material of China."

海关发票是根据进口国海关指定格式出具的特殊单证之一。通常海关发票应包含进口国海关规定的内容,而这些内容在一般的商业发票上是不标示的。

美国、加拿大、新西兰、澳大利亚和一些非洲国家一般要求提供海关发票,其可用于清关,也用于缴纳进口税时核对原产国、比较出口价格和国内价格以及确定反倾销税等。

海关发票的种类有:

(1)加拿大海关发票(见样单6-14)。

(2)美国海关发票。

(3)输往新西兰货物原产地证书格式59A(新西兰海关发票格式59A)。

(4)出口到西非的联合发票和原产地证书格式C(西非海关发票格式C),适用于塞拉利昂和利比里亚等。

(5)牙买加海关发票格式C23,适用于牙买加和洪都拉斯等。

(6)加勒比共同市场海关发票。它适用于加勒比共同体和同市场的成员:牙买加、多米尼加和圭亚那等。

(7)无确定格式的海关发票。这是指海关发票没有特定的名称,适用于马耳他和毛里求斯等。

192 国际商务单证双语教程

Sample 6-14   Canada Customs Invoice
样单 6-14   加拿大海关发票

Revenue Canada Customs and Excise	Revenue Canada Douanes et Accise	CANADA CUSTOMS INVOICE FACTURE DES DOUANES CANADIENNES	Page of de

1.Vendor (name and address) Vendeur (nom et adresse) BEIJING TEXTILE GARMENT CO., LTD. HUARONG MANSION RM2901, NO.85 CHANGAN ROAD,BEIJING, CHINA	2.Date of direct shipment to Canada Date d'expedition directe vers ie Canade AS PER B/L DATE
	3. Other references (include purchaser's order No.) Autres reterences (inclure ie n de commande de Í acheteur) N/A

4.Consignee (name and address) Destinataire (nom et adresse) FASHION FORCE CO., LTD , P.O.BOX 8935 NEW TERMINAL, ALTA,VISTA OTTAWA, CANADA	5.Purchaser's name and address (if other than consignee) Nom et adresse de Í acheteur (s'll differe du destinataire) SAME AS CONSIGNEE
	6.Country of transshipment/Pays de transbordement N/A

	7.Country of origin of goods Pays d'origine des marchandises CHINA	IF SHIPMENT INCLUDES GOODS OF DIFFERENT ORIGINS ENTER ORIGINS AGAINST ITEMA IN12 SIL'EXPEDON COMPREND DES MARCHANDISES D'ORIGINES DIFFERENTES PRECISER LEUR PROVENANCE EN12

8.Transportation give mode and place of direct shipment to Canada Transport preciser mode et point d'expedition directe vercte vers ie Canada SHIPMENT FROM SHANGHAI, CHINA TO MONTREAL, CANADA BY VESSEL	9.Conditions of sale and terms of payment (i.e. consignment shipment, leased goods, etc.) Conditions de vente et modaitites de paiement (p. ex vente, expedition en consignation, location, de marchandises, etc.) CIF MONTREAL BY L/C
	10.Currency of Settlement/Devises du paiement US DOLLAR

11.No. of pkgs. Nore de colis 201 CTNS	12.Specification of commodities (kind of packages, marks and numbers, general description and characteristics, i. e. grade, quality) Designation des articles (nature des colis, marques et numeros, description ger erale et caracteristiques, p.ex classe, qualite) LADIES COTTON BLAZER (100%COTTON, 40×20/140×60) STYLE NO. PO NO. QTY/PCS USD/PC 46-301A 10337 2,550 12.80 PACKED IN 201 CTNS ONLY	13.Quantity (state unit) Quantite (Preciser Í unite) 2,550 PCS	Selling price Prix de vente	
			14.Unit price Prix unitaire USD 12.80	15. Total USD 32,640.00

Continued

18.If any of fields 1 to 17 are included on an attached commercial invoice, check this box Si tout renseignement relatlvement aux zones 1 e 17 ligure sur une ou des tactures ommerciaiesci attachees cocher cette case commercial invoice No.1 N de la factre commerciaie NT001FF004	16. Total weight Poids total		17.Invoice total Total de la facture
	Net 2,010 KGS	Gross Brut 3,015 KGS	USD 32,640.00
19.Exporter's name and address (if other than vendor) Nom et adresse de Í exportateur (s'll differe du vendeur) SAME AS VENDOR	20.Originator (name and address) Expediteur d'origine (nom et adresse) BEIJING TEXTILE GARMENT CO., LTD. HUARONG MANSION RM2901 , NO.85 CHANGAN ROAD, BEIJING, CHINA		
21.Departmental ruling (if applicable) Decision du ministere (s'lly a lieu) N/A	22.If fields 23 to 25 are not applicable, check this box Si ies zones 23 e 25 sont sans objet, cocher cette case ☐		
23. If included in field 7, indicate amount Si compris dans ie total a ie zone 17, preciser Ⅰ. Transportation charges, expense and insurance from the place of direct shipment to Canada Les frais de transport, depenses et assurances a partir du point of expedition directe vers ie Canada USD 4,590.40 Ⅱ. Costs for construction, erection and assembly incurred after importation into Canada Les couts de construction, d' erection et d' assemblage, pres imporaation au. Canada N/A Ⅲ. Export packing Le cout de Í emballage d' exportation N/A	24. If not included in field 17, indicate amount Si non compris dans le total a ie zone 17, preciser Ⅰ.Transportation charges, expense and insurance to the place of direct shipment to Canada Les frais de transport, depenses et assurances Iusqu' au point d' of expedition directd vers ie Canada N/A Ⅱ. Amounts for commissions other than buying commissions Les commissions autres que celles verses Pour Í achat N/A Ⅲ. Export packing Le cout de Í emballage d' exportation N/A		25.Check (if applicable) Cochet (s'lly a liso) Ⅰ.Royalty payments or subsequent proceeds are paid or payable by the purchaser Des redevances ou prodults ont ete ou seront Verses par Í acheteur N/A ☐ Ⅱ. The purchaser has supplied goods or services for use in the production of these goods L'acheteur a fouml des merchandises ou des Services pour ia production des merchandises N/A ☐

西非各国的海关发票的内容和格式几乎都是相同的。如果货物要出口到这些国家,要在海关发票上填写货物的原产国和价值,以证明其可靠性。另外,如果信用证不要求提供海关发票,这些内容就不用填写。澳大利亚海关发票已经停止使用。在发展中国家的商业发票上要注明相关的声明。例如:"兹证明享受特殊税率的货物的制造是在中国进行的,而且货物的加工费和材料费不少于工厂成本的一半。"

6.9 Exporter's Instruction Documents
出口商指示单证

Instruction documents issued by the exporter are generally not required for export, but it is highly recommended to make certain everyone is performing according to the exporter's specific instructions to facilitate the export process.

Exporter's instruction documents include forwarder's instructions, shipping instructions, stowage instructions, hazardous materials/dangerous goods instructions and bank instructions.

1.Forwarder's Instructions

Forwarder's instructions are issued by the consignor and contain instructions for booking the shipment of cargo and completing the transport documents.

2.Shipping Instructions

Shipping instructions are issued by the consignor and give specific instructions to the shipping company or freight forwarder regarding the shipment. They are identical to the forwarder's instructions. The bill of lading is typically drawn up from these information.

3.Stowage Instructions

Stowage instructions are issued by the consignor and contain specific instructions regarding how or where a cargo should be stowed during transport. For example, a shipper can require that the shipment is placed below deck and amidships for greater protection from the elements.

4.Hazardous Materials/Dangerous Goods Instructions

Hazardous materials/dangerous goods instructions are issued by the consignor and contain information regarding a shipment of hazardous materials or dangerous goods. Hazardous material is a substance or product that has been determined to be capable of posing an unreasonable risk to health, safety and property when transported in commerce. Hazardous materials are classified as dangerous goods when transported by air. Hazards are classified as "other regulated materials" and include irritating, corrosive, flammable, radioactive and other life or health threatening materials. Special handling instructions must be provided and containers must be properly emblazoned with warning labels and stickers.

5.Bank Instructions

Bank instructions are issued by the consignor and contain information about how the exporter/seller wishes to have payment secured for a shipment when a documentary collection or documentary letter of credit is used.

出口一般不需要由出口商出具的指示单证,但是强烈推荐根据出口商的明确指示去操作,以便出口过程顺利进行。

出口商指示单证包括货代的指示、装运指示、理舱指示、有害物质/危险货物指示和银行指示。

1.货代的指示

货代的指示由发货人开立,包括订货指示和货运指示单证。

2.装运指示

装运指示是发货人签发的对船公司或货代的特定指示。它们实际上与货代指示相同。提单是典型的以装运指示为基础起草的单证。

3.理舱指示

理舱指示由发货人开立,包含对运输过程中货物应该如何装载或者放哪里的具体说明。例如,托运人可以要求将货物放甲板下面和船中间,以便更好地保护货物。

4.有害物质/危险货物指示

由发货人开立的有害物质/危险货物指示包含有害物质或危险货物的信息。有害物质是一种在运输中可能对人的健康、安全及财产造成不合理风险的物质或产品。航空运输时,有害物质被列为危险品。危险品被划分为"其他管制性物质",包括刺激性、腐蚀性、易燃性、辐射性和其他对生命或健康有威胁的物质。对这些物质必须提供特殊处置指示,集装箱必须恰当贴有警告标签和贴纸。

5.银行指示

由发货人签发的银行指示包含关于当使用跟单托收或跟单信用证时,出口商/卖方希望如何安全付款的信息。

6.10   A Summary of Export Documents
出口单证小结

From the perspective of sellers, documents are not only part of their basic obligations under the contract, but also important tasks concerning the collection of the export cargo proceeds.

Generally speaking, the basic requirements for documents are correctness, completeness, conciseness, cleanness and promptness.

Documents for an export transaction are to be prepared and checked on all the bases such as contract, L/C and original information from the manufacturers.

Any negligence in documents may hinder the fulfillment of the contract and might result in serious problems.

Major export documents include the bill of exchange (draft), invoice, packing list, insurance policy, bill of lading, inspection certificate and certificate of origin, etc.

As is discussed above, different types of documents are required at different stages of the export procedure. But as there are too many different documents involved in too many different stages, to study them one by one may only provide you a squirrel's view of the picture. To help you take a bird's eye of the picture, the main documents are summarized in Table 6-4.

Table 6-4   A Summary of Export Documents

	Goods Preparation	Inspection	Booking Space	Export Clearance	Loading	Insurance	Payment Negotiation
Export License				√			
Sales Contract	√	√		√		√	
Letter of Credit	√	√					√
Commercial Invoice				√		√	√
Packing List				√		√	√
Inspection Application		√					
Inspection Certificate				√			√
Booking Note			√				
Shipping Order					√		
Customs Declaration				√			
Customs Clearance					√		
Shipping Advice							√
Bill of Lading							√
Proposal Form						√	
Insurance Policy							√
Bill of Exchange							√
Certificate of Origin							√
Consular Invoice							√
Customs Invoice							√

　　从卖方的角度来说,单证不仅是合同项下的基本条件,也是收取货款需完成的重要任务。

一般来说,单证的基本要求是正确、完整、简洁、清洁和迅速。

对出口交易而言,制作和核对单证的基础是合同、信用证和制造商提供的原始数据等。任何单证的错误都有可能阻碍合同的履行,甚至可能导致严重的问题。

主要的出口单证包括汇票、发票、装箱单、保险单、提单、检验证书和原产地证书等。

如上所述,不同的单证在出口的不同阶段使用。但是单证的种类和环节太多,如果一个个去学,大家可能会感到困惑。为了使大家能更好地全面了解出口单证,表6-4对主要出口单证做了汇总。

表6-4　　　　　　　　　　　　出口单证汇总表

	备货	检验	订舱	清关	装货	保险	议付
出口许可证				√			
销售合同	√	√		√		√	
信用证	√	√					√
商业发票				√		√	√
装箱单				√		√	√
检验申请表	√						
检验证书				√			
订舱单			√				
装货单					√		
报关申请表				√			
清关单				√			
装船通知							√
提单							√
投保单						√	
保险单							√
汇票							√
原产地证书							√
领事发票							√
海关发票							√

Key Terms

certificate of origin 原产地证书　insurance policy 保险单　shipping advice 装船通知

Exercise

◎ *Case Analysis*

A certain foreign trade company imported a batch of bulk chemical fertilizers, covering ocean marine transportation all risks to insurance companies. After the goods arrived in the port of destination, all were discharged to port warehouse. In the process of unloading, the foreign trade company and the handing company signed a filling and stevedoring agreement, and immediately began filling. One day, the handling company according to the agreement had half of the packed goods piled up at the edge of railway goods yard in the port area, waiting for rail transit to deliver to different buyers. The other half of the goods stayed in the warehouse were yet to be filled the bulk, and suffered from severe wet damage due to typhoon. So, the foreign trade company claimed with the insurance company for the damage, but it was rejected by the insurance company. To this, try to make comments.

某外贸企业进口一批散装化肥,向保险公司投保海运一切险。货抵目的港后,全部卸至港务公司仓库。在卸货过程中,外贸企业与装卸公司签订了一份灌装协议,并立即开始灌装。某日,由装卸公司根据协议将已灌装成包的半数货物堆放在港区内铁路边堆场,等待铁路转运至他地以交付不同买主。另一半留在仓库尚待灌装的散货,因受台风袭击,遭受严重湿损。于是,外贸企业遂就遭受湿损部分向保险公司索赔,被保险公司拒绝。对此,试予评论。

◎ *Practice*

根据下列所给资料,制作一份受益人证明。

L/C NO.: 894010151719

INVOICE, PACKING LIST NO.: SUNJA0306

B/L NO.: N1FBCMAFF996887

BENEFICIARY:CATICO IMPORT AND EXPROT CORP.

　　　　　　 87 LIANHU ROAD,NANJING,CHINA

APPLICANT:FLY TRAVEL GDS I/E GROUP

　　　　　　 OSSERSTRA 12,7256DZ ENSCHEDE, THE NETHERLANDS

DOCUMENTS REQUIRED:

-INVOICE IN TRIPLICATE

-PACKING LIST IN DUPLICATE

-FULL SET OF ORIGINAL CLEAN BILLS OF LADING IN TRIPLICATE

-CERTIFICATE ISSUED BY BENIFICIARY STATING THAT GOODS UNDER ORDER NO. 8561 HAVE BEEN SHIPPED BEFORE MAR. 6, 2019 AND ALL THE REQUIRED DOCUMENTS HAVE BEEN FAXED TO THE APPLICANT IN ONE WEEK AFTER SHIPPING DATE.

Chapter 7

Import Documents
进口单证

Learning Objectives

◆ 重点掌握进口许可证;掌握进口申报;了解进口需要的单证。

Guide Case

Whether It can be Accepted to Print for the Signing

The L/C required manufacturer inspection certificate and it was showed on the right bottom of the manufacturer survey report submitted by the beneficiary that ABC Co., Ltd. as MFR authorized signature Wang Ming. "Wang Ming" obviously was in print. The issuing bank refused to pay for the discrepancies that manufacturer inspection certificate had not been signed.

The beneficiary regarded that UCP600 Article 3(3) provisions - "A document may be signed by handwriting, facsimile signature, perforated signature, stamp, symbol or any other mechanical or electronic method of authentication." Obviously, the name printed in the case should belong to one of "any other mechanical method of authentication", which was supposed to be one kind of signature, and it could be accepted.

Question: Which side is right? The issuing bank or the beneficiary?

签字以打印为之是否可以接受

信用证要求提交制造商检验证书,受益人提交的制造商检验报告的右下方显示"ABC Co., Ltd. as MFR authorized signature Wang Ming",其中,"Wang Ming"明显以打印为之。开证行以"制造商检验证书未被签署"为不符点,提出拒付。

受益人认为，UCP600第3条第3款规定："单证可手签、签样印制、穿孔签字，以及通过盖章、符号表示或任何其他机械或电子证实的方法签署。"显然，本案中打印的名称应属于"任何其他机械认证方式"的一种，从而理应是签署的一种，可以接受。

问题：开证行和受益人哪一方观点正确？

资料来源　天九湾贸易金融圈研究团队．天九湾单证案例2014年度汇编[M].厦门：厦门大学出版社，2015：10.

For many basic transactions, import documents are simple. Importers of non-regulated goods from many countries can present a commercial invoice, a bill of lading and an import declaration, and they are done.

很多基本交易的进口单证都非常简单。对很多国家的进口商来说，如果进口的是非管制类商品，那么只要提交商业发票、提单和进口报关单即可。

7.1　Definition
定　义

Import documents are issued or secured by both an exporter, an importer (or a customs broker working for the importer) or by a third party.

进口单证由出口商、进口商（或为进口商工作的报关员）或第三方开具或者担保。

7.2　Basic Requirements for Making Import Documents
进口制单的基本要求

1.Terms and Conditions

（1）A written or verbal agreement has been made between the parties specifying the product type, quantity, price, delivery date, delivery method and all other conditions of sale including who will pay for shipping, insurance, duties and other costs.

（2）Countries of export and import have normal trade relations.

（3）Country of export is economically and politically stable and does not have excessive international exchange regulations.

（4）Country of import does not require consular certificates or invoices.

（5）Goods traded are unregulated and do not require import licenses or permits.

（6）Buyers are familiar with the goods traded and have no reason to believe that these goods shipped will be anything other than the goods ordered.

（7）Parties to the transaction know each other, have traded successfully in the past, or have no reason to expect duplicity or dishonesty from the other party.

（8）Terms are payment in advance, by cash, check, wire transfer, or credit card, or on open account with future payment by check, wire transfer, or credit card.

2.Basic Import Documents

Import documents include commercial invoice, bill of lading, import declaration, packing list, certificate of origin and insurance policy.

3.Additional Import Documents

While many import transactions require minimal documents, others require that the importer issue or secure additional documents.

(1)Import licenses/permits.

(2)Additional documents required by import authority.

(3)Special transport documents.

(4)Banking and international exchange documents.

1.条款和条件

(1)买卖双方已事先就产品类型、数量、价格、装运日期、装运方式以及其他贸易条件(如谁支付运费、保险费、关税和其他费用等问题)达成书面或口头协议。

(2)出口国和进口国有正常的贸易关系。

(3)出口国经济和政治稳定,无过多的外汇管制。

(4)进口国通关不需领事证书或领事发票。

(5)交易的货物不受管制,不需办理进口许可证。

(6)买方对交易的货物很熟悉,而且相信所装运的货物即所购货物。

(7)交易各方了解彼此,曾经成功合作,或不会怀疑对方口是心非或不诚实。

(8)付款条件是通过现金、支票、银行电汇或信用卡的方式预付货款或者通过支票、银行电汇或信用卡的方式进行远期付款(赊销)。

2.进口单证的基本种类

进口单证包括商业发票、提单、进口报关单、装箱单、原产地证书和保险单。

3.其他进口单证

尽管很多进口贸易都要求单证简单化,但是在某些贸易中,还是要求进口商签发或担保一些额外的单证:

(1)进口许可证。

(2)进口国当局要求的其他单证。

(3)特殊的运输单证。

(4)银行单证和外汇单证。

Sample 7-1   **Import License of the People's Republic of China**

样单 7-1   **中华人民共和国进口许可证**

1.我国对外成交单位 编码 Importer 广州明朗商贸有限公司 52304125596		3.进口许可证编号 License No. CT88661125839		
2.收货单位 52304125596 Consignee 广州明朗商贸有限公司		4.许可证有效期 Validity 2019年 4 月		
5.贸易方式 Terms of trade 一般贸易		8.进口国家(地区) Country where consigned 日本		
6.外汇来源 Terms of foreign exchange 购汇		9.商品原产地 Country of origin 日本		
7.到货口岸 Port of destination 广州		10.商品用途 Use of commodity 外贸自营内销		
11.唛头——包装件数 Marks & numbers-number of packages		EAST SHANGHAI NOSI-500 MADE IN JAPAN		
12.商品名称 Description of commodity 空调		商品编码 Commodity No. 84151021		

13.商品规格、型号 Specification	单位 Unit	14.数量 Quantity	15.单价 Unit Price	16.总值 Amount	17.总值折美元 Amount in USD
制冷量≤4 000大卡/时 分体式空调	台	500	200美元	100 000美元	100 000
18.总计 Total		500			100 000

19.备注 Supplementary details	20.发证机关盖章 Issuing authority's stamp 发证日期 Signature date 2018年 12 月 1 日

商务部监制   本证不得涂改,不得转让

Sample 7-2　Customs Import Declaration of the People's Republic of China

样单7-2　　　　中华人民共和国海关进口报关单

预录入编号: DS9110006　　　　　　　　　　　　　　　　海关编号:

进口口岸 上海浦江海关（2202）	备案号 ×××		进口日期 2018-04-17	申报日期 2018-04-09
经营单位 江苏纺织服装有限公司(5230412559)	运输方式 海运（1）		运输工具名称 VOLENDAM VOY.7524	提运单号 782-02458690
收货单位 江苏纺织服装有限公司	贸易方式 一般贸易（0110）		征免性质 一般征免（1）	征税比例
许可证号 CT88661182569	起运国（地区） 加拿大（501）		装货港 蒙特利尔（CAMTL）	境内目的地 上海（CNSHA）
批准文号 0220215	成交方式 CIF（1）	运费 502/1 300/3	保险费 502/1 000/3	杂费 ×××
合同协议号 F01LCB05127	件数 85	包装种类 纸箱	毛重（千克） 19.00 KGS	净重（千克） 17.00 KGS
集装箱号 CLLU1000752*3(5)	随附单据 INVOICE, PACKING LIST			用途 外贸自营内销（1）

标记唛码及备注
FASHION FORCE
F01LCB05127
CTN NO.
SHANGHAI
MADE IN CANADA

项号	商品编号	商品名称及规格型号	数量及单位	最终目的国 （地区）	单价	总价	币制	征免
1	62043200.90	LADIES COTTON BLAZER 100% COTTON 40×20/140×60	2,550 PCS	中国	12.80	32,640.00	美元	照章 （1）
		总计:　　　2 550件				32 640.00美元		

税费征收情况

税务登记号码　320102134773852

录入员　录入单位	兹声明以上申报无讹 并承担法律责任	海关审单批注及放行日期（签章）	
		审单	审价
	报关员　李平	征税	统计
单位地址　南京市管桥85号，华荣大厦 　　　　　2901室 邮编 210005　电话 025-84715004	申报单位（签章） 江苏纺织服装有限公司 填制日期 2018-04-09	查验	放行

7.3 Import License/Permit and Declaration
进口许可证与进口报关单

All countries seek to control their imports for political, economic or security purpose. Governments also seek to control who imports, what is imported and the country of origin of their imports.

In some cases an outright import ban on a commodity or product might exist. In other cases, import of a product may be banned only from certain countries, while sometimes it may be permissible to import a product only under certain specified conditions. In all cases, governments use various forms of import licenses/permits (Sample 7-1) and declarations (Sample 7-2) to control and track their imports.

1.Import License/Permit (Issued by an Import Authority)

Import license/permit is either general or specific. In some instances, a general license to import and a specific permit to import a restricted product must both be obtained.

2.Dangerous Goods Declaration (Issued by an Importer)

Countries put special procedures in place for handling and documenting shipments of hazardous materials/dangerous goods including biohazardous, toxic and radioactive wastes. This declaration is a formal statement about the contents of a specific shipment and is used by both the import authority and the carrier.

3.Exchange Control Documents

Certain countries (i.e. Russia, Nigeria, and India) seek to control the flow of their national currency by controlling imports and exports. Such countries require that the importer make a statement or declaration that the flow of goods and payments follow prescribed regulations. Importers may be required to apply for prior approval to obtain hard currency to pay for an import shipment.

所有国家都会因为政治、经济或安全的目的而对进口进行管制。除此之外,政府也会控制由谁进口、进口的是什么以及进口商品的原产地。

在某些情况下,某种商品可能会遭遇完全的进口禁令。而有时只是被禁止来自于某些特定国家,或者必须满足某种特定条件才允许进口。但是,所有的政府都会使用不同种类的进口许可证(见样单7-1)和进口报关单(见样单7-2)来管制和追踪进口活动。

1.进口许可证(进口国当局签发)

进口许可证有一般进口许可证和特种商品进口许可证两种。有时候,某种限制进口的商品需要同时提交以上两种证书。

2.危险货物申报单(进口商提交)

对于生物危害物质、有毒物质和放射性废弃物等危险品的装运和制单,每个国家都有特别规定。进口国当局和承运人都会要求提供这类关于装运具体内容正式声明的申报单。

3.外汇管制单证

一些国家(如俄罗斯、尼日利亚、印度)试图通过管制进出口来控制国内货币的流动。这些国家要求进口商做出声明,即商品流动和支付是符合规定的。在这种情况下,进口商如果想得到硬通货来支付一批进口货物的话,可能需要预先审批。

7.4　Additional Documents Required by Import Authorities 进口国当局要求的其他单证

1. Special Certificate of Origin (Issued by a Shipper / Exporter or a Special Authorizing Agency of a Country of Export)

This document certifies the country of a shipment is within the context of a regional trade agreement (e.g. a NAFTA Certificate of Origin).

2. Customs Bond (Issued by an Insurance Company)

This document offers evidence that a financial guarantee by an insurance company has been made to the import authority regarding a particular import shipment.

3. Packing Declaration (Issued by a Shipper/Exporter or Forwarder)

This document certifies that packing materials are free from pests.

4. Certified Consular Invoice (Issued or Certified by a Consulate of a Country of Final Destination Located in a Country of Export)

This document establishes country of origin, description and value of goods shipped.

5. Insurance Certificate

This document offers proof of insurance for a shipment.

6. Inspection Certificate (Generally Issued by a Third Party Independent Testing Company)(Details as Section 6.3.2)

This document certifies product quality, quantity or adherence to certain specifications. These certificates are required by certain nations as a means of controlling techniques commonly used to circumvent exchange control regulations (i.e. overstated quantities or under-declared valuations). An import license usually requires a "clean report of findings" by an authorized inspection organization before goods can clear customs or payment can be made.

7. Quality Certificate (Issued by an Independent Testing Company)

This document certifies that the products continued in the shipment meet the standards of the importing country. Most countries require that this certification be provided by the exporter and be approved and filed by the appropriate governmental control agency (i.e. the exporting country Department of Consumer Safety) prior to shipment.

8. Phytosanitary Certificate (Generally Issued by a Third Party Independent Testing Company)

This document certifies that shipment of imported plants or plant products (i.e. seeds, bulbs, flowers, fruits, vegetables, etc.) is free from pests or disease. This certificate requires on-site inspection of the plants during the growing season and is usually provided by the agricultural ministry or department of the country of export.

9. Fumigation Certificate (Generally Issued by a Third Party Independent Testing Company)

This document certifies that wood-based packing materials; used clothing or packaging (i.e. coffee or cocoa bean bags) and certain other commodities have been fumigated or sterilized to kill any pests. This certificate is issued by private companies authorized to carry out these procedures and includes details of the specific process, temperature range, chemicals and concentrations used.

10. Veterinary Certificate (Generally Issued by a Third Party Independent Testing Company)

This document certifies that a shipment of live animals, fish, chilled and frozen meats (and sometimes even canned meats) has been inspected for disease.

11. Public Health Certificate (Generally Issued by a Third Party Independent Testing Company)

This document certifies that a shipment has been inspected for disease.

12. ATA Carnet (Generally Issued by a Third Party Independent Testing Company or Government Authority)

ATA carnet is an international customs document used for the temporary duty-free admission of certain goods into a country in lieu of the usual customs documents.

13. Free Sale Certificate (Issued by a Local Chamber of Commerce in An Exporter's Country)

This document certifies that certain commodities (i.e. medicines, vitamins, other health products) are freely sold in the country of origin.

1. 专用原产地证书(由托运人/出口商或出口国特别授权机构开立)

这类证书证明装运国属于某个区域性贸易协定的范围之内(如北美自由贸易区原产地证书)。

2. 海关担保(由保险公司签发)

这类证书证明保险公司已经就某个特定批次进口货物向进口国当局出具财务担保。

3. 包装声明书(由托运人/出口商或货运代理签发)

这类单证证明包装材料无虫害。

4. 已证实的领事发票(由驻出口国的最终目的国领事馆签发或证实)

这类单证证明原产国、货物描述和价值。

5. 保险单证

这类单证是货物已被投保的证明。

6. 检验证书(一般由第三方独立的检验机构签发)(详见6.3.2部分)

这类单证证明产品的质量、数量或符合某些特定的规格。由于某些国家的进口商广泛使用一些技术来规避外汇管制(如多报数量或低报价值),因此这些国家当局要求提供检验证书,作为一种控制手段。进口许可证通常要求在货物清关或者付款前由官方检验机构出具清洁检验报告。

7. 品质证书(由独立的检验机构签发)

这类单证证明装运货物满足进口国标准。大多数国家要求,这类证书应在装运前由出口商提供,由适当的政府管理机构批准和存档(如出口国的消费者安全部门)。

8.植物检验检疫证书(一般由第三方独立的检验机构签发)

这类单证证明所进口的植物或植物产品(如种子、鳞茎、花朵、水果、蔬菜等)无虫害或无疾病。要签发这类证书,必须在植物的生长季节做现场检验,通常由出口国的农业部门提供。

9.熏蒸证书(一般由第三方独立的检验机构签发)

这类单证证明木质材料的包装;二手服装或包装(如咖啡或可可豆袋子)和某些特定的其他商品已经被熏蒸消毒,产品上携带的害虫已被杀死。这类证书由被授权实施熏蒸程序的私营企业签发,证书上包括具体程序、温度范围、使用的化学制剂和浓聚物等内容。

10.兽医证书(一般由第三方独立的检验机构签发)

这类单证证明所装运的活动物、鱼、冷冻肉(有时包括罐装肉)已经通过检验,不携带病菌。

11.公共卫生证书(一般由第三方独立的检验机构签发)

这类单证证明所装运货物已经通过检验,不携带病菌。

12.ATA单证册(一般由第三方独立的检验机构或政府机构签发)

ATA单证册是某些特定商品申请临时免税入境时使用的、可替代其他海关单证的国际海关文件。

13.自由销售证书(由出口国本地商会签发)

这类单证证明某些特定商品(如药品、维生素和其他保健品)在原产国是允许自由销售的。

7.5　Special Import Transport Documents
　　特殊的进口运输单证

Special transport documents may be issued in place of a standard ocean bill of lading, used to notify the carrier and import authority of special or dangerous cargo, or be prepared to document certain transactions between the carrier and the consignor or consignee.

1.Special Bills of Lading

For example, the importer, in a letter of credit, may require presentation of an "air waybill" as proof of shipment by air.

2. Shipping Instructions (Generally Issued by a Consignor/Shipper/Exporter, but often at the Request of an Importer/Buyer/Consignee)

This form gives specific instructions to the shipping company about how to handle a shipment. A bill of lading is typically drawn up from this information.

3.Stowage Instructions (Issued by a Consignor/Shipper/Exporter)

This form gives specific instructions to the shipping line about how and where to stow cargo during transport and is typically used when shipping hazardous, oversize, fragile, live or other unusual cargo.

特殊的运输单证可以代替标准海运提单,用以通知承运人和进口国当局所装运货物为特殊货物或危险品,或用以证明承运人与托运人之间或承运人与收货人之间的特殊协议。

1.特殊提单

例如,信用证中的进口商要提交"航空运单"作为空运证明。

2.装运指示(一般由发货人/托运人/出口商签发,但通常以进口商/买方/收货人的要求为前提)

这类单证向装运公司提供了装运的详细指示。提单一般以此说明为基础缮制。

3.装载指示(由发货人/托运人/出口商签发)

这类单证向船公司提供货物运输的详细装载指示,一般用于危险货物、超大货物、易碎货物、活动物或其他非常规商品。

7.6 Banking and International Exchange Documents 银行单证与外汇单证

The importer's contact with banks is determined principally by the terms of payment agreed to with the exporter/seller. If the terms are payment in advance by cash, check, wire transfer, or credit card, or on open account with future payment by cash, check, wire transfer, or credit card, the importer's only contact with the banks will be to write a bank check, to have the bank send a wire transfer of funds to the exporter, or to process a credit card payment.

However, if a documentary collection or documentary letter of credit is used as the payment mechanism, much greater involvement with banks is required.

1.Electronic Filling of Documents

Increasingly, customs documents are required to be filled electronically. Many systems are now in place whereby the same electronic document format may be used for exporting/importing between dozens of different countries. This standardization is proving to be of great benefit to international traders.

2.Customs Brokers

Import documents can be extremely simple or exceedingly complex. Many importers rely upon the services of a customs broker for assistance. Even importers whose goal is to handle all import documents internally often rely upon these professionals until they become well versed in import requirements for their range of commodities.

If you do use a customs broker you will be required to sign a LIMITED POWER OF ATTORNEY. This gives your customs broker the right to act on your behalf with the custom authority and to sign customs documents in your name.

进口商与银行的联系方式主要由进出口双方同意的付款条件决定。如果采用现金、支票、银行电汇或信用卡等方式预付货款或远期支付,那么进口商与银行的业务联系只包括填写支票、让银行向出口商电汇货款或使用信用卡支付。

然而,如果使用跟单托收或跟单信用证的方式,那么进口商要与银行有更多的业务往来。

1.电子填单

目前,使用电子系统填制海关单证的比例逐渐增加。有几十个国家之间的进出口贸易单证查验系统已被电子系统代替。电子系统已被证明能给国际贸易商人带来极大便利。

2.报关行

进口单证可以很简单，也可以很复杂。很多进口商在报关领域主要依赖报关行的服务。即使那些希望独立处理单证的进口商也经常依赖专业报关行的服务，除非他们已对相关商品进口手续的要求非常熟悉。

如果你选择使用报关行服务，那么你需要在"有限授权委托书"上签字。这份委托书将授权相应的报关行以你的名义在海关办理相关手续和签署报关单证。

Training Case 7-1

Must an Inspection Certificate be Indicated the Date of Inspection

Domestic company A exported chemical raw materials to Germany company B. No discrepancy was found after documents were presented to the negotiating bank for examination. So the negotiating bank sent documents to a certain Germany issuing bank. After the issuing bank examined the documents, it found that the date of inspection was not indicated in the inspection certificate and offered to refuse payment.

检验证书是否一定要注明检验日期

国内A公司向德国B公司出口化工原料。单据提交议付行审核后未发现不符点，于是议付行将单据寄给德国某开证行。开证行审单后，发现检验证书没有注明检验日期，遂提出拒付。

Training Case 7-2

A Treatment Case of a Draft Amount in Capital and Small Letter Inconsistent

Bank A issued an irrevocable L/C to bank B. After the beneficiary presented the documents, the bank sent the documents to bank A by courier service. After bank A examined the documents, it found the following discrepancy, hence refused the payment. On the draft the amount in small letter was USD 905,000.00, the amount in capital letter was HONG KONG DOLLARS NINE HUNDRED AND FIVE THOUSAND ONLY, which was inconsistent with each other. After receiving bank A's refusal to pay, bank B thought the discrepancy mentioned is only hand typing mistake, not the substantial discrepancy.

汇票大小写金额不一致的处理

A银行向B银行开出不可撤销信用征。受益人交单后，银行通过快递将单据寄交A银行。A银行审单后发现下述不符点，遂对外拒付。汇票上小写金额为"USD 905,000.00"，大写金额为"HONG KONG DOLLARS NINE HUNDRED AND FIVE THOUSAND ONLY"，金额不一致。收到A银行的拒付电后，B银行认为所述不符点仅是打字手误，非实质性不符点。

Key Terms

import license 进口许可证　　import declaration 进口报关单

Exercise

◎ *Practice*

Practice 1

根据下列资料,制作进口许可证,要求格式清楚、内容完整。

2018 年 10 月 11 日,广东朗悦商贸有限公司(单位编码:52304125596)申请签发编号为 CT88661125839 的进口许可证,从日本进口空调。

品名:空调

规格型号:制冷量≤4 000 大卡/时,分体式空调

商品编码:84151021

单价:208 美元 FOB 广州

数量:300 台

包装:每台装一纸箱

总价:62 400 美元

唛头:EAST

GUANGZHOU

NOS-308

MADE IN JAPAN

商品用途:外贸自营内销

装运港:大阪

目的港:广州

外汇来源:购汇

许可证有效期:2019 年 2 月

中华人民共和国进口许可证
Import License of the People's Republic of China

1.我国对外成交单位 编码 Importer	3.进口许可证编号 License No.
2.收货单位 Consignee	4.许可证有效期 Validity
5.贸易方式 Terms of trade	8.进口国家（地区） Country where consigned
6.外汇来源 Terms of foreign exchange	9.商品原产地 Country of origin
7.到货口岸 Port of destination	10.商品用途 Use of commodity
11.唛头——包装件数 Marks & numbers-number of packages	

续

12.商品名称 Description of commodity			商品编码 Commodity No.		
13.商品规格、型号 Specification	单位 Unit	14.数量 Quantity	15.单价 Unit Price	16.总值 Amount	17.总值折美元 Amount in USD
18.总计 Total					
19.备注 Supplementary details			20.发证机关盖章 Issuing authority's stamp 发证日期 Signature date		

商务部监制   本证不得涂改，不得转让

Practice 2

根据发票及下列资料,制作进口报关单,要求格式清楚、内容完整。

广东纺织服装有限公司从加拿大进口的货物2018年4月17日抵达广州,公司于4月19日填制进口报关单,随附发票、装箱单等向海关进行申报。

广东纺织服装有限公司

地址:广州市中山路85号华荣大厦2901室

邮编:510000

联系电话:020-84715004

经办人:梁鑫

公司经营单位编码:5230412559

税务登记号码:320102134773852

海关预录入编号:DS9110006

船名:Volendam

航次:Voy. 7524

提单号:782-02458690

进口许可证号:CT88661182569

商品编号:62043200.90

数量:2 550件

包装:每30件装一纸箱

商品用途:外贸自营内销

运费600美元,保费50美元,杂费20美元

集装箱号:COSC51246

中华人民共和国海关进口报关单

预录入编号： 　　　　　　　　　　　　　　　　　　海关编号：

进口口岸		备案号		进口日期	申报日期
经营单位		运输方式		运输工具名称	提运单号
收货单位		贸易方式		征免性质	征税比例
许可证号		起运国（地区）		装运港	境内目的地
批准文号		成交方式	运费	保险费	杂费
合同协议号		件数	包装种类	毛重（千克）	净重（千克）
集装箱号		随附单据		用途	

标记唛码及备注

项号	商品编号	商品名称及规格型号	数量及单位	最终目的国（地区）	单价	总价	币制	征免

　　　　　　　　　　　　　　　总计：

税费征收情况

税务登记号码

录入员　录入单位	兹声明以上申报无讹 并承担法律责任	海关审单批注及放行日期（签章）	
		审单	审价
	报关员 申报单位（签章）	征税	统计
单位地址			
邮编　　电话　　填制日期		查验	放行

Chapter 8

Banking Documents
银行单证

Learning Objectives

◆ 重点掌握汇票;掌握各种支付方式、单证存在不符点的处理办法;了解信用证和托收项下单证和货物的流程。

Guide Case

Company A purchased a batch of medical apparatus and instruments from company B, total amount RMB 1.5 million. On the basis of the two sides agreement, on May 28, company A paid the deposit of RMB 300,000 to company B which made delivery on July 8, and company A remitted the balance within 10 days after receiving the goods. On May 28, company A issued a transfer cheque for amount of RMB 300,000 to company B (used in the same city, hereinafter). On June 10, company B reminded the drawee Y to make payment but Y refused to pay. Hence company B asked company A to issue the draft again. Only after company A issued the draft again could company B make payment.

On July 8, company B made delivery on time. On July 12, company A transferred a bank draft endorsed by company C to company B, the sum was RMB 1.2 million. On July 13, company B transferred the draft to company D for repayment of the debt. On July 15, company A found that the goods delivered by company B were false and inferior, hence promptly notified the drawee W to refuse to make payment to the bearer of the bank draft, but when company D presented the draft and asked for the payment to drawee W on July 16, the drawee W still paid the full amount according to the draft value to company D.

Based on the above facts, please answer the following questions respectively:

(1) Was it correct that the drawee Y refused to pay the transfer cheque fare, which was held by to the company B? Why?

(2)Was the draft amount paid by the drawee W to the company D correct?Why?

A公司从B公司购买一批医疗器械,总价为人民币150万元。依据双方约定,5月28日,A公司向B公司支付定金人民币30万元;B公司于7月8日交货,A公司在收货后10日内付汇余款。5月28日,A公司向B公司开出一张金额为人民币30万元的转账支票(同城使用,下同)。6月10日,B公司向付款人Y提示付款,付款人Y拒绝付款。B公司遂向A公司要求重新出票。在A公司重新出票后,B公司方付款。

7月8日,B公司按时交货。7月12日,A公司将从C公司背书受让的一张全额为人民币120万元的银行汇票背书转让给B公司。7月13日,B公司因偿还债务又将该汇票背书转让给D公司。7月15日,A公司发现B公司交付的货物为伪劣产品,遂即通知付款人W拒绝向上述银行汇票的持票人付款,但D公司于7月16日向付款人W提示该汇票请示付款时,付款人W仍然按票面金额向D公司支付了全部票款。

根据上述事实,分别回答以下问题:

(1)付款人Y拒绝向B公司支付所持转账支票票款是否正确?为什么?

(2)付款人W向D公司支付所持银行汇票票款是否正确?为什么?

8.1 Methods of Payments
支付方式

Because international trade always involves the transfer of money between different business entities in different national jurisdictions using different currencies, banks are almost always involved and so are the all-important banking documents. In fact, documents are so much a part of the process that banks refer to them as documentary transaction. Banks rely upon these packets of paper because they spell out every nuance of who, what, where, when and how much money will be paid.

Depending upon the method of payment, bank documents can be minimal or extremely complex.

由于国际贸易的资金转移通常在不同国度的商业实体之间进行,而且通常涉及不同币种,因此一般需要通过银行办理,所以银行单证就变得非常重要。事实上,单证处理在业务中的分量很重,以至于银行通常将其称为单证交易。银行的付款取决于这些单证,因为它们能明确说明付款的对象、内容、地点、时间和金额。

因付款方式的差异,银行的单证业务有简单的,也有复杂的。

8.1.1 *Prepaid/Cash-in-Advance/Cash with Order*
预付/预付现金/订货付现

Prepaid terms are common, especially where the transaction value is not great or where the importer/buyer trusts the exporter/seller sufficiently to prepay for the shipment. Obviously, this is the best arrangement for the exporter/seller.

This is the most straightforward arrangement in the international transaction where the buyer negotiates the purchase of goods and prepays with cash, bank wire transfer, credit card, traveler's check or perhaps even a personal or business check. The importer/buyer either picks up the goods on the spot, or they are shipped after the payment has been received. In this case, the banks are hardly involved other than cashing a check, handling a bank wire transfer, arranging for traveler's check or processing credit card payment.

预付货款的现象很普遍,尤其是在交易金额不高或进口商/买方非常信任出口商/卖方的情况下。很明显,对出口商/卖方来说,这是最好的付款方式。

同时,这是国际贸易中最直接的付款方式。买方与卖方谈好购买事项后即用现金、银行电汇、信用卡或旅行支票的方式预付货款,有时也使用个人或公司支票。进口商/买方要么当场提货,要么允许卖方收到货款后再发货。在这种情况下,银行的业务只包括支票付现、办理电汇、处理旅行支票或办理信用卡支付。

8.1.2 *Open Account*
赊销

Open account terms are also common, especially where the exporter/seller sufficiently trusts that the importer/buyer will pay for the shipment at a later date. Obviously, this is the best arrangement for the importer/buyer.

On open account terms the exporter/seller ships goods to the importer/buyer on the expectation that the payment will be made at a set future date. This can be 30, 60, 90 or even 180 or 360 days after shipment. The payment on the due date may still be made by cash, bank wire transfer, credit card, traveler's check or even a personal or business check.

赊销方式也很普遍,尤其是在出口商/卖方充分信任进口商/买方的情况下,即允许进口商/买方在货物装运后的一段时间内再付款。很明显,对进口商/买方来说,这是最好的付款方式。

在赊销条件下,出口商/卖方将货物装运给进口商/买方,并且相信进口商/买方会在未来的某个日期付款。这个日期有可能是装运后的30天、60天、90天甚至180天或360天。到期付款时,支付的方式有现金、银行电汇、信用卡、旅行支票、个人或公司支票。

8.1.3 *Documentary Collection*
跟单托收

In a documentary collection transaction, the seller uses banks as intermediaries to ensure that the documents conveying title to the shipment are not transferred to the buyer until a payment (or a suitable promise of payment) has been made. It is a "documentary" collection because documents form the basis of the procedure.

Documentary collection transaction requires a great deal of documents.

在跟单托收交易中,卖方委托银行保证在买方付款(或做出合适的付款承诺)前不能将代表货物装运的单证交给买方。由于单证是履行程序的基础,因此此类托收被称为"跟单"托收。

跟单托收交易中需要的单证数量较多。

8.1.4 Documentary L/C
跟单信用证

In a letter of credit transaction, the buyer uses banks as intermediaries to ensure that payment to the seller is made only after certain terms and conditions have been met. All the terms and conditions involve presentation of documents. This is why the technical name for this procedure is "documentary letter of credit" (details as section 8.3).

在信用证交易中,买方委托银行保证仅在信用证的所有条款和条件都得到满足时才付款。所有的条款和条件都与交单相关。这就是为什么此类交易有一个专门的名称"跟单信用证"(详细内容参见8.3部分)。

8.2 International Banking Documents
国际银行单证

8.2.1 Documentary Collection Payment Documents
跟单托收付款单证

The collection order is the key document prepared by the seller specifying the terms and conditions of the documentary collection. It must be prepared with care and precision because banks are permitted to act only upon the instructions given.

The following are the key provisions of the collection order:

(1)Payment type and period as agreed with the buyer;

(2)Name and address of the buyer;

(3)Buyer's bank;

(4)Instructions, if any, about what to do with the accepted bill of exchange;

(5)Notation concerning payment of charges for the documentary collection;

(6)Instructions for the lodging of a protest in the event of non-acceptance or nonpayment;

(7)Instructions for notification of agent or representative in the buyer's country.

托收单是卖方缮制的单证中非常重要的一项,是说明跟单托收的条款和条件的单证。由于它是银行执行托收手续的指示,因此委托书的缮制必须谨慎和精确。

以下是托收单中包含的主要条款:

(1)买方同意的付款方式和期限;

(2)买方的名称和地址;

(3)买方银行;

(4)如有指示,应说明汇票被承兑后应如何处理;

(5)标注跟单托收的手续费支付情况;

(6)买方拒绝承兑或拒付后的处理办法;

(7)向卖方驻买方国家的代理或代表发出通知的指示。

8.2.2　*Documentary Letter of Credit Payment Documents*
跟单信用证付款单证

（1）Letter of credit application (Sample 8-1).

（2）Letter of credit.

（3）Letter of credit advice/notification.

（4）Request for amendment (to the letter of credit).

（5）Amendment (to the letter of credit).

（6）Amendment notification (to the letter of credit).

（7）Negotiable bill of lading.

（8）Document package for the importer/buyer (prepared by the exporter). This is the group of documents that the exporter prepares for the importer and that are needed to secure the shipment from the carrier and clear customs in the country of import. At least, they include a commercial invoice and a certificate of origin, but may also include inspection certificate, insurance policy and other documents. Technically, a negotiable bill of lading is part of the document package.

（9）Draft/bill of exchange.

（1）信用证申请书（见样单8-1）。

（2）信用证。

（3）信用证通知书。

（4）（信用证）修改要求。

（5）（信用证）修改函。

（6）（信用证）修改通知书。

（7）可转让提单。

（8）（出口商）为进口商/买方准备的文件包。这是出口商为进口商准备的单证组合,用以说明货物已在承运人处装运并已办理进口国清关手续。这些单证至少包括商业发票和原产地证书,另外还有可能包括检验证书、保险单和其他单证。严格来说,可转让提单也是文件包的一部分。

（9）汇票。

Sample 8-1　　　　　　　　Irrevocable Documentary L/C Application
样单8-1　　　　　　　　不可撤销跟单信用证申请书

To: BANK OF CHINA, GUANGZHOU BRANCH	Date:
☐Issued by airmail　　☐With brief advice by teletransmission ☐Issued by express delivery ☒Issued by teletransmission (which shall be operative instrument)	Credit No. Date and place of expiry　　　　JULY 30, 2018 IN CHINA
Applicant GUANGDONG FOREIGN TRADE IMP. & EXP. CORP. 15-18/F., GUANGDONG FOREIGN ECONOMIC AND TRADE BUILDING 351 TIANHE ROAD, GUANGZHOU, CHINA	Beneficiary (full name and address) ROYAL TRADERS LTD. 333 BARRON BLVD., INGLESIDE, ILLINOIS (UNITED STATES)
Advising Bank	Amount USD 570,000.00 SAY U. S. DOLLARS FIVE HUNDRED AND SEVENTY THOUSAND ONLY

续

Partial shipments	Transshipment	Credit available with
☐allowed	☐allowed	ANY BANK
☒not allowed	☒not allowed	

Loading on board/dispatch/taking in charge at/from

NEW YORK

Not later than

JULY 15, 2018

For transportation to:

GUANGZHOU, CHINA

By

☐sight payment ☐acceptance ☒negotiation

☐deferred payment at

against the documents detailed herein

☒and beneficiary's draft(s) for 100 % of invoice value

at **** sight

drawn on

☒FOB ☐CFR ☐CIF

☐Or other terms

Documents required: (marked with ×)

1. (×) Signed commercial invoice in __3__ copies indicating L/C No. and Contract No.

2. (×) Full set of clean on board Bills of Lading made out to order and blank endorsed, marked "freight [×] to collect / [ ] prepaid [ ]showing freight amount" notifying THE APPLICANT WITH FULL NAME AND ADDRESS.

    ( ) Air waybills/cargo receipts/copy of railway bills issued by_____ showing "freight [ ] to collect/ [ ]prepaid [ ] indicating freight amount" and consigned to_____.

3. ( ) Insurance Policy/Certificate in_____ copies for_____ % of the invoice value showing claims payable in currency of the draft, blank endorsed, covering All Risks, War Risks and_____.

4. (×) Packing List/Weight Memo in __3__ copies indicating quantity, gross weights of each package.

5. ( ) Certificate of Quantity/Weight in_____ copies issued by_____.

6. ( ) Certificate of Quality in_____copies issued by [ ] manufacturer/[ ] public recognized surveyor_____.

7. (×) Certificate of Origin in __2__ copies .

8. (×) Beneficiary's certified copy of fax/telex dispatched to the applicant within__1__ days after shipment advising L/C No., name of vessel, date of shipment, name, quantity, weight and value of goods.

    ( ) Other documents, if any:

Description of goods:

MEN'S DENIM UTILITY SHIRT

COLOR: MEDDEST SANDBLAS

FABRIC CONTENT: 100% COTTON

QUANTITY: 2,000 CARTON

PRICE TERMS: FOB NEW YORK

COUNTRY OF ORIGIN AND MANUFACTURERS: UNITED STATES OF AMERICA, VICTORY FACTORY

Additional instructions:

1. (×) All banking charges outside opening bank are for beneficiary's account.

2. (×) Documents must be presented within __10__ days after date of issuance of transport documents but within the validity of this credit.

3. ( ) A third party as shipper is not acceptable, Short Form/Blank back B/L is not acceptable.

4. ( ) Both quantity and credit amount_____ % more or less are allowed.

5. (×) All documents must be sent to issuing bank by courier/speed post in one lot.

    ( ) Other terms, if any:

8.2.3 Draft/Bill of Exchange and Acceptance
汇票和承兑

1.Draft/Bill of Exchange

The most common versions of drafts are (1) sight drafts which are payable when presented, and (2) time drafts (usance drafts) which are payable at a future fixed (specific) date or determinable (e.g. 30,60,90 days) date (details as section 6.8.1).

2.Acceptance

Acceptance is a time draft that has been accepted and signed by the drawee (the buyer or the bank) for payment at maturity. If a time draft is accepted by a buyer of merchandise, it is called a trade acceptance. If a time draft is accepted by a bank, it is called a banker's acceptance.

In most cases, obviously, a draft accepted by a bank enjoys higher credit standing than a draft accepted by a company or individual, since a bank is presumed to meet its obligation at maturity, and a company or individual in an international country may not as readily comply with its obligation.

3.Holding or Discounting Acceptance

In documentary transactions, the seller has two options, once its draft is accepted. The seller may either hold it until maturity and collect full face value, or discount the draft, most likely with the accepting bank, and take the net value in cash immediately. In these ways, trade and banker's acceptances often represent the easiest, least expensive way for a seller to provide credit to a buyer, while enjoying the security provided by the documentary transaction.

4.Financing Transaction Using Acceptance

International buyers may indicate that they wish to provide a "time" documentary L/C (rather than a "sight" documentary L/C). In the case of a time documentary L/C, the buyer may agree to allow the seller to increase the sales price slightly in order to offset the acceptance commission and discount costs.

In most cases, the buyer and the buyer's bank will absorb the charges involved, and the seller will receive the full contract sales amount. Since the charges are usually lower than conventional financing charges, the buyer is still better off than if financing had been obtained through a traditional bank loan.

5."Clean" Acceptance

A "clean" acceptance is one that does not have any notations attached that would compromise its value. In a trade acceptance, the customer promises to pay the bank the full amount of the draft no later than the date of maturity, or upon demand of the bank. An accepted draft, when discounted, becomes a negotiable instrument that can be sold in the acceptance market, which is an over-the-counter market of brokers, dealers, and banks.

Banker's acceptances are generally short-term (up to 80 days). Banker's acceptances become money market instruments once they are accepted by a major bank, which means that the bank has undertaken to honor the note at its maturity. Because of this characteristic, banker's acceptances often result in lower financing costs. The difference can range from 1 to 3 percent depending on the transaction and the bank involved. Thus they are important sources of financing.

1.汇票

汇票最普遍的版本包括:(1)即期汇票,即提示后立刻付款;(2)远期汇票,即在未来某个具体的日期或未来某个时间段(如30天、60天、90天)后付款(详细内容参见6.8.1部分)。

2.承兑汇票

承兑汇票是已由受票人(买方或银行)承兑和签字,以保证到期付款的远期汇票。被工商企业者承兑的远期汇票是商业承兑汇票;被银行承兑的远期汇票是银行承兑汇票。

在大多数情况下,因为银行到期履行义务的可能性更大,银行承兑汇票的信用程度明显更高,而国外的公司或个人履行义务的可能性较小。

3.持有或贴现承兑汇票

在跟单交易中,卖方在汇票承兑后有两个选择。卖方可以持有汇票直到到期日收取全额款项,或者对汇票进行贴现(一般在承兑行办理),即刻以提现的方式收取汇票的净值。在这些情况下,商业承兑汇票和银行承兑汇票就属于卖方给买方提供的最简易、最便宜的信用,而同时又能享受跟单交易带来的保证。

4.使用承兑的融资交易

国外买主一般会要求使用"远期"跟单信用证的方式(而不是"即期"跟单信用证)。在远期跟单信用证的情况下,买方有可能同意让卖方稍微提高销售价格,以便抵销承兑和贴现费用。

大多数情况下,相应的费用由买方或买方银行承担,卖方得到的是销售合同的全部金额。因为这些费用低于传统融资的费用,所以相对于传统的银行贷款,托收方式对买方而言还是比较实惠的。

5."清洁"承兑汇票

"清洁"承兑汇票是指不附带任何能让票面价值有协商余地的标注的汇票。在商业承兑汇票中,顾客承诺不晚于到期日向银行支付汇票的全部金额,或根据银行的要求支付。当承兑汇票被贴现时,它就变成一个可以在承兑市场销售的可转让支付工具(承兑市场是经纪人、经销商和银行的场外市场)。

银行承兑汇票通常是短期的(最长80天)。银行承兑汇票成为货币市场工具,一旦它们被一家专业银行接受,就意味着该银行已承诺到期时将履行承兑汇票。由于这个特点,银行承兑常常导致更低的融资成本。融资成本差异的范围是1%~3%,其取决于所涉及的交易和相关的银行。因此,银行承兑汇票是重要的融资资源。

8.3 Documentary L/C
跟单信用证

A letter of credit is the written promise of a bank, undertaken on behalf of a buyer, to pay a seller the amount specified in the L/C provided the seller complies with the terms and conditions set forth in the L/C. The terms and conditions of a documentary L/C revolve around two issues:

(1)the presentation of documents that evidence title to goods shipped by the seller, and (2) payment.

In simple terms, banks act as intermediaries to collect payment from the buyer in exchange for the transfer of documents that enable the holder to take possession of the goods.

An L/C is the historic and popular term used. However, the formal term is "documentary" letter of credit because of the importance of documents in the transaction.

信用证是银行以进口商的名义向卖方开立的书面承诺,只要卖方满足信用证上规定的条款和条件,银行即向卖方支付信用证规定的金额。跟单信用证的条款和条件主要围绕两个主题:(1)提交证明货物由出口商装运的单证;(2)付款。

简单地说,银行以中间人的身份向买方收取货款,作为向其交付可作为提货凭证的单证的条件。

信用证是具有时代意义的、很受欢迎的支付方式。然而,由于单证在业务中非常重要,因此它的正式名称是"跟单"信用证。

8.3.1 *Types of Documentary Letters of Credit*
跟单信用证的分类

1.Revocable,Irrevocable Letter of Credit

A revocable letter of credit gives the buyer and/or the issuing bank the ability to amend or cancel the L/C at any time right up to the moment of intended payment without approval by, or notice to the seller. Revocable letter of credit is, therefore, of great advantage to the buyer.

An irrevocable letter of credit constitutes the L/C as issued. A contractual obligation on the part of the issuing bank to honor the term of payment of the L/C as issued. The buyer and the issuing bank cannot amend or cancel the L/C without the express approval of the seller. An irrevocable L/C is of advantage to the seller. Virtually all documentary letters of credit issued are irrevocable and so state on their face.

2.Confirmed,Unconfirmed Letter of Credit

The payment under an irrevocable letter of credit is guaranteed by the issuing bank. However, from the seller's perspective, this guarantee may have limited value as the issuing bank may be (1) in an international country, (2) beholden to the buyer, (3) small and unknown to the seller, or (4) subject to unknown international exchange control restrictions. The seller, therefore, might wish that another, more local banks add its guarantee (confirmation) of payment to that of the issuing bank.

(1)Unconfirmed letter of credit. In this form of letter of credit, only the issuing bank assumes the undertaking to pay, thus payment is the sole responsibility of the issuing bank.

(2)Confirmed letter of credit. In this form of letter of credit, both the issuing and confirming banks carry the commitment to pay the seller.

The most popular letter of credit for sellers is an irrevocable confirmed letter of credit, because it cannot be cancelled by the buyer, and the second bank (usually the seller's bank) adds its guarantee of payment to that of the buyer's bank.

3.Special Documentary Letter of Credit

(1)Revolving L/C. This is a commitment on bank to restore the credit to the original amount after it has been used or drawn down.

(2)Red clause L/C. This L/C has a special (red) clause that authorizes the confirming bank to make advances to the seller prior to the presentation of the shipping documents, in essence, extending pre-shipment financing to the seller.

(3)Transferable L/C. In this L/C, the original beneficiary transfers all or part of the proceeds of an existing L/C to another party (typically the ultimate supplier of the goods). It is normally used by brokers as a financing tool.

(4)Back-to-back L/C. This is a new L/C opened on the basis of an already existing, nontransferable L/C. It is used by the traders to make payment to the ultimate supplier. A trader receives an L/C from the buyer and then opens another in favor of the supplier. The first L/C is used as collateral for the second L/C. The second L/C makes price adjustments from which come the trader's profit.

1.可撤销信用证和不可撤销信用证

可撤销信用证是指买方和/或开证行在付款前,可在未取得卖方同意或未通知卖方的情况下在任何时间修改或取消的信用证。因此,可撤销信用证对买方比较有利。

不可撤销信用证是指已开出的信用证。开证行对已开出的信用证中的付款条件履行合同义务。未得到卖方同意,买方和开证行都没有修改或取消信用证的权利。不可撤销信用证对卖方有利。事实上,所有的跟单信用证都是不可撤销的,当然,信用证的表面也有相应说明。

2.保兑信用证和不保兑信用证

不可撤销信用证的付款行为由开证行担保。然而,从卖方的角度来说,如果开证行有以下情况,那么保证的程度是有限的:(1)在国外;(2)与买方来往较密切;(3)是一个名不见经传的小银行;(4)受到未知外汇管制的约束。因此,卖方希望有另一家银行,一般来说是本地的,能对信用证的开证行付款责任进行担保(保兑)。

(1)不保兑信用证。在这类信用证项下,只有开证行承担付款责任,也就是说,付款是开证行自己的责任。

(2)保兑信用证。在这类信用证项下,开证行和保兑行一起承担付款责任。

不可撤销保兑信用证是最受卖方欢迎的信用证,因为信用证开出后买方就不能取消,同时又得到第二家银行(通常是卖方银行)对买方银行付款行为的担保。

3.特殊跟单信用证

(1)循环信用证。这是指原始金额被使用之后又自动恢复的信用证。

(2)红条款信用证。信用证上有一个特别的(红色)条款,授权保兑行在卖方提交装运单证前预付货款,这种条款事实上是特别给予卖方的装运前融资。

(3)可转让信用证。在这类信用证项下,第一受益人可以将信用证的全部或部分转让给另一方(通常是实际供货人)使用。它通常是中间商融资的手段。

(4)背对背信用证。这是信用证的新种类,是在已开立的、不可转让的信用证基础上开立的。它是贸易商向实际供货商支付货款的工具。贸易商从买方那里收到信用证之后,再开立一份以实际供货商为受益人的信用证。第一份信用证是第二份信用证的担保。为了从中获益,贸易商将对第二份信用证的价格进行调整。

8.3.2 *Role of Banks*
银行的角色

(1)In a documentary L/C, banks act upon specific instructions given by the applicant (buyer) in the documentary L/C application. Buyer's instructions left out of the L/C by mistake or omitted because "we've always done it in that way" doesn't count. The buyer, therefore, should take great care in preparing the application so that it gives complete and clear instructions.

(2)In a documentary collection, banks act upon specific instructions given by the principal (seller) in the collection order. Seller's instructions left out of the collection order by mistake or omitted because "we've always done it in that way" doesn't count. The principal, therefore, should take great care in preparing the collection order so that it gives complete and clear instructions.

(3)Banks are required to act in faith and exercise reasonable care to verify that the documents submitted appear to be as listed in the letter of credit or the collection order. They are, however, under no obligation to confirm the authenticity of the documents submitted.

(4)Banks are not liable for the acts of third parties. Third parties include freight forwarders, agents, customs authorities, insurance companies and other banks. They also are not responsible for delays or consequences resulting from Acts of God (floods, earthquakes, etc.), or other causes beyond their control.

(5)Banks also assume no liability or responsibility for loss arising out of delays or loss in transit of messages, letters, documents, etc.

(6)Banks assume no responsibility regarding the quantity or quality of goods shipped. They are only concerned that the documents presented appear on their face to be consistent with the instructions in the L/C or the collection order. Any dispute must be settled between the buyer and the seller.

(7)Without explicit instructions, banks take no steps to store or insure the goods. This can be a problem for both the seller and the buyer. A seller who has not received the payment still has the ownership and an insurable interest in the goods.

(8)If a documentary collection remains unpaid or a bill of exchange is not accepted and the collecting bank receives no new instructions with 90 days, it may return the documents to the bank from which it received the collection order.

(9)So long as the documents presented to the banks appear on their face to comply with the terms and conditions of a letter of credit, banks may accept them and initiate the payment process as stipulated in the L/C.

(1)在跟单信用证中,银行根据开证申请人(买方)所提供的跟单信用证申请书上的详细指示办理业务。信用证一旦开出即成立,对于申请书中写错或遗漏的内容,买方不可以"我们一贯都是这么做的"之类的理由要求更改。因此,为了保证申请书的指示是完整和清楚的,买方在填写申请书时应非常仔细。

(2)在跟单托收中,银行根据委托人(卖方)所提供的托收单上的详细指示办理业务。托收单一旦被接受即不可更改,对于托收单中写错或遗漏的内容,卖方不可以"我们一贯都是这么做的"之类的理由要求更改。因此,为了保证托收单的指示是完整和清楚的,卖方在填写托收单时应非常仔细。

(3)银行应该以诚实的态度、合理的方式来核查所收到的单证是否与信用证或托收单上所列明的一致。但是,银行不对所收到的单证的真实性负责。

(4)银行不对第三方的行为所造成的损失负责。第三方包括货运代理、代理商、海关机构、保险公司和其他银行等。另外,对于延误、不可抗力(洪水、地震等)或其他不在控制范围内的原因所造成的损失,银行概不负责。

(5)对于信息、邮件、单证在运送途中的延误或遗失所造成的损失,银行概不负责。

(6)银行不对所装运货物的数量或质量负责。银行只负责核对所提交单证的表面是否与信用证或托收单中的要求一致。除此之外的任何争议都应由买卖双方自行解决。

(7)若无明确指示,银行不负责存储货物或给货物投保。这对买卖双方来说是个难题。未收到货款的卖方仍然拥有货物的所有权以及保险利益。

(8)在跟单托收项下,如果代收行在汇票被拒付或被拒绝承兑后的90天内得不到任何指示,那么代收行将把单证退还给向其发出托收单的银行。

(9)只要所提交单证的表面符合信用证上的条款和条件,银行就必须接受这些单证并开始办理信用证上规定的付款手续。

8.3.3 Electronic Application for a Documentary L/C
跟单信用证的电子申请书

It's becoming more and more common. Buyers install software on their office PCs that enable them to fill out an application and send it to their bank's processing center. Security is provided using encryption and password systems. Electronic applications enable the repeat letter of credit applicant faster turnaround and cut paperwork for everybody.

这类支付方式正日趋普及。买方先在办公室的电脑上安装相应的软件,然后在电脑上填写开证申请书,并通过网络将申请书传送到银行数据处理中心。该程序的安全通过密码来保证。电子申请使重复申请信用证的申请人工作效率更高,减少了纸质工作。

8.3.4 Document Movement for Issuance of an L/C
信用证开立的单证流程

When the two parties of an international trade transaction finalize their deal, a sales contract is established. This document is the basis for the importer to apply for a letter of credit. The content should directly or indirectly reflect the details of the sales contract. Upon its coming into force, however, the L/C will become a completely separate document from the sales contract. The contractual relationship between the exporter and the importer has no impact on the L/C operation what so ever. As a result, the exporter should pay special attention to examining the contents of the L/C so as to avoid any conflicting items.

Typically a letter of credit contains the following contents: name & address of opening bank, date of issuance of L/C, number of L/C, L/C amount, description of goods, type of L/C, full name & address of parties concerned, documents that shall be provided, details of shipment, validity period for L/C, settlement instructions, fee clauses and special clauses, if any.

At the stage of issuance of a documentary L/C, four parties are involved and their relationships are illustrated in Figure 8-1.

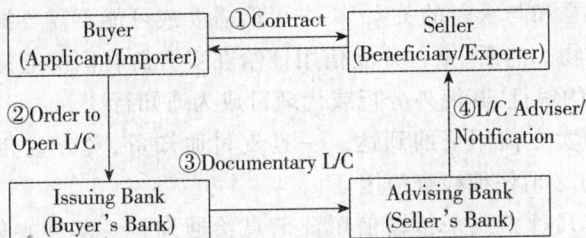

Figure 8-1　Document Movement for Issuance of an L/C

①After signing the sales contract with the seller, the buyer will present to his local bank the contract, the application letter and other documents required for the opening of an L/C. The importer is the applicant of the L/C.

②Depending on the buyer's credibility and relationship with the bank, the buyer may or may not be required to pledge a percentage of the value of the credit in cash funds or cash equivalents. The bank then issues a letter of credit to one of its branches or correspondent banks in the seller's country. The importer's local bank becomes the issuing bank of the L/C and overseas branch or correspondent bank is the advising bank.

③The advising bank will notify the seller of the arrival of an L/C. Once paying an advising fee, the seller will receive the original of the documentary L/C. He has to examine the L/C closely before he accepts it.

An issuing bank can choose several ways to transmit the L/C information to the advising bank. Based on the choice of media, traditionally there are four ways to open an L/C: by airmail, by brief cable and confirmation, by full cable or SWIFT.

贸易双方达成交易后会签订一份销售合同。它是进口商开立信用证的基础。其内容应该直接或间接地反映出销售合同的细节。然而,一旦其生效,信用证将成为一份完全独立于销售合同的单证。出口商和进口商之间的合同关系不会影响信用证业务运作。因此,出口商应该特别注意检查信用证的内容,以避免条款冲突。

通常,信用证包含以下内容:开证行的名称和地址、开立信用证日期、信用证号码、信用证金额、货物描述、信用证的类型、当事人的姓名和地址、应提供的单证、装运细节、信用证有效期、结算指示、费用条款和特殊条款。

在开立跟单信用证阶段,交易四方都要参与,它们的关系如图8-1所示。

①与卖方签订销售合同后,买方将向他的当地银行提交合同、申请书和其他开立信用证的必要文件。进口商是信用证的开证申请人。

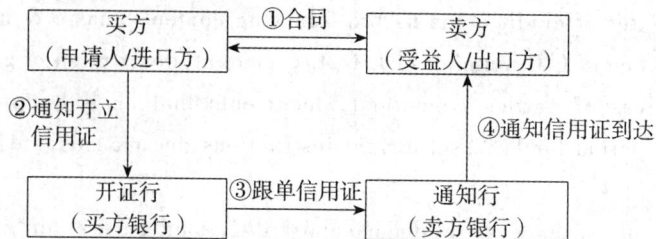

图8-1 信用证开立的单证流程图

②根据买方的信誉和与银行的关系,买方可能需要或可能不需要提供一定比例的信贷现金基金或现金等价物。然后,银行开立信用证给在卖方所在国的通知行。进口商的本地银行成为开立信用证的银行,其海外分行或代理行成为通知行。

③通知行将通知卖方信用证的到达。一旦支付通知费,卖方就会收到正本跟单信用证。在接受之前,卖方必须仔细检查信用证。

开证行可以选择几种方式来传输信用证信息给通知行。基于媒体的选择,传统上有四种方法可以开立信用证:通过航空邮寄开立、通过简电本和确认书开立、通过全电本开立和电开。

8.3.5 *Document Movement for Amendment to an L/C*
信用证修改的单证流程

Due to its emphasis on the importance of documents, when the exporter receives an L/C, it is crucial for him to inspect it thoroughly and carefully. If the beneficiary finds mistakes or terms and conditions which do not comply with the contract of sale, or he cannot fulfill in the future, he must contact the applicant and request for amendment of the L/C without delay. If the applicant agrees to do so, a similar process as issuing an L/C will be carried out again, until the beneficiary receives the amendment to the L/C from the same advising bank. Figure 8-2 shows documents movement for amendment to an L/C.

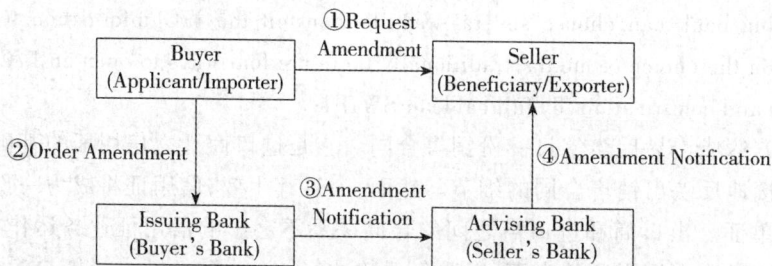

Figure 8-2　Documents Movement for Amendment to an L/C

由于强调单证的重要性,当出口商接收信用证时,彻底仔细检查它对他来说是至关重要的。如果受益人发现信用证有误或条款和条件与销售合同不符,或他在未来不能履行合同义务,他必须联系申请人并要不延误地请求修正信用证。如果申请人同意这样做,类似开立信用证的过程将再次进行,直到受益人收到来自相同通知行的信用证修改书。信用证修改的单证流程如图8-2所示。

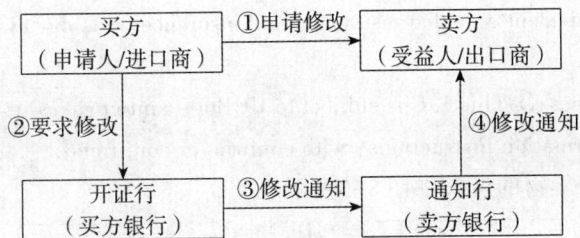

图 8-2　信用证修改的单证流程图

8.3.6　*Document and Goods Movement for Utilization of an L/C*
信用证下单证和货物的流转

Figure 8-3 shows the document and goods movement for utilization of an L/C.

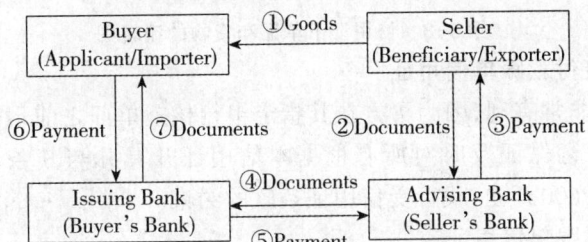

Figure 8-3　Document and Goods Movement for Utilization of an L/C

1.Irrevocable Straight Documentary L/C

Advantage/disadvantage：It is of greatest advantage to the buyer who does not incur a liability to pay the seller until his own bank reviews the documents.

Engagement clauses：① We hereby engage with you that each draft drawn and presented to us under and in compliance with the terms of this documentary L/C will be duly honored by us.②This L/C is subject to UCP600 and engages us in accordance with the terms thereof.

2.Irrevocable Negotiation Documentary L/C

Advantage/disadvantage：This form of L/C is of advantage to the seller who does not have to wait until the buyer's bank reviews the documents to get the L/C paid.

Engagement clauses：① The L/C available with any bank, by negotiation for payment of beneficiary's draft at sight ... ②This L/C is subject to UCP600 and engages us in accordance with the terms thereof.

3.Irrevocable Unconfirmed Documentary L/C

Advantage/disadvantage：There is a slight advantage to the buyer as the buyer is typically responsible for paying the documentary L/C fees. Since confirmation incurs a fee, the buyer would have a small savings.

Engagement clauses：①This L/C is subject to UCP600 and engages us in accordance with the terms thereof. ②The enclosed advice is sent to you without confirmation.

4.Irrevocable Confirmed Documentary L/C

Advantage / disadvantage：This is the most secure L/C for the seller because it adds the guarantee of the second (and usually local) bank to that of the issuing bank. Confirmation by the second bank is the equivalent of added insurance, and insurance costs money, so this form of the L/C is more costly.

Engagement clauses:①This L/C is subject to UCP600 and engages us in accordance with the terms thereof. ②Confirmation instructions: with confirm, or confirmed.

信用证下单证和货物的流转如图8-3所示。

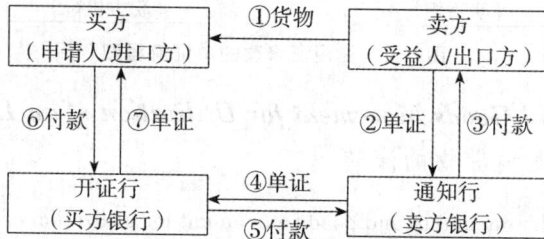

图8-3 信用证下单证和货物的流转图

1.不可撤销直接付款跟单信用证

优缺点:对买方非常有利,因为买方在其指定银行核查单证之前不需承担付款责任。

表示文句:①我行保证及时对所有根据本信用证开具并与其条款相符的汇票兑付。②本信用证根据UCP600开立,我行受信用证条款的约束。

2.不可撤销议付跟单信用证

优缺点:这类信用证对卖方有利,因为卖方在买方银行审核单证之前即可得到货款。

表示文句:①信用证在任何银行都可以根据受益人的即期汇票议付……;②本信用证根据UCP600开立,我行受信用证条款的约束。

3.不可撤销不保兑跟单信用证

优缺点:这类信用证对买方稍有利,因为信用证相关费用通常由买方承担,在不保兑情况下,买方可省去一笔费用。

表示文句:①本信用证根据UCP600开立,我行受信用证条款的约束。②附件中的通知已在未保兑的情况下发送给你方。

4.不可撤销保兑跟单信用证

优缺点:它是对卖方最有保障的信用证,因为有另一家银行(一般是本地的)对信用证的开证行付款责任进行担保。第二家银行的保兑相当于额外的保险,这种保险不是免费的,因此它是最昂贵的信用证。

表示文句:①本信用证根据UCP600开立,我行受信用证条款的约束。②保兑指示:保兑或受保兑。

8.3.7 *Discrepancies with Documents*
单证不符点

If a bank involved in the transaction finds discrepancies in the documents, it has several options:

(1)The advising or confirming bank can refuse to accept the documents and return them to the seller (beneficiary) so that they can be corrected or replaced.

(2)The issuing bank, if it feels the discrepancy is not material to the transaction, can ask the buyer (applicant) for a waiver for the specific discrepancy, but must do so within seven banking days.

(3)The advising or confirming bank can remit the documents under approval to the issuing bank for settlement.

(4)The issuing or confirming bank can return the incorrect documents directly to the seller for correction or replacement and eventually return directly to the issuing or confirming bank.

(5)The confirming bank can proceed with payment to the seller but require a guarantee from the seller for reimbursement if the issuing bank does not honor the documents as presented.

If there is a discrepancy, the buyer and the seller must communicate directly and then inform the banks of their decision. In the case of serious discrepancies, an amendment to the L/C may be necessary.

The seller may request the opening bank to present the documents to the buyer on a collection basis. However, the buyer may refuse to accept the documents/merchandise.

如果银行发现单证的不符点,通常有以下选择:

(1)通知行或保兑行拒绝接受单证并将其退还给出口商(受益人),以便于受益人修改或更换单证。

(2)如果开证行认为不符点对交易影响不大,那么它可以请买方(开证申请人)放弃不符点,但是这个选择必须在7个银行工作日内做出。

(3)通知行或保兑行可以在得到同意的情况下将单证寄给开证行结汇。

(4)通知行或保兑行可以将不正确的单证直接退还给出口商,要求其更正或替换,最后出口商直接将单证寄给开证行或保兑行。

(5)保兑行可以办理付款手续,但是卖方必须出具保函,如果开证行拒付货款,卖方将承担偿付责任。

出现不符点时,买卖双方必须直接沟通并将他们的决定通知银行。如果不符点非常严重,则需要修改信用证。

卖方可能会要求开证行以托收的形式将单证提示给买方。然而,买方一般会拒绝接受这些单证或货物。

8.4　Documentary Collection
跟单托收

Banks act as intermediaries to collect payment from the buyer in exchange for the transfer of documents that enable the holder to take possession of the goods. The procedure is easier than a documentary L/C, and the bank charges are lower. The bank, however, does not act as surety of payment but rather only as collector of funds for documents.

Using a documentary collection, the exporter ships the goods and arranges with his bank for the documents (invoice, bill of lading, insurance policy or certificate and other documents of movement), which often together with a bill of exchange, to be dispatched to an appropriate overseas correspondent bank. Depending on the instructions from the exporter and the terms of his contract with the buyer, the documents are only released upon either payment, or acceptance of the bill of exchange, by the importer. The specific transaction steps are as follows (Figure 8-4):

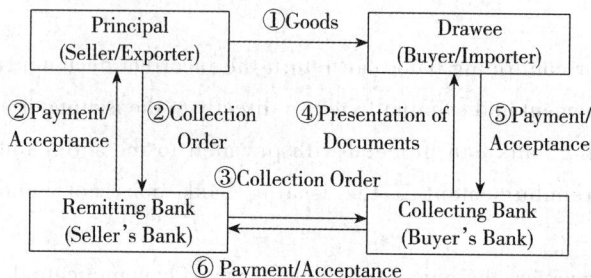

Figure 8-4　Documents and Goods Movement in Documentary Collection

（1）The exporter ships the goods to the importer as agreed in the sales contract and obtains the documents of title from the shipping line.

（2）The exporter submits to his bank - the remitting bank - documents, a draft drawn on the importer, written instructions governing the collection, documents of title (i.e. a complete set of clean, shipped on board bills of lading made out to order and blank endorsed), and other relevant documents (insurance policy or certificate of CIF).

（3）The remitting bank sends the documents, the draft, and the collection order to the collecting/presenting bank in the importer's country which notifies the importer.

（4）If the instruction is D/P, the importer pays the face amount of the draft plus any charges the importer is responsible for, as stated in the collection order, and the collecting/presenting bank releases the documents. If the instruction is D/A, the collecting/presenting bank will release the documents against acceptance of the draft by the importer.

（5）The collecting bank deducts its fee and sends the importer's payment to the remitting bank for credit to the exporter's account for the face value of the draft minus any fees and charges for which the exporter is responsible.

The above transaction flow indicates that the collection procedure is chronological. The banks in a documentary collection transaction do not act until the preceding steps have been completed. This means that the exporter does not receive the payment until its bank has received the funds from its correspondent, collecting bank.

银行以中间人的身份向买方收取货款,转让可用作提货凭证的单证。这种方式比跟单信用证简单,银行费用也更低。然而,虽然银行有凭付款交付单证的义务,但并不承担保证买方付款的责任。

使用这种方法,出口商装运货物并准备银行单证(发票、提单、保险单或凭证和其他单证),这些单证往往连同汇票被寄送到合适的海外通知行。根据出口商指示和与买方签订的合同的相关条款,这些单证仅仅是进口商支付或承兑汇票的凭证。其具体步骤如下(见图8-4):

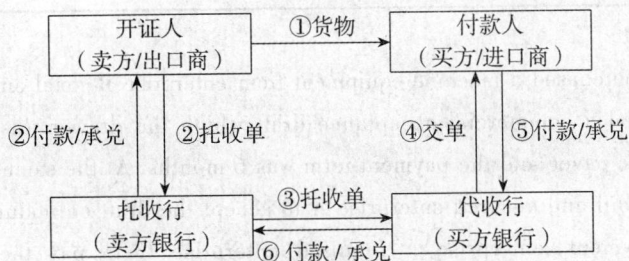

图 8-4　跟单托收下单证和货物的流程图

（1）出口商根据销售合同约定把货物装运给进口商，并且获得船公司的货物装运单证。

（2）出口商向银行（托收行）提交以进口商为抬头的汇票、有关托收的书面指示、货物单证（如凭指示和空白背书的一套完整清洁已装船提单）和其他相关的单证（CIF 保险单或保险凭证）。

（3）托收行发送单据、汇票和托收单给进口国的代收行/提示行，由其通知进口商。

（4）如果是付款交单，进口商支付汇票面值加上任何其负责支付的费用后，如托收单所述，代收行/提示行将放单。如果是承兑交单，代收行/提示行将在进口商承兑汇票后放单。

（5）代收行扣除其费用并把汇票面值款减去出口商需负责支付的任何费用后，将进口商付款打到托收行出口商的账户上。

上述交易流程表明托收过程是按时间顺序排列的。在跟单托收条件下，前面的步骤已经完成后银行才作为。这意味着出口商只有在它所在地的银行收到通知书、代收行的资金后才能收到付款。

8.5　Documentary Collection and Documentary L/C 跟单托收与跟单信用证

There are two major differences between a documentary collection and a documentary letter of credit: (1) the draft involved is not drawn by the seller (drawer) upon a bank for payment, but rather on the buyer (drawee); (2) the seller's bank has no obligation to pay upon presentation but, more simply, acts as a collecting or remitting bank on behalf of the seller, thus earning a commission for its services.

The presenting (collecting) bank reviews the documents making certain they are in conformity with the collection order. Goods are transported, stored, and insured at the expense and risk of the seller until payment or acceptance occurs.

跟单托收和跟单信用证有两个主要区别：（1）相关的汇票不是由卖方（出票人）开给银行，而是开给买方（受票人）；（2）卖方银行没有见票即付的义务，而是以代收行或托收行的身份代表卖方收取货款，并收取相应的服务费用。

代收行应审核单证，保证单证与托收单的规定一致。在买方付款或承兑前，卖方承担货物装运、存储和投保的费用和风险。

Training Case 8-1

Enterprise A purchased a machine equipment from enterprise B, total amount for $500,000. Enterprise A opened a commercial acceptance draft which the drawer was enterprise A and enterprise B was the payee and the payment term was 6 months. At the same time, enterprise C guaranteed for the bill and ensured enterprise A to accept the draft on maturity date. After the expiry date of payment, enterprise A required enterprise C to pay the amount because enterprise A was in financial crisis and unable to pay.

Question: Was enterprise C obligated to pay the amount? why?

A企业从B企业购进一台机器设备，价款50万美元。A企业开出一张由A企业为出票人、B企业为收款人、付款期限为6个月的商业承兑汇票。同时，C企业对汇票做担保，保证A企业到期承兑该汇票。付款期满后，由于A企业财务发生危机，无法付款，A企业要求C企业支付该款。

问题：C企业是否有义务支付该笔款项？为什么？

Key Terms

bill of exchange/draft 汇票

Exercise

◎ *Case Analysis*

A case of two invoices under different payments:

In March 2018, company NR and company CL in country A signed a contract for 10 tons of CF products imported from China, $18 per kilogram and worth $180,000, payment at sight L/C. After company CL opened the L/C, it required two commercial invoices because the international market price might decline, and they could pay less tax for such goods when they made customs declaration. Among them, the invoice of $18 per kilogram was presented with the bill of lading, the bill of exchange, and other documents through bank normally; another invoice for $10 per kilogram was directly mailed to the importer.

In August 2018, company NI signed a contract with company PP in country B for 20 tons of SC products imported from China for the price of $12 per kg, D/P sight payment. The importer requested two invoices, because the government of the import country carries out the actual import valuation system of SC products and the import tariffs standard on the product is: if FOB import price is lower than or equal to $8 per kg, 8 dollars of tariffs will be taxed, and if FOB import price is higher than $8 per kg, it will be taxed according to the actual FOB price clinched. In the past, when FOB price was below $8 per kg in the international market, the importer paid a lot of tariffs and in order to seek a balance, the importer need to make an invoice of $8 per kg, which was directly expressed to the importer for customs clearance. As for the actual payment of import goods, it will still be taxed $12 per kilogram in accordance with the contract signed.

Exporters must seriously consider whether to give importers two invoices. To discriminate the different ways of payments:

①In view of L/C payment, as long as all documents are in conformity with the contract terms and L/C contents, there is not any risk and impact on exporters.

②In view of D/P sight payment, exporters must wait and can send importers the second invoice after importers make payment only if the exporters agreed to make two invoices.

③In view of L/C payment in advance or alternative payment by D/P sight, the second invoice can be sent only after payment received.

④In view of D/A payment or forward other than L/C payment, it is not recommended to make two invoices.

Q: How the exporter deals with the situation that the importer requires two invoices?

不同付款方式下的两张发票案例:

2018 年 3 月,NR 公司与 A 国 CL 公司签订合同,以每千克 18 美元的价格从中国进口 10 吨价值 18 万美元的 CF 产品,付款方式为即期信用证。CL 公司在开出信用证之后,提出要求为其提供两张商业发票,原因是国际市场价格可能下降,这样货到报关时可以少纳税。其中,每千克 18 美元的发票随提单、汇票等其他单证一起通过银行正常交单;另做一张价格为每千克 10 美元的发票,直接邮寄给进口商。

2018 年 8 月,NI 公司与 B 国 PP 公司签订合同,以每千克 12 美元的价格从中国进口 20 吨 SC 产品,付款方式是即期交单。进口商提出要求做两张发票,原因是进口国政府对 SC 产品实行进口海关估价制,对于进口该产品的关税征税标准为:FOB 进口价低于或等于每千克 8 美元,按照 8 美元计价征纳关税;FOB 进口价高于每千克 8 美元,按照实际成交的 FOB 价格征纳关税。过去,国际市场行情低于每千克 8 美元时,进口商缴了很多关税,为了寻求平衡,需要出一张每千克 8 美元的发票,直接快递给进口商用于报关。至于实际进口货物付款,仍然按照合同签订的每千克 12 美元执行。

出口商对于是否给予进口商做两张发票,必须认真考虑。针对不同的付款方式区别对待:

①对于采取信用证付款方式的,只要所有单证与签订的合同条款及信用证内容相符就可以,对出口商没有任何风险和影响。

②对于采用即期交单付款方式的,出口商如果同意做两张发票,必须等进口商将全部货款付讫后,才可以寄送第二张发票。

③对于采用信用证预付或变通的即期交单付款方式的,一定要在收到货款后才可以出第二张发票。

④对于采用承兑交单付款方式或信用证付款方式之外的其他远期付款方式的,建议不要做两张发票。

问题:出口商对进口商要求开两张发票应如何对待?

◎ *Practice*

根据销售合同和其他相关资料,制作一份信用证项下的商业汇票。

浙江省鑫达对外贸易有限公司出口丹麦 INDKOBS FORENTNGEN AF 公司约 4 000 件男式针织套头衫,支付方式为:50% 的发票金额预付货款信用证,50% 的发票金额即期付款交单。

销售合同如下：

SALES CONTRACT

To:INDKOBS FORENINGEN AF   No.ZF12E072323

    964 AMBA, ALBUEN 6-86000 KOLDING, DENMARK

Date: JULY 16, 2018

This sales contract is made between the seller and the buyer whereby the seller agrees to sell and the buyer agrees to buy the undermentioned goods:

Description of Goods	Quantity	Unit Price	Amount
MEN'S KNITTED PULLOVER		CIF AARHUS	
ART NO.5706	4,000 PCS	USD 12.50	USD 50,000.00
55 PCT COTTON 20 PCT LAMBWOOL 20 PCT ANGORA 5 PCT NYLON			
5 PCT MORE OR LESS BOTH IN QUANTITY AND AMOUNT ALLOWED			

Total amount (in words): SAY US DOLLARS FIFTY THOUSAND ONLY.

Packing: 12 PCS IN ONE CARTON

         TOTAL PACKED IN ONE 20′FCL

Delivery: SEA FREIGHT FROM NINGBO TO AARHUS

          PARTIAL SHIPMENTS NOT ALLOWED BUT TRANSSHIPMENT ALLOWED

Shipping Marks: AS PER SELLER'S OPTION

Time of Shipment: ON OR BEFORE 15 SEP., 2018

Terms of Payment: 30 PERCENT OF THE AMOUNT USD 15,000.00 PAID BY T/T BEFORE SHIPMENT AND THE BALANCE USD 3,500,000.00 PAID BY DOCUMENTS AGAINST PAYMENT AT SIGHT IF THE AMOUNT OF USD 15,000.00 NOT ARRIVED IN CHINA BEFORE 31 AUG., 2018, THE SELLER WILL NOT TAKE THE RESPONSIBILITY FOR THE DELAY OF THE SHIPMENT.

Insurance: FOR 110 PCT OF THE INVOICE VALUE COVERING ALL RISKS AS PER CIC OF PICC DATED 01/01/1981 INCLUDING W/W CLAUSE.

Documents required:

1.SIGNED COMMERCIAL INVOICE IN TRIPLICATE

2.FULL SET CLEAN ON BOARD BILL OF LADING MADE OUT TO ORDER OF SHIPPER BLANK ENDORSED MARKED FREIGHT PREPAID NOTIFY THE BUYER

3.DETAILED PACKING ASSORTED LIST IN TRIPLICATE

4.CERTIFICATE OF ORIGIN IN DUPLICATE

5.INSURANCE POLICY IN DUPLICATE

The Seller: The Buyer:

ZHEJIANG XINDA FOREIGN TRADE CORP. LTD.   INDKOBS FORENINGEN AF

        王一峰   KOBE JOHN

　　INDKOBS FORENINGEN AF 公司于 2018 年 8 月 30 日将 30% 的货款 15 000.00 美元打入浙江省鑫达对外贸易有限公司在中国银行杭州支行的账户后,单证员开始按照合同缮制或审核各种单证。2018 年 9 月 19 日,单证员梁波将整套单据交中国银行杭州分行(Bank of China, Hangzhou Branch)托收。

　　其他相关资料:

　　浙江鑫达对外贸易有限公司地址:288 WEST SECOND RING ROAD, HANGZHOU, ZHEJIANG, CHINA

　　实际出货 3 984 件,332 箱

　　发票号码:ZFA0831-Q

　　提单号码:PCESI1206930

　　船名航次:HARMONY V.006W

　　集装箱箱号:KKFU7643630

　　原产地证书号码:CA33424/120079

　　毛重:10.00 千克/箱

　　体积:48×36×40 厘米/箱

　　发票日期:2018 年 8 月 31 日

　　提单日期:2018 年 9 月 14 日

　　1×20′FCL,CY/CY 集装箱封号:B060620

　　税则号:6103.3200

　　净重:8.00 千克/箱

　　保险单号:PIE20183304930000146

　　单色混码包装,每箱男式套头衫的尺码搭配如下:

尺寸	46	48	50	52	54	56
数量	1	2	3	3	2	1	=12 件

　　其中:

　　箱号 1~84 为白色(WHITE),共计 1 008 件;

　　箱号 85~164 为黑色(BLACK),共计 960 件;

　　箱号 165~248 为棕色(BROWN),共计 1 008 件;

　　箱号 249~332 为海军蓝(N.BLUE),共计 1 008 件。

　　唛头:INDKOBSZFI

　　　　2E0723AARHUS

　　　　NO.1-332

BILL OF EXCHANGE

凭
Drawn under _____

不可撤销信用证号
Irrevocable L/C No.

日期
Date_____

按　　息付款
Payable with interest @_____%

号码
No.

汇票金额
Exchange for

杭州
Hangzhou

见票
At _____ days after sight of this FIRST of exchange (Second of exchange being unpaid)

日后（本汇票之副本未付）付交

受款人
Pay to the order of _____

金额
The sum of

此致
To _____
_____

EXCHANGE FOR_____

AT_____DAYS AFTER SIGHT OF THIS FIRST OF EXCHANGE (SECOND OF EXCHANGE BEING UNPAID)

PAY TO THE ORDER OF _____

THE SUM OF _____

TO _____

Chapter 9

Special Documents
特殊单证

Learning Objectives

◆ 重点掌握保险单证；了解贸易优惠单证和检验单证。

Guide Case

A Case that a Buyer's Representative Issued Inspection Certificate of Quality

A certain export company received a letter of credit, other problems were not found after examination, in addition to the inspection certificate. The term of the inspection certificate was: "INSPECTION CERTIFICATE OF QUALITY ISSUED BY THE BUYER'S REPRESENTATIVE, WHOSE SIGNATURE MUST BE VERIFIED BY THE OPENING BANK." The beneficiary contacted the buyer's local representative Mr. ×× and stated that the cargo has been seen and thought it qualified. The buyer's representative issued the quality inspection certificate after shipment. But when the documents reached abroad, they were refused to accept by the issuing bank because the issuer's signature of the inspection certificate of quality was not in complete conformity with the signature mastered by the issuing bank.

Although the buyer admitted that the inspection certificate was provided by their representative, there was something wrong with the goods' quality when they reached the port of destination after several representations by the beneficiary. After several negotiations, the case ended by cutting price.

The main problem of this case is that the beneficiary should not accept the inspection certificate signed by the issuing bank confirmed. The beneficiary and the negotiating bank are unable to grasp if the issuing bank conveniently indicates the signature inconsistent with or the buyer deliberately provides the signature which is not in conformity with the representative of the issuing bank.

买方代表签发品质检验证书的案例

某出口公司接到一张信用证,经审查除检验证书外未发现其他问题。该检验证书条款包含:"由买方代表签发品质检验证书,其签字须由开证行核实。"受益人就本条款与买方驻本地代表××先生联系,称:货已看过,认为合格。买方代表在装运后签发了品质检验证书。但单据到国外被开证行拒收,因品质检验证书签发人的签字与开证行所掌握的签字完全不符。

受益人几经交涉,买方虽然承认所提供的检验证书确系他们代表签发,但货到目的港发现品质有问题。双方多次谈判,最后削价处理才结案。

本案例的主要问题在于受益人不应接受由开证行证实签字的检验证书。开证行随便称签字不符,或买方故意提供与该代表不符的签字交开证行,受益人与议付行均无法掌握。

9.1 Inspection Documents
检验单证

Inspection documents are as followings (details as section 7.4):

(1)Inspection certificate.

(2)Quality certificate.

(3)Phytosanitary certificate.

(4)Fumigation certificate.

(5)Veterinary certificate.

(6)Public health certificate.

检验单证包括如下内容(详见7.4部分):

(1)检验证书;

(2)质量证书;

(3)植物检验检疫证书;

(4)熏蒸证书;

(5)兽医证书;

(6)公共卫生证书。

9.2 Insurance
保 险

9.2.1 *Basic Principles of Insurance*
保险的基本原则

1.Insurable Interest

It may pass from party to party during a transaction depending upon the terms of sale.

2.Utmost Good Faith

When taking out an insurance policy, the insured must disclose any "material circumstance" that may influence the judgement of the insurer in establishing a rate (price) for a specific policy.

3.Indemnity and Subrogation

Indemnity means that the insurer will undertake to compensate the insured for any financial loss suffered due to loss or damage.

Subrogation is the right of the insurer to collect damages from a negligent third party (i.e. the shipping company or ship's owners), and this right is automatically assigned to the insurer by the insured in the policy.

1.保险利益

它取决于销售条款,在交易期间保险利益从一方转到另一方。

2.最大诚信原则

当投保时,被保险人必须披露"投保物的情况",这可能会影响到承保人对具体某个投保率(价格)的判断。

3.赔偿与代位求偿

赔偿是指承保人将承担被保险人任何由于丢失或损坏造成的投保物的损失。

代位求偿是承保人收集来自过失第三方(如船公司或船主)的损失,在保险单里,代位权自动由被保险人分派给承保人。

9.2.2 *Types of Insurances*
保险种类

1.General Marine Insurance

It is now a general term of insurance for any means of transport. Such coverage is often required when payment is by a letter of credit. Different types of insurance policies cover different levels of risk.

Specifically excluded from a Marine Insurance Policy (but often available as supplementary coverage) are losses due to delays, wars, strikes, riots and civil commotions, and unfitness of a conveyance.

Cargo insurance is not available for loss due to misconduct of the insured, ordinary leakage or loss in weight, unsuitable or insufficient packaging, nuclear contamination, and inherent vice (such as natural evaporation of water-based products).

2.Customized Cargo Policy

This coverage may be secured when the nature of the goods excludes their protection under a standard (A, B, C) Marine Insurance Policy. Examples include insurance against product deterioration, refrigeration breakdown, or freezing, insurance for perishable items or time sensitive items, and insurance for equipment that requires special handling.

3.Special Risk Cargo Policy

This coverage is for risk of loss or damage to high-risk cargoes (i.e. computer chips, laptop computers, fine arts, jewelry and antiques). This coverage is also available to high-risk destination and/or for political risk coverage against expropriation, nationalization or confiscation.

4.Open Cargo Policy (Sample 9-1)

This policy is written to cover a number of shipments within a specific time period.

This coverage is also carried by freight forwarders and customs brokers and is made available (for a fee) to their customers for shipments they handle.

5.Export Credit Policy

This policy covers loss due to nonpayment by the importer/buyer. It's often required by the exporter / seller's lender in open account and problematic country of destination transactions. This insurance is often offered by a government or quasi-governmental agency in countries (i.e. India), whose international economic policy is aligned with the encouragement of exports.

1.一般海运险

此为一般保险术语,适用于任何交通工具。信用证作为付款方式时,通常需要投保此险别。不同类型的保险单投保不同的险别。

海运保险单的除外险别(通常可作为附加险别)是针对由于延误、战争、罢工、暴乱、民变和运输工具不适航造成的损失。

货物保险不适用于被保险人操作不当、一般渗漏或失重、不恰当或不足包装、核污染、内在缺陷(如水性产品的自然蒸发)造成的损失。

2.定制的货物保险单

在标准海运保险单下,可投保特定险别使货物免遭损失,如针对产品的变质,制冷故障,冷冻、易腐物品,以及需要特殊处理的设备的保险。

3.特殊风险货物保险单

此险别针对高风险货物(如电脑芯片、笔记本电脑、美术品、珠宝、古玩)。此险别也适用于到高风险目的地的货物及/或有政治风险的货物,如货物可能被征用、国有化或者被没收。

4.预约货物保险单(见样单9-1)

此保险单适用于特定时期大量货物装运的投保。此险别由货运代理人和报关员投保,费用由他们的客户承担。

5.出口信用保险单

此保险单针对由于进口商/买方拖欠付款造成的损失。在往来账户及与有问题的目的地国进行交易时,出口商/卖方的贷方通常需要提供出口信用保险单。出口信用保险适用于鼓励出口的国家(如印度)的政府或国有企业。

9.2.3 Insurance Documents
保险单证

1.Marine Cargo Transportation Insurance Policy (Sample 6-9)

2.Insurance Certificate

3.Beneficiary's Certificate (Sample 9-2)

4.Customs Bond

A bond is a contractual obligation of an insurance company to insure performance of a

Sample 9-1
样单 9-1

Open Cargo Policy
预约货物保险单

合同号：TT150156   2018 年 12 月 17 日

甲　方：上海朗明商贸有限公司

乙　方：中国人民财产保险股份有限公司上海分公司

　　双方就进口货物的运输预约保险拟定以下条款，以资共同遵守：

　　一、保险范围

　　甲方从国外进口全部货物，不论运输方式，凡贸易条件规定由买方办理保险的，都属于本合同范围之内。甲方应根据本合同规定，向乙方办理投保手续并支付保险费。

　　乙方对上述保险范围内的货物负有自动承保的责任，在发生本合同规定范围内的损失时，均按本合同的规定，负责赔偿。

　　二、保险金额

　　保险金额以货物的到岸价格（CIF）即货价加运费加保险费为准（运费可用实际运费，亦可由双方协定一个平均运费率计算）。

　　三、保险险别和费率

　　各种货物需要投保的险别由甲方选定并在投保单中填明。乙方根据不同的险别规定不同的费率。现暂定如下：

货物种类	运输方式	保险险别	保险费率
分体式空调	海运	一切险、战争险	

　　四、保险责任

　　各种险别的责任范围，以乙方制定的"海洋货物运输保险条款""海洋运输货物战争险条款""海运进口货物国内转运期间保险责任扩展条款""航空运输一切险条款"和其他有关条款的规定为准。

　　五、投保手续

　　甲方一经掌握货物发运情况，即应向乙方寄送起运通知书，办理投保。通知书一式五份，由保险公司签认后，退回一份。如不办理投保，货物发生损失，乙方不予理赔。

　　六、保险费

　　乙方按照甲方寄送的起运通知书照前列相应的费率逐笔计收保费，甲方应及时付费。

　　七、索赔手续和期限

　　本合同所保货物发生保险责任范围内的损失时，乙方应按制定的"关于海运进口保险货物残损检验的赔款给付方法"和"进口货物施救整理费用支付方法"迅速处理。甲方应尽力采取防止货物扩大受损面的措施，对已遭受损失的货物必须积极抢救，尽量减少货物的损失。向乙方办理索赔的有效期限，以保险货物卸离海港之日起满一年终止，如有特殊需要可向乙方提出延长索赔期。

　　八、合同期限

　　本合同自 2018 年 12 月 17 日起开始生效。

甲方：   乙方：

上海朗明商贸有限公司   中国人民财产保险股份有限公司上海分公司

　　　王明   张平

principal's obligation as imposed by law or regulation. For example, US customs bond is required by the U.S. Customs to ensure payment of all duties associated with an import shipment.

5.ATE Carnet (Issued by National Chambers of Commerce Affiliated with the Paris-Based International Chamber of Commerce (ICC))

This is an international customs document that may be used for the temporary duty-free admission of certain goods (e.g. samples for a trade show, cars for an automobile race, musical instruments for a music concert) into a country in lieu of the usual customs documents. Technically, an ATE carnet is a form of insurance or bond. It guarantees that import duties and fees will be paid if the goods are not re-exported within a stated time.

1.海洋货物运输保险单(见样单6-9)

2.保险凭证

3.受益人证明(见样单9-2)

Sample 9-2   Beneficiary's Certificate

样单9-2   受益人证明

<table>
<tr>
<td colspan="4" align="center">GUANGZHOU TEXTILE GARMENT CO., LTD.
HUARONG MANSION RM2901 NO.85 GUANJIAQIAO,GUANGZHOU,CHINA
CERTIFICATE</td>
</tr>
<tr>
<td>To</td>
<td>FASHION FORCE CO., LTD.
P.O.BOX 8935 NEW TERMINAL, ALTA,
VISTA OTTAWA, CANADA</td>
<td>Invoice No.</td>
<td>NT01FF004</td>
</tr>
<tr>
<td></td>
<td></td>
<td>Date</td>
<td>MAR. 20, 2019</td>
</tr>
<tr>
<td colspan="4">WE CERTIFY HEREBY THAT ORIGINAL CERTIFICATE OF ORIGIN FORM A, ORIGINAL EXPORT LICENSE, COPY OF COMMERCIAL INVOICE, DETAILED PACKING LISTS AND A COPY OF BILL OF LADING WERE SENT DIRECTLY TO APPLICANT BY COURIER WITHIN 5 DAYS AFTER SHIPMENT. THE RELATIVE COURIER RECEIPT IS ALSO REQUIRED FOR PRESENTATION.

GUANGZHOU TEXTILE GARMENT CO., LTD.
张欢</td>
</tr>
</table>

4.海关担保

担保是保险公司的合同义务,其确保在法律或法规下委托人义务的实施。例如,美国海关要求海关担保,以确保相关进口货物关税的支付。

5.ATE通关卡(由总部设在巴黎的国际商会下属的各国家商会出具)

这是一份国际海关证明,可以用于临时进入某国的免税货物(比如贸易展览品、汽车比赛用的汽车、音乐会乐器等),以代替通常的海关单证。从技术上讲,ATE通关卡是一张保险单或担保单。在规定的时间内,货物没有复出口,它保证支付进口关税和费用。

9.3　Trade Agreements and Trade Preference Documents
贸易协定与贸易优惠单证

1.Certificate of Origin (Details as Section 6.8.2)

2.Export/Import Declaration (Sample 6-6,Sample 7-1)

3.Procedure of Import-Export Customs Clearance

Application-examination and inspection-levying duties-release.

4.Documents Presented during Customs Declaration

（1）Export customs declaration form (details as section 6.5.1);

（2）Commercial invoice and packing list;

（3）Shipping order;

（4）Export customs clearance bill;

（5）Export license/certificate of quota;

（6）Processing trade registration book.

1.原产地证书(详见6.8.2部分)

2.进出口报关单(见样单6-6和样单7-1)

3.进出口清关程序

申报—查验—征税—放行。

4.办理清关时需提交的单证

（1）出口报关单(详见6.5.1部分)；

（2）商业发票和装箱单；

（3）装货单；

（4）出口清关单；

（5）出口许可证/配额证明；

（6）加工贸易登记簿。

Training Case 9-1

A Loss Case because Commodity Inspection Certificate not in Conformity with Provisions

On October 15, 2018, a certain British bank issued an L/C for our agricultural products export company A. The relevant clauses are as following: "Amount: $918,000.00 ... 1,800 M/T (QUANTITY 5% MORE OR LESS ALLOWED) OF ROUND SHAPED WHITE RICE, $510.00 PER M/T NET CIF LIVERPOOL. FULL SET ORIGINAL CLEAN 'ON BOARD' OCEAN BILLS OF LADING MADE OUT TO ORDER AND ENDORSED IN BLANK MARKED 'FREIGHT PREPAID' NOTIFYING DOBSON CO., LTD. 42 KING'S AVENUE, LIVERPOOL TWYISJ BRITAIN ... INSPECTION CERTIFICATE OF QUALITY IN TRIPLICATE, INSPECTED AT THE TIME OF SHIPMENT ISSUED BY CID LOSS IF ANY PAY TO DOBSON CO., LTD."

After receiving the L/C, company A got the goods ready at once. On October 25, all goods were shipped and the documents were prepared to the negotiating bank for negotiation. The negotiating bank did not agree to negotiation after the examination of documents. The reason was the negotiation amount exceeded the total amount of the L/C. The total amount of the L/C was $918,000, but the invoice amount and the draft amount both were $945,540. The extra amount was $27,540.

Company A believed that the L/C regulated 1,800 metric tons and allowed 5% more or less,which was 1,800 metric tons plus 5%, the highest could be filled with 1,890 metric tons. We actually only delivered 1,854 metric tons, only added 3% (1,800×(1+3%)). It was allowed in the terms of the L/C. The unit price USD 510/MT multiplied by 1,854 metric tons, the total amount was $945,540.

The negotiating bank still did not agree to negotiation because the total amount of the L/C was not allowed to increase or decrease although the L/C allowed to increase or decrease 5%. So even if the quantity conformed to the stipulations of the L/C and it was absolutely not allowed if the negotiating amount beyond the total amount limit of the L/C. The negotiating bank advised, since the cargo had been shipped out, and could not be changed, it could only be available by payment against presentation of guarantee. What is called payment against presentation of guarantee was that the company issued guarantee documents and took the responsibility of all the consequences and risks when the issuing bank or the applicant refused to pay or refuse the documents. Under these conditions, the negotiating bank sent the documents to the issuing bank and actively listed inconsistent situation in the sending letter:

"(1)The bill of lading indicated that the shipment date was on October 25, the issuing date of the inspection certificate of quality was on October 23, which showed that your inspection time was not at the time of shipment.

"(2)The notify party column on the bill of lading: TWYISJ BRITAIN correctly should be TW6ISJ BRITAIN.

"Documents are temporarily retained. Please inform your processing opinion as soon as possible."

By checking the copy of the documents, company A thought that the above two "discrepancies" proposed by the issuing bank were unreasonable, especially for item 2 in the bill of lading notify party column that TWY should be TW6. It was strange. Repeatedly against the L/C regulation, the L/C opened by the other side was TWY, TW6 didn't exist. Our documents were completely consistent. On November 14, company A put forward to the issuing bank through the negotiating bank:

"This lot of goods actually was shipped on October 23. CID made a comprehensive inspection on this batch of goods on October 23 and thought it qualified to loading. So our inspection certificate of quality was issued on October 23. According to CID, it meaned that the date of issuance of the certificate was the date of inspection for the goods. The shipment started on

October 23, the inspection was made on October 23, which conformed to the stipulations of the L/C 'inspected at the time of shipment'.

"The notify party I submitted in the bill of lading, Dobson Co., Ltd. 42 King's Avenue, Liverpool, TWYISJ BRITAIN, completely conforms to the stipulations of the L/C. With regard to the notify party you proposed should be TW6, please check carefully the L/C opened. It is TWY on the earth, not TW6.

"To sum up, our documents completely conform to the requirements of the L/C. The discrepancies do not exist. Please make payment on time. "

On November 18, the issuing bank replied:

"Firstly, we shall apologize to you for the mistake of the address of the notify party in the bill of lading. After our bank checking, our telex machine obstacles TW6 for TWY by mistake when we open the L/C. Therefore the applicant accepted the bill of lading on this question.

"The number for this shipment is for 1,854 metric tons, more than the amount of the L/C. You require paying the excess amount on collection basis. I'm negotiating with the applicant for the acceptance. But the documents under the key items exist unconformities with the L/C. Although your problem is not in this and your correspondence on November 14 has explained, we think the discrepancy is obvious.

"According to your reply, the goods under the L/C were shipped on October 23, so the inspection certificate of quality was issued on October 23. We can only determine the shipment time according to the shipping documents. UCP600 regulates that on board or shipment to the ship or the shipped to the named vessel can be printed in advance on the bill of lading to indicate that the goods have been put on a named vessel. In this case, the issuing date of the bill of lading shall be deemed to be the date of shipment. So according to the regulation, the issuing date of the bill of lading you submitted is on October 25, which is the date of shipment of goods. According to your reply, CID believes that the issuing date of the certificate is the date of goods inspection. That is to say, your certificate was issued on October 23, the goods were inspected on October 23 and were shipped on October 25. How can it meet the requirements of the L/C 'inspected at the time of shipment'? So this obviously is a discrepancy of the documents.

"So we can't pay and hope to inform the documents processing opinion. "

Company A studied the opinion of the issuing bank with the related personnel of the negotiating bank and thought that the statement by the other party that the inspection certificate of company A did exist discrepancies in addition to the bill of lading notify party address. Finally company A directly negotiated with the buyer, in settlement of $490 per ton and took a loss $37,080 and the case ended.

This case involves more issues, but mainly reflects on the processing of the documents.

商检证与规定不符致损案

2018年10月15日,英国某银行开给我农产品出口公司A一张信用证,有关部分条款如下:"总金额918 000美元……1 800公吨,数量允许5%增减。圆粒白大米,每公吨净重价格为 510 美元,CIF 利物浦。全套清洁已装上船的正本海运提单,做成空白抬头、空白背书,注明"运费预付"通知不列颠利物浦 TWYISJ 皇室大街 42 号多布逊有限公司……商品检验司签发的品质检验证书一式三份,在装运时检验。保险如发生赔偿,请付给多布逊有限公司。"

A 公司接到信用证后即备货,10 月 25 日全部货物装运完毕,并备妥单据向议付行交单办理议付。议付行经审单后不同意议付,其理由为议付金额超出信用证总金额,信用证总金额为 918 000 美元,发票和汇票金额却为 945 540 美元,超出 27 540 美元。

A 公司认为,信用证规定货量为 1 800 公吨,并允许 5% 增减装,也就是最多可以装 1 890 公吨(1 800 公吨加 5%)。我们实际只装 1 854 公吨,仅增装 3%(1 800×(1+3%))。这是信用证规定条款允许的。每公吨单价 510 美元乘以 1 854 公吨,总金额就是 945 540 美元。

议付行仍不同意议付,因信用证虽规定货量允许增减装 5%,但信用证总金额并未允许增减。所以即使数量符合信用证规定,议付的总金额超出信用证总金额限度也是绝对不允许的。议付行建议,既然货已装运完,无法更改,只能凭担保议付。所谓凭担保议付即公司出具担保文件,承担开证行或开证申请人提出拒付款或拒受单据时所发生的一切后果及风险。在这种条件下,议付行向开证行寄单并在寄单面函中主动列明单证不符情况:

"(1)提单上表明的装运日为 10 月 25 日,品质检验证书的签发日期为 10 月 23 日,说明你方并不是装运时检验的。"

"(2)提单上通知人栏中的 TWYISJ BRITAIN 正确表述应为 TW6ISJ BRITAIN。"

"单据暂保留。速告处理意见。"

A 公司经核对留底单据,认为开证行所提出以上两条"不符点"是没有道理的,尤其对第二项提单通知人栏中的 TWY 应为 TW6,觉得奇怪,再三对照信用证规定,对方开来信用证就是 TWY,根本不存在 TW6,我方单证完全相符。A 公司于 11 月 14 日即通过议付行向开证行提出:

"本批货物实际于 10 月 23 日全部装运完毕。商品检验司于 10 月 23 日对本批货物全面进行检验,认为合格才装运上船,所以我品质检验证书于 10 月 23 日签发。据商品检验司称,其证书的出具日期即表示为该货的检验日期。10 月 23 日开始装运,23 日检验,已符合信用证规定'于装运时检验'的要求。

"我方所提交的提单上通知人 Dobson Co. Ltd. 42 King's Avenue, Liverpool, TWYISJ BRITAIN, 完全符合信用证规定。至于你行提出应为 TW6,请你行仔细核对所开立的信用证,该证根本是 TWY,并非 TW6。

"综上所述,我方单据完全符合信用证要求。其不符点是不存在的,请你行按时付款。"

11 月 18 日开证行回复:

"对于提单通知人地址错字问题,首先向你方表示歉意。我行经查核,由于我行电传机发生障碍,将 TW6 误为 TWY。因此申请人对此问题表示接受该提单。

"对于本批货物装运数量为 1 854 公吨,超过我方信用证金额,其超额部分你方以托收方式要求付款,我方正与申请人商洽要求承兑。但其主要关键项下的单据存在与证不符点。虽然你方认为问题不在此并在11月14日来电做了一些解释，但我们认为其不符点是明显存在的。

"根据你方回复，信用证项下的货物于10月23日开始装运，所以品质检验证书出具日期为10月23日。我行只能从装运单证上来确定装运时间。UCP600规定：已装船或装运于船上或已装运于具名船只，可以在提单上用预先印就的文字表明货物已被装上具名船只。在这种情况下，提单的签发日期即视为装运日期。所以按上述规定，你方所提交的已装船提单其出单日期为10月25日，也就是本批货物的装运日期。按你方回复，商品检验司认为其证书出具日期即为货物检验日期。也就是说，你证书于10月23日出具，即于10月23日检验，10月25日装运，怎能符合信用证要求的'于装运时检验'的规定？所以这一点显然是单证不符点。

"因此我行无法付款，希望速告单据处理意见。"

A公司对开证行的意见与议付行有关人员研究，认为根据对方所述，除提单通知人地址以外，A公司的检验证书确实存在不符点。A公司最后直接与买方洽商，以每吨降价490美元结算、承担损失37 080美元而结案。

本案涉及的争议问题较多，但主要反映在单据的处理上。

Key Terms

Insurance Document 保险单证

Exercise

◎ *Practice*

2018年3月9日，广东大通国际货运代理有限公司通知广州纺织服装有限公司其所订舱位已经确认，该批货物将于3月20日装上由广州开往加拿大蒙特利尔港的"HUA CHANG"轮第09981船次。在得到了船公司关于确认订舱的配舱回单后，广州纺织服装有限公司即于3月16日按照信用证的有关规定填写"投保单"，并随附商业发票向中国人民财产保险股份有限公司广州分公司办理保险手续。请根据下列信用证要求填写出口货物运输保险投保单和海洋货物运输保险单。

2018 JAN. 31 15:23:4		
MT S700 　　**ISSUE OF A DOCUMENTARY LETTER OF CREDIT**	LOGICAL TERMINAL　E102	
	PAGE　00001	
	FUNC　MSG700	
	UMR　06607642	
MSGACK DWS765I AUTH OK，KEY B110106173BAOC53B，BKCHCNBJ BNPA**** RECORO		
BASIC HEADER	F 01 BKCHCNBJA940 0542 725524	
APPLICATION HEADER	0 700 1122 010129 BNPACAMMAXXX 4968 839712 010130 0028 N	
	*BNP PARIBAS (CANADA)	
	*MONTREAL	

续

```
USER HEADER          SERVICE CODE 103:

                     BANK PRIORITY 113:

                     MSG USER REF. 108:    (银行盖信用证通知专用章)

                     INFO. FROM CI 115:
```

SEQUENCE OF TOTAL 27:1 / 1

FORM OF DOC. LETTER OF CREDIT 40A:IRREVOCABLE

DOC. LETTER OF CREDIT NUMBER 20:63211020049

DATE OF ISSUE 31C:20180129

EXPIRY 31D:DATE 20180410 PLACE IN BENEFICIARY'S COUNTRY

APPLICANT 50:FASHION FORCE CO., LTD.

P.O.BOX 8935 NEW TERMINAL, ALTA, VISTA, OTTAWA, CANADA

BENEFICIARY 59:GUANGZHOU TEXTILE GARMENT CO.,LTD.

HUARONG MANSION RM2901 NO.85 ZHONGSHAN ROAD, GUANGZHOU, CHINA

AMOUNT 32B:CURRENCY USD AMOUNT 32,640

AVAILABLE WITH/BY 41D: ANY BANK BY NEGOTIATION

DRAFT AT 42C:SIGHT

DRAWEE 42D: BNPACAMMAXXX

*BNP PARIBAS (CANADA)

*MONTREAL

PARTIAL SHIPMENTS 43P:NOT ALLOWED

TRANSSHIPMENT 43T:ALLOWED

LOADING ON CHARGE 44A:CHINA

FOR TRANSPORTATION TO 44B:MONTREAL

LATEST DATE OF SHIPMENT 44C: 20180325

DESCRIPTION OF GOODS 45A:

SALES CONDITIONS: CIF MONTREAL/CANADA

SALES CONTRACT NO. F01LCB05127

LADIES COTTON BLAZER (100% COTTON, 40×20/140×60)

STYLE NO.	PO NO.	QTY/PCS	USD/PC
46-301A	10337	2,550	12.80

DOCUMENTS REQUIRED 46A:

+COMMERCIAL INVOICES IN 3 COPIES SIGNED BY BENEFICIARY'S REPRESENTATIVE.

+CANADA CUSTOMS INVOICES IN 4 COPIES.

+FULL SET OF ORIGINAL MARINE BILLS OF LADING CLEAN ON BOARD PLUS 2 NON-NEGOTIABLE

COPIES MADE OUT OR ENDORSED TO ORDER OF BNP PARIBAS (CANADA) MARKED FREIGHT

续

PREPAID AND NOTIFY APPLICANT'S FULL NAME AND ADDRESS.

+DETAILED PACKING LISTS IN 3 COPIES.

CHARGES 71B:OUTSIDE COUNTRY BANK CHARGES TO BE BORNE BY THE BENEFICIARY

OPENING BANK CHARGES TO BE BORNE BY THE APPLICANT

CONFIRMATION 49:WITHOUT

INSTRUCTIONS 78:

+WE SHALL COVER THE NEGOTIATING BANK AS PER THEIR INSTRUCTIONS.

+FORWARD DOCUMENTS IN ONE LOT BY SPECIAL COURIER PREPAID TO BNP PARIBAS (CANADA)

1981 MCGILL COLLEGE AVE., MONTREAL QC H3A2W8, CANADA.

SEND TO REC. INFO. 72:

THIS LETTER OF CREDIT IS SUBJECT TO UCP FOR DOCUMENTARY CREDITS (2007 REVISION) ICC

PUBLICATION NO. 600 AND IS THE OPERATIVE INSTRUMENT.

TRAILER ORDER IS <MAC:> <PAC:> <ENC:> <CHK:> <TNG:> <PDE:>

MAC:F344CA36

CHK:AA6204FFDFC2

出口货物运输保险投保单

发票号码		投保条款和险别
被保险人	客户抬头	(　　) PICC CLAUSE
		(　　) ICC CLAUSE
		(　　) ALL RISKS
		(　　) W.P.A./W.A.
		(　　) F.P.A.
		(　　) WAR RISKS
	过户	(　　) S.R.C.C.
		(　　) STRIKE
		(　　) ICC CLAUSE A
		(　　) ICC CLAUSE B
		(　　) ICC CLAUSE C
保险金额	USD (　　　)	(　　) AIR TPT ALL RISKS
	HKD (　　　)	(　　) AIR TPT RISKS
	(　) (　　　)	(　　) O/L TPT ALL RISKS
起运港		(　　) O/L TPT RISKS

续

目 的 港		( ) TRANSSHIPMENT RISKS
转 内 陆		( ) W TO W
开 航 日 期		( ) T.P.N.D.
船 名 航 次		( ) F.R.E.C.
赔 款 地 点		( ) R.F.W.D.
赔 付 币 别		( ) RISKS OF BREAKAGE
正 本 份 数		( ) I.O.P.
其 他 特 别 条 款		

以 下 由 保 险 公 司 填 写			
保单号码		费 率	
签单日期		保 费	

投保日期：   投保人签章：

中国人民财产保险股份有限公司

The People's Insurance (Property) Company of China, Ltd.

发票号码   保险单号次

Invoice No.   Policy No.

海 洋 货 物 运 输 保 险 单
MARINE CARGO TRANSPORTATION INSURANCE POLICY

被保险人：

Insured：

中国人民财产保险股份有限公司(以下简称本公司)根据被保险人的要求及其所缴付约定的保险费,按照本保险单承担险别和背面所载条款与下列特别条款承保下列货物运输保险,特签发本保险单。

This policy of Insurance witnesses that the People's Insurance (Property) Company of China, Ltd. (hereinafter called the "Company"), at the request of the Insured and in consideration of the agreed premium paid by the Insured, undertakes to insure the under mentioned goods in transportation subject to the conditions of the Policy as per the Clauses printed overleaf and other special clauses attached hereon.

保险货物项目 Description of Goods	包装 Packing	单位 Unit	数量 Quantity	保险金额 Amount Insured

承保险别 Conditions	货物标记 Marks of Goods

续

总保险金额 Total Amount Insured				
保费 Premium		装载运输工具 Per Conveyance S.S.		开航日期 Slg. on or abt.
起运港 From			目的港 To	

所保货物,如发生本保险单项下可能引起索赔的损失或损坏,应立即通知本公司下述代理人查勘。如有索赔,应向本公司提交保险单正本(本保险单共有____份正本)及有关文件。如一份正本已用于索赔,其余正本则自动失效。

In the event of loss or damage which may result in a claim under this Policy, immediate notice must be given to the Company's Agent as mentioned hereunder. Claims, if any, one of the Original Policies which has been issued in_____original(s) together with the relevant documents shall be surrendered to the Company. If one of the Original Policies has been accomplished, the others to be void.

赔款偿付地点 Claim payable at		
日期 Date		在 At
地址 Address		

Chapter 10

Electronic Commerce and International Trade Documents
电子商务与国际贸易单证

Learning Objectives

◆ 重点掌握电子单证;掌握电子支付;了解国际贸易中的电子单证。

Guide Case

A certain amount of import and export business agreed to ship in two lots, payment for an irrevocable L/C at sight. After the first batch of goods were sent, the buyer dealt with the formalities of payment. But after getting goods, it was found that the goods' quality didn't agree seriously with the contract stipulations, and the issuing bank was asked to inform the negotiating bank for the second batch of shipping documents under an L/C not for negotiation, but the bank ignored. Later, the negotiating bank was still in the negotiation for the second batch of shipping documents under the L/C. After the negotiating bank made negotiation, the paying bank notified the buyer to get documents against payment, but the buyer refused. Q:

(1) Was the method handled by the bank appropriate?

(2) What was the advisable way for the buyer to deal with this matter?

某笔进出口业务,约定分两批装运,支付方式为即期不可撤销信用证。第一批货物发送后,买方办理了付款赎单手续。但收到货物后,买方发现货物品质与合同规定严重不符,便要求开证行通知议付行对信用证项下的第二批货运单据不要议付,但银行忽视了。后来议付行对信用证项下的第二批货运单据仍予以议付。议付行议付后,付款行通知买方付款赎单,遭到买方的拒绝。问题:

(1)银行处理方法是否合适?

(2)买方应如何处理此事为宜?

10.1　E-Commerce and International Trade
电子商务与国际贸易

Electronic commerce, commonly known as e-commerce, consists of the buying and selling of products or services over electronic systems such as the Internet and other computer networks. The amount of trade conducted electronically has grown extraordinarily since the spread of the Internet. A wide variety of commerce is conducted in this way, spurring and drawing on innovations in electronic funds transfer, supply chain management, Internet marketing, online transaction processing, electronic data interchange (EDI), inventory management systems, and automated data collection systems. Modern electronic commerce typically uses the World Wide Web at least at some point in the transaction's lifecycle, although it can encompass a wider range of technologies such as e-mail as well.

E-commerce's influence to international trade is as following:

(1)E-commerce improves international trade.

(2)The emergence of virtual market changes the environment of international trade.

(3) The emergence of virtual company makes difference of the operating bobby of international trade.

(4)The operation and management of international trade change a lot.

电子商务,通常指通过电子系统买卖产品或服务,如互联网和其他计算机网络。互联网普及后,电子贸易的数量飞快增长。电子商务应用于各式各样的商业活动中,促进了电子资金转账、供应链管理、网络营销、在线交易处理、电子数据交换(EDI)、库存管理系统和自动数据采集系统的革新和发展。在交易过程中,现代电子商务一般采用万维网,当然它还包含更广泛的技术,如电子邮件。

电子商务对国际贸易的影响:

(1)电子商务使国际贸易得到发展。

(2)虚拟市场的出现改变了国际贸易的环境。

(3)虚拟公司的出现使国际贸易操作的监管产生差异。

(4)国际贸易管理和运作改变了很多。

10.2　E-Documents and E-Payment
电子单证与电子支付

10.2.1　E-Documents
电子单证

1.EDI Network

EDI is widely-used technology for the automated exchange of documents between dissimilar applications. It allows value chain partners to exchange purchase orders, invoices, advanced shipment notices, and other business documents directly from one business system to the other, without human intervention. Proven advantages are fewer errors, lower administrative costs, and faster order-to-cash cycles.

2.eUCP

eUCP is not an amendment to UCP, but is a supplement to UCP.

3.Problems in E-Documents

(1)Security;

(2)Reality;

(3)Legality.

4.Electronic Bill of Lading

1.电子数据交换网络

电子数据交换是在不同领域广泛应用的文件自动交换技术。它允许贸易伙伴直接从一个业务系统到另外一个业务系统交换采购订单、发票、提前装船通知和其他商业文件,无须人工干预。它已被证实的优点是错误更少、办公成本更低、处理订单–现金流程更快。

2.UCP电子交单增补

它不是UCP的修订本,而是补充。

3.电子单证的问题

(1)安全性;

(2)真实性;

(3)合法性。

4.电子提单

10.2.2 E-Payment

电子支付

1. Electronic Money

Electronic money refers to exchanging a certain amount of cash or deposits from the issuer and obtaining data representing the same amount, or transferring the balance in the bank through some electronic means through the fast payment service launched by banks and third parties, so that transactions can be conducted.

2.Development of E-Payment

E-payment has a rapid development due to the fast growth of e-commerce. Up to December 2017, China have reached 772 million netizen according to the 41th China Internet Network Development State Statistic Report released on January 31, 2018 by China Internet Network Information Center (CNNIC), which increased 40.74 million than that of the end of 2016. Internet penetration is 55.8% and the growth rate reached 2.6% than that of the end of 2016. Up to December 2017, China shopping user scale of network payment transactions reached 533 million, which rose by 14.3% than that of 2016 and making up 69.1% of the total Internet users. Shopping user scale of mobile network reached 506 million, which increased 14.7% year on year and the using proportion increased from 63.4% to 67.2%.

1.电子货币

电子货币是指用一定金额的现金或存款从发行者处兑换并获得代表相同金额的数据或者银行及第三方推出的快捷支付服务,通过使用某些电子化途径将银行中的余额转移,从而能够进行交易。

2.电子支付的发展

由于电子商务的快速发展,电子支付得到了迅速发展。据2018年1月31日中国互联网络信息中心(CNNIC)第41次《中国互联网络发展状况统计报告》,截至2017年12月,我国网民规模达7.72亿,全年共计新增网民4 074万人。互联网普及率为55.8%,较2016年年底提升2.6个百分点。截至2017年12月,我国网络购物用户规模达到5.33亿,较2016年增长14.3%,占网民总体的69.1%。手机网络购物用户规模达到5.06亿,同比增长14.7%,使用比例由63.4%增至67.2%。

10.3　Electronic Documents in International Trade
国际贸易中的电子单证

EDI is widely used in international trade documents. Now, along with the fast development of computers and Internet, more and more companies use computers to make out documents.

Future developments in electronic documents will be diverse. The technology used is shifting from page-based to XML-based documents, and even further to databases containing indexed documentary units. Multi-agent models are also in use for the development of documents.

EDI is the computer-to-computer interchange of strictly formatted messages that represent documents other than monetary instruments. EDI implies a sequence of messages between two parties. The formatted data representing the documents may be transmitted from originator to recipient via telecommunications or physically transported on electronic storage media.

In EDI, the usual processing of received messages is by computer only. Human intervention in the processing of received messages is typically intended only for error conditions, for quality review, and for special situations. For example, the transmission of binary or textual data is not EDI as defined here unless the data is treated as one or more data elements of EDI message and are not normally intended for human interpretation as part of on-line data processing.

EDI已在国际贸易单证中广泛使用。当前,随着计算机与互联网的快速发展,越来越多的公司开始使用计算机来缮制单证。

未来电子单证的发展将多样化。使用的技术将从基于页面的单证扩展到基于XML(可扩展标识语言)的单证,甚至是包含索引单证的数据库。多智能体模型也被应用于单证上。

EDI是严格的格式化信息在计算机间的交换,这些信息代表的是单证而不是货币工具。EDI蕴含一系列买卖双方之间的信息。代表单证的格式化数据可通过无线电通信或者电子存储介质由发起者传递给接收者。

就EDI而言,通常信息的接收过程是仅通过计算机进行处理的。在对接收到的信息进行处理的过程中,人工干预通常只在接收有误、质量审核和特殊情况下使用。例如,除非数据被视为EDI信息的一个或多个数据元素,否则传输的二进制或文本数据并不是在此所定义的EDI数据,并且一般都不适合作为在线数据进行处理。

Key Terms

electronic commerce 电子商务

Exercise

◎ *Practice*

请根据以下资料制作信用证指定的议付单证。

发票号码:SH25586

发票日期:2018-04-20

单位毛重:15.40 KGS/CTN

单位净重:13.00 KGS/CTN

单位尺码:60×40×50 CM/CTN

船名:DAFENG V3336

提单号码:SH223545

提单日期:2018-05-15

ISSUE OF A DOCUMENTARY L/C	
ISSUING BANK	ROYAL BANK, TOKYO
SEQUENCE OF TOTAL	1/1
FORM OF DOC. L/C	IRREVOCABLE
DOC. L/C NUMBER	JST-AB12
DATE OF ISSUE	20180405
EXPIRY	DATE 20180615 PLACE CHINA
APPLICANT	WAV GENEAL TRADING CO., OSAKA, JAPAN
BENEFICIARY	XINHONG TRADING CO., LTD. 224 JINLING ROAD, NANJING, CHINA
AMOUNT	CURRENCY USD AMOUNT 10,300.00
AVAILABLE WITH/BY	BANK OF CHINA BY NEGOTIATION
DRAFT AT	SIGHT FOR FULL INVOICE VALUE
DRAWEE	ROYAL BANK, TOKYO
PARTIAL SHIPMENTS	ALLOWED
TRANSSHIPMENT	ALLOWED
LOADING IN CHARGE	NANJING PORT
FOR TRANSPORTATION TO	OSAKA, JAPAN
LATEST DATE OF SHIPMENT	20180531

GOODS DESCRIPTION	LADIES GARMENTS AS PER S/C NO.SHL553
	PACKING：10 PCS/CTN
	ART NO. QUANTITY UNIT PRICE
	STYLE NO. ROCOCO 1,000 PCS USD 5.50
	STYLE NO. ROMANTICO 1,000 PCS USD 4.80
	CIF OSAKA
	SHIPPING MARKS：ITOCHU/OSAKA/NO.1-200
DOCUMENTS REQUIRED	*3/3 SET OF ORIGINAL CLEAN ON BOARD OCEAN BILLS OF LADING MADE OUT TO ORDER OF SHIPPER AND BLANK ENDORSED AND MARKED "FREIGHT PREPAID" NOTIFY APPLICANT (WITH FULL NAME AND ADDRESS).
	*ORIGINAL SIGNED COMMERCIAL INVOICE IN 5 FOLD.
	*INSURANCE POLICY OR CERTIFICATE IN 2 FOLD ENDORSED IN BLANK, FOR 110 PCT OF THE INVOICE VALUE COVERING THE INSTITUTE CARGO CLAUSES (A), THE INSTITUTE WAR CLAUSES, INSURANCE CLAIMS TO BE PAYABLE IN JAPAN IN THE CURRENCY OF THE DRAFTS.
	*GSP CERTIFICATE OF ORIGIN FORM A IN 1 ORIGINAL AND 1 COPY.
	*PACKING LIST IN 5 FOLD.
ADDITIONAL COND.	1. T.T. REIMBURSEMENT IS PROHIBITED.
	2. THE GOODS TO BE PACKED IN EXPORT STRONG COLORED CARTONS.
DETAILS OF CHARGES	ALL BANKING CHARGES OUTSIDE JAPAN INCLUDING REIMBURSEMENT COMMISSION ARE FOR ACCOUNT OF THE BENEFICIARY.
PRESENTATION PERIOD	DOCUMENTS TO BE PRESENTED WITHIN 10 DAYS AFTER THE DATE OF SHIPMENT, BUT WITHIN THE VALIDITY OF THE L/C.
CONFIRMATION	WITHOUT
INSTRUCTIONS	THE NEGOTIATING BANK MUST FORWARD THE DRAFTS AND ALL DOCUMENTS BY REGISTERED AIRMAIL DIRECTLY TO U. S. IN TWO CONSECUTIVE LOTS, UPON RECEIPT OF THE DRAFTS AND THE DOCUMENTS IN ORDER, WE WILL REMIT THE PROCEEDS AS INSTRUCTED BY THE NEGOTIATING BANK.

References
参考文献

I. References of Books

[1]谢娟娟.对外贸易单证实务与操作[M].北京:中国人民大学出版社,2017.

[2]余世明.国际商务单证[M].7版.广州:暨南大学出版社,2014.

[3]周瑞琪,王小鸥,徐月芳.国际贸易实务[M].3版.北京:对外经济贸易大学出版社,2015.

[4]刘启萍,周树玲.外贸英文制单[M].2版.北京:对外经济贸易大学出版社,2013.

[5]黎孝先,王健.国际贸易实务[M].6版.北京:对外经济贸易大学出版社,2016.

[6]全国外经贸单证专业培训考试办公室.国际商务单证理论与实务[M].北京:中国商务出版社,2017.

[7]易露霞,方玲玲,陈原.国际贸易实务双语教程[M].3版.北京:清华大学出版社,2011.

[8]赖红清.外贸单证操作教程[M].武汉:华中科技大学出版社,2017.

[9]李贺,奚伟东.外贸单证实务[M].2版.上海:上海财经大学出版社,2017.

[10]刘慧,杨志学,徐兰,等.国际商务单证项目教程[M].北京:清华大学出版社,2017.

[11]姚大伟.国际商务单证理论与实务[M].5版.上海:上海交通大学出版社,2018.

[12]天九湾贸易金融研究汇.国际结算单证热点疑义相与析[M].北京:中国海关出版社,2018.

[13]李辉,魏弘.国际贸易单证实务[M].2版.北京:对外经济贸易大学出版社,2018.

[14]王利平,程文吉,张帆,等.外贸单证[M].杭州:浙江大学出版社,2018.

[15]何源.跟单信用证一本通[M].2版.北京:中国海关出版社,2018.

[16]林晓静,曹玮.国际贸易单证实务[M].北京:北京理工大学出版社,2018.

[17]许晓冬.国际商务单证实务[M].北京:中国纺织出版社,2017.

[18]陆洲艳,钱华,陆泽西.国际商务单证[M].北京:清华大学出版社,2017.

[19]芮宝娟.进出口单证实务[M].3版.北京:中国人民大学出版社,2017.

[20]吴国新,李元旭,何一红.国际贸易单证实务[M].4版.北京:清华大学出版社,2017.

[21]胡涵景,洪岩,杨青海,等.国际贸易单证标准化实务[M].2版.北京:中国质检出版社,中国标准出版社,2017.

[22]成丽.国际贸易单证实务[M].北京:中国人民大学出版社,2017.

[23]章安平,牟群月.外贸单证操作[M].4版.北京:高等教育出版社,2017.

[24]陈红兵,聂钟鸣.国际结算、支付与单证理论与实务[M].天津:天津大学出版社,2017.

[25]吴穗珊.外贸单证实务学习指导与练习[M].2版.北京:电子工业出版社,2017.

[26] HINK E G,李月菊,王立非.国际贸易单证简明教程[M].上海:上海外语教育出版社,2017.

[27]布朗奇.国际贸易实务[M].孔雁,蔡荣生,译.5版.北京:清华大学出版社,2007.

[28] HINKELMAN E G. International trade documents[M]. 3rd ed. Novato: World Trade Press,2008.

[29] JOHNSON T E. Export/Import procedures and documents[M]. 4th ed. New York: Ama. com,2002.

II. References of Internet Resource

[1]中华人民共和国商务部.

[2]中华人民共和国海关总署.

[3]阿里巴巴.

[4]中国企业在线.

[5]中华大黄页.

[6]中国出口商品网.

[7]世界贸易组织网.

[8]中国国家税务总局.

[9]中国展览网.

[10]中国国际展览中心集团公司.

[11]中国展览交易网.

[12]南京世格软件有限公司.

[13]中国反倾销反补贴保障措施网上图书馆.

[14]中国税务通.

[15]中国法律在线.

[16]中华人民共和国对外经济法律法规汇编.

[17]中国国际货运代理协会.

[18]东方海外货柜航运有限公司(OCCL).

[19]马士基集团(A. P. MOLLER-MAERSK GROUP).

[20]铁行渣华(P & O NEDLLOYD).

[21]Find Law International Trade Law Sources.

[22]Business Guide to the Web.